Modern Bridge Bidding Complete

INTRODUCING THE
ROTH POINT COUNT

MODERN
Bridge Bidding
COMPLETE

Introducing the
ROTH POINT COUNT

BY

Alvin Roth and Jeff Rubens

WITH A FOREWORD BY EDGAR KAPLAN

Funk & Wagnalls   New York

CONTENTS

(vi)

FOREWORD

Skillful bridge bidding depends on how well you evaluate your hand and what system (partnership understandings) you use. Each topic has been the subject of many books, but this book is remarkable in that it covers both. Furthermore, for the first time the expert's approach to evaluation and system is presented in a way that the average player can understand.

Point-count evaluation is so popular that many (erroneously) consider it a part of the laws of bridge. It is so ingrained in our minds that although the standard point count has been shown to be one of the primary causes of poor results, no one has thought (or had the nerve) to challenge it. Here, in what the authors aptly call a revolution, the inadequacies of the standard count are fully exposed, and corrective measures are proposed. To be sure, this is a breath of fresh air which is most welcome in our stagnant bridge atmosphere. But there is an even greater achievement in this book, for we find also an explanation of the limitations of *any* point count, even the spectacularly effective Roth Point Count.

The reader will feel the effects of not one revolution but two when he also learns that there is more to bidding than counting points—and that the art can be a fascinating one indeed.

On matters of system and partnership understanding Al Roth has no superior either as a theorist or as a practical player. He has won so many national and international honors, with so many different partners, that it would be futile to attempt to list them. He advocated and helped popularize the first successful break away from traditional American bidding, and the record shows that his ideas are sound. It is significant that almost all American experts, including those who do not follow the complete system, employ many of Roth's techniques in their own favorite methods.

There are few bridge writers (outside of myself) whose every book I consider a must, but Al Roth is one of those few. I know from experience that it is foolish to disregard anything he has to say about the game. This book has not disappointed me. It should be required reading for anyone anxious to improve his bridge.

EDGAR KAPLAN

New York
August, 1968

INTRODUCTION

This book is about contract bridge bidding. The subject of bidding can be divided into two parts: how to evaluate your hand and what bidding methods to employ. Accordingly, the book is divided into two parts, the first dealing with evaluation and the second with bidding methods (or "system").

When hand evaluation by point count (rather than by honor tricks, the first universal method of hand evaluation) became popular, it marked the beginning of a period in which the level of bidding skill of the average player rose enormously. This rise was due primarily to a more precise method of hand evaluation than the mere counting of honor tricks. However, in recent years the average level of bidding skill has remained constant. This indicates that the limitations of point count evaluation *under the present system* have been reached. Bridge authorities have realized for many years that point count bidding yields only a restricted degree of accuracy. Beyond this, expert judgment is needed in order to obtain best results. Flaws and inaccuracies in the standard point count method can be corrected only by top players who, through their experience, knowledge and skill, are able to replace point count with their own expert judgment when necessary. Several changes in the popular point count have been suggested over the years, but none of these changes corrected more than a fraction of the ills of this evaluation method, and the bridge-playing public, consequently, once having mastered what we will call traditional point count methods, seems to have been unable to progress further.

Clearly the present method of hand evaluation has too many built in limitations and inaccuracies to remain viable. Clearly, it is time for a change, time for further improvements in methods of evaluation.

If everyone is to share the experts' secrets, expert bidding methods must be translated into terms that can be understood by players at all levels of experience. If you ask an expert why he bid so strongly with a hand that seems (under the traditional point count) to be too weak to justify his actions, he will probably tell you that he "liked his hand." In other words, he *knows* that the traditional point count value of his hand was wrong, but he cannot explain why in a way that a non-expert can understand.

In Part One of this book, we will show how *expert evaluation techniques can be expressed in terms of point count,* simply by *extending* and improving the traditional point count.

The idea of expressing expert evaluation in terms of points was first developed by Alvin Roth. Accordingly, we call this evaluation method the Roth Point Count. This technique is *not* an entirely new point count. The High Card Points used by almost all bridge players (4 points for an ace, 3 points for a king, etc.) is the basis of the Roth Point Count.

The Roth Point Count consists of various *adjustments* in the standard point count *which express in terms of points the adjustments made by experts when they evaluate their hands.* In other words, the new count translates expert thinking from the "intuitive genius" of the super-player into the same point count that everyone —from beginner to expert—uses to express the value of his hand. Thus, by using the Roth Point Count, you can see your hand through the eyes of an expert.

To achieve this, you need learn no more than some extensions of the present point count. It would be unfair to say that the Roth Point Count is as easy to master as the standard point count—it isn't. But neither is it very difficult. For one thing, it starts out with the standard point count which most bridge players of any experience are familiar with. It should be no deterrent that the Roth Point Count is a little more complicated than the ordinary, for it offers a vast improvement in hand evaluation.

In order to make the learning process as simple as possible, we have organized Part I (in which the Roth Point Count is presented) as though it were a description of Standard American bidding. The purpose of this is two-fold: first, to enable the reader to learn the Roth Point Count in a setting most familiar to him; second, to prepare for a comparison of old-fashioned bidding methods with the more modern ones presented in Part II. *It should be noted that the bidding methods presented in Part I are not necessarily recommended.*

Despite this method of presentation, it may appear to some readers that the Roth Point Count is very complicated, perhaps unnecessarily so. We wish to make two points in this regard:

First, you get what you pay for. That is, the more techniques you learn (methods of counting points included) the better your results will be. In particular, the more refinements of the Roth Point Count you learn, the better you will evaluate your hand. In this book we present a point count that is complete enough for expert evaluation. Perhaps you will want to learn it all, perhaps not. Regardless, the more you learn about the Roth Point Count (and the reasons behind it—which are also presented) the more accurately you will be able to evaluate your hand and the more you will know about bridge.

Second, whether you know it or not, the standard point count is almost as complicated as the Roth Point Count! The difference is mainly in appearance, for standard point—counting manuals hide the special rules and exceptional cases, apparently not daring ever to present the reader with the entire package lest he reject the material as too complicated. In this book, we develop the Roth Point Count step by step. After each addition we give a summary of the entire method developed to that point. When we have finished describing the Roth Point Count, the final summary table shows it *all.* We ask the reader to follow the logical development of the count chapter by chapter. We have a higher opinion of bridge players than other authors. We believe an average player, *or even a relative beginner,* can learn the entire Roth Point Count as easily as he can learn the traditional count! We ask only that you proceed one step at a time and at your own proper pace.

Throughout this book and particularly in Part I we make certain simplifications, both in approach and language, designed to simplify the learning process for the reader. Since these conveniences represent an abuse of language, we wish to set the record on them straight at the very outset.

Very often, in relating a number of points to a bid, we say that the bidding indicates, for example, that "game is definite," or that "slam is impossible." Expressions such as these, when relating to point totals, are not to be taken literally but rather to be interpreted as meaning that the point count evaluation indicates that certain actions should or should not be taken. For example, when we say that "26 points are required for game" we do not mean that it is impossible to make a game contract without a combined holding of 26 points, nor do we mean that if you have 26 points, and do bid game, that you are certain to fulfill your contract. What *is* meant is that it will, in general, be a good policy to contract for game when and only when your partnership possesses 26 points. Similarly, the phrase "game is impossible" means only that the combined point count indicates that game should not be bid, that a game contract will (probably) not have a good chance of success. It does not mean, of course, that you won't be able to make game (with, let us say, favorable breaks) on occasion. Similar phrases should be interpreted in like manner.

In Part I, which introduces the Roth Point Count within the context of Standard American bidding, we make two simplifications which are not, in fact, standard.

First, we have done away with the notion of "biddable suit." This concept, with its long lists of requirements and exceptions to exceptions, has plagued aspiring bridge students since the Culbertson era (when it was first introduced). In our view, the potential gains available through making use of this concept are far outweighed by the confusion it evokes, particularly for the beginner or inexperienced player. Further, there are so many exceptions to the biddable-suit rules and their applications, that the space required by a comprehensive discussion is almost prohibitive. Previous books on bidding which make use of rules regarding the honor strength required for a suit to be biddable casually disregard the difficulties caused when the exceptional cases arise, leaving the student to flounder with no guide when he picks up such a hand.

Second, in the matter of opening the bidding, we have adjusted our rules so that an opening bid in a major suit is not made on a four-card suit. Now this is not standard, and we are not attempting to claim it is. The requirement of five or more cards for a major-suit opening is used in Part I of this book not just because we feel this is a superior method (although, as it happens, we do), but rather because this rule allows the choice of suits for an opening bid to be expressed completely in 12 lines rather than 12 pages.

There is a great unending debate among experts about the soundness of the "five-card majors" rule. Disregarding our personal views, the violent split of expert opinion on this topic, judged objectively, must be taken to indicate that there is merit to both sides of the argument. Thus, whether one style or the other is in fact superior, the margin of superiority cannot be great. As far as we are concerned, this decides the issue, for the amount of simplification gained by the use of "five-card majors" is almost immeasurable. In any event, we heartily recommend it for inexperienced players, for it will make learning so much easier. (When you become experienced, and more fully understand the advantages and disadvantages of the rule, you can then formulate your own opinion of its soundness. But by then you will not be interested in simplicity.)

We have made certain other abridgments of standard bidding, again for the sake of clarity. These are minor changes, and are generally explained in footnotes to the text, so that the reader may know the full story, regardless of what he is (perhaps temporarily) learning for his own use.

Part II of this work differs considerably from Part I. In Part II, we have assumed that the reader is familiar with Standard American bidding methods and attempt to convince him to abandon them in favor of the Roth approach. This part of the book deals with choice of system; except for a few fine points, evaluation is a secondary consideration and it is assumed that the reader has mastered the Roth Point Count in Part I.

This somewhat unusual format is deliberate. We have two things to bring forward in this book: the Roth Point Count and the Roth approach to bidding—and we want them to be considered separately on their own merits. Thus, you can use the Roth Point Count profitably regardless of the system you use; similarly, the Roth method can be employed with any evaluation method. To keep the topics separate, we first present the point count in a familiar framework before continuing with a discussion of system. Some readers will profit mainly from Part I; some will be more interested in Part II; the overwhelming majority, we hope, will profit from both parts. The two-part breakdown is our way of indicating recognition of evaluation and system as two independent aspects of bidding. By covering both in detail, we hope we have made this the first truly complete book on bidding.

Thus, when you approach this book, we recommend that you consider it as two separate books. Part One is about hand evaluation; the description of Standard American bidding, though valuable to the aspiring student, is incidental to the main theme. Part Two is about a bidding system, the Roth Approach to Bidding. This delves deeper into bidding theory and attempts to solve some of the common problems that beset standard bidders. Do not think that Part I will not be of use in learning Part II, for (aside from the evaluation techniques which will be useful whatever system you decide to you) the value of the Roth approach cannot be fully appreciated unless you have learned (preferably played) Standard American methods.

Although parts of this book resemble a law brief (The Case Against Traditional Point Count) and others a political manifesto (Standard American Bidding Must Go!) it is actually a textbook, designed to instruct. The reader is requested to keep this in mind throughout. In particular, we wish to issue a warning against going through the contents too quickly. The material presented in this book is meant to be read, perhaps reread, *and then studied.* For example, the Roth Point Count (presented in Part I), while based on standard point count techniques, contains many new principles and ideas. It would be foolish to attempt to learn them all at one sitting.

As an aid to the learning process, hundreds of illustrative examples are presented in full detail. Furthermore, you, the reader, are given numerous opportunities to test your own progress with quizzes after each section, as well as review quizzes at the end of each chapter. You can make best use of these if you are completely honest with yourself in taking them. A poor score on a quiz is a warning that you passed over some of the material too quickly. There is nothing to be ashamed of (neither bridge nor the material in this book is particularly easy), but you should heed the warning and review those points you missed before proceeding further. When, ultimately, you find yourself bidding better than your friends, it won't matter how many times you had to read a particular chapter!

Finally, a word of encouragement. By reading this book you are taking part in a great experiment, the results of which, we believe, will lead to a true revolution in point count evaluation, perhaps even to a reexamination of Standard American bidding concepts. As a participant, you will play a part in determining the outcome of the experiment. So we sincerely urge you to give the ideas in this book a full and fair test. *We are convinced that every bridge player can significantly improve his bidding skills by following the principles of this book.*

Good luck.

A REMINDER

Part I of this book is a complete delineation of the dynamic new Roth Point Count. Part II of this book presents the Roth Bidding Method.

Hand evaluation, the burden of Part I, is and should be the same regardless of the bidding method used. It is not necessary, therefore, for the reader to consider the Roth Point Count and the Roth Bidding Method inextricably bound together. *No matter what bidding methods you may use, we believe that your employment of the Roth Point Count in evaluating your hand will make your* present *bidding methods more efficient and more accurate.*

In order to present Roth Point Count in the clearest and simplest manner possible, we have elected to do so in the context of Standard American bidding because Standard American is the most widely used although not, we believe, by any means the best approach to bidding. As you will see, Roth Point Count does make Standard American—or any other system—a better system.

In Part II of this book we will present what we believe to be the best of all bidding methods.

CHAPTER

1

Revolution in Point-Count Bidding

The cards have been shuffled and dealt; you are ready to begin an evening of bridge. Your first hand offers interesting prospects:

♠5   ♡52   ◇AJ872   ♣KJ852

To find out just how good this hand is, you count your points: four for the ace, three for the king, one for each jack, two for the singleton, and one for the doubleton. This adds up to 12 points—not a bad hand at all! Since your partner, the dealer, is taking his own good time about choosing a bid, your mind wanders a bit, and it occurs to you that not even a world champion could have evaluated this hand any better than you did. To be sure, world champions may use highly complicated bidding systems, but point count itself is *not* a system. It is a tool used by almost all bridge players—experts and novices alike—to determine how good or bad a hand is. Armed with the knowledge that your hand is worth exactly 12 points, you look forward confidently to a triumphant success in the bidding.

You are pleased to hear your partner open the bidding with **one spade.** Your right-hand opponent passes and you respond **two diamonds.** You know that this bid promises a minimum of 10 points, and you make a mental note that you have two points in reserve. Your left-hand opponent passes, and partner rebids **two spades.** Since he may have as many as 15 points for this bid, and since you have learned that a total of 26 points is required for game, you can see that game is certainly not out of the question. You therefore try once more by bidding **three clubs.** (The opponents, perhaps muttering something about "never getting any cards," continue to pass throughout the auction.) Sure enough, partner contracts for game by bidding **three notrump,** which you pass.

The opening lead is made, and you put down the dummy. As the hand is played out, you observe that your opponents' pile of tricks grows at an alarming rate. Your partner struggles grimly; he applies every technique of declarer play he has ever learned; but he can take no more than seven tricks, and your three notrump contract is set two. You are somewhat annoyed until partner tells you his hand:

♠ AQ872   ♡ AK4   ♢ 53   ♣ 643

You can see that his bidding was above reproach. He had 14 points: four for each ace, three for the king, two for the queen, and one for the doubleton. His 14 points and your 12 points did in fact add up to the 26 points needed for game. Yet, as you study the two hands, you realize that there was nothing wrong with partner's play of the hand; three notrump was a virtually hopeless contract from the start. But how on earth could you stop in a makeable part-score with 26 points between the two hands? It may occur to you that your singleton and doubleton, which represented 3 of your 12 points, weren't very useful for playing at notrump. This is indeed unfortunate, but what could you have done about it? You had no way of knowing that the hand would be played at notrump until partner bid three notrump, by which time it was far too late to arrive at any makeable contract.

The game continues, and a few deals later you pick up:

♠ K98754   ♡ K542   ◇ 53   ♣ 9

Once again, you count your points: three for each king, one for
the doubleton, and two for the singleton, for a total of 9 points.
You are a bit surprised to hear partner open the bidding with **one
spade,** but you dutifully respond **two spades,** showing 7 to 10
points. This is quickly followed by three passes. To your chagrin,
you find that you have missed an ice-cold game, for partner's
hand is:

♠ AQ1063   ♡ A83   ◇ A7   ♣ 862

Partner was correct to pass two spades. He knew that the *most*
the two hands could produce was his 15 points plus 10 (your highest
possible value) or 25, one point less than the 26 needed for game.
Had you held only 6 points, it might not have been easy to take
even eight tricks, so partner wisely stopped at two spades once
the magic total of 26 could not be reached. Yet the game was there
for the taking!

At the end of the evening, while you are congratulating the opponents on their victory, it occurs to you that the laurels *could*
have been yours. There seemed to be quite a few hands totaling
23 or 24 points on which game could have been made, but was not
bid; and hands totaling 26 or 27 points on which game was bid,
but could not be made. Since it is decidedly more pleasant to
have the opponents congratulate you on your victory, you resolve
to do better in the future.

Unfortunately, however, your determination is not likely to be
rewarded with success, because you—and all bridge players except
the greatest experts—do not realize that the problem is *not* just one
of judgment. It is the point count method that is to blame. *The
traditional method of counting points is deficient, fallacious, and
misleading, and leads the bridge player into incorrect contracts
through no fault of his own.* It *is* true that 26 points usually produce
game, but the points must be counted properly. It is time for a

revolution in point count bidding; time to discard the inaccurate, outmoded method and to adopt a new, effective, yet easy to use, method which we are calling *Roth Point Count*. As we will see in later chapters, the hand with which you went down two at three notrump *actually adds up to only 22 Roth Points*—not nearly enough for game! The hand you bid to two spades, which was cold for ten tricks, *adds up to 29 Roth Points*—more than enough for game! *The traditional point count method produced the wrong total in both cases.* Roth Point Count—which involves **just a few simple changes** in the point count method you know and use— will guide you to the correct contract on a far higher percentage of hands.

The traditional point count method was popularized in the late 1940s. Point count made it possible for bridge players to arrive at an approximate hand evaluation with an ease never before possible. It was relatively more accurate than the methods of hand evaluation that preceded it. Subsequent experience and analysis has taught us, however, that the traditional point count method also has its weaknesses. The Roth Point Count is designed to eliminate them. It is as much more accurate as traditional point count was to what preceded it.

As the general quality of bridge improves, many players realize that they must change some of their bidding methods in order to compete with the growing number of at least reasonably good players. In the process they experiment with large numbers of conventional bids. These often have colorful names—"South African Transfer," "Fragment Bids," "Astro," to name just a few—but the results they produce are not always beneficial. It can be quite disconcerting to try to remember that in certain situations, a club bid really shows hearts, or a jump in diamonds shows a singleton spade. The sheer memory work involved often hurts the player's overall bidding—and his declarer play and defense as well. Furthermore, these conventions generally deal with unusual kinds of hands and specific and relatively infrequent situations, and one can grow old and gray waiting until the right time to use them comes along.

Any real bidding improvement must come from better bidding of the "bread-and-butter" hands—the cold games that don't add up to "26 points," or the "27-point" hands on which game can't be made. But most important, these conventions are for the most part based on the same deficient point count method that most bridge players use. Thus, while special conventions may have their place, real improvement must come from better bidding of *all* hands.

A few bridge theorists have tried to improve their accuracy by changing the basic 4–3–2–1 point count. Unfortunately, these new point count procedures were so complicated that only a professor of mathematics was apt to be able to cope with them. For example, one expert suggested counting aces as 4 and ½ points and tens as ½ point, and making numerous "corrections" for specific good and bad holdings. After a few tries at counting up to 15 and ½, 13 and ⅞, and other unlikely totals, gloom and depression began to set in, and his readers retreated to the far more comfortable (if slightly less accurate) standard method. So would we!

Experts realize that the standard point count method is often inaccurate. Therefore, they make various adjustments *during the bidding*. They may decide that a hand that appears to be worth 15 points is really worth less because of "a bad fit with partner" or "wasted values," or that an innocent-looking 14-point hand is really worth much more because of "an excellent fit" or "all the right cards." All experts do this, *yet none can define—in terms of points —how they do it*. Some bridge writers have tried to hint at this by teaching the reader to make "corrections" in his point count in certain situations. None show how to do this in *all* situations; none help the bridge player to bid better *on each and every hand*.

In this book, we will show how you, *using the same basic 4–3–2–1 point count you now use*, can bid as well as the experts do by applying a few simple rules. All you will be required to do is: first, count your *Roth Points;* second, *adjust your point count during the bidding*—deducting points under certain clearly defined circumstances, and adding points under others. Bidding will become an exciting and dynamic process: *You will see the value of your hand change before your very eyes as a result of the bids you and your partner make!* You will learn to think the way the expert does. There will be no fractions, no higher mathematics, no long lists of principles to memorize—just a few easy rules to learn and apply. You will bid better on *every* hand, and have more fun doing it! As a result, you will have a *real* advantage at the bridge table.

The Revolution at Work

The Roth Point Count is the first complete method showing how point count changes during the bidding of every hand. It is even easier to use than techniques which require changing the point count only in certain specialized situations, and it is far more accurate because *it applies to all hands.*

The first thing you will do, after sorting your cards, is count your Roth Points. Since Roth Point Count uses the same 4–3–2–1 count that you are familiar with, this will be fast and easy, as well it should be. Bridge would be quite a dull game if everyone had to take five or ten minutes during the bidding simply to count up his points! Then, while the bidding is going on, you will adjust your point count in one of the following three ways:

1. PROMOTE your point count—*add* points when good things happen during the bidding. You will see your voids, singletons, and doubletons take on extra value when you have good trump support for partner; see your hand improve in total value when partner bids a suit for which you have good support. The expert does these things by "feel"; you will do exactly the same thing by *promoting* your point count when your hand improves during the bidding.

2. KEEP the same point count when the bidding neither improves nor weakens your hand.

3. DEMOTE your point count—*deduct* points when the auction takes a turn for the worse. You will see your voids, singletons, and doubletons *lose* value when you have little or no trump support for partner; see the overall value of your hand go down when partner bids a suit you don't like. Once again, you will be doing just what

the expert does, only you will be doing it by using Roth Point
Count—a simple and accurate guide to the *true* value of your hand
at every stage of the auction.

Recall the first hand in this chapter:

$$♠5 \quad ♡52 \quad ◇AJ872 \quad ♣KJ832$$

Before the bidding begins, this hand *is* worth 12 points. But a
bad thing happens: Partner opens with **one spade**, a suit for which
you have no support. *Demote! Your hand is no longer worth 12
points.*

On the second example hand, you held:

$$♠K98754 \quad ♡K542 \quad ◇53 \quad ♣9$$

Before the bidding begins, this hand *is* worth 9 points. But a
very good thing happens: Partner opens with **one spade**, thus bidding a suit for which you have excellent trump support. *Promote!
Your hand is now worth much more than 9 points.*

Suppose you hold:

$$♠AK3 \quad ♡A1054 \quad ◇K86 \quad ♣KJ7$$

You open **one notrump**, showing 16–18 points, and partner raises
to **two notrump**. *Keep* the same point count. Your hand was worth
18 points before the bidding started. Nothing very bad or very
good has happened; your hand is still worth 18 points. Partner is
simply inviting game in notrump, and his bid does not affect the
value of your hand, which was judged in terms of notrump to
begin with. Naturally, you accept partner's invitation by bidding
three notrump, since you have the maximum possible total—18
points.

Of course, your point count will not always change with every
bid. In later chapters, we will see exactly when and how much to
add or subtract. The purpose of these examples is to give you a
general idea of the dynamics of Roth Point Count in action. Bidding
this way is an exciting adventure. For the first time, you will see
your hand change in value during the bidding! Like the experts,
you will promote and demote your hand according to the way the

auction develops. No longer will you find yourself trapped by the traditional method of counting points; your bidding will be more accurate, and you will enjoy it more!

How to Use This Book

Please do *not* try to rush through this book in one evening. Read a little at a time. Learn the material in each section thoroughly before proceeding to the next.

Each chapter contains one or more sets of quizzes to test your understanding of the material in each section. When you have finished a section, take the quiz carefully. If you get more than one wrong answer, you should go back and read through the section again. Since later sections build on the principles developed in the earlier sections, it is helpful to have a clear understanding of what you have read before moving on. To help you in your quest for knowledge, "capsule summaries" will be presented at strategic points in the book to provide brief reviews and serve as convenient references should you wish to check back. Review quizzes at the end of each chapter will enable you to evaluate your progress. A good score indicates that you can proceed with confidence; a lower score suggests that you would do well to go back over the chapter once more.

As you abandon the traditional point count method and begin to use the Roth Point Count, you will find yourself bidding and thinking like the experts do. The rewards will be great, but it is up to you to make it work. Good luck!

CHAPTER
2
The Opening Bid

The game is under way and you are first to call (the dealer). You have sorted your cards and are ready to begin. What now?

Step 1 / Count your Roth Points

The first thing you do is to count your Roth Points. There are three factors for you to evaluate: *High-Card Points,* for which we will use the abbreviation HCP; *Distribution Points;* and *Length Points.*

HIGH-CARD POINTS (HCP) are counted in the usual fashion:

$$
\begin{aligned}
\text{Ace} &= 4 \\
\text{King} &= 3 \\
\text{Queen} &= 2 \\
\text{Jack} &= 1
\end{aligned}
$$

DISTRIBUTION POINTS are also counted in the familiar way:

$$
\begin{aligned}
\text{Void} &= 3 \\
\text{Singleton} &= 2 \\
\text{Doubleton} &= 1
\end{aligned}
$$

LENGTH POINTS are the only new feature you need to learn at present. Long suits have a way of taking extra tricks—more tricks than one would expect just from counting the high-card points in that suit. Therefore, we add extra points for particularly long suits. We will have to be careful, however, when *minor suits* are involved. Since game in a minor suit—five clubs or five diamonds—requires 11 tricks, it is obviously harder to make than game in a major, which requires only 10 tricks, or game in notrump, which requires only 9 tricks. Therefore, hands with long minor suits are often best played at notrump. It can be rather trying to attempt to run off a suit such as ♣A98742 opposite ♣63 as notrump. Your opponents have an unfortunate tendency to develop their own suits, and they may succeed in defeating the contract before you can get that suit set up. Furthermore, when you do decide to play for the 11-trick minor-suit game you can afford only two losers, and a shaky trump suit will doom you to defeat even before you get started. Therefore, we will add points only for "good" minor suits: those which contain two top honors (ace-king, ace-queen, or king-queen). The rules that we will follow are:

Major suits:	*Any* six-card major suit	= 1
	Any seven-card major suit	= 2
Minor suits:	Any *good* six-card minor suit	= 1
	Any *good* seven-card minor suit = 2	

As you can see, *the addition of points for long suits is the only change from the usual point count procedure.*

Now that we have covered the basic rules, let's look at a few examples. For a while, we will present the Roth Point Count in detail, but rest assured that the entire counting process will soon become automatic.

		HCP	Dist.	Length	Total
1.	♠2	0	2	0	2
	♡KQ42	5	0	0	5
	◇J832	1	0	0	1
	♣A754	4	0	0	4
		10	2	0	12

		HCP	Dist.	Length	Total
2.	♠ AJ6532	5	0	1	6
	♡ 54	0	1	0	1
	♢ K632	3	0	0	3
	♣ 3	0	2	0	2
		8	3	1	12

Remember to count an "extra" point (Length Point) for the six-card spade suit.

		HCP	Dist.	Length	Total
3.	♠ 3	0	2	0	2
	♡ 54	0	1	0	1
	♢ K632	3	0	0	3
	♣ AJ6532	5	0	0	5
		8	3	0	11

Do *not* add a point for the six-card club suit, as it is *not good*. (Headed by two top honors). (Compare with the previous hand).

		HCP	Dist.	Length	Total
4.	♠ K53	3	0	0	3
	♡ 2	0	2	0	2
	♢ 62	0	1	0	1
	♣ AQ107432	6	0	2	8
		9	3	2	14

Do add 2 points for the seven-card club suit, as it *is good*— headed by two top honors.

		HCP	Dist.	Length	Total
5.	♠ A5	4	1	0	5
	♡ ---	0	3	0	3
	♢ 9432	0	0	0	0
	♣ AKQ8543	9	0	2	11
		13	4	2	19

Do add 2 points for the seven-card club suit, as it *is good*.

Capsule Summary: Roth Points for the Opening Bid

HIGH-CARD POINTS	DISTRIBUTION POINTS	LENGTH POINTS	
		Majors	Minors
Ace = 4	Void = 3	6-card suit: = 1	= 1 if suit is *good*
King = 3	Singleton = 2		
Queen = 2	Doubleton = 1		
Jack = 1		7-card suit: = 2	= 2 if suit is *good*

A *good* suit is one which includes two of the top three honors.

QUIZ

For each of the following hands, count your Roth Points (HCP, Distribution Points, and Length Points). What is the total for each hand?

1. ♠842 ♡K104 ◇72 ♣AKJ84
2. ♠A4 ♡AK ◇J84 ♣Q98732
3. ♠--- ♡AQ8742 ◇A843 ♣J98
4. ♠9874 ♡732 ◇AJ2 ♣K43
5. ♠A4 ♡53 ◇AJ86532 ♣98
6. ♠A108742 ♡A109876 ◇5 ♣---
7. ♠5 ♡--- ◇A108742 ♣A109876
8. ♠K87 ♡K2 ◇4 ♣AQJ8742
9. ♠432 ♡3 ◇542 ♣AKQ432
10. ♠A432 ♡43 ◇QJ874 ♣K2

SOLUTIONS

1. 12 points. 11 HCP and 1 point for the doubleton.

2. 16 points. 14 HCP and 1 point for *each* doubleton (*no* Length Points).

3. 15 points. 11 HCP, 3 points for the void, and 1 point for length (6-card major suit).

4. 8 points. 8 HCP.

5. 12 points. 9 HCP and 1 point for each doubleton (*no* Length Points).

6. 15 points. 8 HCP, 3 points for the void, 2 points for the singleton, and 1 point *each* for length in spades and hearts (6-card major suits).

7. 13 points. 8 HCP, 3 points for the void, and 2 points for the singleton (*no* Length Points).

8. 18 points. 13 HCP, 2 points for the singleton, 1 point for the doubleton, and 2 points for length (*Good* 7-card minor suit).

9. 12 points. 9 HCP, 2 points for the singleton, and 1 point for length (*Good* 6-card minor suit).

10. 12 points. 10 HCP, and 1 point for *each* doubleton.

If you got more than one wrong, go back and study the points that caused you trouble. With just a little practice, you should be able to count Roth Points easily and quickly. If you scored 9 or 10 correct, you may proceed with confidence to the next section.

Step 2 / Bid or Pass?

Now that you have counted your Roth Points, you are ready to proceed to the second step: Should you open the bidding, or should you pass? While it is certainly more fun to bid, discretion requires that you pass when you do not have more than your fair share of the cards. Let's ignore for the moment the question of *what* to open with, and concentrate on the question that comes first: Should you open at all?

REQUIREMENTS FOR THE OPENING ONE-BID*

To open the bidding with a one-level bid, you must hold *14 to*

---

* Technically, these rules apply only to an opening in first or second position—i.e., when partner has not passed. The "standard" rules for third- and fourth-position openings, however, are so vague and confusing that we prefer to avoid a detailed discussion of this topic until Part II. The high-card point requirements given for opening bids replace the traditional "two defensive tricks" rule. Experience has shown that 10 HCP will usually produce at least two defensive tricks. We therefore are simplifying this traditional requirement by expressing it entirely in terms of HCP.

21 points, including at least 10 in high-card points (HCP). Be sure that you have the required 10 HCP! On those happy occasions when your hand is *too strong* for a one-level opening bid, special opening bids will be used. (These will be described in later chapters.) Thus, our rule concerning opening is quite simple:

13 points or less: Pass.

14 or more points, but less than 10 HCP: Pass.

14 or more points, and at least 10 HCP: Open.

In the Roth Point Count, there is no vague "middle ground" in which hands may or may not be opened as there is in the traditional method; no "optional" opening bids (which, presumably, are decided by consulting the ceiling or your daily horoscope). Any problems concerning distribution, suits, and high cards are taken care of by the Roth Point Count. All you need do is count your Roth Points and your HCP. With 14 or more Roth Points and at least 10 HCP, open; otherwise pass. What could be simpler?

Let's look at a few examples:

		HCP	Dist.	Length	Total
1.	♠ J873	1	0	0	1
	♡ J873	1	0	0	1
	♢ AK4	7	0	0	7
	♣ A6	4	1	0	5
		13	1	0	14

You have 14 Roth Points, *and* at least 10 HCP. You *must* open.

		HCP	Dist.	Length	Total
2.	♠ AK5	7	0	0	7
	♡ K62	3	0	0	3
	♢ 983	0	0	0	0
	♣ K764	3	0	0	3
		13	0	0	13

You have only 13 Roth Points. You must pass.

		HCP	Dist.	Length	Total
3.	♠ A75432	4	0	1	5
	♡ A65432	4	0	1	5
	◇ 2	0	2	0	2
	♣ ---	0	3	0	3
		8	5	2	15

You have 15 Roth Points, but only 8 HCP. You need at least 10 HCP to open. Therefore, you *must* pass.

		HCP	Dist.	Length	Total
4.	♠ K42	3	0	0	3
	♡ 62	0	1	0	1
	◇ 62	0	1	0	1
	♣ AKJ432	8	0	1	9
		11	2	1	14

You have 14 Roth Points and at least 10 HCP. You *must* open.

QUIZ

On each of the following hands, you are the dealer (first to speak). Do you open or pass?

1. ♠ AK865 ♡ AQ3 ◇ 52 ♣ 864
2. ♠ KQ10 ♡ A543 ◇ Q72 ♣ J63
3. ♠ Q86432 ♡ AJ7432 ◇ 2 ♣ ---
4. ♠ AK8653 ♡ A32 ◇ 65 ♣ 82
5. ♠ A842 ♡ 732 ◇ 6 ♣ AK753
6. ♠ KQJ65 ♡ KQ3 ◇ A82 ♣ 32
7. ♠ 65 ♡ 82 ◇ AKQ643 ♣ K32
8. ♠ 86 ♡ 74 ◇ A5 ♣ KQJ7643
9. ♠ A86432 ♡ AQ643 ◇ 3 ♣ 3
10. ♠ AKQJ643 ♡ 6 ◇ 7 ♣ 8432

SOLUTIONS

1. Open. You have at least 10 HCP and a total of 14 points (13 HCP and 1 for the doubleton).

2. Pass. You have a total of only 12 points.

3. Pass. While your total is 14 (7 HCP, 3 for the void, 2 for the singleton, 1 each for the spade and heart length), you do *not* have the necessary 10 HCP.

4. Open. You have at least 10 HCP and a total of 14 points (11 HCP, 1 for each doubleton, and 1 for the spade length).

5. Pass. You have only 13 points (11 HCP and 2 for the singleton).

6. Open. You have 16 points (15 HCP and 1 for the doubleton) and at least 10 HCP.

7. Open. You have 12 HCP, plus 1 for each doubleton and 1 for the diamond length (*Good* 6-card minor)—total 15.

8. Open. You have 10 HCP, plus 1 for each doubleton and 2 for the club length (*Good* 7-card minor)—total 15.

9. Open. You have 10 HCP, plus 2 for each singleton and one for the spade length—total 15.

10. Open. You have 10 HCP, plus 2 for each singleton and 2 for the spade length (7-card major)—total 16.

Remember that the quizzes in this book are designed not only to train you in the use of the Roth Point Count but also to help you develop your skill until counting becomes automatic. A good score is assurance that you have learned the Roth Point Count, the first and most important step on the road to bidding like an expert.

Step 3 / Notrump or Suit?

You have counted your Roth Points, and you find that you have at least 10 HCP and 14 total points. (If you don't, of course, you pass, and are no longer concerned with problems of the opening bid.) The next thing you must do is determine whether you should open with 1 NT or with one of a suit.

(17)

REQUIREMENTS FOR THE 1 NT OPENING BID

There are three requirements for the 1 NT opening bid. If your hand satisfies all three, you should open 1 NT. If your hand fails to meet *any one* of the three requirements (yet contains 14 or more total points and at least 10 HCP), you *may not* open 1 NT, but *must open* with one of a suit. The requirements for the 1 NT opening bid are:

1. 16–18 HCP.
2. Balanced suit distribution: 4–3–3–3, 4–4–3–2, 5–3–3–2.
3. High-card points in *at least three* of the four suits.

Once you have decided to open 1 NT, *do not count Distribution Points*. Some examples:

		HCP	Dist.	Length	Total
1.	♠AQ5	6	0	0	6
	♡KJ72	4	0	0	4
	◇Q86	2	0	0	2
	♣A103	4	0	0	4
		16	0	0	16

You have 16 HCP, balanced suit distribution (4–3–3–3), and high-card points in at least three suits. *Open 1 NT.*

		HCP	Dist.	Length	Total
2.	♠AQ6	6	0	0	6
	♡KQ72	5	0	0	5
	◇AQJ6	7	0	0	7
	♣84	0	1 → 0	0	1 → 0
		18	1 → 0	0	19 → 18

You have 18 HCP, balanced distribution (4–4–3–2), and high-card points in at least three suits. *Open 1 NT.* Do not count a Distribution Point for the doubleton club for bidding notrump.

		HCP	Dist.	Length	Total
3.	♠ A864	4	0	0	4
	♡ KQ72	5	0	0	5
	◇ AQJ7	7	0	0	7
	♣ 5	0	2	0	2
		16	2	0	18

You have 16 HCP and high-card points in at least three suits, but you may not open 1 NT without balanced distribution. *Open with one of a suit.* Since you are bidding a suit and *not* notrump you *do* count the 2 Distribution Points for the singleton club.

		HCP	Dist.	Length	Total
4.	♠ A83	4	0	0	4
	♡ K7	3	1	0	4
	◇ K2	3	1	0	4
	♣ AQ8642	6	0	1	7
		16	2	1	19

You have 16 HCP and high-card points in at least three suits, but you may not open 1 NT without balanced distribution. *Open with one of a suit*, being sure to count your Distribution Points.

		HCP	Dist.	Length	Total
5.	♠ AQJ4	7	0	0	7
	♡ K82	3	0	0	3
	◇ AQ2	6	0	0	6
	♣ K63	3	0	0	3
		19	0	0	19

You may not open 1 NT with more than 18 HCP. *Open with one of a suit.*

		HCP	Dist.	Length	Total
6.	♠ A86	4	0	0	4
	♡ QJ84	3	0	0	3
	◇ AKJ2	8	0	0	8
	♣ 64	0	1	0	1
		15	1	0	16

You may not open 1 NT with less than 16 HCP. *Open with one of a suit.*

		HCP	Dist.	Length	Total
7.	♠ AQ864	6	0	0	6
	♡ KQ2	5	0	0	5
	◇ Q43	2	0	0	2
	♣ A4	4	1 → 0	0	5 → 4
		17	1 → 0	0	18 → 17

You have 17 HCP, balanced distribution (5–3–3–2), and high-card points in at least three suits. *Open with 1 NT.* Notice that the Distribution Point is not counted when you bid notrump.

		HCP	Dist.	Length	Total
8.	♠ AKQ2	9	0	0	9
	♡ AK3	7	0	0	7
	◇ 542	0	0	0	0
	♣ 863	0	0	0	0
		16	0	0	16

You have 16 HCP and balanced distribution, but you do not have high-card points in three suits. *Open with one of a suit.*

————————————————————————————————

Capsule Summary: When to Open 1 NT

You must have: 1. 16–18 HCP.

2. Balanced suit distribution: 4–3–3–3, 4–4–3–2, or 5–3–3–2.

3. High-card points in at least three suits.

If you meet these requirements, and open 1 NT, do not count points for distribution.

————————————————————————————————

QUIZ

On each of the following hands, you are the dealer. You must decide if you (1) Pass; (2) Open 1 NT; (3) Open with one of a suit. Remember that the *first* thing you do is count your Roth Points!

1. ♠ KQJ4 ♡ AJ42 ◇ K42 ♣ A8
2. ♠ QJ2 ♡ AK5 ◇ KQJ42 ♣ 97
3. ♠ K52 ♡ AQ864 ◇ K96 ♣ 82
4. ♠ KQJ2 ♡ 763 ◇ AKQJ ♣ 63
5. ♠ AKQ ♡ KQ5 ◇ A642 ♣ Q42
6. ♠ AJ6542 ♡ K4 ◇ K2 ♣ 876
7. ♠ QJ102 ♡ KQJ3 ◇ AKJ5 ♣ 4
8. ♠ --- ♡ AJ8642 ◇ A9643 ♣ 73
9. ♠ AQ64 ♡ K43 ◇ K64 ♣ KJ2
10. ♠ 53 ♡ KQ2 ◇ AJ32 ♣ AJ74

SOLUTIONS

1. Open 1 NT. You have 18 HCP, balanced distribution, and high-card points in at least three suits. Although you have 19 points, do not count any Distribution Points for the doubleton club once you have decided to bid notrump.

2. Open 1 NT. You have 16 HCP, high-card points in at least three suits, and balanced distribution. (You have 17 points, but only 16 points for purposes of bidding notrump.)

3. Pass. You have only 13 points.

4. Open with one of a suit. You may not open 1 NT without high-card points in at least three suits. (Total points: 17)

5. Open with one of a suit. You may not open 1 NT with more than 18 HCP. (Total points: 20)

6. Open with one of a suit. You must open as you have 14 points: 11 HCP, 1 for each doubleton, and 1 for length (6-card major suit).

7. Open with one of a suit. You may not open 1 NT without balanced distribution. (Total points: 19)

8. Pass. You may not open the bidding with less than 10 HCP. (Total points: 14)

9. Open with 1 NT. Your hand meets all three requirements. (Total points: 16)

10. Open with one of a suit. You lack the 16 HCP required to open 1 NT even though you have 16 total points.

For each hand, check to see that you counted your Roth Points correctly. Remember that you *do* count Distribution Points when opening with one of a suit, but *do not* count Distribution Points if you decide to open 1 NT. Do not hesitate to go back and review if anything is unclear!

Step 4 / Which Suit to Open?

As we have seen, the opening bid of 1 NT is a very *limited* bid, subject to exact requirements. This is a big advantage: with just one bid, we succeed in conveying to partner a great deal of information about our hand. However, because the requirements for opening 1 NT are so severe, we will much more often open with one of a suit. This brings us to the final question: which suit should we bid?

WHICH SUIT TO OPEN

The first thing to do is locate your *longest* suit. Then, just follow these simple steps:

1. If your *longest* suit is 5 cards or more, bid it! In case of ties, do not award duplicate prizes; pick the *higher-ranking* suit (with spade and club suits each 5 cards in length, bid 1 ♠; with heart and diamond suits each 6 cards in length, bid 1 ♡; and so on.)
2. If your *longest* suit contains 4 cards, bid your *longer* minor.

In case of ties, choose your *stronger* minor. (If your minors
are virtually identical, open 1 ♣.) Notice that a two-card or
shorter suit is *never* opened.

Here's how the rules work:

		HCP	Dist.	Length	Total
1.	♠ K5	3	1	0	4
	♡ AQ8642	6	0	1	7
	◇ K96	3	0	0	3
	♣ A2	4	1	0	5
		16	2	1	19

Your longest suit has 6 cards. Bid it. *Open 1 ♡.*

		HCP	Dist.	Length	Total
2.	♠ Q9876	2	0	0	2
	♡ AK987	7	0	0	7
	◇ A5	4	1	0	5
	♣ 3	0	2	0	2
		13	3	0	16

With two 5-card suits, bid the *higher-ranking* one. *Open 1 ♠.*

		HCP	Dist.	Length	Total
3.	♠ K98765	3	0	1	4
	♡ 5	0	2	0	2
	◇ AQJ654	7	0	1	8
	♣ ---	0	3	0	3
		10	5	2	17

With two 6-card suits, bid the *higher-ranking* one. *Open 1 ♠.*

		HCP	Dist.	Length	Total
4.	♠ K42	3	0	0	3
	♡ A	4	2	0	6
	◇ Q987	2	0	0	2
	♣ AJ876	5	0	0	5
		14	2	0	16

Your longest suit has 5 cards, so bid it. *Open 1 ♣.*

		HCP	Dist.	Length	Total
5.	♠ J872	1	0	0	1
	♡ J873	1	0	0	1
	◇ AK3	7	0	0	7
	♣ A6	4	1	0	5
		13	1	0	14

Your longest suit has 4 cards, so you must bid your *longer minor*.
Open 1 ◇.

		HCP	Dist.	Length	Total
6.	♠ A652	4	0	0	4
	♡ A873	4	0	0	4
	◇ 7	0	2	0	2
	♣ K853	3	0	0	3
		11	2	0	13

Your longest suit has 4 cards, but where are your 14 points?
Pass.

		HCP	Dist.	Length	Total
7.	♠ A652	4	0	0	4
	♡ 7	0	2	0	2
	◇ AQ73	6	0	0	6
	♣ A853	4	0	0	4
		14	2	0	16

Your longest suit has 4 cards, so you must bid your longer minor.
Since they are equal in length, bid the stronger one. *Open 1 ◇.*

		HCP	Dist.	Length	Total
8.	♠ AQ74	6	0	0	6
	♡ AJ3	5	0	0	5
	◇ KQ2	5	0	0	5
	♣ 432	0	0	0	0
		16	0	0	16

Your longest suit has 4 cards, but this time it does not matter.
With 16 HCP, balanced distribution, and high-card points in at

(24)

least three suits, *open 1 NT*. Do not forget to open 1 NT when you meet the three requirements for this bid!

		HCP	Dist.	Length	Total
9.	♠ K872	3	0	0	3
	♡ KJ9	4	0	0	4
	◊ A72	4	0	0	4
	♣ A62	4	0	0	4
		15	0	0	15

Your longest suit has 4 cards, so you must bid your longer minor. Since the minor suits are equal in length, you must bid the stronger. Unfortunately, they are almost identical in strength! Do not try to make fine distinctions by looking at sixes and sevens. *Open 1 ♣.*

Capsule Summary: Which Suit to Open

LONGEST SUIT HAS 5 OR MORE

1. Bid your *longest suit*.
2. Ties: Bid the *higher-ranking* suit.

LONGEST SUIT HAS 4 CARDS

1. Bid your *longer minor*.
2. Ties: Bid the *stronger minor*.
2a. If tie is still not broken (minors equal in length *and* strength) bid 1 ♣.

Capsule Summary: The Four Steps for Opening

Step 1. Count your Roth Points.
Step 2. Decide whether to open the bidding or pass.
    A. With less than 14 total points *or* less than 10 HCP, *Pass.*
    B. With 14 or more total points and at least 10 HCP, continue to Step 3.
Step 3. Decide whether to open with 1 NT or one of a suit.
    A. With 16–18 HCP, high-card points in at least three suits and balanced distribution, *open 1 NT*. (Do *not* count Distribution Points if you open 1 NT.)

B. Otherwise, continue to Step 4. (Where you *do* count Distribution Points!)

Step 4. Select the proper suit in which to make your opening bid.

A. If your longest suit has 5 cards or more, bid it. Bid the higher-ranking suit in case of ties.

B. If your longest suit has 4 cards, bid your longer minor. If the minors are equal in length, bid the stronger. If the minors are equal in length *and* strength, open with 1 ♣.

Remember: Points? Open? Notrump? Suit?

You are now ready to take the final review quiz for this chapter. This quiz will test the degree to which you understand the Roth Point Count thus far. If your score is high, you may go on to Chapter 3 with full assurance. If you make several errors, however, go back and review the relevant sections in this chapter. *It is essential to understand the material in this chapter before proceeding further.* So don't be upset over a wrong answer. The quiz is simply an aid to evaluating your progress.

REVIEW QUIZ FOR CHAPTER 2

On each hand, you are the dealer. First, count your Roth Points; second, decide what action to take.

					POINTS	BID
1.	♠82 ♡J63 ◇AKQJ76 ♣54				_____	_____
2.	♠7 ♡AQJ865 ◇K86432 ♣---				_____	_____
3.	♠K842 ♡QJ53 ◇AKQ ♣62				_____	_____
4.	♠AQJ2 ♡K3 ◇J842 ♣AK2				_____	_____
5.	♠AK3 ♡Q8543 ◇72 ♣Q82				_____	_____
6.	♠AJ3 ♡7 ◇AQJ642 ♣A53				_____	_____
7.	♠Q86542 ♡--- ◇AQ6543 ♣2				_____	_____
8.	♠8 ♡AQ863 ◇AQ9754 ♣2				_____	_____
9.	♠KQJ ♡AKQJ ◇742 ♣632				_____	_____
10.	♠A765432 ♡K2 ◇K3 ♣52				_____	_____
11.	♠K63 ♡A85 ◇K63 ♣K764				_____	_____
12.	♠A763 ♡K842 ◇7 ♣KQ43				_____	_____
13.	♠K65 ♡QJ2 ◇AQ962 ♣A3				_____	_____

14.	♠7 ♡K32 ◇AQJ8643 ♣62		____	____
15.	♠KJ95 ♡A983 ◇976 ♣AK		____	____
16.	♠KJ32 ♡AKQ ◇K3 ♣K842		____	____
17.	♠987 ♡A8 ◇K987 ♣AK42		____	____
18.	♠6 ♡73 ◇KJ865 ♣AK542		____	____
19.	♠AQ87 ♡43 ◇KJ2 ♣AQJ2		____	____
20.	♠83 ♡AQ642 ◇AQ3 ♣KJ3		____	____
21.	♠87432 ♡AKQ6 ◇Q84 ♣2		____	____
22.	♠AK87 ♡K32 ◇5 ♣AQ872		____	____
23.	♠98763 ♡AKQJ4 ◇A3 ♣6		____	____
24.	♠83 ♡A82 ◇K3 ♣AKQ632		____	____
25.	♠5 ♡AQ1086 ◇--- ♣KJ97654		____	____
26.	♠K3 ♡Q82 ◇A765 ♣A432		____	____
27.	♠AK987 ♡6 ◇5 ♣AJ5432		____	____
28.	♠KQJ9 ♡KQJ9 ◇A9873 ♣---		____	____
29.	♠AKQ2 ♡AK87 ◇52 ♣643		____	____
30.	♠AQ7 ♡KJ64 ◇32 ♣AQ97		____	____

SOLUTIONS

		POINTS			BID	
	HCP	Dist.	Length	Total		
1.	11	2	1	14	1◇	11 HCP, 1 for each doubleton, 1 for the diamond length. Your longest suit has 5 or more cards; bid it.
2.	10	5	1	16	1♡	10 HCP, 3 for the void, 2 for the singleton, 1 for the heart length. With two 6-card suits, bid the higher-ranking.
3.	15	1	0	16	1◇	You may not bid 1 NT with only 15 HCP. Since your longest suit has 4 cards, bid your longer minor.

	POINTS			BID	
	HCP	Dist.	Length	Total	
4.	18	1 → 0	0	18	1 NT	18 HCP. Do not count Distribution Points once you have decided to bid notrump.
5.	11	1	0	12	Pass	You may not open with less than 14 points.
6.	16	2	1	19	1 ◇	Your longest suit has 5 or more cards; bid it.
7.	8	5	2	15	Pass	You have 15 points (8 HCP, 3 for the void, two for the singleton, and 1 each for the length in spades and diamonds) but may not open with less than 10 HCP.
8.	12	4	1	17	1 ◇	Your longest suit has 5 or more cards. Bid it.
9.	16	0	0	16	1 ♣	You may not open 1 NT without high-card points in three suits. Since your longest suit has 4 cards, you must bid your longer minor. Since the minors are equal in length, you look at the strength. That is also "equal," so bid 1 ♣.
10.	10	3	2	15	1 ♠	Do not forget to add 2 points for the 7-card spade suit. Since your longest suit has 5 or more cards, bid it.

	HCP	Dist.	Length	Total	BID	
		POINTS			BID	
11.	13	0	0	13	Pass	You must have 14 points to open.
12.	12	2	0	14	1 ♣	Since your longest suit has 4 cards, bid your longer minor.
13.	16	1 → 0	0	16	1 NT	This hand meets the three requirements for a 1 NT opening. Remember *not* to count Distribution Points once you have decided to bid notrump.
14.	10	3	2	15	1 ◇	You have 10 HCP, 3 Distribution Points, and 2 points for the *good* 7-card minor. Bid your longest suit when it has 5 or more cards.
15.	15	1	0	16	1 ◇	You may not open 1 NT with only 15 HCP. Since your longest suit has 4 cards, bid your longer minor.
16.	19	1	0	20	1 ♣	You may not open 1 NT with more than 18 HCP. Since your longest suit has 4 cards, bid your longer minor.
17.	14	1	0	15	1 ♣	Since your longest suit has 4 cards, you look for your longer minor. The minors are equal in length; so bid the stronger one.

	POINTS			BID	
	HCP	Dist.	Length	Total	
18.	11	3	0	14	1 ♢	Your longest suit has 5 cards. Break the tie by bidding the higher-ranking one.
19.	17	1 → 0	0	17	1 NT	Remember not to count Distribution Points when you have decided to bid no-trump.
20.	16	1 → 0	0	16	1 NT	Your hand meets the three requirements.
21.	11	2	0	13	Pass	You must have 14 points to open.
22.	16	2	0	18	1 ♣	You have 16 HCP, but may not open 1 NT without balanced distribution. Bid your 5-card suit.
23.	14	3	0	17	1 ♠	Your longest suit has 5 cards. Break the tie by bidding the higher-ranking one.
24.	16	2	1	19	1 ♣	You have 16 HCP, but may not open 1 NT without balanced distribution. Do not forget to add 1 point for the *good* 6-card club suit.
25.	10	5	0	15	1 ♣	Your longest suit has 5 cards or more; bid it.
26.	13	1	0	14	1 ♣	Your longest suit has 4 cards, so you look for your longer minor. The minors are equal in

	POINTS			BID	
HCP	Dist.	Length	Total		
					length, so you try to break the tie by considering strength. Since this is also "equal," bid the lower minor.
27. 12	4	0	16	1 ♣	Bid your longest suit when it has at least 5 cards.
28. 16	3	0	19	1 ◇	Bid your longest suit when it has at least 5 cards.
29. 16	1	0	17	1 ♣	You may not open 1 NT without high-card points in three suits. Since your longest suit has 4 cards, bid your longer minor.
30. 16	1 → 0	0	16	1 NT	Bid 1 NT with 16 HCP, a balanced hand, and high-card points in at least three suits; but do not count Distribution Points once you have decided to bid notrump.

Rate yourself:

29–30: Excellent work! You are more than ready for the next chapter.

25–28: Very good. Review briefly the ones you missed before going on.

20–24: You are still uncertain in some areas. Reread the relevant sections.

Below 20: It's not as hard as it looks. Try this chapter again next week.

CHAPTER

3

The First Response

It is always a cheery occasion when your side opens the bidding. By opening, you take charge of the auction at the outset, and strike the first blow on the battlefield. Of course, even when you are fortunate enough to be able to open, your partnership will not always be victorious in the fight to win the final contract; but a definite advantage has been gained.

In the previous chapter, you learned how to make the first critical decisions: *when* to open and *what* to open. But, just as often, fate will smile on partner, showering him with aces and kings—and he will be the first to speak for your side. Therefore, let us move across the table, and face the challenge of making the first *response*— what to do after your partner has opened the bidding. In this chapter, we will discuss what to do after partner opens with *one of a suit;* responses to other openings will be covered in subsequent chapters.

Step 1 / Count your Roth Points

Partner is the dealer, and there is a pause while he stops to count his Roth Points. (Naturally, you wish to play with a partner who is also astute enough to use Roth Point Count, so as to inflict the maximum amount of carnage upon your hapless opponents. This is not essential, however; Roth Point Count works perfectly well when played with a partner using traditional point count. Remember that Roth Point Count is *not* a system, but a method of evaluation. Whatever your system, you will bid better using this counting method because you will be able to determine the *true* value of your hand. In Part II, we will describe a *system* (The Roth Method), part or all of which you may wish to adopt. You will have no trouble communicating with partner, as your "system" has not been changed; but you *will* bid consistently better than he does, which may prove a trifle embarrassing).

Do you mix another drink? Tie your shoelace? Admire the furniture? Not at all; *you count your Roth Points.* Partner and your right-hand opponent may both pass, in which case it will be up to you to pass or open the bidding, so have your Roth Points counted as soon as possible. Furthermore, if partner opens the bidding, you may be required to *adjust* your Roth Point Count in various ways. Like the ballplayer who can't hit what he can't see, you can't adjust what you haven't counted. So—no matter what your position at the bridge table—always count your Roth Points as soon as you have sorted your cards, following the procedures given in the previous chapter.

Step 2 / *Adjust* Your Roth Points

The distinguishing feature of the Roth Point Count is that it enables you to do what experts do by "feel"—adjust the value of your hand according to the bids you and your partner have already made.

Let's see how it works in practice. When partner opens the bidding with one of a suit, the first thing you look at is *the number of cards you hold in his suit.* Trumps are priceless; the more trumps you have, the more points your hand is worth. A short side suit— a void, a singleton, or even a doubleton—promises a limitation on the tricks that can be lost in that suit; things can never get entirely out of control since you will eventually be able to ruff in and prevent the opponents from taking an unpleasantly large number of tricks. However, without the security of *length* in trumps, that promise may never be fulfilled. In order to ruff in, you need trumps to do the ruffing; short suits will not do you much good if you do not have very many trumps. Even worse, those disagreeable opponents may seize the initiative by leading trumps themselves, preventing you from ever doing any ruffing at all, and they may add insult to injury by ruffing away your winners, since they may hold enough trumps to make life quite unpleasant.

The Distribution Points that you count represent the trick-taking power of voids, singletons and doubletons in hands played at suit contracts. The combination of short suits and trumps produces tricks through "ruffability." Consequently, the more trumps, the more power; and the more power, the more tricks. The Distribution Points are justified *only* if you have enough trumps with which to do the ruffing. *Extra* trumps mean *extra* power and *more* points; *fewer* trumps mean *less* power and *fewer* points.

Therefore, if partner opens the bidding in a suit in which you have some length, optimism is the spirit of the day. But if partner selects a suit in which you are short—one in which you have a void, singleton, or doubleton—you must tread softly. Players using traditional point count must use intuition and guesswork to decide. when to be optimistic or pessimistic; players using Roth Point Count have no such problems, because the required degree of optimism and pessimism is *built right into the point count itself!*

To avoid the dangers of hands with poor support for partner, and to take into account the extra power of hands with especially good support for partner's suit, simply follow these rules:

1. With 0, 1, or 2 cards in the suit in which partner has opened, do *not* count *any* Distribution Points. A bad thing has happened: partner has selected a suit that you look upon with great distaste.

"Ruffability" is lacking. *DEMOTE* your hand by reducing any and all Distribution Points to zero.

2. With three cards in the suit in which partner has opened, *KEEP* the same point count. Three-card support is considered standard; the fact that partner has selected such a suit for his opening bid is neither particularly good nor particularly bad.

3. If partner's suit is one in which you hold four or more cards, you have cause for unbridled optimism. Trumps abound in plentiful supply; and even if you eventually play the hand in a different suit (or in notrump), the fact that both partners have length in the same suit will probably make the hand easier to play. Therefore, *PROMOTE* your hand—add points, as follows:

A. With four cards in the suit in which partner opens, add *one* point for *each* void or singleton. Add *one* point for *one* doubleton (even if you hold more than one *doubleton,* add just one point).

B. With five or more cards in the suit in which partner opens, add *two* points for *each* void or singleton. Add *one* point for *one* doubleton.

Here's how the rules work:

1. Partner opens 1 ◇ and you hold:

	HCP	Dist.	Length	Total
♠3	0	2	0	2
♡AJ42	5	0	0	5
◇J83	1	0	0	1
♣K10532	3	0	0	3
	9	2	0	11

KEEP the same Roth count. With the standard three-card holding in partner's suit, no adjustments need be made. Your hand is worth 11 points, the same as before partner's opening bid.

2. Partner opens 1 ♡, and you hold the same hand:

	HCP	Dist.	Length	Total
♠ 3	0	2 → 3	0	2 → 3
♡ AJ42	5	0	0	5
◇ J83	1	0	0	1
♣ K10532	3	0	0	3
	9	2 → 3	0	11 → 12

You have four cards in the suit in which partner opened. PROMOTE your hand by adding an extra point for the singleton spade.

3. Partner opens 1 ♠, and once again you hold:

	HCP	Dist.	Length	Total
♠ 3	0	2 → 0	0	2 → 0
♡ AJ42	5	0	0	5
◇ J83	1	0	0	1
♣ K10532	3	0	0	3
	9	2 → 0	0	11 → 9

This time, an unfortunate event has occurred; partner has chosen a suit which you very much dislike. With a singleton in the suit in which partner has opened, DEMOTE your hand by reducing all Distribution Points to zero. After partner has opened 1 ♠, this hand is worth only 9 points.

4. Finally, suppose partner opens 1 ♣:

	HCP	Dist.	Length	Total
♠ 3	0	2 → 4	0	2 → 4
♡ AJ42	5	0	0	5
◇ J83	1	0	0	1
♣ K10532	3	0	0	3
	9	2 → 4	0	11 → 13

With five or more cards in the suit partner has opened, PROMOTE your hand by adding *two* points for the singleton. Your hand is now worth 13 points. The more trumps—the more points!

In these examples, note how the effects of good and bad holdings in partner's suit are built into the Roth Point Count. Experts know that the value of a hand depends on the bids partner has made; the Roth Point Count is the first method that makes it possible for *you* to bid the way the experts do!

5.	IF PARTNER OPENS 1 ♡:				IF PARTNER OPENS 1 ◇:			
	HCP	Dist.	Length	Total	HCP	Dist.	Length	Total
♠ AJ6	5	0	0	5	5	0	0	5
♡ 53	0	1→0	0	1→0	0	1→2	0	1→2
◇ KQJ432	6	0	1	7	6	0	1	7
♣ 74	0	1→0	0	1→0	0	1	0	1
	11	2→0	1	14→12	11	2→3	1	14→15

Before partner opens, this hand is worth 14 points: 11 HCP, 1 for each doubleton, and 1 Length Point for the six-card minor headed by two of the top three honors. If partner opens 1 ♡--a suit for which you have poor support—you DEMOTE your hand by reducing *all* Distribution Points to zero. Your hand is now worth only 12 points. (Similarly, your hand would be demoted to 12 points if partner opened 1 ♣.)

If partner opens 1 ◇, a suit in which you hold more than three cards, you PROMOTE your hand. However, never promote more than one *doubleton*. You have added one point for the heart doubleton; do not add another for the club doubleton.

Had partner opened 1 ♠, a suit for which you have standard (three-card) support, you would KEEP your original count of 14 points.

6.	IF PARTNER OPENS 1 ♣:				IF PARTNER OPENS 1 ♡:			
	HCP	Dist.	Length	Total	HCP	Dist.	Length	Total
♠ ------	0	3→0	0	3→0	0	3→5	0	3→5
♡ K98762	3	0	1	4	3	0	1	4
◇ A98762	4	0	0	4	4	0	0	4
♣ 5	0	2→0	0	2→0	0	2→4	0	2→4
	7	5→0	1	13→8	7	5→9	1	13→17

Very distributional hands are strongly affected by whether or not partner's suit is agreeable to you. Before partner opens, this hand is worth 13 points: 7 HCP, 3 points for the spade void, 2 points for the singleton club, and 1 Length Point in hearts. (Do not count a Length Point for diamonds, as this is not a good minor suit). If partner opens 1 ♣, danger signals shriek out a warning—you don't like opener's suit, and he may not like yours. DEMOTE your hand by reducing *all* Distribution Points to zero. The severe reduction of your hand—from 13 points to 8—is caused by the very poor support for partner's suit. The result would be exactly the same had partner opened 1 ♠ instead of 1 ♣. (Of course, this demotion may be only temporary. If it develops later that partner likes one of your suits, the value of your hand will increase accordingly).

If, however, partner opens 1 ♡ (or 1 ◇), a suit for which you have excellent support, PROMOTE your hand. Since your support is more than four cards in length, add 2 points for the spade void and 2 points for the club singleton. Your hand is now worth 17 points—your powerful trump support represents a great asset to the combined partnership holdings.

If you held this hand, wouldn't you prefer your partner to bid 1 ♡ rather than 1 ♣?

At the beginning of this discussion of how to adjust your Distribution Points, we mentioned that these points represent the trick-taking power of short suits in hands *played at suit contracts*. Obviously, if a hand is played at notrump short suits have no trick-taking power at all. Therefore, while the adjustments described above will give you the correct value of your Distribution Points *for purposes of suit bidding*, your short suits will *never* have any value at notrump. Therefore, regardless of the bids partner has made, *if you are making a response in notrump do not count Distribution Points.*

It will be observed that this rule is consistent with the one given in the previous chapter for counting points when *opening* with one notrump. We noted that once you have decided to open with one notrump you should not count any Distribution Points. As we have now seen applications of this principle by both opener and responder, we can state it as a general rule in the following simplified

form: WHEN BIDDING NOTRUMP, DEMOTE ALL DISTRIBU-
TION POINTS TO ZERO.

Capsule Summary: Roth Points for the First Response

1. Always *count your Roth Points* first.

2. If partner opens the bidding with one of a suit, look at the
number of cards you hold in that suit:

NUMBER OF CARDS IN PARTNER'S SUIT	ADJUSTMENT IN ROTH POINT-COUNT BY RESPONDER FOR PURPOSES OF SUIT BIDDING
0, 1, or 2	DEMOTE *all* Distribution Points to zero.
3	KEEP the same point count.
4	PROMOTE: Add 1 for *each* void Add 1 for *each* singleton Add 1 for *one* doubleton
5 or more	PROMOTE: Add 2 for *each* void Add 2 for *each* singleton Add 1 for *one* doubleton

Never promote more than one doubleton.

Note that only Distribution Points are affected by these adjustments.

3. (General rule) When bidding notrump, demote all Distribution Points to zero.

QUIZ

In each of the following situations, partner's opening bid is given
together with your hand. What is your adjusted Roth Point Count
for suit bidding in each case?

	PARTNER OPENS:	YOU HOLD:				Adjusted point count
1.	1 ♠	♠5	♡52	◇AJ872	♣KJ852	
2.	1 ♠	♠K98754	♡K542	◇53	♣9	
3.	1 ♡	♠Q64	♡KJ87	◇K43	♣A74	
4.	1 ♣	♠87	♡6	◇AQ9764	♣KJ43	
5.	1 ♡	♠8	♡AQ84	◇Q9642	♣973	
6.	1 ◇	♠84	♡72	◇A873	♣K9642	
7.	1 ◇	♠84	♡72	◇K9642	♣A873	
8.	1 ♠	♠8	♡AQ9762	◇AKQ5	♣A2	
9.	1 ♡	♠97	♡----	◇AJ652	♣K75432	
10.	1 ♠	♠K86	♡AJ532	◇8742	♣2	
11.	1 ♠	♠A8765	♡Q87654	◇42	♣--	
12.	1 ♠	♠A876	♡Q876543	◇42	♣--	
13.	1 ♣	♠A9765	♡Q1032	◇4	♣KJ7	
14.	1 ◇	♠A843	♡Q842	◇5432	♣2	
15.	1 ♠	♠AK	♡Q8643	◇K742	♣42	

SOLUTIONS

		HCP	Dist.	Length	Total	
1.	9 points.	9	3→0	0	9	DEMOTE when you have a void, singleton or doubleton in the suit partner opens by reducing *all* Distribution Points to zero.
2.	13 points.	6	3→6	1	13	With five or more cards in partner's suit, PROMOTE by adding 2 points for the singleton and 1 point for the doubletons.
3.	13 points.	13	0→0	0	13	With four cards in partner's suit, PROMOTE—

	HCP	Dist.	Length	Total	
					but you have no voids, singletons, or doubletons to promote!
4. 16 points.	10	3 → 5	1	16	With four cards in partner's suit, PROMOTE by adding 1 point for the singleton and 1 point for the doubleton. Do not forget to count 1 Length Point for the *good* six-card minor.
5. 11 points.	8	2 → 3	0	11	PROMOTE by adding 1 point for the singleton with four cards in partner's suit.
6. 10 points.	7	2 → 3	0	10	When you PROMOTE, never add points for a *second doubleton.*
7. 10 points.	7	2 → 3	0	10	Doubletons do not gain in power when you have a fifth trump; add 1 point for *one* of the doubletons.
8. 20 points.	19	3 → 0	1	20	Good heavens. Partner opened! Do not get so excited that you forget to DEMOTE your Distribution Points when you have a singleton in partner's suit.
9. 8 points.	8	4 → 0	0	8	With a void in partner's suit, DEMOTE all Distribution Points to zero. Do not count a Length Point for the six-card *minor,* as it is not *good.*

	HCP	Dist.	Length	Total	
10. 10 points.	8	2	0	10	KEEP the same point count with 3-card support for partner.
11. 14 points.	6	4→7	1	14	With five-card support for partner, PROMOTE by adding 2 for the void and 1 for the doubleton.
12. 14 points.	6	4→6	2	14	With four-card support for partner, PROMOTE by adding 1 point for the void and 1 point for the doubleton. Remember to count *two* Length Points for the 7-card major.
13. 12 points.	10	2	0	12	KEEP the same point count with 3-card support for partner.
14. 9 points.	6	2→3	0	9	PROMOTE. Add 1 point for the singleton with 4-card support for partner.
15. 12 points.	12	2→0	0	12	DEMOTE your Distribution Points to zero with a doubleton in partner's suit—even a very good doubleton!

Step 3 / Respond or Pass?

When partner opens the bidding with one of a suit, you know that he holds between 14 and 21 points. This is quite a wide range. It is possible that despite partner's opening, your side does not have more points than the opponents. If, for example, partner has 15 points and you have only 2 points, the total for your side is 17. Since there are 40 total points in the deck, the opponents have 23—

and you certainly do not want to get very ambitious with the balance of strength stacked against you! Therefore, you do not *always* respond when partner opens; there are times when discretion requires that you pass before you get into trouble.

How should you decide whether to respond or pass? The rule to follow is that *as long as there is a reasonable chance for game, keep the bidding open.* Games are "gold" to the bridge player; by making two of them before the opponents do, you win the rubber. As in life, opportunity in bridge may knock but once, and if you fail to bid a game that you can make, you may find that fortune favors the opponents on subsequent deals, with the result that they make two games before you do and take home the laurels.

Experience has shown that a *total of 26 points* is usually enough to produce a game. (However, 29 points is apt to be needed for a game in a *minor* suit, which requires 11 tricks.) Therefore, there is no need to respond to partner's opening bid unless you have *6 points* or more.* Since partner may have 21 points, and 21 plus 5 equals 26, why not respond with 5 points? The answer is that hands do not play well when most of the points are in one hand, so there is probably no game when partner has 21 points and you have only 5. (Also, on a percentage basis, partner is unlikely to hold 21 points.) Otherwise, continue to keep the bidding open whenever the magic total of 26 is within reach—which means that you *must* respond whenever you have 6 points or more. Similarly, you must pass with 5 points or fewer, since the magic total is beyond your reach. (Never mind that you cannot help partner's suit. A one-level contract, undoubled, cannot come to much harm.)

Capsule Summary: When to Respond to Suit Bids

RESPONDER'S
POINTS

6 or more	You *must* respond.
5 or less	You *must* pass.

----

* For purposes of deciding whether or not to respond, count your points *for suit bidding.*

On each of the following hands, do you respond or pass?

	PARTNER'S OPENING:	YOU HOLD:			
1.	1 ♠	♠4	♡A763	◊9852	♣5432
2.	1 ♡	♠4	♡A763	◊9852	♣5432
3.	1 ◊	♠2	♡42	◊J654	♣A86432
4.	1 ♣	♠J764	♡9843	◊42	♣A62
5.	1 ♡	♠A532	♡42	◊J32	♣10972

SOLUTIONS

1. PASS. Your hand is worth only 4 points. Do not count any Distribution Points when you have poor support for partner's suit.

2. RESPOND. Your hand is worth 7 points—4 HCP and 3 for the PROMOTED singleton.

3. RESPOND. Your hand is worth 10 points—5 HCP, 3 for the PROMOTED singleton, and 2 for the PROMOTED doubleton.

4. RESPOND. Your hand is worth 6 points—5 HCP and 1 for the doubleton. KEEP the same point count with three-card support for partner.

5. PASS. This hand is worth only 5 points after you DEMOTE your Distribution Points.

Step 4 / What Do You Respond?

If you have 5 points or less and pass, your chance to bid is over for the time being. If, however, the result of the previous step indicates that a response is in order, the question of *what to respond* arises. Inasmuch as partner's hand may be anywhere from 14 to 21 points, you are in no position to make a unilateral decision as to what the final contract should be. Your job is to give partner as much information as you can, so that the partnership can proceed on as enlightened a basis as possible. Certain bids that you can make convey a great deal of information, and you should make such bids whenever your hand meets the requirements for one of them. If your hand does *not* satisfy the requirements for the more informative bids,* you must then look further down the scale of priorities until you find the most descriptive bid suitable to the hand that you hold. The list of priorities is as follows:

1. *Raise partner's major suit.* If partner has opened 1 ♡ or 1 ♠, you should raise his suit if your hand meets the requirements.

2. *Jump to 2 NT or 3NT.* If you cannot raise partner's major—either because your hand is unsuitable or because partner didn't happen to open with one of a major—the next thing you check is whether or not your hand meets the requirements for a jump to 2 NT or 3 NT.

3. *Bid a new suit.* If you are unable to either raise partner's major or jump to 2 NT or 3 NT, your next preference is to bid a new suit.

4. *Raise partner's minor.* If partner has opened 1 ♣ or 1 ◊ and your hand is not suitable for any of the three prior categories, a raise of his suit may be just what the doctor ordered.

5. *Bid 1 NT.* If your hand is unsuitable for any of the above responses, you must fall back on the response of 1 NT.

Experts know that giving preference to the high-priority bids in the above list leads to easier bidding and sounder contracts. Now let's consider the requirements for each response in turn, remembering that should your hand *not* be suitable for the response under consideration, you will then have to look at the category following next on the list.

Raising Partner's Major Suit

The very first requisite for raising partner's major is that he *open* with one of a major! Obviously, you will have to skip this category

---

* We will see later that these informative bids are called "limit bids." In general, it is always best to make a limit bid if possible. This is primarily because limit bids allow you to describe your hand accurately *in one bid.* An opening bid of one notrump, described in the previous chapter, is a limit bid; suit openings of one are *not* limit bids.

any time partner's opening is any bid other than 1 ♡ or 1 ♠. When partner does open 1 ♡ or 1 ♠, however, raise whenever your hand meets any of the following requirements:

Raise to two holding 7 to 10 Roth Points, including at least three-card support for partner's major. Three-card support is sufficient for a single raise since we know partner must have at least five cards in a major suit to open with one of that suit. *Eight trumps between the two hands insure a suitable trump fit,* and your three plus partner's minimum of five make up at least the necessary total.

Raise to three holding 13 to 15 Roth Points, including *at least 10 HCP,* and at least *four-card support* for partner's major.

Raise to four holding 11 to 15 Roth Points, *fewer than 10 HCP,* and *five-card support* for partner's major (or *very good* four-card support). (This bid is preemptive, not strength-showing*).

Here are a few examples to illustrate these raises:

1. Partner opens 1 ♠:

	HCP	Dist.	Length	Total
♠ A87	4	0	0	4
♡ K963	3	0	0	3
◇ 52	0	1	0	1
♣ 8762	0	0	0	0
	7	1	0	8

Raise to 2 ♠. You have 8 Roth Points and three-card support for partner's major. (Remember to KEEP the same point count with the standard three-card holding in partner's suit.)

---

* It may seem unusual that the responder should bid four spades with only 11 points, while a raise to *three* spades requires 13 pts. However, this makes sense if we examine the purposes of these bids. A raise to four spades is an attempt to shut the opposition out of the bidding. A raise to three spades (which is *forcing*) shows some values and leaves opener room to try for slam if he wishes.

2. Partner opens 1 ♡ :

	HCP	Dist.	Length	Total
♠ AJ87	5	0	0	5
♡ J872	1	0	0	1
◇ 6	0	2 → 3	0	2 → 3
♣ A432	4	0	0	4
	10	2 → 3	0	12 → 13

Raise to 3 ♡. You have four-card heart support, 10 HCP, and 13 Roth Points. Remember to PROMOTE the singleton diamond since you hold four cards in partner's suit.

3. Partner opens 1 ♠ :

	HCP	Dist.	Length	Total
♠ A9876	4	0	0	4
♡ 52	0	1 → 2	0	1 → 2
◇ 3	0	2 → 4	0	2 → 4
♣ K10764	3	0	0	3
	7	3 → 6	0	10 → 13

Raise to 4 ♠. You hold 13 Roth Points, fewer than 10 HCP, and five-card support—an ideal hand for the raise to four.

4. Partner opens 1 ♡ :

	HCP	Dist.	Length	Total
♠ A63	4	0	0	4
♡ K842	3	0	0	3
◇ 62	0	1 → 2	0	1 → 2
♣ Q1098	2	0	0	2
	9	1 → 2	0	10 → 11

Do not raise. Your total of 11 Roth Points is too many for a raise to 2 ♡ and too few for a raise to 3 ♡. Your hand does *not* meet the requirements for raising partner's major, and you will therefore have to look elsewhere down the priority list for a response.*

---

* It may occur to the reader that this procedure is unnatural, for one cannot raise despite excellent support for partner's major suit. And so it is. In Part II of this book, we will see that *Roth bidding* methods *do* call for a heart raise with this hand.

5. Partner opens 1 ♠ :

	HCP	Dist.	Length	Total
♠ A7	4	1 → 0	0	5 → 4
♡ KQ63	5	0	0	5
◇ A872	4	0	0	4
♣ 942	0	0	0	0
	13	1 → 0	0	14 → 13

Do not raise. While you have 13 Roth Points, your spade holding is far short of the minimum four-card support needed to raise to 3 ♠.

6. Partner opens 1 ♠ :

	HCP	Dist.	Length	Total
♠ AJ62	5	0	0	5
♡ 2	0	2 → 3	0	2 → 3
◇ K87432	3	0	0	3
♣ 74	0	1 → 2	0	1 → 2
	8	3 → 5	0	11 → 13

Raise to 4 ♠. You have 13 Roth Points, but may not raise to 3 ♠ with fewer than 10 HCP. Your four-card support is very good, however, so a raise to 4 ♠ is justified.

Capsule Summary: Raising Partner's Major

RAISE TO:	IF YOU HOLD:
Two	7–10 Roth points*; at least 3-card support.
Three	13–15 Roth points; at least 10 HCP; at least 4-card support.
Four	12–16 Roth points; *fewer* than 10 HCP; 5-card support (or very good 4-card support).

---

* The observant reader may have detected still another flaw here. What if the responder has only 6 points and support for opener's major suit? He must respond, yet cannot raise—another artificial procedure! It would not help to make the point zone of the single raise 6–10, for the bid would then not limit responder's hand accurately. A procedure which does away with all these flaws will be presented in Part II.

(48)

YOU MAY *NOT* RAISE, AND MUST SELECT ANOTHER RE-
SPONSE, IF YOU FAIL TO MEET ANY OF THE NECESSARY
REQUIREMENTS.

QUIZ

On each of the following hands, first count your Roth Points;
then decide whether or not you raise. If you do raise, state whether
it is to two, three or four.

	PARTNER OPENS:	YOU HOLD:
1.	1 ♡	♠ AJ87 ♡ 87 ◇ K983 ♣ 964
2.	1 ♠	♠ A87 ♡ Q9876 ◇ J872 ♣ 5
3.	1 ♠	♠ A87 ♡ AQ962 ◇ J87 ♣ 54
4.	1 ♡	♠ 987 ♡ KQ42 ◇ 72 ♣ AQ42
5.	1 ♠	♠ K8765 ♡ 73 ◇ 32 ♣ AK72
6.	1 ♡	♠ 87 ♡ Q432 ◇ J432 ♣ 852
7.	1 ♡	♠ 7 ♡ A10963 ◇ K8642 ♣ 63
8.	1 ♠	♠ A83 ♡ A87642 ◇ 742 ♣ 8
9.	1 ♡	♠ Q86 ♡ A72 ◇ 98763 ♣ 32
10.	1 ♠	♠ KQ43 ♡ A974 ◇ AK32 ♣ 3

SOLUTIONS

1. *Do not raise.* You may never raise with fewer than three cards
in support. (Total points: 8, DEMOTING because of the shortness in partner's suit.)

2. *Raise to 2 ♠.* You have 9 Roth Points and three-card support.

3. *Do not raise.* With 12 Roth Points, you are too strong to raise
to 2 ♠ and too weak to raise to 3 ♠.

4. *Raise to 3 ♡.* You have 13 Roth Points (11 HCP, and 2 points
for the PROMOTED doubleton) and four-card support.

5. *Raise to 3 ♠.* You may not raise to 4 ♠ with 10 or more HCP.
Your total is 13 Roth Points (10 HCP, 2 points for the doubletons,
and 1 PROMOTION point for *one* doubleton—never promote a
second doubleton.) 13 points and five-card support meet the requirements for the raise to three.

6. *Pass.* You may not respond with fewer than 6 points.

7. *Raise to 4 ♡*. You have 13 Roth Points (7 HCP, 4 points for the PROMOTED singleton, and 2 points for the PROMOTED doubleton), fewer than 10 HCP, and five-card support.

8. *Do not raise*. You have 11 Roth Points—8 HCP, 2 for the singleton, and 1 length point for the six-card major. You are therefore not within the acceptable point range for either a raise to 2 ♠ or a raise to 3 ♠.

9. *Raise to 2 ♡*. You have 7 Roth Points and three-card support.

10. *Do not raise*. You have 19 Roth Points (16 HCP and 3 points for the PROMOTED singleton)—too much for a raise. Responses with hands with great strength—18 points or more—will be discussed later on.

Jumping to 2 NT or 3 NT

When you are able to raise partner's major and you make the appropriate bid, the turn passes to your left, and you can sit back and await developments. If you cannot raise partner's major, however, you must find a different bid. The next thing to check is whether or not you can *jump to 2 NT or 3 NT*. These bids have very exacting requirements. You will not be able to make them often, but when you can, partner will get a very accurate picture of your hand. Therefore, assuming you are unable to raise partner's major, you should always give preference to these bids when your hand meets the requirements. The requirements are:

To jump to 2 NT: 1. 13–15 HCP;
                    2. Balanced suit distribution (4–3–3–3, 4–4–3–2, or 5–3–3–2 where the five-card suit is a *minor*);
                    3. Stoppers in all unbid suits.

To jump to 3 NT*:   1. 16–18 HCP;
                    2. Balanced suit distribution (preferably 4–3–3–3);
                    3. Stoppers in all unbid suits.

---

* These classic requirements are presented for the sake of completeness. Actually, most experts eschew the response of 3 NT—with good reason, as we will see later.

Stoppers—which make it unlikely the opponents can run a suit—are A, K x, Q xx, any four cards in a suit, or better.

Remember that we do not count Distribution Points when bidding notrump (either as opener *or* as responder). *Some examples:*

1. Partner opens 1 ♠. You hold:

	HCP	Dist.	Length	Total
♠ 32	0	1 → 0	0	1 → 0
♡ KQ4	5	0	0	5
◇ KJ107	4	0	0	0
♣ AJ64	5	0	0	5
	14	1 → 0	0	15 → 14

Jump to 2 NT. You have 14 HCP, balanced suit distribution, and stoppers in all unbid suits. Note that you DEMOTE your Distribution Points to zero when bidding notrump.

2. Partner opens 1 ♡. You hold:

	HCP	Dist.	Length	Total
♠ AQ8	6	0	0	6
♡ 742	0	0	0	0
◇ AK86	7	0	0	7
♣ 643	0	0	0	0
	13	0	0	13

Do not jump in notrump. While you have 13 points and balanced suit distribution, you do not have a stopper in the unbid club suit.

3. Partner opens 1 ◇. You hold:

	HCP	Dist.	Length	Total
♠ AK7	7	0	0	7
♡ K103	3	0	0	3
◇ KQ2	5	0	0	5
♣ Q1084	2	0	0	2
	17	0	0	17

Jump to 3 NT. This is an ideal hand for the bid—17 HCP, 4-3-3-3 distribution, and stoppers in all unbid suits.

4. Partner opens 1 ♣. You hold:

	HCP	Dist.	Length	Total
♠ K874	3	0	0	3
♡ A2	4	1 → 0	0	5 → 4
◇ KQJ84	6	0	0	6
♣ 62	0	1 → 0	0	1 → 0
	13	2 → 0	0	15 → 13

Do not jump in notrump. While you have 13 HCP and stoppers in all unbid suits, you do not have balanced suit distribution. Many experts prefer not to respond 2 NT to a minor-suit opening *any time* they hold a four-card major suit. This procedure—bidding the major suit rather than 2 NT—is recommended, but it is not clear whether or not it can be considered "standard."

5. Partner opens 1 ♠. You hold:

	HCP	Dist.	Length	Total
♠ AQ64	6	0	0	6
♡ K83	3	0	0	3
◇ K72	3	0	0	3
♣ Q104	2	0	0	2
	14	0	0	14

Do not jump in notrump. Raise to 3 ♠! Always raise partner's major when you meet the requirements for a raise.

- -

Capsule Summary: Jumps in Notrump

Jump to 2 NT: 13–15 HCP; balanced suit distribution; stoppers in all unbid suits.

Jump to 3 NT: 16–18 HCP; balanced suit distribution; stoppers in all unbid suits.

(DO NOT JUMP IN NOTRUMP IF YOU CAN RAISE PARTNER'S MAJOR INSTEAD.)

- -

QUIZ

Count your Roth Points and decide whether or not you jump in notrump. As usual, name your exact response *whenever you can do so.*

	PARTNER OPENS:	YOU HOLD:
1.	1 ◇	♠ A97 ♡ K86 ◇ 432 ♣ AQJ2
2.	1 ♠	♠ KQ2 ♡ QJ96 ◇ AQ3 ♣ K104
3.	1 ♣	♠ Q106 ♡ KJ84 ◇ Q32 ♣ A32
4.	1 ♡	♠ A76 ♡ K432 ◇ K743 ♣ K2
5.	1 ♠	♠ 64 ♡ AJ875 ◇ AQ3 ♣ K43
6.	1 ◇	♠ AQ64 ♡ 74 ◇ K83 ♣ KJ87
7.	1 ♡	♠ K876 ♡ 109 ◇ AK876 ♣ K3
8.	1 ♠	♠ 86 ♡ KQ10 ◇ AQ64 ♣ K842
9.	1 ♡	♠ AKQ ♡ 87 ◇ KQJ2 ♣ A1072
10.	1 ♡	♠ Q86 ♡ A842 ◇ 98764 ♣ 2

SOLUTIONS

1. *Jump to 2 NT.* You have 14 HCP, balanced suit distribution, and stoppers in all unbid suits.

2. *Jump to 3 NT.* You have 17 HCP, balanced suit distribution, and stoppers in all unbid suits.

3. *Do not jump in notrump.* You have only 12 HCP—not enough to jump to 2 NT. (12 Roth Points)

4. *Raise to 3 ♡.* You have 15 points—13 HCP and 2 points for the PROMOTED doubleton. Always raise partner's major when you have the appropriate hand.

5. *Do not jump in notrump* with a five-card *major* suit. (14 Roth Points)

6. *Do not jump in notrump.* You do not have stoppers in all unbid suits. (14 Roth Points)

7. *Do not jump in notrump.* You do not have balanced suit distribution. (13 Roth Points)

8. *Jump to 2 NT.* You have 14 HCP, balanced suit distribution, and stoppers in all unbid suits.

9. *Do not jump in notrump.* You have 19 HCP—too many for a jump to 3 NT. (19 Roth Points)

10. *Raise to 2 ♡.* You have 9 Roth Points—6 HCP and 3 points for the PROMOTED singleton—and adequate trump support.

Bidding a New Suit

More often than not, you will not be able to raise partner's major suit or jump in notrump. According to the list of priorities, your next best choice is to bid a new suit. Whereas few hands qualify for the first two categories, very many hands qualify for a response in a new suit and this is the most frequent form of response.

The requirements for bidding a new suit are:

11 or more Roth Points, or

6 or more Roth Points and a suit of four or more cards which you can bid *at the one-level.*

Always bear in mind that *with 6–10 Roth Points you may bid a suit at the one-level, but* NOT *at the two-level.*

The level of the bid you make in a new suit is determined by this rule: Assuming you meet the requirements for a bid in a new suit, make a simple (non-jump) response (e.g.: 1 ♣—1 ♠; 1 ♡—2 ◊) with 6 to 17 Roth Points and a *single jump* response* (e.g.: 1 ♣—2 ♠; 1 ♡—3 ◊) with 18 or more Roth Points.

When bidding a new suit, bid your longest new suit, breaking ties in favor of the higher-ranking suit with suits of five or more cards, and in favor of the lower-ranking suit with four (or fewer) cards in each suit. (Note that only in rare circumstances—in particular, when you have support for partner but do not qualify for a direct raise—will you be forced to choose from three-card suits for your two-level response. See Example 10 below. The necessity

* The single jump response will be given a different meaning in The Roth Method (described in Part II).

to bid "phony" suits will disappear in the Roth Method presented in Part II.)

The following examples show the rules for bidding new suits in action.

1. Partner opens 1 ♣:

	HCP	Dist.	Length	Total
♠ AQJ76	7	0	0	7
♡ A962	4	0	0	4
◇ 53	0	1 → 0	0	1 → 0
♣ 42	0	1 → 0	0	1 → 0
	11	2 → 0	0	13 → 11

Respond 1 ♠. Bid your longest suit. As usual, the Roth Point Count "builds in" pessimism because partner opened in a suit for which your support is below standard, and Distribution Points are DEMOTED to zero.

2. Partner opens 1 ♣:

	HCP	Dist.	Length	Total
♠ AK86	7	0	0	7
♡ 5432	0	0	0	0
◇ A87	4	0	0	4
♣ 32	0	1 → 0	0	1 → 0
	11	1 → 0	0	12 → 11

Respond 1 ♡. The question of raising partner's major does not arise for the simple reason that he did not open in a major suit; and you may not jump in notrump with only 11 HCP. You may (in fact, must), however, bid a new suit. When your longest suits contain four cards, choose the *lower-ranking*. This method of bidding is called "up the line" because by bidding one heart you leave partner the chance to bid spades *at the one-level.* You need not fear bidding so weak a suit. As we shall see later, partner will not raise without at least four. If he does raise, therefore, you can be assured that there will be at least that ideal eight-card "fit" between you and all will be well.

3. Partner opens 1 ♣:

	HCP	Dist.	Length	Total
♠ QJ765	3	0	0	3
♡ 62	0	1 → 0	0	1 → 0
◇ AK862	7	0	0	7
♣ 2	0	2 → 0	0	2 → 0
	10	3 → 0	0	13 → 10

Respond 1 ♠. When your longest suit is five cards or more, bid the higher-ranking in case of ties.

4. Partner opens 1 ◇:

	HCP	Dist.	Length	Total
♠ A874	4	0	0	4
♡ K43	3	0	0	3
◇ 987	0	0	0	0
♣ 653	0	0	0	0
	7	0	0	7

Respond 1 ♠, your longest suit.

5. Partner opens 1 ♡:

	HCP	Dist.	Length	Total
♠ A76	4	0	0	4
♡ 653	0	0	0	0
◇ AQ872	6	0	0	6
♣ 73	0	1	0	1
	10	1	0	11

Respond 2 ◇. You have 11 Roth Points. Therefore, bid your longest suit. (Compare with Examples 7 and 8).

6. Partner opens 1 ♠:

	HCP	Dist.	Length	Total
♠ J1092	1	0	0	1
♡ A4	4	1 → 2	0	5 → 6
◇ K3	3	1	0	4
♣ A9654	4	0	0	4
	12	2 → 3	0	14 → 15

Raise to 3 ♠. Do not bid a new suit when you meet the requirements for raising partner's major. Remember *not* to PROMOTE a second *doubleton*.

7. Partner opens 1 ♠ :

	HCP	Dist.	Length	Total
♠ 32	0	1 → 0	0	1 → 0
♡ Q86	2	0	0	2
◇ 654	0	0	0	0
♣ KQJ42	6	0	0	6
	8	1 → 0	0	9 → 8

Do not bid a new suit. You have only 8 Roth Points and no suit of four or more cards to bid at the one-level.

8. Partner opens 1 ◇ :

	HCP	Dist.	Length	Total
♠ Q1032	2	0	0	2
♡ 86	0	1 → 0	0	1 → 0
◇ 32	0	1 → 0	0	1 → 0
♣ AJ742	5	0	0	5
	7	2 → 0	0	9 → 7

Respond 1 ♠. You may not bid 2 ♣ without at least 11 Roth Points, but you do have a four-card suit to bid at the one-level (where the minimum requirement is only 6 points).

9. Partner opens 1 ◇ :

	HCP	Dist.	Length	Total
♠ KQ2	5	0	0	5
♡ AJ3	5	0	0	5
◇ 532	0	0	0	0
♣ K1075	3	0	0	3
	13	0	0	13

Jump to 2 NT. You have 13 HCP, balanced suit distribution, and stoppers in all unbid suits. Do not bid a new suit at the two-level when you satisfy the requirements for the higher-priority 2 NT bid.

10. Partner opens 1 ♡:

	HCP	Dist.	Length	Total
♠ 64	0	$1 \to 2$	0	$1 \to 2$
♡ K8642	3	0	0	3
◇ A74	4	0	0	4
♣ K105	3	0	0	3
	10	$1 \to 2$	0	$11 \to 12$

Respond 2 ♣. You do not meet the requirements for any heart raise, but you have more than the necessary 11 points. With two suits of four or fewer cards, break the tie by bidding the *lower-ranking*. This example is included to show how artificial Standard American bidding can be.

Capsule Summary: Responding in a New Suit

When responding in a new suit, bid your longest suit (higher-ranking of two five-card or longer suits; lower-ranking of two four-card or shorter suits) without a jump if you have 11–17 Roth Points; with 18 or more Roth Points, follow the same rules but *jump* in the indicated suit; with 6–10 Roth Points, bid a new suit only if you have a four-card or longer suit which can be named at the level of one.

(DO NOT BID A NEW SUIT IF YOU CAN RAISE PARTNER'S MAJOR SUIT OR BID TWO NOTRUMP OR THREE NOTRUMP.)

QUIZ

For each of the hands shown below, first count your Roth Points; then decide on your response.

	PARTNER OPENS:	YOU HOLD:
1.	1 ♡	♠ AJ87 ♡ 5 ◇ K9832 ♣ 964
2.	1 ♣	♠ 987 ♡ AJ3 ◇ Q872 ♣ 642
3.	1 ♡	♠ A872 ♡ K963 ◇ 52 ♣ 876

4.	1 ♠	♠3 ♡62 ♢QJ876 ♣AKJ72
5.	1 ♢	♠843 ♡A432 ♢7 ♣J8642
6.	1 ♣	♠Q8432 ♡AKJ72 ♢43 ♣8
7.	1 ♡	♠Q43 ♡32 ♢A8765 ♣J43
8.	1 ♢	♠K85 ♡AQ2 ♢642 ♣AQ85
9.	1 ♡	♠Q76 ♡42 ♢KQJ2 ♣A742
10.	1 ♣	♠98 ♡AJ874 ♢Q872 ♣42
11.	1 ♣	♠AQ87 ♡54 ♢6 ♣J98432
12.	1 ♢	♠A5 ♡J87 ♢Q9832 ♣543
13.	1 ♣	♠AQ64 ♡8732 ♢J83 ♣32
14.	1 ♡	♠432 ♡KQ64 ♢876 ♣AQJ
15.	1 ♡	♠8 ♡AQ62 ♢K64 ♣J10875

SOLUTIONS

1. *Respond 1 ♠.* Your longest suit is diamonds, but you may not bid at the two-level with only 8 points. Therefore, bid your four-card suit at the one level.

2. *Respond 1 ♢.* Bid your longest suit. (7 points)

3. *Raise to 2 ♡.* You have 9 Roth Points (7 HCP and 2 points for the PROMOTED doubleton) and adequate trump support. Always prefer a raise in partner's major when you meet the requirements.

4. *Respond 2 ♢.* You have 11 Roth Points (even after DEMOTING your Distribution Points) and may therefore bid at the two-level. With two five-card suits, bid the higher-ranking.

5. *Pass.* You have only 5 points and need 6 to respond.

6. *Respond 1 ♠.* With two five-card suits, bid the higher ranking. (10 points)

7. *Do not bid a new suit.* You may neither bid at the two-level with only 7 points nor bid the three-card spade suit.

8. *Jump to 2 NT.* You have 15 HCP, balanced suit distribution, and stoppers in all unbid suits. Do not bid a new suit when you meet the requirements for a higher-priority jump in notrump.

9. *Respond 2 ♣.* With 12 points, you may bid at the two-level.

With two-four suits, bid the lower-ranking.

10. *Respond 1 ♡*. Your longest suit is five cards; bid it. (7 points)

11. *Respond 1 ♠*. Bid your longest *new* suit. (You have 13 Roth Points—7 HCP, 4 for the PROMOTED singleton, and 2 for the PROMOTED doubleton.)

12. *Do not bid a new suit.* You have no suit of four or more cards to bid at the one-level and you are not strong enough to bid at the two-level. (9 points)

13. *Respond 1 ♡*: With two four-card suits, bid the lower-ranking. (7 points)

14. *Respond 2 ♣*. The rare case where a bid of a new three-card suit is acceptable: 11 to 12 points, support for partner's suit, and no 4-card or longer new suit to bid. (12 points)

15. *Raise to 3 ♡*. You have 13 Roth Points (10 HCP and 3 for the PROMOTED singleton) and four-card support. Raising partner's major always takes priority over bidding a new suit.

The "Catchall" Bids: Raising Partner's Minor and Bidding One Notrump

Whenever possible, you should raise partner's major, jump in notrump, or bid a new suit. Sometimes, however, you do not have a hand that meets the requirements for any of these bids. This will usually happen when you have less than 11 points and no suit to bid at the one-level, as hands with 11 or more points will, in general, be suitable for one of the first three response categories. For these hands, you have two weapons left in your arsenal: the raise of partner's minor and the response of one notrump.

Having eliminated a raise of partner's major, a jump in notrump, or a bid in a new suit, you must check whether or not you can raise partner's minor.

*The raise to two of a minor** promises 7–10 Roth Points and at

---

* The raise to *three* of a minor is a very sore spot in Standard American bidding, and has been deferred until Chapter 12 for the sake of simplicity.

least four-card support. If you cannot raise partner, jump in no-trump, or bid a new suit, but must respond (6 or more points) bid *one notrump*. (This response will work out to show 6–10 points.)

Here's how these rules work:

1. Partner opens 1 ♡. You hold:

	HCP	Dist.	Length	Total
♠ Q43	2	0	0	2
♡ 32	0	1 → 0	0	1 → 0
◇ A8765	4	0	0	4
♣ J43	1	0	0	1
	7	1 → 0	0	8 → 7

Respond 1 NT. You have 7 HCP and balanced suit distribution. You cannot raise, jump in notrump, or bid a new suit (not enough points to bid at the two-level). Of course, you DEMOTE your Distribution Points to zero when bidding notrump.

2. Partner opens 1 ◇:

	HCP	Dist.	Length	Total
♠ A5	4	1 → 2	0	5 → 6
♡ J87	1	0	0	1
◇ Q9832	2	0	0	2
♣ 543	0	0	0	0
	7	1 → 2	0	8 → 9

Raise to 2 ◇. You PROMOTE the doubleton spade plus your 7 HCP makes for a total of 9 points with good support for diamonds.

3. Partner opens 1 ♠:

	HCP	Dist.	Length	Total
♠ 2	0	2 → 0	0	2 → 0
♡ 863	0	0	0	0
◇ QJ75	3	0	0	3
♣ KJ842	4	0	0	4
	7	2 → 0	0	9 → 7

Respond 1 NT. You may not bid at the two-level with less than 11 points, and bid you must as you have more than enough for a response.

Capsule Summary: The "Catchall" Responses

1. RAISE PARTNER'S MINOR TO TWO with 7–10 points and at least four-card support.

2. OTHERWISE BID ONE NOTRUMP (shows 6–10 points, nothing else to do).

DO *NOT* USE THE "CATCHALL" RESPONSES IF YOU MEET THE REQUIREMENTS FOR A RAISE OF PARTNER'S MAJOR, A JUMP IN NOTRUMP, OR A BID IN A NEW SUIT.

QUIZ

After counting your Roth Points, decide your response on each of the following hands:

	PARTNER OPENS:	YOU HOLD:			
1.	1 ♠	♠52	♡863	◇QJ1043	♣AJ2
2.	1 ◇	♠A86	♡Q32	◇Q432	♣652
3.	1 ♣	♠653	♡72	◇J84	♣AQ765
4.	1 ◇	♠QJ103	♡842	◇A832	♣65

SOLUTIONS

1. *Respond 1 NT*. You may not bid at the two-level with only 8 points.

2. *Respond 2 ◇*. You have 8 points and four-card support.

3. *Respond 2 ♣*. Here you have 9 points if you raise to 2 ♣ (7 HCP and 2 for the PROMOTED doubleton). Note you would have only 7 points if you responded 1 NT, for Distribution Points are not counted when bidding notrump.*

4. *Respond 1 ♠*. Do not raise diamonds when you meet the requirements for a bid in a new suit, which has higher priority. (9 points)

---

* Note that the Roth Point Count will sometimes show that a hand has different values for bids in different denominations! This theme will be more fully developed in later chapters.

Capsule Summary: The First Response

Step 1. *Count* your Roth Points.

Step 2. *Adjust* your Roth Points according to the number of cards you hold in partner's suit:

LENGTH IN PARTNER'S SUIT	ADJUSTMENT (for purposes of suit bidding)
0–2 cards	DEMOTE *all* Distribution Points to zero.
3 cards	KEEP the same point count.
4 cards	PROMOTE: Add 1 for *each* void or singleton Add 1 for *one* doubleton
5 or more cards	PROMOTE: Add 2 for *each* void or singleton Add 1 for *one* doubleton

Never PROMOTE *more than one doubleton.*

Step 3. Do you respond?

| 5 points or less; | PASS |
| 6 or more points: | RESPOND continue to Step 4 |

Step 4. What do you respond?

1. FIRST CHOICE: RAISE PARTNER'S MAJOR

RAISE TO:	HOLDING:
Two	7–10 points; at least 3-card support
Three	13–15 points; at least 10 HCP: at least 4-card support
Four	11–15 points; less than 10 HCP; at least 5-card support (or very good 4-card support)

If unable to raise partner's major, consider:

2. SECOND CHOICE: JUMP IN NOTRUMP
JUMP TO: HOLDING:
2 NT   13–15 HCP; balanced suit distribution; stoppers in all unbid suits
3 NT   16–18 HCP; balanced suit distribution; stoppers in all unbid suits

If unable to jump in notrump, consider:

3. THIRD CHOICE: BID A NEW SUIT

Bid your longest new suit (higher-ranking of five-card or longer suits; lowest-ranking of four-card or shorter suits). Jump in the indicated suit with 18 or more points. With 6–10, bid a new suit (four or more cards) only at the one-level.

4. FOURTH CHOICE: RAISE PARTNER'S MINOR OR BID ONE NOTRUMP

RAISE PARTNER'S MINOR:
To *two* with 7–10 points and at least 4-card support, otherwise bid one notrump.

REVIEW QUIZ FOR CHAPTER 3

On each hand, partner's opening bid is indicated. First, count your Roth Points; then decide what action to take.

PARTNER OPENS:	YOU HOLD:				POINTS	BID
1. 1 ♠	♠5	♡52	◇AJ872	♣KJ852		
2. 1 ♠	♠Q9875	♡A542	◇53	♣94		
3. 1 ♠	♠K98754	♡K542	◇53	♣9		
4. 1 ♡	♠KQ3	♡52	◇AQ62	♣K843		
5. 1 ♣	♠J98632	♡5	◇AKQ54	♣4		

6.	1 ♠	♠A87 ♡AQ962 ◊J87 ♣54	_____	_____
7.	1 ◊	♠632 ♡8 ◊J8543 ♣A852	_____	_____
8.	1 ♣	♠9876 ♡A32 ◊8432 ♣85	_____	_____
9.	1 ◊	♠KQ75 ♡5432 ◊QJ2 ♣A7	_____	_____
10.	1 ♠	♠A6 ♡Q9873 ◊Q8763 ♣5	_____	_____
11.	1 ♠	♠Q10742 ♡A83 ◊7 ♣KJ43	_____	_____
12.	1 ◊	♠KQ3 ♡AJ2 ◊Q72 ♣AJ107	_____	_____
13.	1 ♡	♠K876 ♡74 ◊KQ975 ♣A10	_____	_____
14.	1 ♡	♠A874 ♡--- ◊J872 ♣96432	_____	_____
15.	1 ♠	♠K432 ♡AJ103 ◊10987 ♣6	_____	_____
16.	1 ♣	♠74 ♡AQJ2 ◊K653 ♣KJ5	_____	_____
17.	1 ♣	♠AQ87 ♡Q83 ◊543 ♣432	_____	_____
18.	1 ♠	♠32 ♡KJ943 ◊KQ2 ♣AJ5	_____	_____
19.	Pass	♠J62 ♡A98 ◊KQ9432 ♣7	_____	_____
20.	1 ♡	♠A3 ♡Q1072 ◊KQ83 ♣Q85	_____	_____
21.	1 ♡	♠A1062 ♡Q83 ◊72 ♣8643	_____	_____
22.	1 ◊	♠Q63 ♡85 ◊72 ♣AJ7432	_____	_____
23.	1 ◊	♠64 ♡92 ◊J854 ♣A8765	_____	_____
24.	1 ♣	♠KJ107 ♡QJ82 ◊A963 ♣2	_____	_____
25.	1 ♡	♠A8642 ♡Q874 ◊842 ♣2	_____	_____
26.	1 ♡	♠A8642 ♡Q8743 ◊65 ♣3	_____	_____
27.	1 ♠	♠32 ♡6 ◊J8763 ♣A8642	_____	_____
28.	1 ◊	♠KJ875 ♡AQ9642 ◊85 ♣--	_____	_____
29.	1 ♠	♠52 ♡AJ964 ◊53 ♣J763	_____	_____
30.	1 ♣	♠QJ6 ♡AJ7 ◊K105 ♣QJ64	_____	_____

SOLUTIONS

	HCP	Dist.	Length	Total	Bid
1.	9	3→0	0	9	1 NT

In Chapter 1 (page 1), the player using traditional point count thought he had 12 points. We now see this

	HCP	Dist.	Length	Total	Bid

hand is worth only 9 Roth Points—and only a bid of 1 NT! (You must have 11 points to bid a new suit at the two-level.)

| 2. | 6 | 2→3 | 0 | 9 | 2 ♠ |

With 9 Roth Points and excellent trump support, you have an ideal raise to 2 ♠. Remember never to promote a second *doubleton*.

| 3. | 6 | 3→6 | 1 | 13 | 4 ♠ |

Back in Chapter 1, the traditional player thought he had 9 points—he raised to 2 ♠ and *missed game*. But we know this hand is worth 13 Roth Points and therefore a raise to 4 ♠! In the Roth Point Count, the more *trumps*—the more points.

| 4. | 14 | 1→0 | 0 | 14 | 2 NT |

Do not bid a new suit when your hand meets all the requirements for a jump to 2 NT: 13–15 HCP, balanced suit distribution, and all unbid suits stopped.

| 5. | 10 | 4→0 | 1 | 11 | 1 ♠ |

Bid your longest suit.

| 6. | 11 | 1 | 0 | 12 | 2 ♡ |

You do not meet the requirements for a spade raise or notrump jump, but you can and should bid your longest suit.

| 7. | 5 | 2→4 | 0 | 9 | 2 ◊ |

You meet all requirements.

| 8. | 4 | 1→0 | 0 | 4 | Pass |

You have fewer than 6 points.

	HCP	Dist.	Length	Total	Bid	
9.	12	1	0	13	1 ♡	You may not jump in no-trump with only 12 HCP. Bid your lower-ranking four-card suit, remembering to KEEP the same point count with standard three-card support for partner's suit.
10.	8	3 → 0	0	8	1 NT	After DEMOTING your Distribution Points, you may not bid at the two-level since you have only 8 points.
11.	10	2 → 4	0	14	3 ♠	With 14 points (including 4 for the PROMOTED singleton), 10 HCP, and five-card support, you have an excellent raise to 3 ♠. Do not bid a new suit when you can raise partner's major.
12.	17	0	0	17	3 NT	You have 17 HCP, balanced suit distribution, and all unbid suits stopped.
13.	12	2 → 0	0	12	2 ♢	You may bid at the two-level with 11 points or more, so bid your longest suit.
14.	5	1 → 0	0	5	Pass	You need 6 points to respond.
15.	8	2 → 3	0	11	2 ♢	This hand is too strong for a raise to 2 ♠ once you PROMOTE your singleton. Bid your lowest-ranking new four-card suit.

	HCP	Dist.	Length	Total	Bid
16.	14	1	0	15	1 ◇
17.	8	0	0	8	1 ♠
18.	14	1 → 0	0	14	2 ♡
19.	10	2	1	13	Pass
20.	13	1 → 2	0	15	3 ♡
21.	6	1	0	7	2 ♡
22.	7	2 → 0	0	7	1 NT

16. You may not jump in no-trump without a spade stopper. With two four-card suits, bid the lower-ranking.

17. Always prefer a response in a new suit to a 1 NT response when you meet the requirements for bidding a new suit.

18. Do not jump in notrump with a five-card *major* suit.

19. When partner passes, you become the opening bidder. You do not have the minimum 14 points to open, and should pass.*

20. Your hand meets all the requirements.

21. Do not bid a new suit when your hand meets the requirements for a raise of partner's major suit.

22. You may not bid at the two-level with less than 11 points, and you have no suit to bid at the one-level. Do not count any Distribution Points when bidding notrump.

---

* In Standard American theory, the requirements for third- and fourth-position opening bids are reduced. This allows, for example, lead-directional bids in third position. We have not emphasized this point for the sake of simplicity. However, while it is natural to want to take action on this hand, a one-bid will be misleading to partner. A more intelligent (and *much* more effective) approach to this problem will be presented in Part II.

	HCP	Dist.	Length	Total	Bid	
23.	5	2 → 3	0	8	2 ♦	You cannot bid 2 ♣ with only 8 points.
24.	11	2 → 0	0	11	1 ♦	Bid the lowest-ranking four-card suit.
25.	6	2 → 3	0	9	2 ♡	With 9 Roth Points and good support, you have an ideal raise to 2 ♡.
26.	6	3 → 6	0	12	4 ♡	In order to justify a jump to game on this hand, traditional point count recommends "taking a chance with lots of trumps and unusual distribution." Using Roth Point Count, there is no such vague guesswork. 12 Roth Points, fewer than 10 HCP, and 5-card support equals a jump to game—no problem! The more trumps—the more points.
27.	5	3 → 0	0	5	Pass	You do not have the required 6 points.
28.	10	4 → 0	1	11	1 ♡	Bid the longer suit.
29.	6	2 → 0	0	6	1 NT	You may not bid at the two-level without 11 points. Count no Distribution Points when bidding notrump.
30.	14	0	0	14	2 NT	Your hand meets all the requirements.

The reader may find it useful to review the Roth Point Count in capsule form at various stages of its development through this book. Accordingly, a chart summarizing the principles thus far explained will be found at strategic points throughout Part I—in particular, at the end of a chapter in which new ideas are explained. Here is the first such chart.

ROTH POINT COUNT (thus far described)

	HIGH-CARD POINTS	DISTRIBUTION POINTS	LENGTH POINTS
BASIC COUNT	Ace 4 King 3 Queen 2 Jack 1	Void 3 Singleton 2 Doubleton 1	6-card major 1 *good* 6-card minor 1 7-card major 2 *good* 7-card minor 2 (*good* suits include two of the top 3 honors.)
FOR SUIT BIDDING	KEEP	If partner shows a suit: *Fit* *Adjustment* 0–2 DEMOTE to zero 3 KEEP 4(5+) ADD 1 for *one* doubleton ADD 1(2) for EACH void or singleton	
FOR NO-TRUMP BIDDING		DEMOTE to zero	

CHAPTER

4

Rebids by Opener

Thus far, the procedures used to evaluate hands through the Roth Point Count have differed from standard methods, but only slightly. The differences might, in fact, be classified as minor improvements. This chapter includes the "make-or-break" portions of the revolution in point-count bidding. For it is here that we will introduce those facets of the Roth Point Count method which represent the most drastic changes from classical evaluation techniques. It is these changes that, for the most part, represent the enormous improvement of the Roth Point Count over traditional Standard American point counting.

But at the same time, these aspects of the Roth Point Count are also the most complex, and thus the most difficult to learn. One would, after all, expect a more accurate high-powered method to be more difficult, and there is no denying that the techniques described in this chapter are more complicated than those previously introduced. You can't expect to get something for nothing, and you will be required to expend extra energy to learn how to bid through the eyes of an expert. But the rewards are great, for your bidding will improve immeasurably. Furthermore, we will explain the theoretical reasoning behind each of the adjustments in Roth Points, and you will be able to increase your understanding of the underlying structure of bridge bidding. You will know not only *how* the experts achieve bidding accuracy, but *why* their techniques work. And it will all be translated into a simple point count, so that you can evaluate your hand as well as anyone else.

The crucial adjustments in the Roth Point Count are being presented in the chapter on "Rebids by Opener" because it is in this area of bidding that they are first needed to a significant degree. Because of the relative difficulty of this material, we are departing from our usual format and breaking this chapter into two parts. The first, Chapter 4A, will describe the crucial adjustments in the Roth Count, and give you adequate chance to practice these methods before confronting actual bidding situations. We call this subchapter "The Heart of the Matter," because it presents what we consider the most important features of the Roth Point Count. In Chapter 4B, "The Revolution in Action," we show how these adjustments are applied in practice, by discussing techniques for opener's rebid.

The reader is on warning that the point-counting methods presented in this chapter will require more study and practice than the others in this book, and is requested to act accordingly by spending proportionally more time on this material. Your results will show that it is time well spent.

CHAPTER
4A

The Heart of the Matter

In the previous chapter, responder had a great deal of fun promoting, keeping, and demoting his point count in accordance with his partner's opening bid. It would certainly be grossly unfair if only the responder ever knew the excitement of looking at his cards through the eyes of an expert and seeing his point count vary according to the bids he and his partner make. Fortunately, the opening bidder does get his chance to get into the act, for in the Roth Point Count *both* partners become "responders" after the opening bid has been made, and *each* adjusts his point count in accordance with the degree of optimism or pessimism indicated by the auction. So let us now move back across the table and consider how you should evaluate your hand for purposes of making the opener's rebid—the call made by opener after the opening bid and first response.

1/When Partner Bids a New Suit

If responder bids a new suit, you should first look at the number of cards you hold in his suit. (If misfortune strikes and partner has to pass your opening bid, you will usually have to retire and fight again another day.) Since you have already counted your Roth Points before making your opening bid, all you need do is follow the same basic rules as the responder in adjusting your Distribution Points for purposes of suit bidding. (If you bid notrump, you still DEMOTE all Distribution Points to zero.)

If partner has bid a new suit:

LENGTH IN PARTNER'S SUIT	ADJUSTMENT (for purposes of suit bidding)
0–2 cards	DEMOTE *all* Distribution Points to zero.
3 cards	KEEP the same point count.
4 cards	PROMOTE: Add 1 point for *each* void or singleton; Add 1 point for *one* doubleton.
5 or more cards	PROMOTE: Add 2 points for *each* void or singleton; Add 1 point for *one* doubleton.

These are the same rules responder follows in adjusting his point count after the opening bid. There is one additional thing that you must know, however: *Do not count Length Points in your own suit when you PROMOTE for good support in partner's suit.* If you PROMOTE for good support in partner's suit, you will have four or more cards in that suit and thus will want to raise your partner. This rule therefore conforms to the more general rule: *When raising partner, do not count Length Points in your own suit.*[*]

Suppose you hold

♠ AJ42   ♡ AQ9763   ♢ 62   ♣ 7

You open **one heart** since you have 15 Roth Points (11 HCP, 3 Distribution Points, and 1 Length Point). If partner responds **one spade,** you PROMOTE: since you have four cards in his suit, you add 1 point for the singleton and 1 point for the doubleton. Bridge rules strictly prohibit playing a contract in two suits at once, however, so you may not name both hearts and spades as trumps! Since spades are carrying the day, do *not* count your Length Point in hearts. Your new Roth count is 16 (11 HCP, 3 for the PROMOTED singleton, and 2 for the PROMOTED doubleton —and *no* Length Points).

Thus, when partner bids a new suit, you simply evaluate your hand as a responder would do—with the one added factor regarding Length Points.

2/When Partner does *not* Bid a New Suit

If partner does not bid a new suit, there are three things that he can do: raise your suit; make a notrump response that promises balanced suit distribution; or make a notrump response that does *not necessarily* promise balanced suit distribution. The distinction between the two kinds of notrump bids brings us to the most difficult part of the Roth Point Count. The relative complexity of the adjustments that you will make in each case is justified by the fact that they represent *the most significant improvement over traditional point counting methods* and are essential for accurate hand evaluation.

We have seen that *a notrump bid does not always show a balanced hand.* To be sure, there are many cases where one bids notrump only when holding balanced suit distribution; the opening bid of one notrump and the response of two notrump to an opening suit bid of one are examples of notrump bids which *do* show balanced hands. But there are some notrump bids, such as the response of *one* notrump to a suit bid, which do not (necessarily) indicate balanced suit distribution, as was shown in the preceding chapter. The Roth Point Count, being the only truly accurate point-count method, is the *only* method which takes this important dis-

---

* To be strictly accurate, the responder, at his first turn, also should follow the rule not to count Length Points when raising partner. We avoided such examples in Chapter 3 so as not to present too many new ideas at once, but we now adopt the general rule.

tinction into account and builds it right into the point count itself.

Let us look first at what happens to your Length Points for each of the three kinds of bids responder can make (raise of your suit, "balanced" notrump bid, or "unbalanced" notrump bid).

1. *If you are bidding a suit:*

PARTNER'S ACTION   LENGTH POINT ADJUSTMENT

Raise of your suit
PROMOTE by *adding 1 point for each card over four in your suit.* (If your suit is only 3 or 4 cards in length, KEEP the same point count.)

"Balanced" notrump bid
PROMOTE by adding 1 point for each card over four in your longest suit. (With suits of equal length, PROMOTE only one).

"Unbalanced" notrump bid
KEEP the same point count.

2. *If you are bidding notrump:*

First follow the rules in (1) above to determine the Length Points in each suit. Then, KEEP Length Points only for suits that are GOOD; DEMOTE to zero Length Points in suits that are not GOOD.

A suit of five or more cards that is supported by partner gains in power. If partner raises your suit, therefore, you PROMOTE by adding one point *for each card over four.* If partner makes a "balanced" notrump bid, he cannot have a void or singleton in any suit, and is in effect "supporting" all suits.* Consequently, you

---

* Since the "support" in this case *may* be only a doubleton, this adjustment will sometimes lead to a slight overevaluation. The distinction, however, is too fine to delineate in the present work. It would be necessary to introduce fractions in order to express this adjustment precisely.

PROMOTE for your long suit just as though partner had raised it directly. With two long suits, PROMOTE only one. You can expect support for one of your suits, but not both. If partner makes an "unbalanced" notrump bid, he may not have support for your suit, and your Length Points are unaffected by this "neutral" bid. You therefore KEEP the same point count.

If you are now bidding a suit, you have finished adjusting your Length Points. If, however, your bid is in notrump, matters change somewhat. Long suits are useful for taking tricks at notrump *provided that they are sufficiently strong* (see the discussion of Length Points in Chapter 2, page 10, for an explanation of why Length Points for bidding notrump are counted only if your suit is strong enough). Therefore, if you bid notrump you should KEEP Length Points *only* if they are based on a GOOD suit (recall that this means a suit headed by two of the top three honors).* This rule applies whether your suit is a major or a minor, though it will more often be a minor (for with a long major suit you usually prefer to try for a major-suit contract rather than a notrump contract).

Now that we have taken care of the Length Point situation, let us see how your Distribution Points are affected as a result of the three kinds of responses we have been discussing. The first thing that you must do is determine whether or not your side holds an 8-card or longer suit fit.** Do not attempt to do this by walking around the table and looking at partner's hand; the opponents are liable to take a dim view of such behavior. Besides, it is much more

---

* Technically, the rule to KEEP your Length Points with a GOOD suit when bidding notrump could have been introduced in Chapter 3, when we discussed the response of one notrump. We omitted this both for the sake of simplicity and because the rule is rarely applicable to the response of one notrump.

** Since the existence of an 8-card or larger fit guarantees a satisfactory trump suit, it is logical that your hand is worth more when such a fit is assured. The Roth Point Count takes this crucial factor into account!

fun (and considerably more legal) to don the guise of Sherlock Holmes and attempt to deduce the necessary information. Let's try it:

	YOU	PARTNER	YOU HOLD
1.	1 ♡	2 ♡	♠ K6 ♡ QJ854 ◇ AK3 ♣ J104

Your side must hold at least an 8-card fit in hearts, as partner must have at least 3-card support to raise.

	YOU	PARTNER	YOU HOLD
2.	1 ♣	2 ♣	♠ AK87 ♡ Q642 ◇ 42 ♣ AJ5

An 8-card fit is *not* assured. Partner could have only four cards in clubs for his raise.

	YOU	PARTNER	YOU HOLD
3.	1 ♠	3 ♠	♠ KQ654 ♡ AJ4 ◇ A83 ♣ 82

Your side must hold at least an 8-card fit in spades. In fact, at least a 9-card fit is assured as partner must have four-card support for the double raise.

	YOU	PARTNER	YOU HOLD
4.	1 ♠	2 NT	♠ AQ9764 ♡ AQJ ◇ 1043 ♣ 2

Your side must hold at least an 8-card fit in spades. The reason? Partner is not permitted to respond 2 NT with a void or singleton and must have at least two cards in spades.

	YOU	PARTNER	YOU HOLD
5.	1 ♠	2 NT	♠ KJ865 ♡ A7 ◇ KQ953 ♣ 6

Once again, your side must hold at least an 8-card fit. Partner is not permitted to respond 2 NT with *two* doubletons (as he would then have unbalanced suit distribution), so he must have at least three cards in at least one of your two five-card suits.

6.   1 ♡   2 NT   ♠ KJ3   ♡ AKQ54   ◇ 43   ♣ A108

You cannot conclude that your side has an 8-card fit. Partner could have a doubleton heart.

7.   1 ◇   2 NT   ♠ QJ6   ♡ A42   ◇ K1043   ♣ A107

You cannot conclude that your side has an 8-card suit fit. Partner could have, for example, four cards in clubs and three cards in each of the other three suits.

Having determined whether an 8-card suit fit is definite or not definite, simply follow these rules for adjusting your Distribution Points *if you are bidding a suit*:

8-CARD FIT IS:	DISTRIBUTION POINT ADJUSTMENT
Definite	KEEP your Distribution Points.
Not definite	DEMOTE *all* Distribution Points to zero.

As always, if you are bidding notrump, DEMOTE all Distribution Points to zero, regardless of other considerations.

The reason for these rules is that Distribution Points are used to take into account the factor of ruffability. In general, full point value should be awarded for ruffability only when an adequate trump fit, which experience has shown to be eight or more cards, is guaranteed. Therefore, unless an 8-card (or better) trump fit is assured, all Distribution Points should be DEMOTED to zero, for the promise of ruffability given by the short suits is unlikely to be fulfilled due to the shortage of trumps with which to ruff. If you are bidding notrump, there will of course be no trumps and no ruffability, so you DEMOTE all Distribution Points to zero even if an 8-card or longer suit fit is assured.

With a little practice, these adjustments will seem far less formidable. Let's look at some examples:

YOU	PARTNER		HCP	Dist.	Length	Total
1. 1 ♠	2 ♠		13	2	$0 \to 1$	16
	♠ AKQ32	♡ A543	◇ 32	♣ 32		

An 8-card fit is assured, as partner must have at least three-card support to raise. PROMOTE the fifth spade and KEEP your Distribution Points.

2. 1 ♠	1 NT		13	$2 \to 0$	0	13
	♠ AKQ32	♡ A543	◇ 32	♣ 43		

An 8-card fit is not definite since partner may be short in spades, hearts, or both. Therefore, DEMOTE your Distribution Points. You cannot make any PROMOTION for Length Points as your suit has not been supported.

3. 1 ♠	2 NT		13	$2 \to 0$	$0 \to 1$	14
	♠ AKQ32	♡ A543	◇ 32	♣ 32		

An 8-card fit is not definite, for partner could have only two spades and three hearts. Therefore, DEMOTE all Distribution Points to zero. You should PROMOTE the fifth spade as partner's "balanced" notrump bid implies support for all suits.

4. 1 ♡	1 NT		13	3	$1 \to 3$	19
	♠ AKQ432	♡ A432	◇ 32	♣ 3		

Partner must have at least two cards in spades for his two no-trump response, so an 8-card fit is assured. PROMOTE by adding one point for each card over four in your "supported" spade suit and KEEP your Distribution Points. Note that this hand counts *five points higher* than the previous one, even though only one change was made (switching a small club to a small spade). *This evaluation is completely in keeping with expert methods.* Look at all that happened as a result of this change: (i) a loser in clubs was eliminated; (ii) a virtually sure winner in spades was added; (iii) the existence of a satisfactory trump fit became guaranteed; (iv) the chances of running the spade suit without loss became greatly increased, thus increasing the value of the fourth and fifth spades as well as the sixth.

5. 1 ♠   2 NT   13   3   0 → 1   17

♠ AKQ32   ♡ A5432   ◇ 43   ♣ 2

Since partner may not respond 2 NT with two doubletons, he must have at least three cards in one of the major suits, and an 8-card fit is therefore assured. Therefore, PROMOTE by adding one Length Point for the fifth spade (but not for the fifth heart also). Again the evaluation is good, for this hand is in fact less valuable than the one in example 4, yet clearly better than the hand in example 3.

6. 1 ◇   2 ◇   13   1 → 0   0   13

♠ KJ86   ♡ AQ54   ◇ K83   ♣ 42

An 8-card diamond fit is not certain since partner could have only four for his raise. Therefore, DEMOTE your Distribution Points to zero. With only three cards in diamonds, you have no length to PROMOTE.

7. 1 ♠   1 NT   15   2 → 0   1   16 (suit)
                               15   2 → 0   1 → 0   15 (NT)

♠ AJ5432   ♡ A5   ◇ K4   ♣ K43

This hand is evaluated for both suit and notrump. For suit bidding, Distribution Points are DEMOTED to zero because there is no guaranteed 8-card fit, while the Length Point is kept. For notrump bidding, Distribution Points are demoted to zero (as usual) and the Length Point is also DEMOTED because the spade suit is not GOOD. Although a hand will sometimes have different values for different denominations, the Roth Point Count does not always determine *what* you bid.* It does, however, tell you how much your hand is worth in the denomination you choose to bid, and thus will always help you to bid to the right *level* in the proper denomination.

8. 1 ♠   3 ♠   12   3   0 → 1   16

♠ AK753   ♡ 84   ◇ 3   ♣ AJ642

Partner's double raise promises four-card support, so a fine suit fit exists. KEEP your Distribution Points and PROMOTE the fifth spade.

9. 1 ♠   2 NT   12   3   0 → 1   16

♠ AK753   ♡ 84   ◇ 3   ♣ AJ642

Partner cannot have two doubletons, so an 8-card fit must exist in either spades or clubs (or both). PROMOTE the fifth spade, but not the fifth club.

10. 1 ♠   1 NT   12   3 → 0   0   12

♠ AK753   ♡ 84   ◇ 3   ♣ AJ642

---

* It might fairly be said, however, that *if possible* you should bid in (or towards) the denomination in which your Roth Point Count is highest.

As is usually the case when partner responds 1 NT, there is no reason to suspect the existence of an 8-card fit. DEMOTE all Distribution Points to zero. KEEP the same Length Point total, which in this case is zero.

The following chart summarizes the adjustments which have just been described:

	HCP	DISTRIBUTION POINTS	LENGTH POINTS
FOR SUIT BIDDING	(KEEP)	If partner does not show a new suit: With known 8-card trump fit, KEEP; otherwise DEMOTE to zero.	When raising partner's suit, do not count Length Points. If partner shows support, ADD 1 for each card over 4 in each supported suit.
FOR NOTRUMP BIDDING	(KEEP)	(DEMOTE to zero).	ADD 1 for each card over 4 in a supported suit; if partner shows a balanced hand, assume he has supported your longest suit. KEEP only if based on GOOD suit; otherwise DEMOTE to zero.

The entries enclosed in parentheses were described previously and are included to complete the table. Your adjustment of Distribution Points for suit bidding depends on whether or not partner has bid a suit. If he has, follow the procedures outlined on page 86; if he has not, use the rule stated above.

You will probably agree that we weren't fooling when we said this was the hardest part of the Roth Point Count. It would be surprising if anyone could master these rules the first time around. Before you go on to the examples of counting Roth Points for opener's rebid (which make use of these rules), why not review the entire section? It should be worth your while, for if you can master the principles of point counting just described you will know 90% of the Roth Point Count. There are only a few more things to learn and they are a lot easier than what you have already accomplished.

Now let's take a look at more examples of the adjustments for opener's rebid in action. In each case, we will compute the Roth Point Count *for suit purposes.*

	HCP	Dist.	Length	Total
1. ♠ Q53 ♡ AKJ32 ◇ K864 ♣ 2	13	2	0	15

With 15 Roth Points, including 10 HCP, you open the bidding with **one heart.** Consider various responses that partner can make and see how your point count is affected.

	HCP	Dist.	Length	Total
Partner responds 1 ♠ :	13	2	0	15

KEEP the same point count for distribution with the standard three-card holding in partner's suit.

	HCP	Dist.	Length	Total
Partner responds 1 NT:	13	2 → 0	0	13

DEMOTE all Distribution Points to zero as there is no certain 8-card trump fit.

Partner responds 2 ♣:   13   **2 → 0**   0   13

DEMOTE all Distribution Points to zero whenever you hold fewer than three cards in the suit partner bids.

Partner responds 2 ◇:   13   **2 → 3**   0   16

PROMOTE with four cards in partner's suit by adding one point for the singleton.

Partner raises to 2 ♡:   13   2   **0 → 1**   16

PROMOTE by adding one point for the fifth heart as the suit was "supported" by partner. Note that you KEEP your Distribution Points because partner "did not show a new suit" and at least an 8-card heart fit is assured. (Here we see why the rule was phrased "if partner does not show a new suit . . . ," for you are certainly entitled to count for distribution with ruffability available.)

Partner jumps to 2 NT: 13   **2 → 0 0 → 1**   14

Partner has a good hand, but this does not affect the rule of DE-MOTING all Distribution Points to zero when partner has not bid a suit and no 8-card fit is assured. But you do assume that hearts are "supported."

You may have noticed that in some of the above situations, the value of your hand dropped to 13 Roth Points, or *less* than the minimum required to open the bidding! Do not be disturbed; the minimum standards for opening the bidding are sufficiently high so that you will usually be able to withstand the misfortune of partner's making a bid which doesn't suit your hand. However, caution is clearly indicated when this occurs. As you will see, it is possible that partner's *next* bid will be right down your alley with the result that your Roth points go *up*—but until this happens, your reduced Roth point count shows that you must proceed slowly.*

---

* As noted in Chapter 2, the Roth Point Count will not always affect each individual bid. In fact, as we have seen, the count often depends on which bid is chosen.

Here is another example to show how the rules work:

			HCP	Dist.	Length	Total
2. ♠ KJ42 ♡ 43 ◇ AK9763 ♣ 7			11	3	1	15

Your original total is 15 Roth Points (remember to add 1 Length Point for the *good* six-card minor), so you open the bidding with 1 ◇.

Partner responds 1 ♡: 11 3 → 0 1 12

Help! You must DEMOTE all Distribution Points to zero since you have only two-card support for partner, leaving you with only 12 points! Thank goodness the Length Point is not affected by partner's bid in a suit for which we do *not* have good support, and hence do not intend to raise.

	HCP	Dist.	Length	Total
Partner responds 1 ♠:	11	3 → 5	1 → 0	16

With four-card support for partner, PROMOTE by adding one point for the doubleton and one point for the singleton. Since it is illegal to play a hand in both spades and diamonds, do *not* count a Length Point in diamonds. Your total therefore is 16 points.

	HCP	Dist.	Length	Total
Partner responds 1 NT:	11	3 → 0	1	12

Yes, this is a time for caution! We must DEMOTE all Distribution Points for there may be no 8-card trump fit. The Length Point stays, however.

Partner responds 2 ♣: 11 3 → 0 1 12

DEMOTE your Distribution Points with shortness in partner's suit.

Partner raises to 2 ◇: 11 3 1 → 3 17

PROMOTE whenever a suit of five cards or longer is supported by adding one point for each card over four. Be sure to *add* this to the Length Point you have already counted in diamonds; your new

Length total is 3 points. Note that you KEEP your Distribution Points because partner has not bid a new suit and there *is* a certain 8-card (in fact, longer) fit in diamonds.

Once again, observe how the Roth Point Count builds in the required degree of optimism or pessimism, based on partner's response. On some hands, you are sorry you opened the bidding (for the time being, at least) because partner has selected a particularly "inappropriate" bid; on others, your hand is improved because you and partner are on the same wavelength. You *see* this happen— *see* your hand the way an expert would—when you use the Roth Point Count!

Capsule Summary: Roth Points for Opener's Rebid

1. PARTNER BIDS A NEW SUIT:

LENGTH IN PARTNER'S SUIT	ADJUSTMENT (of Distribution Points for suit bidding purposes)
0–2 cards	DEMOTE to zero.
3 cards	KEEP the same point count.
4 cards	PROMOTE: Add 1 point for *each* void or singleton; Add 1 point for *one* doubleton.
5 or more cards	PROMOTE: Add 2 points for *each* void or singleton; Add 1 point for *one* doubleton.

When raising partner, do not count Length Points.

2. PARTNER SUPPORTS YOUR SUIT:

LENGTH OF YOUR SUIT	ADJUSTMENT (of Length Points)
3–4 cards	KEEP the same point count.
5 or more	PROMOTE: add 1 point for each card over 4 in the supported suit.

3. PARTNER DOES NOT BID A NEW SUIT:

DEMOTE *all* Distribution Points to zero if no 8-card or better trump fit is certain. KEEP Distribution Points if an 8-card (or better) fit is assured.

REVIEW QUIZ FOR CHAPTER 4 A

In each of the hands shown below, your opening bid and partner's response are shown. How many Roth Points do you have for suit bidding purposes:

	YOU	PARTNER	YOU HOLD:
1.	1 ◇	1 ♡	♠ A742 ♡ 53 ◇ KQ86 ♣ KJ8
2.	1 ♠	3 ♠	♠ KQ9654 ♡ AJ4 ◇ K843 ♣ ---
3.	1 ♡	1 NT	♠ 7 ♡ AK10874 ◇ K85 ♣ Q107
4.	1 ◇	2 ♣	♠ 6 ♡ 85 ◇ AKJ974 ♣ KQ84
5.	1 ♡	2 NT	♠ 8 ♡ KQ9853 ◇ A642 ♣ A2
6.	1 ♣	1 ♡	♠ A6 ♡ K87 ◇ 6432 ♣ AK109
7.	1 ♠	2 ♡	♠ KQ875 ♡ 32 ◇ AQ1062 ♣ 2
8.	1 ♠	2 ◇	♠ KQ875 ♡ 32 ◇ AQ1062 ♣ 2
9.	1 ♡	2 NT	♠ K83 ♡ AQ1096 ◇ K1074 ♣ 7
10.	1 ◇	2 ◇	♠ J1074 ♡ 6 ◇ AK108 ♣ AQ82

SOLUTIONS

	HCP	Dist.	Length	Total	
1.	13	1 → 0	0	13	DEMOTE all Distribution Points to zero when you have 0–2 cards in partner's suit.
2.	13	3	1 → 3	19	PROMOTE by adding 1 point for each card over four when partner supports a suit

of five or more cards. Do not forget the original Length Point for a six-card major suit. Keep Distribution Points since an 8-card fit is assured.

3. 12 2 → 0   1   13

DEMOTE all Distribution Points to zero for there may be no 8-card trump suit.

4. 13 3 → 5   1 → 0   18

PROMOTE by adding 1 point for the singleton and 1 point for the doubleton when you have four cards in partner's suit, but do *not* count Length Points in your own suit, since you will want to raise clubs.

5. 13 3   1 → 3   19

You have 13 HCP, 3 Distribution Points (partner has at least two hearts), and 3 Length Points (hearts have been "supported").

6. 14 1   0   15

KEEP the same Distribution Point count with three cards in partner's suit.

7. 11 3 → 0   0   11

DEMOTE all Distribution Points to zero with only two cards in partner's suit. You now have only 11 points— the Roth Point Count shows you that caution is in order! (Compare with Example 8.)

8. 11 3 → 6   0   17

With five-card support for partner, PROMOTE by adding two points for the singleton and one for the doubleton. When you have good support for partner, the Roth Point Count goes up—optimism prevails, and this is shown *in the point count!* (Compare with Example 7.)

9. 12 2 → 0 0 → 1 13 DEMOTE all Distribution Points to zero, for partner need not have 3 hearts. But you *can* consider hearts "supported" and PROMOTE a Length Point.

10. 14 2 0 16 KEEP the same Length count when a *four*-card suit is raised by partner. The minor-suit raise shows 4-card support, so the Distribution Points may also be kept.

ROTH POINT COUNT (thus far described)

	HIGH-CARD POINTS	DISTRIBUTION POINTS	LENGTH POINTS
BASIC COUNT	Ace 4 King 3 Queen 2 Jack 1	Void 3 Singleton 2 Doubleton 1	6-card major 1 GOOD 6-card minor 1 7-card major 2 GOOD 7-card minor 2
FOR SUIT BIDDING		If partner shows a suit: *Fit* *Adjustment* 0–2 DEMOTE to zero 3 KEEP 4(5+) ADD 1 for *one* doubleton ADD 1(2) for EACH void or singleton If partner does not show a suit: KEEP with known 8-card or better trump fit; otherwise DEMOTE to zero	When raising partner's suit do not count Length Points in your own suit SUIT BID-DING If partner shows support,* ADD 1 for each card over 4 in the supported suit
FOR NO-TRUMP BIDDING	KEEP	DEMOTE to zero	KEEP (and adjust as for suit bidding) only if based on a *good* suit (otherwise DEMOTE to zero)

A GOOD suit is one containing two of the top three honors.

---

* If partner shows a balanced hand, assume he has supported your longest suit.

CHAPTER

4B

The Revolution in Action

Now that you have learned how to evaluate your hand properly and are well on your way towards bidding as well as the experts do, it is time to discuss opener's rebid—what bid opener should select at his second turn to bid.

Step 1 / Adjust your Roth Points

Once you have heard partner's response to your opening bid, the first thing that you do is adjust your Roth Points in accordance with the procedures given in the previous chapter. As promised, you see the value of your hand change right before your eyes, in accordance with the degree of optimism or pessimism warranted by partner's action.

Step 2 / Is Partner's Response "Limited" or "Unlimited"?

After you have adjusted your Roth Points, you are ready to continue the "game hunt." Game requires a partnership total of 26 points. Your opening bid plus partner's response represent the evidence available so far, and determine whether game is definite, possible, or totally out of the question. Sometimes you will not have enough information to decide after just two bids, and you will need more clues. In such cases, your best procedure is to make the most informative bid, so that you and your partner will have as much data as possible at each step of the auction.

Frequently, however, partner makes a bid that has clearly defined limits. When this happens, you can narrow down the game prospects to the categories "definite," "possible," or "impossible." For example, suppose you open **one heart** and partner raises to **two hearts.** Partner's raise is a *limited* bid, as he is known to possess between 7 and 10 points (and support for hearts). Therefore, if you have 15 points or less, your powers of deduction should tell you that game is out of the question. Even if partner has his maximum holding of 10 points, your side cannot hold more than 15 plus 10 or 25—not enough for game. If instead you hold 17 points, prospects are uncertain. If partner holds a maximum—9 or 10 points—26 points and game are there; but if partner has only a minimum 7 or 8 points, you cannot have more than 25 total points between you. Thus, game is *possible*. Finally, if you hold 19 or more points, you can deduce that game is *definite*. Even if partner has the minimum possible holding for his bid (7 points), the combined total of the two hands is 19 plus 7 or 26—game!

Should you open **one diamond** and partner respond **one spade,** not even Sherlock Holmes could make an intelligent deduction with so little information. Partner could have as few as 6 points for his bid, or as many as 17; his bid of **one spade** is *unlimited*— not tied to a narrow point range. In such cases, the only thing you can do is collect more evidence. You make the most informative bid possible, expecting that a decision regarding game prospects will be reached later.

Therefore, it is important to know which bids are limited and which bids are unlimited. Over *limited* bids, you will make a substantial part of the decision as to whether or not game is on the horizon; but over *unlimited* bids, you will instead add to the available data by making the most informative rebid possible, waiting until more of the evidence is in before reaching any decision. In general, each partner should describe his hand as well as possible. Eventually, one or the other will become "captain" and decide where to place the contract.

This table enumerates limited and unlimited responses:

LIMITED RESPONSES	UNLIMITED RESPONSES
Any raise of your suit	*Any* bid in a new suit.
Single raise: 7–10	
Double raise: 13–15	
Triple raise: 11–15	
Any notrump bid	
1 NT: 6–10	
2 NT: 13–15	
3 NT: 16–18	

QUIZ

In each of the following auctions, state whether partner's response is a *limited* bid or an *unlimited* bid. If it is *limited,* state the range of points partner holds.

	YOU	PARTNER			YOU	PARTNER
1.	1 ◇	2 ♣		6.	1 ♠	2 ♠
2.	1 ♡	4 ♡		7.	1 ♡	2 NT
3.	1 ♠	1 NT		8.	1 ◇	2 ◇
4.	1 ♣	1 ◇		9.	1 ♡	3 ♡
5.	1 ♣	3 NT		10.	1 ◇	1 ♠

SOLUTIONS

1. Unlimited.
2. Limited (11–15 points).
3. Limited (6–10 points).
4. Unlimited.
5. Limited (16–18 points).

6. Limited (7–10 points).
7. Limited (13–15 points).
8. Limited (7–10 points).
9. Limited (13–15 points).
10. Unlimited.

Step 3A / Bidding over a Limited Response

We have seen that after a *limited* response, you are able to deduce whether game is impossible, possible, or definite. Now we must consider what to do in each of these cases. Part of the fascination of bridge stems from the fact that verbal statements such as "no game, partner" are prohibited, and the bidding must convey this and other messages—it is up to you and your partner to keep the bidding language clear and the message coherent.

If game is out of the question, and there is no possibility that the combined partnership holdings add up to 26 points, you should find the *cheapest playable contract.* There is no bonus for playing a contract of 3 ♡ as opposed to a contract of 2 ♡ (except possibly for your opponents, if they are able to limit you to eight tricks). However, you must be sure that the contract is *playable.* It is quite possible to make a game by combining two or three part scores, and you certainly do not want to go down in the wrong part-score contract when a different contract would have resulted in a plus score for your side.

If game is possible, you should *invite* game—suggest to partner that he bid game with a hand toward the maximum end of his range, and that he stop short of game with a minimal hand.

If game is definite, you must make *certain* that game is reached. One possible way to do this is to bid game yourself. Sometimes, however, you will not be sure *which* game to bid, and in such cases you must be sure to make a bid that partner is not permitted to pass. You may know that game is certain, but partner does not; so do not give him a chance to go wrong by allowing him to pass before game is reached.

Let us now consider the various limited bids that partner can make, and see how to convey the necessary message to partner.

BIDDING OVER A 1 NT RESPONSE

When partner responds 1 NT, you know that he has 6–10 points. After DEMOTING all Distribution Points to zero, your next task is to decide on the likelihood of game. The examples below show how this is done:

	YOU	PARTNER	DECISION
1.	1 ♠	1 NT	NO GAME (13 Roth Points for notrump or suit)

♠ AQ865 ♡ K83 ◇ A94 ♣ 32

	YOU	PARTNER	DECISION
2.	1 ◇	1 NT	DEFINITE GAME (20 Roth Points for notrump)

♠ 32 ♡ AK85 ◇ KQ85 ♣ AKJ

	YOU	PARTNER	DECISION
3.	1 ♡	1 NT	POSSIBLE GAME (17 Roth Points for notrump or suit)

♠ KJ5 ♡ AQJ62 ◇ AQ87 ♣ 3

	YOU	PARTNER	DECISION
4.	1 ◇	1 NT	NO GAME (14 Roth Points for notrump)

♠ K853 ♡ A53 ◇ AK876 ♣ 3

In Example 1, you know that there is no game. You have 13 Roth Points (after DEMOTING your Distribution Points to zero) and partner has at most 10 points; the maximum possible is 23 points—less than the 26 required for game.

In Example 2, you can deduce that game should be bid. You have 20 points and partner must have at least 6 points; so no matter whether partner has a minimum or maximum, the combined total is at least 26 points.

In Example 3, game is possible. Your total is 17 points. If partner has 9 or 10 points, game should be bid; if he has only 7 or 8, game should not be bid. Therefore, you should *invite* game.

Finally, in Example 4, the evidence indicates that there is no chance for game. You have 14 points, and partner can have at most 10; the maximum possible combined total is 24.

Since partner must have between 6 and 10 points, we can assign point ranges to the above categories. (It is, however, unnecessary to memorize these ranges.) Game is *out of the question* if you have 15 points or less—only a person in need of remedial training in mathematics can produce a total of 26 opposite partner's maximum of 10 points. If you have 16–19 points, game is *possible;* and if you have 20 or more points, game is *definite*. Having evaluated the evidence, what bid do you make?

If game is out of the question (you hold 15 points or less):
1. Rebid a six-card suit *or* bid a suit of four or more cards if it is lower ranking than your original suit.
2. Otherwise *pass.*
Examples:

	YOU	PARTNER	YOU HOLD
1.	1 ♡	1 NT	♠ 32 ♡ AK865 ◊ K32 ♣ K85

Pass. Game is out of the question (you have 13 Roth Points) and you have no six-card suit or lower-ranking four-card suit.

2.	1 ◊	1 NT	♠ K964 ♡ 32 ◊ AK962 ♣ K3

Pass. Again, you have 13 Roth Points and game is out of the question. You may not bid a new suit that is *higher*-ranking than your original own suit (for this would invite game).

3.	1 ♠	1 NT	♠ Q10865 ♡ 3 ◊ AKJ7 ♣ A53

Bid 2 ◊. With 14 points, there is no game. Partner already knows you have five spades and might like to hear about the diamonds.

4.	1 ◊	1 NT	♠ 8 ♡ A63 ◊ AK875 ♣ QJ32

Bid 2 ♣. You have a lower-ranking four-card suit.

	YOU	PARTNER	YOU HOLD
5.	1 ♠	1 NT	♠ AQ10643 ♡ 32 ◊ A832 ♣ 7

Bid 2 ♠. Give preference to rebidding a strong six-card suit over bidding a new four-card suit.

6.	1 ♣	1 NT	♠ K865 ♡ AQ83 ◊ 2 ♣ AJ43

Pass. You have no lower-ranking four-card suit to bid.

If game is possible (you hold 16–19 points):
1. With no void or singleton, raise to 2 NT. (This raise asks partner to pass with a minimum and bid 3 NT with a maximum.)
2. With a *void* or *singleton,* your hand is not well oriented towards play in notrump. Therefore, bid a suit, according to the following priorities:

A. Bid a *new five-card* suit;

B. *Jump rebid* a six-card suit;

C. Bid a new four-card suit, whether it ranks above or below your original suit.

Examples:

YOU	PARTNER	YOU HOLD:
1. 1 ♠	1 NT	♠ AQ1086 ♡ 6 ◇ AK875 ♣ A2

Bid 2 ◇. Whenever possible, bid a new *five*-card suit.

2. 1 ♡	1 NT	♠ 3 ♡ AQ10962 ◇ AQ82 ♣ A5

Bid 3 ♡. With no new five-card suit but with your original suit six cards, *jump* in your original suit. You should not bid only 2 ♡ because partner would think you are simply trying to find the cheapest playable contract and pass. You would bid 2 ♡ with

♠ 3   ♡ AQ10642   ◇ A842   ♣ 65

where game is impossible, so you must *jump* to tell partner that you have 16–19 points and game is *possible.* He will then know that he should bid a game with a maximum and pass with a minimum.

3. 1 ◇	1 NT	♠ AK72 ♡ 83 ◇ AK432 ♣ A8

Bid 2 NT. You have 18 points and no void or singleton. Do not bid 2 ♠. Partner would have bid 1 ♠ rather than 1 NT if he had four spades.

4. 1 ◇	1 NT	♠ Q832 ♡ --- ◇ AKJ85 ♣ AQ102

Bid 2 ♣. You may not raise notrump with a void, so bid a new four-card suit. (You bid the lower-ranking as you are not strong enough to bid the higher-ranking.)

If game is definite (you hold 20 or more points):

1. If you hold a seven-card (or longer) major suit, or a very strong six-card suit, jump to four of the major.

2. With a balanced hand, or no new suit to bid, raise to 3 NT.

3. Holding a new suit of four or more cards, *jump* in the new suit.

Examples:

YOU	PARTNER	YOU HOLD
1. 1 ♡	1 NT	♠ 3 ♡ AK10854 ◇ AKQ2 ♣ 3

Jump to 3 ◇. Game is definite, so let partner know by jumping in your new suit. The reason that you do not jump to game yourself is that 3 NT, 4 ♡ or 5 ◇ (and possibly 6 ◇) could be the correct contract. Partner's next bid will "clue" you as to your best game.

| 2. 1 ♠ | 1 NT | ♠ KQJ86 ♡ AK8 ◇ KJ7 ♣ A3 |

Raise to 3 NT. With a balanced hand, raise to game in notrump. You know that game is certain because your 21 points plus partner's minimum of 6 adds up to 27, or 1 point more than the 26 points needed for game.

| 3. 1 ◇ | 1 NT | ♠ KQ8 ♡ 83 ◇ AKJ875 ♣ AK |

Raise to 3 NT. Your 21 points (keep the Length Point for notrump with a *good* suit) plus partner's minimum of 6 points ensures that the necessary total of 26 points is there, and you have no new four-card suit to bid.

Capsule Summary: Opener's Rebid After a 1 NT Response

OPENER'S POINTS	OPENER'S DISTRIBUTION	OPENER'S REBID
15 or less (NO GAME)		1. Rebid a six-card suit; 2. Bid a new four-card suit if it is *lower-ranking* than your first suit; 3. Otherwise pass.
16–19 (POSSIBLE GAME)	No void or singleton	Raise to 2 NT.

	At least one void or singleton	1. Bid a new five-card suit; 2. *Jump* rebid a six-card suit; 3. Bid a new suit (regardless of rank).
20–21 (DEFINITE GAME)	Very strong major	Jump to 4 of major.
	Balanced hand or no new suit to bid	Raise to 3 NT
	New suit of 4 or more cards	Jump in new suit.

QUIZ

On each of the following hands, your opening bid is indicated, and partner responds 1 NT. First, adjust your Roth Points; second, decide whether game is impossible, possible, or definite; and finally, select your rebid.

	YOU	PARTNER	YOU HOLD:
1.	1 ♣	1 NT	♠8 ♡KJ7 ◇AQ8642 ♣KJ2
2.	1 ♡	1 NT	♠K8 ♡AQ1063 ◇AK3 ♣KJ8
3.	1 ♠	1 NT	♠KQ10864 ♡AKQ2 ◇A3 ♣2
4.	1 ◇	1 NT	♠K83 ♡AQ2 ◇KQ864 ♣42
5.	1 ♠	1 NT	♠AK10943 ♡2 ◇AKQ7 ♣A5
6.	1 ◇	1 NT	♠K874 ♡AQ32 ◇AJ94 ♣10
7.	1 ♣	1 NT	♠AKQ3 ♡KQ2 ◇J2 ♣AQ84
8.	1 ♡	1 NT	♠3 ♡AJ865 ◇AQ863 ♣42
9.	1 ♠	1 NT	♠K9764 ♡--- ◇KJ84 ♣AJ92
10.	1 ♠	1 NT	♠AQ8732 ♡AQ7 ◇K3 ♣K2
11.	1 ♠	1 NT	♠AKQ32 ♡K83 ◇K52 ♣32
12.	1 ◇	1 NT	♠K1043 ♡2 ◇AK8653 ♣43
13.	1 ◇	1 NT	♠AQ102 ♡K63 ◇AJ85 ♣K2
14.	1 ♡	1 NT	♠--- ♡KQ9653 ◇932 ♣AJ73
15.	1 ◇	1 NT	♠KQ85 ♡AKJ2 ◇KJ3 ♣A2

SOLUTIONS

1. *2 ◊*. You have only 15 Roth Points for notrump so game is impossible there. Rebid your six-card suit.

2. *3 NT*. Your 20 points plus partner's minimum of 6 ensure that the magic total of 26 must be present. With balanced suit distribution, raise to game in notrump.

3. *3 ♠*. With 19 points, you are in the possible game range. With no new five-card suit, your next priority is to jump in a six-card suit. You must jump to be sure that partner knows you are inviting game, rather than just looking for the cheapest playable contract.

4. *Pass*. With only 14 points, game is out of the question, and you have no six-card suit or lower-ranking four-card suit to bid.

5. *3 ◊*. Your 21 points make game definite. Indicate this to partner by jumping in your new four-card suit.

6. *Pass*. There is no game when you have only 14 points, so you may not rebid a four-card suit that is higher-ranking than your first-bid suit.

7. *3 NT*. You have 21 points, so game is definite, and you have balanced distribution.

8. *2 ◊*. Since you have only 11 points, there is no game. Bid your new five-card suit. (This bid invites partner to pass or correct to hearts, but game may yet be reached if partner can re-evaluate his hand in support of diamonds.)

9. *2 ♣*. You can deduce that there is no game since you have only 12 points. Bid your lower-ranking new four-card suit. (Once again, partner may be able to revalue—See Example 8.)

10. *2 NT*. With 19 points, game is possible. With no void or singleton, invite game by raising to 2 NT. (Keep the Length Point for notrump purposes as the spade suit is *good*.)

11. *Pass*. There is no game when you have only 15 points, and you have balanced suit distribution.

12. *2 ◊*. Your total of 11 Roth Points shows that there is no game. You may not bid a new suit that is higher-ranking than your first suit, so simply rebid your six-card minor. Partner has

already had a chance to value his hand in diamonds, so he will probably pass. (Compare with 8 and 9.)

13. *2 NT.* Game is possible since you hold 17 points. With no void or singleton, invite game by raising to 2 NT.

14. *2 ♡.* There is no game when you have only 11 Roth Points. Rebid your six-card suit.

15. *3 NT.* With balanced suit distribution and 21 points, you have an ideal raise to 3 NT.

BIDDING AFTER NOTRUMP JUMPS

If partner jumps in notrump, your action is relatively straightforward. Both you and partner know that game is definite, for even if partner has the minimum for his bid, the two hands add up to 26 points.* The first thing you should do is check to see if *slam* is a possibility. If the two hands can add up to 33 *points,* you are in the slam range. If partner jumps to 2 NT and you have 17 points or less, slam is out of the question since partner's maximum is 15 points; if partner jumps to 3 NT and you have 14 points or less, slam is similarly impossible as partner's maximum is 18 points. Techniques for dealing with hands in the slam range will be discussed in the chapter on slam bidding; here we will be concerned only with those hands on which there is *no chance for slam.*

With balanced suit distribution, raise partner's 2 NT jump to 3 NT or pass if his jump is to 3 NT. You should rarely bid over a jump to 3 NT (assuming your hand is not in the slam range, of course) unless your hand is very distributional and you are most averse to playing in notrump. It is always safe to rebid a six-card major suit, as partner must have at least two-card support (he may not jump in notrump with a singleton). However, you should not

---

* Strictly speaking, this will not always be true, as partner might have 13 points and you might have a DEMOTED Roth Point Count of 12 (or less). Since you cannot bid 2–1/2 NT to find out if partner is maximum or minimum, however, just treat all notrump jumps as indicating a definite game. Usually it will be there anyway.

go exploring into new areas unless you are under extreme provocation, as 3 NT will most often be the best contract. Thus, with

♠3　♡AQ10642　◇AJ42　♣32,

you would be fully justified in bidding 3 ♥ over partner's jump to 2 NT or 4 ♥ over his jump to 3 NT. But if you hold

♠32　♡AQ654　◇AQ65　♣32,

open 1 ♥, and hear partner jump to 3 NT, you should pass. You do not have any more hearts than partner expects, and if he wanted to play in hearts, he would not have jumped to 3 NT. Only wild-eyed optimists would see any point in exploring the possibility of playing in the four-card diamond suit, especially since minor-suit games require *29 points*. Thus, when not under extreme provocation, simply raise 2 NT to 3 NT or pass at 3 NT.

Over a jump to 2 NT, where you may bid below the level of 3 NT, you should show a new four-card (or longer) *major* suit, since partner may also have four cards in that suit. Some examples:

	YOU	PARTNER	YOU HOLD:			
1.	1 ♠	2 NT	♠AK865	♡Q83	◇KJ3	♣32

Raise to 3 NT. You have balanced suit distribution.

2.	1 ◇	2 NT	♠K3	♡Q85	◇AQ10642	♣Q7

Raise to 3 NT. There is no point in rebidding the long minor when you have a relatively balanced hand, high-card points in all suits, and no chance for slam.

3A.	1 ◇	3 NT	♠K1087	♡Q109	◇AQ42	♣K3
3B.	1 ◇	2 NT	♠K1087	♡Q109	◇AQ42	♣K3

A. *Pass.* You have only 14 Roth Points and balanced suit distribution.

B. *Bid 3 ♠.* Show a four-card major if you can do so below 3 NT.*

4.   1 ♠   2 NT   ♠ AJ10975 ♡ KQ864 ◇ 3 ♣ 3

Bid 3 ♡. You certainly do not like notrump with such an unbalanced hand. Bid your new five-card suit.

5.   1 ♡   3 NT   ♠ --- ♡ KQJ432 ◇ A432 ♣ 932

Bid 4 ♡. Do not play in notrump with a void. It is always safe to rebid a six-card major over a notrump jump.

Capsule Summary: Bidding Over Notrump Jumps

1. OVER 2 NT

OPENER'S POINTS	OPENER'S DISTRIBUTION	OPENER'S REBID
18 or more	---	*See chapter on Slam Bidding*
17 or less		1. Bid a new five-card suit.
		2. Rebid a six-card suit;
		3. Bid a four-card major suit;
		4. Otherwise bid 3 NT.

2. OVER 3 NT

OPENER'S POINTS	OPENER'S DISTRIBUTION	OPENER'S REBID
15 or more	Relatively Balanced	See chapter on Slam Bidding
14 or less	---	Pass.
	Unbalanced	1. Bid a new five-card suit.
		2. Rebid a six-card major.
		3. Bid a new four-card suit (usually only with a void elsewhere in the hand).

----

* This procedure can be omitted if the partnership has agreed not to respond two notrump when holding a four-card major.

QUIZ

On each of the hands below, your opening bid and partner's jump in notrump are shown. Count your Roth Points and determine your rebid.

	YOU	PARTNER	YOU HOLD:			
1.	1 ♣	2 NT	♠ K863	♡ 3	◇ Q1084	♣ AKJ3
2.	1 ♡	2 NT	♠ 864	♡ AQ1053	◇ AQJ2	♣ 3
3.	1 ♠	2 NT	♠ AJ10432	♡ 2	◇ KQ32	♣ 75
4.	1 ◇	3 NT	♠ KQJ2	♡ AJ103	◇ KQ42	♣ 2
5.	1 ♡	2 NT	♠ ---	♡ KQ107432	◇ 95	♣ AJ63
6.	1 ◇	2 NT	♠ ---	♡ AJ42	◇ KQ543	♣ J842
7.	1 ◇	3 NT	♠ 65	♡ K2	◇ AQ10543	♣ Q32
8.	1 ♠	2 NT	♠ AQ1065	♡ AQ432	◇ 32	♣ 10
9.	1 ♣	2 NT	♠ K432	♡ QJ102	◇ 32	♣ AK3
10.	1 ♣	2 NT	♠ 3	♡ AK107	◇ 1064	♣ KQJ32

SOLUTIONS

1. 3 ♠. Show your four card major suit. (13 points. No Distribution Points because there may be no 8-card suit fit.)

2. 3 ◇. You are not in the slam range since you hold only 14 Roth Points, and though your hand is not wildly unbalanced, all your strength is in the red suits so you should give partner a choice of contracts.

3. 3 ♠. With unbalanced suit distribution, rebid your six-card major suit.

4. *Do not pass.* With 16 points, you are in the slam range, since the total partnership point count will reach 33 if partner has 17 or 18 points. (See Chapter 9.)

5. 4 ♡. We did not discuss what to do with a *seven*-card major, and a rebid of 3 ♡ would not be wrong; but you will not want to play 3 NT if partner now bids it because of your spade void.

Since you would bid 4 ♡ even if partner were to bid notrump again, why not bid it right away?

6. *3 ♡.* You do not want to raise notrump with unbalanced suit distribution. Bid your new four-card major suit.

7. *Pass.* Your hand is relatively balanced and there is no chance for slam. (14 points for notrump, keeping the 3 PROMOTED Length Points with a GOOD suit.)

8. *3 ♡.* You do not have balanced suit distribution. Bid your new five-card suit. (16 points.)

9. *3 ♡.* You must show a four-card major, and a bid of three hearts gives partner a chance to bid spades if he wishes.

10. *3 ♡.* You can show the major suit below the level of 3 NT.

BIDDING OVER A RAISE OF YOUR SUIT

When partner raises your suit, you receive two important items of information. First, you have quite a good idea about how strong his hand is; you know that he must have 7–10 Roth Points for a raise to two or 13–15 Roth Points for a raise to three, and if partner raises to four of a major you know that he has 11–15 points and fewer than 10 HCP. Second, you know that you have succeeded in locating a playable trump suit. Given this information, you are in a position to make a most valuable contribution to the partnership auction by determining whether game is definite, possible, or impossible, and conveying this information to your partner as follows:

1. *Over raises of a major suit:*

CHANCES FOR GAME	TYPICAL EXAMPLE	YOUR ACTION
Impossible	Partner raises to two and you have 15 points or less	*Pass.* You have found the cheapest playable contract; stay there!
Possible	Partner raises to two and you have 17–19 points	*Invite* game by bidding three of your major suit.

| Definite (but no *slam*) | Partner raises to two and you have 20 or more points; partner raises to three or four and you have 17 points or less | Bid game in your major suit (or pass if partner jumped to four of the major). |

If partner raises to three or four of the major and you hold 18 or more points, you are in the slam range. Such hands will be discussed in the chapter on slam bidding.

2. *Over raises of a minor suit:*

Our rules in this situation will be influenced by the fact that when game is possible or definite, it is best to first try to play in 3 NT. Provided we have all suits stopped, game in notrump is usually easier to make than game in a minor, as shown by the fact that it takes only 26 points to make game in notrump but 29 points to make game in a minor suit.

CHANCES FOR GAME	TYPICAL EXAMPLE	YOUR ACTION
Impossible	Partner raises to two and you have 16 points or less	*Pass.* Stop in your cheapest playable contract.
Possible	Partner raises to two and you have 16–18 points	1. With relatively balanced suit distribution and stoppers in all unbid suits, bid 2 NT. 2. If unable to bid notrump, bid a new four-card or longer suit. 3. If unable to bid notrump or a new suit, continue to three of your minor suit.
Definite (but no *slam*)	Partner raises to two and you have 19 points or more	1. With balanced suit distribution and stoppers in all unbid suits, bid 3 NT.

2. With balanced suit distribution but with one or more suits unstopped, bid a suit you have stopped (provided it is *below* the level of 3 NT) so that partner may bid 3 NT if he has the other suits stopped. Such a suit may if necessary be only three cards in length (e.g., AQ5).

3. With highly unbalanced distribution and no interest in notrump, bid five of your minor suit.

Here's how these rules work:

YOU	PARTNER	YOU HOLD
1. 1 ♠	2 ♠	♠ AQJ86 ♡ KQ86 ◇ 32 ♣ 32

Pass. You have 15 Roth Points (PROMOTING by adding one point for the supported five-card major suit) and partner has *at most* 10 points for his raise to 2 ♠. Since the maximum possible is 25, there is no game.

2. 1 ♡	2 ♡	♠ Q86 ♡ AKJ976 ◇ Q83 ♣ 2

Bid 3 ♡. You have 17 Roth Points (12 HCP, 2 points for the singleton club, one Length Point for the six-card major, and two PROMOTED Length Points for a supported six-card suit). Game is possible if partner has 9 or 10 points (the total will be 26 or more) but impossible if he has only 7 or 8 points (the total will then be less than 26). *Invite* game by bidding 3 ♡ and let partner decide.

3. 1 ♠	2 ♠	♠ KQJ85 ♡ 2 ◇ AKQ8 ♣ Q102

Bid 4 ♠. You have 20 Roth Points (17 HCP, two points for the heart singleton, and one point for PROMOTING the supported five-card major). Game is definite, as even if partner has his minimum 7 points, the total for your side will reach the magic total of 26. You also know that you are not in the slam range, as your 20 points plus partner's maximum of 10 points add up to 30, far short of the 33 points needed for slam. Therefore, simply raise to game in spades.

4.   1 ◇   2 ◇   ♠ KJ107   ♡3   ◇ AQ86   ♣ Q1085

Pass. You have 14 Roth Points (12 HCP and two points for the singleton heart). Even if partner has his maximum of 10 points, game is out of the question.

5.   1 ◇   2 ◇   ♠ KJ3   ♡ A86   ◇ AKJ82   ♣ K3

Bid 3 NT. You have 20 Roth Points for notrump (19 HCP plus one PROMOTED Length Point in diamonds which you keep for notrump because the suit is GOOD. So game is likely even if partner has only 6 or 7 points. With balanced suit distribution and stoppers in all unbid suits, jump to three notrump.

6.   1 ♣   2 ♣   ♠ KJ87   ♡ Q1032   ◇ 32   ♣ AK3

Pass. Since you have only 13 Roth Points (no Distribution Point since partner may have only 4 clubs), there is no game. Do not worry about the fact that your club suit is only three cards in length; partner's raise promises support for clubs, and there is no reason to believe he will like either of your other suits. Since game is impossible, pass and stay out of trouble.

7.   1 ◇   2 ◇   ♠ 3   ♡ A98   ◇ AKQ85   ♣ K1074

Bid 3 ♣. Game is possible since you have 19 Roth Points (16 HCP, two points for the singleton spade, and one for the supported five-card suit). Bid your longest new suit.

Capsule Summary: Bidding After a Raise of Your Suit

1. OVER RAISES OF A MAJOR SUIT

CHANCES FOR GAME	YOUR ACTION
Impossible	*Pass.*
Possible	*Invite* game by bidding three of your major.
Definite	Bid game in your major suit.

2. OVER RAISES OF A MINOR SUIT

CHANCES FOR GAME	YOUR ACTION
Impossible	*Pass.*
Possible	1. With balanced suit distribution and stoppers in all unbid suits, bid 2 NT.
	2. Bid a new four-card or longer suit.
	3. Continue to three of your minor.
Definite	1. With balanced suit distribution and stoppers in all unbid suits, bid 3 NT.
	2. With balanced suit distribution but with one or more suits unstopped, bid a suit you do have stopped *below* the level of 3 NT.
	3. With highly unbalanced distribution, bid five of your minor. (*29 points* needed for game!)

QUIZ

In each of the following problems, count your Roth Points and decide your action.

	YOU	PARTNER	YOU HOLD
1.	1 ♠	2 ♠	♠KQJ864 ♡AQ85 ◇Q53 ♣---
2.	1 ♣	2 ♣	♠KQ86 ♡2 ◇QJ73 ♣AKJ2
3.	1 ♡	2 ♡	♠3 ♡AQ865 ◇KQ842 ♣43
4.	1 ♠	3 ♠	♠K8543 ♡A102 ◇AQ2 ♣32

5.	1 ◇	2 ◇	♠Q1083	♡KJ72	◇AK3	♣107
6.	1 ♠	4 ♠	♠KQ865	♡2	◇AQ84	♣K83
7.	1 ♡	3 ♡	♠K83	♡AK1097	◇AQ86	♣3
8.	1 ♠	2 ♠	♠KJ1086	♡75	◇AQ96	♣A3

SOLUTIONS

1. *Bid 4 ♠.* You have 20 Roth Points (14 HCP, 3 points for the club void, 1 Length Point for the six-card major suit, and a 2-point PROMOTION for the supported six-card suit) and partner must have at least 7 points. Therefore, your side has at least 26 points and game is definite.

2. *Bid 2 ◇.* You have 18 Roth Points (16 HCP and two points for the singleton) so game is possible. Bid your lower-ranking new suit. Do *not* promote a supported *four*-card suit.

3. *Pass.* Since you have only 15 Roth Points (11 HCP, 3 Distribution Points, and 1 point PROMOTION for the supported major) game is out of the question. (Partner has 10 points at most.)

4. *Bid 4 ♠.* Game is definite since partner has at least 13 points and you have 15, but there is clearly no chance for slam as partner cannot have more than 15. Just bid game in spades.

5. *Pass.* Do not be afraid to pass with a three-card minor when game is out of the question. (13 points)

6. *Pass.* You have 17 Roth Points (14 HCP, two for the singleton, one for the supported five-card major) and partner cannot have more than 15, so you are not in the slam range.

7. *Do not bid 4 ♡.* You have 19 Roth Points (16 HCP, two points for the singleton, and one for the supported five-card major). If partner has 14 or 15, you will have the 33 points required for slam; so you may not bid 4 ♡, a bid that tells partner that slam is out of the question. See Chapter 9 on Slam Bidding.

8. *Bid 3 ♠.* You have 17 Roth Points (14 HCP, two Distribution Points, and one point PROMOTION for the supported five-card major) and there should be a game if partner has 9 or 10 points. Therefore, you must *invite* game.

Step 3B / Bidding over an Unlimited Response

We have seen that when partner makes a limited response, you are in an excellent position to decide the fate of your partnership's game hunt. Partner's hand is limited to such a narrow point range that you can make some very shrewd deductions regarding the likelihood of game; you can then convey the results of your detective work to partner by the bid you make—passing or "signing off" when there is no game, inviting game when game is possible, and bidding game or making a bid partner cannot pass when game is definite.

When, however, partner bids a new suit in response to your opening bid, the available clues are much more scanty. To be sure, you know that partner must have at least 6 points (he would have passed with fewer) and no more than 17 points (he would have *jumped* in a new suit with more); but this is not sufficient for purposes of deciding on game. Only with 20 or more points can you be confident, since you know that your side must have game opposite partner's minimum of 6 points. With 12 to 18 points, game is possible (remember that while you may not open the bidding with only 12 points, your hand may originally qualify for an opening but now be worth only 12 points after DEMOTING for partner's response). Yet you cannot afford to get too industrious—if partner has a very bad hand, you surely do not want to reach too high a contract as the opponents may exact a penalty.

Thus, the combined total of your hand and partner's hand could be as much as 38 (you could have 21 points plus his maximum of 17) or as little as 18 (your approximate minimum of 12 plus his minimum of 6). Not even a World Champion could reach a sensible decision regarding game prospects with such a lack of information! Therefore, the best contribution you can make to the partnership auction is to make the most informative bid possible. After hearing your rebid, partner may be in a position to reach a conclusion about game, or he may continue to contribute information until a sensible decision can be reached.

Which bids will be most informative to partner? You will undoubtedly best appreciate this after considering his point of view, as given in the next chapter. For now, however, be aware that in the next chapter you move once again to the other side of the table and consider responder's rebid. So, give both yourself and your partner a break by following this list of priorities:

1. *Raise partner's major:* If partner has bid a major suit at the one-level,
   A. Raise to two with 16 points or less and at least four-card support;
   B. Raise to three with 17–19 points and at least four-card support;
   C. Raise to four with 20 or more points and at least four-card support.

If you open 1 ♠ and partner bids 2 ♡, raise to 3 ♡ with 16 points or less and at least three-card support and raise to 4 ♡ with 17–19 points and at least three-card support. Note that a *single* major raises shows 16 points or less and a *double* major raise shows 17–19 points.

You need four-card support when partner responds at the one-level because he may have only a four-card suit himself, and it is best to have a total of eight or more trumps when possible. When partner bids 2 ♡ over 1 ♠, however, he must have at least five hearts (unless he is planning to support spades, in which case you have a playable trump suit in spades and need not be overly concerned about hearts), so you need only three-card support to guarantee the minimum needed eight trumps.

Bridge would be a dull game if it consisted simply of a series of rules to memorize, and there are always exceptions. With

♠ AK3   ♡ 52   ◇ Q832   ♣ AJ86

open 1 ♣ (the stronger minor in case of ties) and if partner bid 1 ♠, mix a club in with your spades and raise to 2 ♠! It is improper to rebid a four-card suit, and it is unsatisfactory to rebid 1 NT with weakness in an unbid major suit—opponents "in the know" like to lead unbid majors against notrump. Since the spades are very good, prefer the raise.

2. If partner bids one of a major and you cannot raise,

    A. Bid a four-card or longer spade suit at the one-level;

    B. If you cannot bid a new suit at the one-level and have balanced suit distribution, bid 1 NT with 15 points or less, 2 NT with 19 to 20 points, and 3 NT if you are fortunate enough to hold 21 or more points.*

    C. If you cannot do either of the above, you may bid a new suit of four or more cards at the two-level *if* it is lower ranking than your first suit.** If you have 18 or more points, you may bid a new suit at the two-level regardless of its rank.

    D. Finally, if you do not qualify for any of the above, you should rebid your original suit: at the two-level with 16 points or less; at the three-level with 17 points or more.

3. If partner bids one of a minor (you open 1 ♣ and he responds 1 ◇), the priorities are very similar:

    A. Bid a new suit at the one-level;

    B. Bid notrump if you cannot bid a new suit at the one-level and have balanced suit distribution;

    C. Raise diamonds with four or more cards in support (to two with 16 points or less; to three with 17–19 points);

    D. Jump in a new suit with 20 or more points (remember, game is certain);

    E. Rebid your own suit as in 2D above.

You should not be in a hurry to raise partner's *minor*, as game in a minor is harder to make than game in notrump or in a major.

4. If partner's new suit is bid at the two-level, the priorities are

---

* Do not be concerned about balanced hands with 16–18 points. You would have *opened* 1 NT with such a hand. Also, in Part II we will note that a better use can be made of the 3 NT rebid, based on a change in the 2 NT opening range.

** This allows partner to go back to your first suit *at the two-level*. You will appreciate being in only two if he has a minimum response. You may bid a new suit that is *higher ranking* than your first suit only if you hold 18 or more points. Partner must bid at the three-level to return to your first suit, but you will still be safe if you have substantial extra values.

(114)

much the same. Bidding a new suit at the *two*-level (lower ranking than your original) now has the top priority. However, you know he has at least 11 points (he may not bid at the two-level with less). Here, a 2 NT rebid shows 14–15 points and a 3 NT rebid shows 19 to 21 points—*plus* balanced suit distribution.

The following examples should clarify the above rules:

YOU	PARTNER	YOU HOLD
1. 1 ♡	1 ♠	♠K83 ♡K96542 ◇AK3 ♣3
?		

Rebid 2 ♡. You may not raise partner's major with only three-card support (except in emergencies) and you have no new suit to bid. Therefore, rebid your own suit. Since you hold only 16 Roth Points, bid only 2 ♡.

2. 1 ◇	1 ♠	♠7 ♡K864 ◇AQJ32 ♣K43
?		

Rebid 2 ◇. Do not forget to DEMOTE your Distribution Points when you hold a singleton in partner's suit; your hand is now worth only 13 Roth Points. You may not bid the higher-ranking heart suit (such a bid of a higher-ranking suit is commonly called a "reverse") since you do not have the required 18 points.

3. 1 ♣	1 ♠	♠AK73 ♡K83 ◇2 ♣AJ742
?		

Raise to 3 ♠. You have 18 Roth Points (14 HCP and 3 points for the PROMOTED singleton—remember to PROMOTE when you have four-card support for partner) and four-card support for partner's major. Your first duty is to raise partner's major, and with 17–19 points the proper raise is to 3 ♠.

4. 1 ◇	1 ♡	♠K1072 ♡32 ◇AK73 ♣QJ2
?		

Bid 1 ♠. You may not raise partner's major with only a doubleton in support, but you do satisfy the next most immediate priority—

bidding a new suit at the one-level. Your hand is worth 13 Roth Points after DEMOTING your Distribution Points.

5. 1 ◇   1 ♠   ♠84 ♡KQ7 ◇AJ103 ♣A983
    ?

Bid 1 NT. Bidding notrump takes priority over bidding a new suit at the *two*-level. You meet the requirement of balanced suit distribution.

6. 1 ♣   1 ◇   ♠Q1074 ♡3 ◇K1097 ♣AKJ7
    ?

Bid 1 ♠. Bidding a new suit at the one-level takes priority over raising partner's *minor*. After PROMOTING your singleton (since you have four cards in partner's suit) your hand is worth 16 Roth Points.

7. 1 ◇   1 ♠   ♠--- ♡KQ84 ◇A10973 ♣K742
    ?

Bid 2 ♣. After DEMOTING, your hand is worth only 12 Roth Points, so you may not bid the higher-ranking heart suit. You also may not bid notrump with such unbalanced distribution. Bid your new lower-ranking four-card suit; this is far more informative to partner than just rebidding your own suit. Partner has already heard about the diamonds and might like to know about the clubs.

8. 1 ◇   1 ♡   ♠KQ3 ♡Q103 ◇KQJ3 ♣AQ8
    ?

Bid 2 NT. With 19 points, balanced suit distribution, and all unbid suits stopped, you have an ideal hand for this bid. Did you first ask yourself if you could raise partner's major? Good! Raising partner's major does take priority over jumping in notrump—but you may not raise with only three-card support.

9. 1 ♠   2 ◇   ♠KQ1085 ♡KJ87 ◇AQ3 ♣2
    ?

Bid 2 ♡. Showing a new four-card suit that is lower-ranking than your first suit is much more informative than rebidding your own suit. You are not in a hurry to raise partner's minor suit, as game in a major (or notrump) is much easier to make and you want to try for that first.

10. 1 ◇   2 ♣   ♠KQ87   ♡3   ◇AQJ97   ♣AQ3
      ?

Bid 2 ♠. KEEP the same point count with three-card support for partner; your hand is worth 20 points (18 HCP plus 2 points for the singleton heart). You may bid the higher-ranking spade suit since you have more than 18 points. Had you held instead

♠KQ87   ♡3   ◇AQJ97   ♣432,

you would rebid 2 ◇, since your 14 Roth Points would not justify a bid of a suit ranking above the suit of your original bid.

Capsule Summary: Bidding After an Unlimited Response

1. RAISE PARTNER'S ONE-LEVEL MAJOR-SUIT RESPONSE:
   To *two* with 16 points or less and at least four-card support;
   To *three* with 17–19 points and at least four-card support;
   To *four* with 20 or more points and at least four-card support.
   After 1 ♠—2 ♡: Raise to 3 ♡ with 16 points or less and at least three-card support;
   Raise to 4 ♡ with 17–19 points and at least three-card support.

2. BID A NEW SUIT AT THE ONE-LEVEL (must be at least four cards in length).

3. BID NOTRUMP WITH BALANCED SUIT DISTRIBUTION
   Over a one-level response: 1 NT = 15 points or less;
                                2 NT = 19–20 points;
                                3 NT = 21 or more points.
   Over a two-level response   2 NT = 14–15 points;
                                3 NT = 19–21 points.

4. BID A NEW *LOWER*-RANKING SUIT AT THE TWO-LEVEL
   Exception: You may "reverse" (bid a new higher-ranking suit at the two-level) if you have *18 points* or more.

(117)

5. RAISE PARTNER'S MINOR

After 1 ♣—1 ◇ : Raise to two with 16 points or less and at least
four-card support;

Raise to three with 17–19 points and at least
four-card support.

6. REBID YOUR OWN SUIT (must be at least five cards in
length)

At the two-level with 16 points or less;

At the three-level with 17–19 points.

QUIZ

For each of the hands below, count your Roth Points and select
your rebid. It is best to try to work out each problem based on
what you have learned and logical reasoning, and to go back to the
previous text only *after* the quiz to check on any problems you
may have missed.

	YOU	PARTNER	YOU HOLD
1.	1 ◇	1 ♠	♠K83 ♡Q94 ◇AJ1063 ♣K10
2.	1 ♡	2 ♣	♠KJ87 ♡AK543 ◇43 ♣K3
3.	1 ♣	1 ♠	♠Q1084 ♡2 ◇AQ3 ♣AQ942
4.	1 ♣	1 ◇	♠KQ102 ♡5432 ◇2 ♣AKJ5
5.	1 ♠	2 ◇	♠AQ1064 ♡K43 ◇3 ♣KQ85
6.	1 ♠	2 ◇	♠AQ1064 ♡AK3 ◇3 ♣KQ85
7.	1 ◇	1 ♡	♠KJ3 ♡74 ◇AK865 ♣AKJ
8.	1 ◇	1 ♡	♠KQ102 ♡AK53 ◇KQ83 ♣8
9.	1 ◇	1 ♠	♠3 ♡AK97 ◇KJ42 ♣Q1032
10.	1 ♡	1 ♠	♠8742 ♡AK1063 ◇KJ85 ♣---
11.	1 ♠	2 ♡	♠KQJ32 ♡K109 ◇AK6 ♣32
12.	1 ◇	2 ♣	♠A1032 ♡3 ◇AQ1096 ♣AQ7
13.	1 ♣	1 ♠	♠AQ3 ♡32 ◇5432 ♣AKJ3

SOLUTIONS

1. *Bid 1 NT*. You have 13 Roth Points (do not count Distribution Points when bidding notrump), and balanced suit distribution. Bidding notrump takes precedence over rebidding a five-card suit.

2. *Bid 2* ♡. You have 14 Roth Points (after DEMOTING your Distribution Points with only two-card support for partner) so you may not "reverse" by bidding spades (a suit ranking above hearts). With no lower-ranking new suit to bid, rebid your five-card major; any five-card suit may be rebid in an emergency situation.

3. *Bid 3* ♠. You have 17 Roth Points (14 HCP and 3 points for the PROMOTED singleton) and four-card spade support.

4. *Bid 1* ♡. Bid your lowest-ranking new four-card suit. Note that this bid allows partner to bid spades at the one-level, but he cannot mention hearts at the one-level if you bid 1 ♠.

5. *Bid 2* ♠. With only 14 Roth Points, you may not bid a new suit at the *three*-level, which requires 18 points (being equivalent to a reverse).

6. *Bid 3* ♣. Any hand strong enough for a "reverse" (18 points or more) is strong enough to bid a new suit at the three-level. You have 18 Roth Points even after DEMOTING your Distribution Points.

7. *Bid 2 NT*. With 19 points, balanced suit distribution, and all unbid suits stopped, your hand is ideal for this bid.

8. *Bid 4* ♡. You have 20 Roth Points in support of hearts—17 HCP and three points for the PROMOTED singleton. With four-card suport for partner's major, your primary obligation is to raise, and you should raise to four with 20 or more points.

9. *Bid 2* ♣. You may not bid 1 NT with unbalanced suit distribution; nor may you "reverse" with only 13 Roth Points.*

---

* Although two clubs is the "standard" answer, many experts prefer to avoid naming a new suit at the two-level with such a minimum hand. Thus, it is acceptable to "mix a club in with your spades" and rebid one notrump.

10. *Bid 2 ♠*. Raising partner's major takes priority over bidding a new suit or rebidding your own suit. (15 points)

11. *Bid 4 ♡*: Three-card support is sufficient when partner's major is bid at the two-level, and you should raise to four with 17–19 points. (17 points)

12. *Bid 2 ♠*. You have 18 points (KEEPING the same point count with three-card support for partner) and may therefore reverse.

13. *Bid 2 ♠*. An emergency case where a raise of a one-level major suit response with only three cards in support is permissible. You may not rebid the four-card club suit, and bidding notrump with both hearts and diamonds unstopped is likely to mislead partner, who may expect you to prevent the opponents from enjoying an uninterrupted run of tricks in these suits. Since your three-card spade support is very good, raising spades is the least of evils. What about a pass? You may *never* pass an unlimited response—you have no reason to believe that game is out of the question for your side! (15 points)

Capsule Summary: Opener's Rebid

IF RESPONDER'S BID IS LIMITED
ADD your points to partner's minimum and maximum holdings and determine if game is impossible, possible, or definite. Then, bid as follows:

CHANCES FOR GAME	PARTNER'S RESPONSE	YOUR ACTION
IMPOSSIBLE	1 NT	1. Rebid a six-card suit. 2. Bid a new lower-ranking suit of four or more cards; otherwise Pass.
	Raise of your suit	Pass.
POSSIBLE	1 NT	Balanced suit distribution: Bid 2 NT.

		Unbalanced suit distribution: 1. Jump rebid a six-card suit; 2. Bid new lower-ranking suit;
	Single raise of your major suit	Bid three of the major.
	Single raise of your minor suit	Balanced suit distribution and stoppers in all unbid suits: bid two notrump; Bid a suit you have stopped. With unbalanced suit distribution: bid three of your minor.
DEFINITE (But no slam)	1 NT	Balanced suit distribution: Bid 3 NT. Unbalanced suit distribution: Jump in a new suit or jump to game in a six-card or longer major.
	2 NT	Balanced suit distribution: Bid 3 NT. Unbalanced suit distribution: Bid a new suit or rebid a six-card major.
	3 NT	Pass or rebid a six-card major.
	Raise of your major	Bid game in the major.
	Raise of your minor	Balanced suit distribution and all unbid suits stopped: Bid 3 NT; Show a stopper below the level of 3 NT; Bid a new suit; Jump to five of minor (29 points needed for game).

If Responder's Bid Is Unlimited

Do not attempt to determine game chances at this time. Bid according to the following priority.

1. RAISE PARTNER'S MAJOR

PARTNER'S RESPONSE	YOUR POINTS	YOUR DISTRIBUTION	YOUR ACTION
1 ♡ or 1 ♠	16 or less	4-card or longer support	Raise to two;
	17–19	"	Raise to three;
	20–21	"	Raise to four.
2 ♡ after 1 ♠	16 or less	3-card or longer support	Raise to 3 ♡;
opening	17–19	3-card or longer support	Raise to 4 ♡.

(Note that a *single* raise shows 16 or less; a *double* raise shows 17–19.)

2. BID A NEW SUIT AT THE ONE-LEVEL

   The suit must be at least four cards in length.

3. BID NOTRUMP WITH BALANCED SUIT DISTRIBUTION

PARTNER'S RESPONSE	YOUR POINTS	YOUR ACTION
1 of a suit	13–15	1 NT;
	19–20	2 NT;
	21 or more	3 NT.
2 of a suit	14–15	2 NT;
	19–21	3 NT.

4. BID A NEW LOWER-RANKING SUIT AT THE TWO-LEVEL

   You may *reverse* (bid a higher-ranking suit) or bid a suit at the three-level only with 18 or more points.

5. RAISE PARTNER'S MINOR

PARTNER'S RESPONSE	YOUR POINTS	YOUR DISTRIBUTION	YOUR ACTION
1 ◇ after 1 ♣	16 or less	4-card support	Raise to 2 ◇.
opening	17–19	"	Raise to 3 ◇.

6. REBID YOUR OWN SUIT

At the two-level: Up to 16 points.
At the three-level: 17–19 points.

REVIEW QUIZ FOR CHAPTER 4

For each of the following problems: First, count your Roth
Points; second, decide if partner's response is limited or unlimited;
and third, decide on your action. Try to reason out each situation
rather than rely on a memorized set of rules.

YOU	PARTNER	YOU HOLD			
1. 1 ♣ ?	1 ♡	♠Q97	♡87	◇KJ105	♣AQJ8
2. 1 ◇ ?	1 NT	♠987	♡AQJ	◇KQJ7	♣AK7
3. 1 ♣ ?	1 ♡	♠KQ108	♡J83	◇72	♣AK109
4. 1 ♡ ?	2 ♡	♠9	♡AQJ105	◇KJ74	♣J52
5. 1 ♠ ?	2 ♡	♠AKQ32	♡Q53	◇K74	♣86
6. 1 ♠ ?	2 NT	♠AQ9765	♡2	◇J954	♣A7
7. 1 ◇ ?	2 ◇	♠A86	♡AQ2	◇AQ875	♣K3
8. 1 ♣ ?	2 ♣	♠AK85	♡432	◇Q83	♣AQ8
9. 1 ♠ ?	2 ◇	♠AKJ976	♡3	◇K107	♣AQ2
10. 1 ◇ ?	1 NT	♠42	♡KQ105	◇AJ97	♣KJ4
11. 1 ♡ ?	2 ◇	♠3	♡AQ976	◇KQ1042	♣98
12. 1 ♡ ?	3 ♡	♠AQ8	♡K9765	◇AK72	♣4

	YOU	PARTNER	YOU HOLD
13.	1 ◇	1 ♡	♠ KJ10 ♡ 765 ◇ AKJ9 ♣ AKJ
	?		
14.	1 ◇	1 NT	♠ 1074 ♡ 3 ◇ AQ1086 ♣ AQJ7
	?		
15.	1 ♣	1 ♠	♠ KQ85 ♡ 3 ◇ KQ8 ♣ AK954
	?		
16.	1 ♡	1 ♠	♠ 7 ♡ KJ9652 ◇ A83 ♣ AJ7
	?		
17.	1 ♠	2 ♠	♠ A10975 ♡ AQ7 ◇ Q102 ♣ K8
	?		
18.	1 ♠	1 NT	♠ K10865 ♡ 3 ◇ K954 ♣ AK7
	?		
19.	1 ♣	1 ♠	♠ 85 ♡ KQ8 ◇ AQ7 ♣ AKJ86
	?		
20.	1 ♣	3 NT	♠ Q86 ♡ 32 ◇ K874 ♣ AKQ2
	?		
21.	1 ♣	1 ♡	♠ K1086 ♡ K1086 ◇ 2 ♣ AQ42
	?		
22.	1 ♡	2 ♣	♠ --- ♡ KQ865 ◇ Q862 ♣ A542
	?		
23.	1 ♠	2 ♣	♠ Q10865 ♡ KJ97 ◇ 2 ♣ AKQ
	?		
24.	1 ◇	1 ♠	♠ 10987 ♡ AK3 ◇ AK975 ♣ 2
	?		
25.	1 ♠	1 NT	♠ KJ975 ♡ Q83 ◇ AKJ ♣ A2
	?		
26.	1 ♣	2 ♣	♠ AQ8 ♡ KQ7 ◇ K3 ♣ AJ974
	?		
27.	1 ♡	2 NT	♠ K83 ♡ AQ1097 ◇ A83 ♣ 72
	?		
28.	1 ◇	1 ♠	♠ Q83 ♡ 865 ◇ KQ107 ♣ AK8
	?		
29.	1 ◇	1 ♡	♠ K107 ♡ 8 ◇ AQ10642 ♣ A82
	?		

	YOU	PARTNER	YOU HOLD
30.	1 ♣ ?	1 NT	♠ KJ10 ♡ AQ ◇ AQ ♣ KJ10742
31.	1 ♡ ?	1 ♠	♠ K97 ♡ KJ875 ◇ --- ♣ AQ1042
32.	1 ♣ ?	3 NT	♠ AQ97 ♡ --- ◇ A32 ♣ KQ10763
33.	1 ♡ ?	1 NT	♠ 8 ♡ AK10742 ◇ AKJ2 ♣ K3
34.	1 ♠ ?	3 ♠	♠ AQJ109 ♡ AJ865 ◇ 32 ♣ 2
35.	1 ♠ ?	2 ♡	♠ KJ975 ♡ AK32 ◇ A32 ♣ 10
36.	1 ♣ ?	1 NT	♠ K1074 ♡ KQ85 ◇ 3 ♣ AQ42
37.	1 ♡ ?	4 ♡	♠ 7 ♡ KQJ97 ◇ AJ83 ♣ K107
38.	1 ♡ ?	2 ♣	♠ K1086 ♡ AQ975 ◇ 3 ♣ A83
39.	1 ♠ ?	2 ♠	♠ AQJ965 ♡ KQ87 ◇ A83 ♣ ---

SOLUTIONS

	POINTS	BID	
1.	13	1 NT	With balanced suit distribution, prefer the 1 NT rebid to bidding a new suit at the *two*-level.
2.	20	3 NT	Game is definite as partner must have at least six points. With balanced suit distribution, raise to 3 NT. You do not need stoppers in all unbid suits when partner has already bid notrump.
3.	14	1 ♠	You may not raise hearts with only three-card support, but you are able to satisfy the next highest pri-

	POINTS	BID	
			ority: showing a new suit at the *one*-level.
4.	15	Pass	Even after adding one point for a supported five-card suit, game is still out of the question, as partner cannot have more than 10 points.
5.	15	3 ♡	Supporting partner's major takes precedence over rebidding your own suit, and three-card support is sufficient when partner's major is bid at the *two*-level.
6.	17	3 ♠	It is always safe to rebid a six-card major over a jump in notrump.
7.	20	3 NT	With balanced suit distribution and all unbid suits stopped, prefer the notrump game to game in a minor since the latter requires 29 points. You have 19 HCP plus one point for a supported five-card good suit, but do not count a Distribution Point for the doubleton club when bidding notrump.
8.	15	Pass	Game is out of the question since partner cannot have more than 10 points. Do not bid simply because you are worried about having only three clubs. Partner has promised good club support, and there is no guarantee that any other suit (or notrump) will be better.
9.	20	3 ♠	Rebidding a good six-card major is more important than supporting partner's minor. With a booming 20 points, jump to let partner know that you have a fine hand. You should let your judgment overcome the rules on exceptional cases such as this.

	POINTS	BID	
10.	14	Pass	Game is out of the question.
11.	17	3 ◇	You have 17 Roth Points (11 HCP, 4 for the PROMOTED singleton, and 2 for the PROMOTED doubleton). Supporting partner's minor takes precedence over rebidding a five-card suit.
12.	19	---	Do not simply bid 4 ♡ as you are in the slam range. Slam should be bid if partner has 14 or 15 points, so you may not make the "wet blanket" 4 ♡ bid that requires partner to pass. (See Chapter 9.)
13.	20	2 NT	You have balanced suit distribution and all unbid suits stopped.
14.	13	2 ♣	You may not pass with unbalanced suit distribution when a lower-ranking four-card suit is available.
15.	20	4 ♠	After PROMOTING your singleton, your hand is worth 20 Roth Points and a jump to *four* spades.
16.	14	2 ♡	Even with the Length Point for the six-card major, you have only 14 Roth Points, so rebid your suit at the two-level.
17.	17	3 ♠	Game is possible if partner has 9 or 10 points. Invite by raising to 3 ♠.
18.	13	2 ◇	Though there is no chance for game, you should not pass with unbalanced suit distribution. Bid your new lower-ranking four-card suit.
19.	19	2 NT	You have balanced suit distribution and all unbid suits stopped.
20.	14	Pass	There is no chance for slam as

	POINTS	BID	
			partner cannot have more than 18 points.
21.	15	2 ♡	Do not forget to PROMOTE for your singleton when you have four cards in partner's suit. Raising partner's major is far more helpful to him than bidding a new suit.
22.	15	2 ◇	On the other hand, bidding a new suit is more helpful than raising partner's *minor*. Don't forget to PROMOTE your void which is now worth four points.
23.	17	2 ♡	Bidding a new four-card suit takes precedence over raising partner's minor.
24.	17	3 ♠	After PROMOTING your singleton club, your hand is just worth the double raise.
25.	18	2 NT	Game is possible if partner has 8–10 points. With balanced suit distribution, invite game by bidding 2 NT.
26.	19	3 NT	Game seems definite. Suggest that it be played in notrump.
27.	14	3 NT	Game is definite and your hand is suitable for notrump. Why complicate the issue? Just bid 3 NT. The PROMOTED Length Point counts for notrump since the heart suit is *good*.
28.	14	1 NT	While you have no heart stopper, your hand is perfectly balanced and your spades are only moderate. This is not an emergency case; do not bid 2 ♠.
29.	14	2 ◇	Do not bid notrump with such un-

	POINTS	BID	
			balanced distribution, especially when you have a fine six-card minor to rebid.
30.	20	3 NT	Though neither the Length Points nor Distribution Points count for notrump (clubs not *good*), you still have enough to ensure game. With stoppers in all unbid suits, bid the notrump game rather than trying for game in clubs, which requires 29 points.
31.	16	2 ♣	KEEP the same point count with three-card support for partner, and bid your new lower-ranking (five-card) suit.
32.	21 (suit) 18 (notrump)	---	A pass would defy all logic. First of all, your hand is wildly unbalanced and unsuited for play in notrump. Second, with 15 HCP, you are on the verge of slam in high cards alone (partner's maximum of 18 will give your side a total of 33), and if you can induce partner to play in a suit you have all sorts of Distribution Points to PROMOTE, making slam even more likely. You would probably make 3 NT, but bigger and better things are very likely. (See Chapter 9.)
33.	19	3 ♡	Though you must DEMOTE your Distribution Points, you still have quite a fine hand. Let partner know by jumping in your *six*-card major.
34.	16	4 ♠	Slam is out of the question as partner cannot have more than 15

	POINTS	BID	

points. A heart bid is pointless; you have found a playable trump suit and there is no bonus for finding an extra one.

35. 18 4 ♡ Your first obligation is to support partner's major suit. Remember to jump to 4 ♡ when you have 17–19 points.

36. 14 Pass Your hand is not perfectly balanced, but you may not rebid a four-card suit or "reverse" with fewer than 18 points.

37. 17 Pass Even after PROMOTING by adding one point for your supported five-card major, you can dismiss slam possibilities, as partner's maximum is 15 points.

38. 15 2 ♡ You may not reverse with only 15 Roth Points.

39. 22 4 ♠ Do not forget to count 1 a Length Point for the six-card major and PROMOTE by adding an additional 2 points when the six-card suit is supported by partner. Game is definite and slam is impossible, so simply bid 4 ♠.

This is the longest and most difficult quiz we have had so far, and you have done quite well if you scored 30 or more correct. Even if your score was less, do not be discouraged, as opener's rebid is a considerable challenge. Come back to this chapter in a day or two and review the points you missed, and you will be surprised at how soon you are able to handle well the techniques of bidding after your partner's first response.

CHAPTER

5

Responder's Rebid

Now that both opener and responder have learned how to enjoy the advantages of the adjustments of Roth Point Count, it is time once again to shift to the other side of the table. This time we will consider the responder's rebid—the action responder should take on his second turn to bid. In point of fact, however, this shift across the table is more a matter of practice than a matter of theory. After the opening bid, both partners are "responders" for purposes of counting Roth Points. Thus, while we will continue to refer to the player making the first bid as opener and his partner as responder, *both partners will follow the previously discussed point-count rules throughout the duration of the auction.*

This means that *you already know how to count Roth Points for purposes of making responder rebid*—and every further bid throughout the auction.* If you combine the rules you have previously learned with a dose of logic and a pinch of common sense, you should have no trouble making the Roth Point Count work for you at every stage of the auction.

---

* With one exception: if opener has bid *two* suits. This is the first point at which we face a situation in which partner may have bid two suits.

For example, suppose you hold

♠ KJ107 ♡ 3 ◇ AQ8542 ♣ 86

which (before the bidding begins) you evaluate as being worth 14 Roth Points (10 HCP, 3 Distribution Points, and 1 Length Point for the *good* six-card minor). Partner opens **one club,** so you DEMOTE your Distribution Points to zero; your hand is now worth only 11 points. You respond **one diamond,** bidding your longest suit at the one-level. Partner rebids **one spade.** How many points is your hand worth now?

If you will recall the rules we have discussed previously, you will remember that you should PROMOTE your Distribution Points when you hold four cards in partner's suit *and* DEMOTE any Length Points in your own suit since it is not permitted to play in two trump suits at once. You now have 10 HCP, 3 points for the PROMOTED heart singleton, and 2 points for the PROMOTED club doubleton—total 15 points. Note that your hand goes *up* in value now that you and partner have discovered that spades will make a good trump suit; partner must have at least four spades to bid the suit, so your side must have at least eight trumps—enough for a highly satisfactory trump suit. Your hand is worth just as much as if partner had opened in spades. It took you a little longer to find the spade fit, but find it you did, and your hand value increased accordingly.

As a second example, suppose that you hold

♠ A10765 ♡ K1064 ◇ J83 ♣ 2

which starts at 10 points. Partner opens **one heart,** and you PROMOTE your club singleton by adding a point, making your total 11. You are too strong to raise to two hearts (which shows 7–10 points) and too weak to raise to three hearts (which shows 13–15 points), so you follow the next highest priority by bidding **one spade**— showing a new suit at the one-level. Partner rebids **one notrump.** How do you evaluate your hand now?

If you demoted your Distribution Points, your logic is faulty. You still have four cards in your partner's heart suit and certainly plan to bid some number of hearts this time to let him know about it. Your hand is still worth 11 points—the four-card heart support has not gone away!* You have located a playable trump suit in a major and have no intention of playing in notrump. The time you *do* demote your Distribution Points is shown in the following example:

PARTNER	YOU	YOU HOLD
1 ♣	1 ♡	♠ J83 ♡ A9762 ◇ Q32 ♣ K4
1 NT	?	

With balanced suit distribution, you are well satisfied to play in notrump and have no reason to consider supporting partner's clubs or rebidding your five-card heart suit. Partner could easily have only a doubleton heart, so you have no reason to believe that any suit will fulfill the eight-card requirement for a satisfactory trump suit. Since you plan to play in notrump (because you have no outstanding suit fit with partner), DEMOTE your Distribution Points to zero. Your hand is worth 10 Roth Points—10 HCP. (The PROMOTED Length Point in hearts after partner's "balanced" notrump bid does not count for notrump since the heart suit is not *good*.)

If you hold

♠ 732 ♡ AQ865 ◇ 2 ♣ J976

you have 9 Roth Points; but when partner opens **one diamond**, you DEMOTE your Distribution Points and now have only 7 Roth Points. Your correct response is **one heart**, showing the new suit at the one-level. Now suppose partner rebids **one notrump**. While you do not like notrump (and, as we will see later, should bid **two clubs** to convey this information to partner), your heart suit must find some help in partner's balanced hand so you PROMOTE your hand to 8 points. What if partner had opened **one club**, you responded **one heart**, and he rebid **one notrump**? When partner bids clubs, your hand is worth 10 points—7 HCP, and 3 points for the PROMOTED diamond singleton. You should not let partner's no-

---

* Although partner has made a "balanced" notrump bid, do *not* count a PROMOTED Length Point in spades. You plan to support hearts and therefore should not count Length Points in your own suit.

trump rebid affect your point count, since a good fit has been found. KEEP the same 10 points for purposes of bidding clubs.

If partner supports your suit, be sure to count your Distribution Points since a good trump suit has been found. In the previous example, if partner opens **one diamond** and raises you to **two hearts** (instead of rebidding notrump), your hand is now worth 10 Roth Points: 7 HCP, 2 Distribution Points, and one point for a supported five-card suit. Once again, note how the Roth Point Count keeps track of how the bids you and your partner make affect the value of your hand. If partner rebids **one notrump,** indicating that no good suit fit is yet apparent, less optimism is in order. When partner raises your suit, however, the value of your hand increases. The Roth Point Count *builds in* the adjustments right into the point-count itself, where it belongs, so that you can bid the way the experts do.

Whenever you locate a fit of 8 or more cards in one of partner's suits (either his first suit or his second suit), you will usually find it most logical to use the point total based on this suit as trump. But *if partner bids two suits and you still cannot see a good (8-card or better) fit, use the point total arrived at after partner's opening bid.** With

♠ J83   ♡ 432   ♢ AQ965   ♣ 32

you have 8 Roth Points until partner opens **one club,** after which you DEMOTE your Distribution Points and adjust your total to 7 points. You bid **one diamond** and partner rebids **one spade.** Since partner may well have only four spades for this bid, the spade suit may be one card short of the minimum necessary for a superior trump suit. Keep your 7 point total at this time. (You would have 8 points if partner *opened* 1 ♠ because his opening spade bid would guarantee at least five spades, and your three spades would ensure that the minimum of eight is present.)

Thus, all you need do is consider the available evidence at any point in the auction. If a good trump fit has been found (which will

---

* This rule covers the exceptional cases noted at the beginning of this chapter.

usually be the case when you have four-card or longer support for partner), follow the usual rules regarding Distribution Points. However, DEMOTE your Distribution Points with unfavorable holdings in partner's suit. (Also, be sure not to count Distribution Points for purposes of bidding notrump.)

As a quick check on your understanding of the Roth Point Count for responder's rebid, here is a short quiz. Decide how many points each hand is worth *after* partner's rebid.

QUIZ

	PARTNER	YOU	YOU HOLD
1.	1 ♣ 1 ♡	1 ♢	♠K1074 ♡3 ♢Q832 ♣A1064
2.	1 ♢ 1 NT	1 ♠	♠AQ1064 ♡AJ75 ♢43 ♣82
3.	1 ♢ 1 NT	1 ♠	♠A10975 ♡2 ♢KQ83 ♣Q94
4.	1 ♢ 2 NT	1 ♡	♠A83 ♡Q1084 ♢42 ♣Q975
5.	1 ♠ 2 ♠	2 ♡	♠Q83 ♡AQ876 ♢Q85 ♣32
6.	1 ♠ 2 ♣	1 NT	♠53 ♡Q87 ♢AQ106 ♣J864
7.	1 ♣ 1 ♠	1 ♢	♠Q1086 ♡2 ♢KJ87 ♣AQ97
8.	1 ♡ 2 ♣	1 ♠	♠Q10953 ♡2 ♢KJ87 ♣AQ9
9.	1 ♡ 2 ♣	1 ♠	♠K832 ♡Q97 ♢32 ♣AQ65
10.	1 ♣ 2 ♠	1 ♠	♠KQJ32 ♡K85 ♢A83 ♣32

SOLUTIONS

1. 12 points (in clubs). 9 HCP and 3 points for the singleton which you PROMOTE with four cards in partner's (first) suit.

2. 12 points. DEMOTE your Distribution Points with no good fit with partner (no proven 8-card fit), even though you do not plan to pass 1 NT. The PROMOTED Length Point in spades counts both for purposes of bidding a new suit (which you plan to do) *and* bidding notrump because the spade suit is *good*.

3. 14 points (in diamonds). 11 HCP, 3 points for the singleton, but no Length Points in spades because you plan to support partner's suit. The good diamond fit has not gone away just because partner bid notrump.

4. 8 points. You have no good suit fit with partner; also, you like notrump with balanced suit distribution. So DEMOTE your Distribution Points to zero and count only the 8 HCP.

5. 11 points. KEEP the same distribution point count with three-card support for partner.

6. 11 points. Your hand was worth only 9 points after the 1 ♠ opening since you must DEMOTE your Distribution Points with only two cards in partner's suit. However, partner has now mentioned a new suit and you hold four-card support for it. Evaluate your hand much as if he had opened 1 ♣—your PROMOTED doubleton is worth two points.

7. 15 points. After partner opens 1 ♣, a suit for which you have four-card support, your hand is worth 15 points—12 HCP and 3 points for the PROMOTED singleton. The fact that you also have four-card support for partner's second suit is therefore ir-relevant—your total of Roth Points remains the same.

8. 12 points. When partner opens 1 ♡, you DEMOTE your Dis-tribution Points. With only three-card support for his second suit, there is no reason to become optimistic. Partner may have only four clubs. Since no 8-card fit is assured, value in terms of part-ner's first bid suit.

9. 13 points. Here you have *four*-card support for partner's sec-ond suit, so your PROMOTED diamond doubleton is now worth two points. Even if you select hearts as your final trump suit, that fourth club is very likely to prove helpful.

10. 15 points. You have 13 HCP, one point for the club double-ton, and one PROMOTION point for the supported five-card suit.

Bidding When Partner's Hand is Limited

In the previous chapter, we saw that opener was in a position to decide whether game was definite, possible, or impossible if responder made a *limited* bid. When responder's bid was unlimited, opener was in no position to make any unilateral decisions, and contented himself with making the most descriptive bid possible. The same process will continue throughout the auction. Each player, at his turn to bid, must decide whether or not his partner's bidding shows a limited hand. If so, a decision regarding game prospects should be made, and this information conveyed to partner. If not, it is necessary only to make the most informative bid possible and await further evidence before reaching a decision about game chances.

Let us first consider which rebids by opener are *limited*. In what situations can *responder* play detective and make sound deductions about the partnership's game prospects? Examples of limited rebids by opener are shown below. They are all similar in that *opener's possible point range is confined to narrow limits.*

	OPENER	RESPONDER	
1.	1 ◇ *1 NT*	1 ♠	Opener's point range is limited to 13 to 15 points when he rebids 1 NT.
2.	1 ♣ *3 ♡*	1 ♡	Opener's range is limited to 17–19 points when he jump raises a major.
3.	1 ◇ *2 NT*	1 ♠	Opener has 19–20 points when he jumps to 2 NT.
4.	1 ♣ *2 ◇*	1 ◇	Opener has 16 points or less when he raises your suit to two.
5.	1 ♠ *2 ♠*	2 ◇	Opener has 16 points or less when he rebids his own suit without jumping.

6.	1 ♡	1 ♠	Opener has 17–19 points when he jump rebids his own suit.
	3 ♡		
7.	1 ♣	1 ♠	Opener has 20 or more points for the triple major-suit raise.
	4 ♠		
8.	1 ♠	2 ♡	Opener's hand is limited to 16 points or less.
	3 ♡		

A little experimentation will convince you that opener's rebid is limited unless it is a bid in a new suit. Note that opener's hand must fall within narrowly defined point limits in each of the above examples. We will now consider the appropriate bids over some of the possible limited rebids that partner can make.

WHEN OPENER REBIDS 1 NT

Partner's 1 NT rebid limits his hand to 15 points or less. While he needs 14 points to open, it is possible that he now has only 13 since he may have DEMOTED his hand after your response.

Knowing that partner has 13–15 Roth Points, you are in a position to decide if game is definite, possible, or impossible. For example, you hold:

♠ K83   ♡ Q10865   ◊ A83   ♣ 32

Partner opens 1 ♣, you respond 1 ♡, and partner rebids 1 NT. You have 9 points, for notrump, and even if partner has his maximum of 15, you will be short of the 26 points needed for game. Therefore, you can tell that game is impossible. If you hold

♠ K83   ♡ KJ965   ◊ A72   ♣ 73

game is possible. You have 11 Roth Points for notrump and there will be a game if partner has 15 (or a very good 14), but no game if he has only 13. Finally, if you hold

♠ KQ3   ♡ KQ965   ◊ A72   ♣ 73

game is definite. Your 15 points (including a PROMOTED Length Point for the *good* heart suit) plus partner's minimum of 13 add up to the total necessary for game—in fact, you have at least 2 points to spare.

In *all* situations where partner has limited his hand (not only when he rebids 1 NT), your first duty is to determine the chances for game, just as you did when you were the opener and partner's response was limited. Do not try to memorize complex lists of point requirements for impossible, possible, and definite game chances. You should be able to work out each situation at the table, and it is certainly more fun to apply your powers of deduction than to try to become a memory expert. However, you must know how many points each of partner's bids shows; a detective cannot work in the absence of clues! Fortunately, you have already learned this in the previous chapter, but do not hesitate to review from time to time. *Nobody* learned all these point ranges the first time through. You need to know the point requirements for the various bids not only so that you will bid correctly, but also so that you will read *partner's* messages accurately.

So, getting back to business, when partner rebids 1 NT, you judge your game chances. Then, simply do as follows:

GAME CHANCES	YOUR ACTION
IMPOSSIBLE	Balanced suit distribution: Pass.
	Unbalanced suit distribution: Rebid a six-card suit or bid a new lower-ranking suit (the change of suit by responder is *not* forcing when opener rebids 1 NT*).
POSSIBLE	Balanced suit distribution: Raise to 2 NT.
	Unbalanced suit distribution: Bid a new suit, *jump* rebid a six-card suit, or jump in partner's suit.

* In the Roth method (see Part II), the change of suit by responder remains forcing even when opener rebids 1 NT.

DEFINITE   Balanced suit distribution: Raise to 3 NT.

Unbalanced suit distribution: *Jump* in a new suit, or jump to game in your own suit or partner's suit.

Going back to the previous examples, suppose you hold:

♠ K83   ♡ Q10865   ◇ A83   ♣ 82

Partner opens 1 ♣, you respond 1 ♡, and partner rebids 1 NT. You should *pass*. Game is impossible and you have balanced suit distribution. There is no point in rebidding the heart suit, since partner may have only a doubleton heart, which would leave your side in a trump suit of only seven cards and a level higher than you need to be. If you hold

♠ K83   ♡ KJ965   ◇ A72   ♣ 73

raise to 2 NT. Game is possible, and your raise tells partner to bid game with a maximum hand but to pass with a minimum. An especially enlightened partner whose hand calls for a game bid will bid 3 ♡ "on the way" to 3 NT if he holds good three-card support, so that you may bid 4 ♡ if you have a five-card suit (as you do here). Finally, if you hold

♠ KQ3   ♡ KQ965   ◇ A72   ♣ 73

game is definite, and you should simply bid 3 NT as your suit distribution is balanced.

WHEN OPENER JUMPS IN NOTRUMP

Life becomes fairly simple when partner jump rebids in notrump, since game is usually definite. You should, however, check quickly to be sure that *slam* is not possible (remember, slam is likely if your side holds a total of 33 or more points). If slam is impossible, decide *where* to play the hand. With any relatively balanced hand, the best course is to bid 3 NT (or pass if partner has jumped to 3 NT). With a very unbalanced hand, you may rebid a long suit or bid a new suit. For example, suppose you hold

(140)

♠ 983   ♡ K98652   ◇ 843   ♣ 2

Partner opens 1 ◇, and you KEEP your 6 Roth Points. You respond 1 ♡, and partner jumps to 2 NT, showing 19–20 points. Your hand is now worth only 3 points in notrump since Distribution Points do not count for notrump purposes. What do you do?

You might want to pass, since the partnership cannot have the 26 points quired for game in notrump. This is illogical. Partner—when he bid 2 NT—had no way of knowing that you had *six* hearts. There is still every reason to believe that hearts will be a playable trump suit. (Partner cannot rebid 2 NT with a void or singleton in hearts.) If you play in hearts, your hand is worth 8 points, and you will be well over the minimum 26 needed for game. So, try for the heart game by bidding 3 ♡. Even if partner rebids 3 NT, we recommend going on to 4 ♡. (If you have been compelled to partner an unruly bidder who might bid notrump on just about anything, discretion would suggest a pass over 3 NT, but the care and feeding of uninhibited partners would require a book by itself. We are assuming that your partner, while he need not necessarily use Roth Point Count, follows reasonably standard bidding principles.) Since you know that your side has the required eight-card trump suit, you are justified in insisting on the heart contract; but do not jump to 4 ♡ directly over 2 NT or partner may get very excited and try for slam, thinking you have a better hand. This illustrates the general principle that you should *evaluate your hand in all possible denominations before bidding*. The Roth Point Count may bring light where only darkness appeared before.

WHEN OPENER RAISES YOUR MAJOR

If partner raises your major suit, your action is straightforward. If game is definite, bid game in the major; if game is possible, invite by bidding three of the major; if game is impossible, pass (since you must be in a playable contract).

WHEN PARTNER RAISES YOUR MINOR

When partner raises your minor-suit bid, you should again pass if game is impossible. If, however, game is possible or definite, your first priority is to aim for *game in notrump,* which takes only 26 points as opposed to the 29 points required for making 5 ♣ or 5 ◇. If game is possible and you have all unbid suits stopped, bid two notrump. With

♠ K83   ♡ K65   ◇ AJ1086   ♣ 32

you respond 1 ◇ to partner's 1 ♣ opening and partner raises to 2 ◇. Your 11 HCP will be enough for game in notrump if partner has his maximum of 15 or 16. (Do not count Distribution Points for notrump purposes.) Since you have stoppers in the unbid suits, bid 2 NT. Partner can pass with a minimum (or return to 3 ◇ if his hand is highly unbalanced) or raise to 3 NT with a maximum. With

♠ K83   ♡ 765   ◇ AJ1086   ♣ K2

we would bid 2 ♠. You may bid a new *three*-card suit in an emergency of this sort, for you cannot bid 2 NT without a heart stopper. The fact that you are bidding on alerts partner to the fact that game is possible, and he also knows that his first duty is to try for game in notrump (if he has a heart stopper). Don't worry about a spade raise—partner denied four spades when he raised your *minor* suit.

WHEN OPENER REBIDS HIS OWN SUIT

When partner rebids his own suit without jumping, he is known to have 16 points or less *and* at least five cards in his suit, since he may not rebid a four-card suit. If there is no chance for game, it is usually best to pass *even if the combined trump suit appears unappetizing.* Suppose you have:

♠ Q864   ♡ 3   ◇ KJ108   ♣ 5432

Partner opens 1 ♡ and you respond 1 ♠ because you have 6 Roth Points even after DEMOTING your Distribution Points. If partner rebids 2 ♡, pass and take your medicine. You may not rebid a four-card suit, and any other bid would be interpreted as a try for game. Even with

♠ Q8643 ♡ 3 ◇ KJ108 ♣ 543

you should still pass partner's 2 ♡ rebid. Partner has at least five hearts *and might have more*, and his heart suit is probably better than your spade suit. Good players know when to pass—they bail out before the bidding gets out of hand. With

♠ AK8643 ♡ 3 ◇ 5432 ♣ 43

however, you would be quite correct to rebid 2 ♠ over 2 ♡. You have a good six-card suit, and spades are likely to be at least as good as hearts. Furthermore, opener may now be able to raise spades, and you could get to game (13 revalued Roth Points).

If game is possible, you should have some idea where to play it. If notrump looks attractive (you have relatively balanced suit distribution and all unbid suits stopped), bid two notrump. With three-card (or better) support for partner, raise his suit. With balanced suit distribution and *some* (but not all) unbid suits stopped, or with an unbalanced hand, bid a new suit. Thus, with

♠ KJ86 ♡ 32 ◇ AQ86 ♣ Q43

partner opens 1 ♡ and rebids 2 ♡ over your 1 ♠ response. Your total of 12 points indicates that game is possible (not definite, for partner may have less than 14 points after your response), so bid 2NT. With

♠ KJ86 ♡ 32 ◇ AKJ3 ♣ Q43

you would jump to 3 NT since game is definite. With

♠ AQ863 ♡ 3 ◇ KQ107 ♣ J75

partner opens 1 ♡ and rebids 2 ♡ over your 1 ♠ response. Be careful! If you simply rebid 2 ♠, partner will not know that game is possible. In fact, he'll think you are trying to warn him against further action (unless he fits spades) with a hand such as

♠ AK8643 ♡ 3 ◇ 5432 ♣ 32

If you rashly bid 3 ◇ you are committing the hand to too high a level (a new-suit bid by responder is forcing) when game is only *possible*. (You don't really want to pass 3 ♡ if partner bids it, since you don't like hearts any more than you did before, and if partner doesn't like spades he must bid notrump at the three-level.) Discretion suggests a 2 NT bid. This suggests the *possibility* of game to partner, and allows him to pass a two-level contract if he judges that game is impossible. Finally, suppose you hold

♠ AQ86 ♡ 3 ◇ KJ875 ♣ Q32

and partner opens 1 ♡; you bid 2 ◇, whereupon partner rebids 2 ♡. Here a 2 ♠ bid is cheap and descriptive and the best solution to your problem. Had you held

♠ Q864 ♡ 3 ◇ KJ875 ♣ Q32

what would you do if partner opened 1 ♡, you bid 2 ◇, and he bid 2 ♡? You would apologize for your error! This hand is worth only 8 Roth Points when partner opens 1 ♡, and you need 11 points to respond at the two-level. Your correct first-round response was 1 ♠, and you should pass if partner then rebids 2 ♡ since game is impossible.

If game is *definite*, you must be sure that partner cannot pass your bid unless you are able to bid game directly. Partner may not pass *any new suit* that you bid, so with a hand such as

♠ KQJ76 ♡ 3 ◇ AKJ7 ♣ 432

you may safely bid 3 ◇ on the sequence 1 ♡—1 ♠—2 ♡? Partner will let you know if he can support spades or bid 3 NT, and you will pass his 3 NT bid or raise his 3 ♠ bid to 4 ♠.

Capsule Summary: When Opener's Rebid Is Limited

OPENER'S REBID	GAME CHANCES	YOUR DISTRIBUTION	YOUR ACTION
1 NT	Impossible	Balanced	Pass.
		Unbalanced	Rebid a six-card suit; Bid a new lower-ranking suit.

OPENER'S REBID	GAME CHANCES	YOUR DISTRIBUTION	YOUR ACTION
	Possible	Balanced	Raise to 2 NT (unless you can support opener's suit).
		Unbalanced	Jump rebid a six-card suit or in opener's suit; Bid a new suit (four cards or more);
	Definite (but no slam)	Balanced	Raise to 3 NT.
		Unbalanced	Jump in a new suit or jump to game in your own first suit or partner's suit.
2 NT	Definite (but no slam)	Balanced	Bid 3 NT.
		Unbalanced	Rebid a five-card or longer suit, bid a new suit, or support partner's suit.
3 NT	Definite (but no slam)	Balanced	Pass.
		Unbalanced	Rebid a six-card major suit. Bid a new suit (only if your hand is very unbalanced). Pass.
RAISE OF YOUR MAJOR	Impossible		
	Possible		Bid three of the major.

OPENER'S REBID	GAME CHANCES	YOUR DIS-TRIBUTION	YOUR ACTION
	Definite (but no slam)		Bid game in the major.
RAISE OF YOUR MINOR	Impossible		Pass.
	Possible	Balanced, all unbid suits stopped	Bid 2 NT.
		Balanced, some unbid suits un-stopped	Bid a suit you have stopped.
		Unbalanced	Bid three of the minor.
	Definite (but no slam)	Balanced, all unbid suits stopped	Bid 3 NT.
		Balanced, some unbid suits un-stopped	Bid a stopper be-low the level of 3 NT.
		Very unbal-anced	Bid five of the mi-nor.
REBID OF OWN SUIT	Impossible	Good six-card suit	Rebid suit.
		Otherwise	Pass.
	Possible	Good six-card suit	Jump in your suit.
		Balanced	Bid notrump or raise partner to three.
		Unbalanced	Bid new suit.
	Definite		Bid new suit or bid some directly.

QUIZ

For each problem, first count your Roth Points (making all adjustments in light of partner's bidding); then decide on your game chances; finally, select your rebid.

	PARTNER	YOU	YOU HOLD
1.	1 ◇ 2 ♠	1 ♠ ?	♠ A1086 ♡ Q83 ◇ 2 ♣ J10875
2.	1 ♣ 1 NT	1 ◇ ?	♠ 875 ♡ AQ86 ◇ AK43 ♣ 32
3.	1 ♠ 3 ♣	2 ♣ ?	♠ 6 ♡ Q106 ◇ KJ75 ♣ AQJ62
4.	1 ♠ 3 ♡	2 ♡ ?	♠ K7 ♡ KJ1065 ◇ AJ85 ♣ 106
5.	1 ◇ 1 NT	1 ♠ ?	♠ KQ865 ♡ AKJ85 ◇ 864 ♣ ---
6.	1 ◇ 3 NT	1 ♡ ?	♠ 65 ♡ Q8642 ◇ 73 ♣ A1054
7.	1 ♣ 3 ♡	1 ♡ ?	♠ K86 ♡ KQJ32 ◇ AK7 ♣ 74
8.	1 ♣ 2 ◇	1 ◇ ?	♠ K1087 ♡ 32 ◇ A854 ♣ 1073
9.	1 ◇ 2 NT	1 ♡ ?	♠ K86 ♡ AQ853 ◇ 8765 ♣ 3
10.	1 ◇ 1 NT	1 ♠ ?	♠ Q8654 ♡ 2 ◇ 74 ♣ AJ864
11.	1 ◇ 2 ♡	1 ♡ ?	♠ K986 ♡ AK65 ◇ 743 ♣ 32
12.	1 ♡ 2 NT	1 ♠ ?	♠ A10643 ♡ 3 ◇ QJ432 ♣ 32
13.	1 ♠ 2 ♠	2 ◇ ?	♠ 83 ♡ K864 ◇ AQJ2 ♣ Q73
14.	1 ♡ 1 NT	1 ♠ ?	♠ K843 ♡ AJ62 ◇ Q83 ♣ 32
15.	1 ◇ 2 ◇	1 ♠ ?	♠ A743 ♡ Q83 ◇ 42 ♣ Q962

SOLUTIONS

1. *Pass.* You have only 9 points, so there is no chance for game. Do not add a point when a *four*-card suit is supported.

2. *Bid 3 NT.* Game is definite, since your 13 points plus partner's minimum of 13 adds up to 26. With balanced suit distribution, a notrump contract is indicated.

3. *Bid 3 NT.* You have 14 points for notrump, relatively balanced suit distribution, and stoppers in all unbid suits. Perfectly balanced distribution is not required at this stage so long as all unbid suits are stopped and the hand is not extremely unbalanced.

4. *Bid 4 ♡.* You have 15 Roth Points (12 HCP, 2 Distribution Points, and one point for a supported five-card suit). Game is definite and slam is out of the question. There is no bonus for "showing" diamonds on the way to game—except for the opponents, who will have a better idea what to lead.

5. *Bid 3 ♡. Jump* in a new suit to tell partner that game is definite, but do not meekly accept a notrump contract with such an unbalanced hand (17 points, counting 1 PROMOTED Length Point for one of your 5-card suits and 3 Distribution Points because you should have an 8-card fit in one of your long suits).

6. *Pass.* There is no chance for slam and no reason to rebid hearts (partner may have only a doubleton). (6 points)

7. *Do not bid 4 ♡.* Partner has 17–19 points and you have 18, so *slam* is not only possible but definite (your side must have at at least 35 points). Partner must pass if you bid 4 ♡. (See Chapter 9.)

8. *Pass.* There is no chance for game since you hold only 8 points and partner has at most 16.

9. *Bid 3 ◇.* Why rush into 3 NT? Aside from the fact that your hand is worth 12 points in diamonds but only 10 in notrump, partner might support hearts this time around. You should pass if he now bids 3 NT, however.

10. *Bid 2 ♣.* Game in notrump is out of the question since you have only 7 Roth Points for notrump, but you violently dislike

notrump and wish to suggest to partner that the hand be played in one of your suits.

11. *Bid 3 ♡*. You have 11 Roth Points, so game is possible if partner has a maximum.

12. *Bid 3 ◊*. Game is definite, since partner's jump to 2 NT promises 19–20 points, but *where* to play it is another question. Spades, notrump, or even an unlikely diamond game might be best. Get more information from partner before deciding—you will raise a 3 ♠ bid to 4 ♠, pass 3 NT, and raise a 4 ◊ bid to 5 ◊. Your hand is worth 7 points in notrump but much more if partner can support spades or diamonds.

13. *Bid 2 NT*. Game is possible if partner has 14 or more points since your total is 12. (Remember that partner may have demoted from his original total.) Had you held

♠ 83   ♡ KQ64   ◊ AQJ2   ♣ Q73

you would jump to 3 NT since game would be definite.

14. *Bid 2 ♡*. Your hand is worth 11 points in support of hearts and you intended to support hearts all along, so don't change your mind now!

15. *Pass*. With only 8 Roth Points, game is out of the question. Any attempt to find a better trump suit is likely to make matters even worse, so pass and hope for the best.

Bidding When Partner's Hand is Unlimited

Whenever partner's hand is unlimited—regardless of the number of prior bids that have been made—you are sometimes not in any position to make decisions concerning game, and should instead make the most informative possible bid.* This is not new; you followed the same general strategy when you were the opening bidder and responder's bid was unlimited. Thus, we need only briefly review the priorities that you should follow, and mention a few new added attractions that will help you select your action in each case. The list of priorities is as follows:

---

* With 13 or more points, however, you *can* judge that game is *definite*, since opener is assumed to have at least 13 points.

1. Raise partner's major
2. Bid a new major
3. Bid notrump
4. Bid a new minor
5. Raise partner's minor
6. Rebid your own suit

RAISING PARTNER'S MAJOR

The most informative bid that you can make is to raise your partner's major suit. You must first be sure that you have enough cards in his suit so that a minimum total of eight will be present. If partner has promised a five-card suit by *opening* with one of a major, three-card support will be sufficient; otherwise, four-card support is required. For example, if the auction goes 1 ♣—1 ◇— 1 ♠, you need *four*-card support to raise spades, as partner could have only four spades himself.

If you have the necessary trump support, simply count your points and take action as shown below:

POINTS	YOUR ACTION
6–7	Pass (unless partner has *jumped* the bidding). Partner needs 19 or more points for game, and he will usually take stronger action with such hands than simply bidding a new suit without jump with a hand that strong.
8–11	Raise partner's major to two. Partner could have as few as 14 Roth Points, so game is not definite.
12 or more.	Raise to three. Game is definite, but you need not raise all the way to four because *partner is not permitted to pass this bid.*

BIDDING A NEW MAJOR SUIT

If you are unable to raise a major suit partner has bid, your next choice is to bid a new major suit of your own. To do so, your hand must satisfy two conditions: the new suit must be at least four cards in length, and you may not *reverse* (bid a *higher*-ranking suit at the *two*-level) unless you are sure that game is definite even though little is known about partner's hand—in other words, unless you have at least 13 Roth Points. For example, you hold

♠ K964   ♡ 32   ◇ AQ1085   ♣ 32

Partner opens 1 ♣, you respond 1 ◇, and partner bids 1 ♡. Bid 1 ♠, as it is perfectly proper to bid a new four-card major suit at the one-level even with less than 13 points. However, if you hold

♠ K964   ♡ AQ1098   ◇ 32   ♣ 32

and partner opens 1 ◇ and rebids 2 ♣ over your 1 ♡ response, you may *not* bid 2 ♠. Bidding a *higher*-ranking suit at the *two*-level is a reverse and requires that game be definite. With only 9 Roth Points, game is certainly not definite!

It is very important for you to know that you are *not* required to bid unless partner *jumps* in a new suit. With the second example hand given above, you should bid 2 ♡ after opener's 2 ♣ rebid, since the five-card heart suit is a very good one and you want partner to know that hearts may be a playable trump suit. Thus, you do not pass when you have something constructive to say and a reasonable hand (more than your rock-bottom minimum of 6 or 7 points). But change the hand to

♠ KJ64   ♡ Q6432   ◇ 2   ♣ 432

and you should pass the 2 ♣ rebid. You have the absolute minimum 6 Roth Points needed to respond (and nothing partner has bid has caused you to PROMOTE your hand). Clubs may not be a very good trump suit, but there is no reason to believe any other will be better. Stop while you can! Of course, you may not bid 2 ♠ since you are far short of the minimum 13 Roth Points required for this reverse.* With

---

* A reverse by *opener* requires 18 points because responder may have as few as 6 points. However, a reverse by *responder* requires only 13 points because that is enough to ensure that the 26 point total needed for game is present.

♠ KJ64   ♡ Q6432   ◇ 432   ♣ 2

you would bid 2 ◇, since diamonds must be a better trump suit than clubs.

BIDDING NOTRUMP

A notrump bid usually shows balanced suit distribution and all unbid suits stopped. The point requirements are as follows:

PREVIOUS LEVEL OF BIDDING	BID	POINTS	EXAMPLE	
one-level	1 NT	8–11	1 ♣	1 ◇
			1 ♠	*1 NT*
	2 NT	12–15	1 ◇	1 ♡
			1 ♠	*2 NT*
	3 NT	16–18	1 ♣	1 ♡
			1 ♠	*3 NT*
two-level	2 NT	11–12	1 ♡	2 ♣
			2 ◇	*2 NT*
	3 NT	13–16	1 ♠	2 ♣
			2 ◇	*3 NT*

BIDDING A NEW MINOR SUIT

The rules for bidding a new minor suit are much the same as those for bidding a new major: you must have at least four cards in the suit you bid and you may not reverse or bid at the three-level unless game is definite. The reason for placing this bid in a separate category is to make clear that it is less informative than bidding a new major suit or bidding notrump, and should therefore be avoided whenever you meet the requirements for one of the higher-priority bids.

RAISING PARTNER'S MINOR

To raise partner's minor, you should have four-card support and 8 or more points. Since you do not want to get past the level of 3 NT, you will most often just make a single raise. In other words, if you hold

♠K843　♡A853　◇2　♣J862

and partner opens 1 ◇, your hand is worth 8 Roth Points after DEMOTION, and you can correctly respond 1 ♡. Partner rebids 2 ♣. You may not bid 2 ♠ (a reverse), even though your hand is now worth 11 Roth Points. Just raise to 3 ♣.

REBIDDING YOUR OWN SUIT

Too many players overemphasize the importance of rebidding their own suits because they forget that partner is on the same team. When they hold

♠AK865　♡32　◇KJ42　♣87

and the bidding goes 1 ♡--1 ♠--2 ◇, they look at their good five-card major, possibly decide that they want to play the hand, and rebid spades. When their partner shows up with a singleton spade and the hand goes down a few tricks, they complain about a bad trump split—neglecting to note that the opponents held so many trumps that they *had* to split badly! You know better, as raising partner's minor takes precedence over rebidding a five-card suit. Partner has diamonds, you have diamonds, and you're on the same side!

There are times, however, when it is quite proper to rebid your own suit. This will most often happen when you hold a six-card suit or a very good five-card suit *and* are unable to make any of the higher-priority bids. For example, if you hold

♠AKJ95　♡43　◇106　♣9853

and the auction proceeds 1 ♡--1 ♠--2 ◇, you cannot support hearts and you may not bid 3 ♣ with only 8 Roth Points, since moving up to the three-level requires 13 or more points. Therefore, rebid 2 ♠. The simple 2 ♠ rebid flashes a warning sign to partner, and tells him not to go on unless he has appreciably more than a minimum opening. Thus, with

♠AKQ85　♡32　◇106　♣A832

do *not* rebid 2 ♠, as partner will not know you have such a good hand. Here you may bid 3 ♣ as you have the required 13 Roth points. With

$$♠AKJ85 \quad ♡32 \quad ◇32 \quad ♣A83$$

jump to 3 ♠. Once again, a simple 2 ♠ rebid would tell partner to "go slow" and your hand is much too good for such a message. (With the Length Point for a six-card major, you have 13 Roth Points.)

So, you rebid your own suit without jumping if you cannot do anything else and wish to give partner the stop sign; of course, partner *may* continue bidding, particularly with a fit for your suit; and you *jump* if you have a hand good enough for game and a strong suit.

Capsule Summary: When Opener's Rebid Is Unlimited

1. RAISE PARTNER'S MAJOR:	Single raise with 8–12 points Four-card or longer support Double raise with 13 or more points
2. BID A NEW MAJOR SUIT:	But you must have 13 or more points to *reverse* or bid at the three-level
3. BID NOTRUMP (Balanced suit distribution and all unbid suits stopped)	Over a one-level bid: 1 NT = 8–11 points. 2 NT = 12–15 points. 3 NT = 16–18 points. Over a two-level bid: 2 NT = 11–12 points. 3 NT = 13–16 points.
4. BID A NEW MINOR SUIT:	But do not reverse or bid at the three-level unless you have 13 or more points.
5. RAISE PARTNER'S MINOR:	Usually to three (four-card or longer support), with 8–11 points.

6. REBID YOUR OWN SUIT: Simple rebid with 10 points or less jump rebid with 13 points or more.

YOU ARE ALWAYS PERMITTED TO PASS UNLESS PARTNER JUMPS IN A NEW SUIT, AND SHOULD DO SO WITH A MINIMUM (6–7 POINTS) AND NO USEFUL BID TO MAKE.

QUIZ

Once you have learned the order of priority and the point count requirements listed above (including those for reverses), let logic rather than a formal list of rules be your guide. First, count your Roth Points; then decide on your action.

	PARTNER	YOU	YOU HOLD
1.	1 ◇	1 ♡	♠ K1086 ♡ KQ54 ◇ 43 ♣ 432
	1 ♠	?	
2.	1 ♡	1 ♠	♠ KJ865 ♡ 32 ◇ 532 ♣ Q83
	2 ♣	?	
3.	1 ♣	1 ◇	♠ KJ74 ♡ AQ65 ◇ Q864 ♣ 2
	1 ♡	?	
4.	1 ◇	1 ♡	♠ 32 ♡ K864 ◇ J53 ♣ KJ107
	1 ♠	?	
5.	1 ♡	2 ♣	♠ KJ3 ♡ 74 ◇ 853 ♣ AQJ64
	2 ◇	?	
6.	1 ◇	1 ♠	♠ KQ8653 ♡ J63 ◇ 32 ♣ 32
	2 ♣	?	
7.	1 ♣	1 ◇	♠ K1064 ♡ 32 ◇ KQ83 ♣ Q83
	1 ♡	?	
8.	1 ♡	1 ♠	♠ QJ32 ♡ 8 ◇ QJ653 ♣ J63
	2 ♣	?	
9.	1 ◇	1 ♡	♠ AQ3 ♡ K1064 ◇ AJ42 ♣ 32
	2 ♣	?	
10.	1 ◇	1 ♠	♠ KJ86 ♡ 832 ◇ 85 ♣ KJ107
	2 ♡	?	

SOLUTIONS

1. *Bid 2 ♠*. You have 10 Roth Points and four-card support.

2. *Pass.* You have only 6 points and no constructive action to take. For all you know, partner has a singleton spade.

3. *Bid 3 ♡*. Counting the PROMOTED singleton, your hand is worth 15 Roth Points in support of hearts.

4. *Bid 1 NT*. You have 8 points for notrump, balanced suit distribution, and stoppers in all unbid suits. Here you have a constructive action to take—getting partner out of a probably inadequate spade contract into a potentially attractive notrump contract.

5. *Bid 2 NT*. You have 11 HCP, balanced suit distribution, and a stopper in the unbid suit. A rebid of 3 ♣ might leave partner concerned about a spade stopper, and would overstate the club strength.

6. *Bid 2 ♠*. Here you are justified in preferring your own suit, and you rebid simply to flash a potential stop sign to partner. (7 points)

7. *Bid 1 ♠*. Show the new major suit at the one-level. (10 points)

8. *Pass.* Remember that partner must keep bidding any time you bid a new suit. With only 7 Roth Points, don't encourage him any further!

9. *Bid 3 NT*. Bidding notrump takes priority over raising partner's minor. With 14 HCP and stoppers in all unbid suits, game is definite, so bid it. Partner could pass a 2 NT rebid with minimum values.

10. *Bid 2 NT*. A trap question! Did you notice that partner *reversed?* He bid a new *higher-* ranking suit at the two-level, which promises least 18 points. Thus, the regular requirements for a 2 NT rebid are immaterial— your 8 points plus partner's minimum of 18 indicates that the 26 point game total is present. With balanced suit distribution and stoppers in all unbid suits, suggest that game be played in notrump. Do not worry if you missed this question—I just do not want you to think that you know *all* the answers at this point!

Capsule Summary: Responder's Rebid

IF OPENER'S REBID IS LIMITED:

First, determine chances for game. *Then:*

CHANCES FOR GAME	YOUR ACTION
IMPOSSIBLE	*Pass* if you have no constructive action to take or if you are in a playable contract.
	Go back to partner's first suit if that will be a better trump suit.
	Rebid your own suit if is six or more cards long and you cannot play notrump or any of partner's suits.
	Bid a new lower-ranking suit *only* if partner's rebid was 1 NT, your hand is very unsuited for notrump, and you have no six-card or longer suit to rebid.
POSSIBLE	*Invite* game by raising the appropriate trump suit or notrump.
	Bid notrump if your hand meets the requirements (stoppers in unbid suits).
	Bid a new lower-ranking suit (but do *not* reverse)
	Jump rebid a six-card suit.
DEFINITE	Bid an indicated game (partner's major; your major; notrump).
	Bid a new suit (jump if partner's rebid was 1 NT).

IF OPENER'S REBID IS UNLIMITED:

Unless you hold 13 or more points and game is definite, you cannot reach any decision regarding game. Follow these priorities:

1. RAISE PARTNER'S MAJOR   (to two = 8–12 points; to three = 13 points or more)
2. BID A NEW MAJOR SUIT
3. BID NOTRUMP
4. BID A NEW MINOR SUIT
5. RAISE PARTNER'S MINOR   (to three = 8–11 points)

6. REBID YOUR OWN SUIT   (*jump* with 13 points or more)
BUT *PASS* WITH 6–7 POINTS AND NO USEFUL BID TO
MAKE.

REVIEW QUIZ FOR CHAPTER 5

In each problem, first count your Roth Points; then decide whether
partner's hand is limited or unlimited; then select your action.

	PARTNER	YOU	YOU HOLD
1.	1 ♣	1 ◇	♠ KJ87 ♡ KQ43 ◇ A742 ♣ 2
	1 ♡	?	
2.	1 ♣	1 ♡	♠ 74 ♡ A9865 ◇ Q102 ♣ Q63
	1 ♠	?	
3.	1 ◇	1 ♡	♠ A865 ♡ J874 ◇ 863 ♣ K2
	2 ♡	?	
4.	1 ◇	1 ♡	♠ QJ106 ♡ K875 ◇ AQ3 ♣ 32
	1 NT	?	
5.	1 ♠	2 ◇	♠ 8 ♡ AQ4 ◇ Q10865 ♣ KQ32
	3 ◇	?	
6.	1 ♣	1 ♡	♠ 32 ♡ AJ1097 ◇ 743 ♣ K83
	2 NT	?	
7.	1 ◇	1 ♠	♠ K1096 ♡ AQ3 ◇ 32 ♣ K1085
	2 ◇	?	
8.	1 ♣	1 ◇	♠ 5432 ♡ 7 ◇ AQ86 ♣ A1074
	1 ♠	?	
9.	1 ♣	1 ♡	♠ 3 ♡ Q10865 ◇ A8642 ♣ 84
	1 NT	?	
10.	1 ◇	1 ♠	♠ KJ1064 ♡ 3 ◇ 654 ♣ AJ84
	2 ♣	?	
11.	1 ◇	1 ♡	♠ 654 ♡ AQ765 ◇ 432 ♣ 103
	3 ♡	?	
12.	1 ♣	1 ♠	♠ QJ1065 ♡ A73 ◇ 853 ♣ 102
	1 NT	?	
13.	1 ♣	1 ◇	♠ J1065 ♡ KQ8 ◇ A942 ♣ 73
	1 ♡	?	

	PARTNER	YOU	YOU HOLD
14.	1 ♡ 2 ♡	1 ♠ ?	♠KJ65 ♡84 ◇A843 ♣1076
15.	1 ◇ 1 ♠	1 ♡ ?	♠Q1086 ♡AQ86 ◇743 ♣32
16.	1 ◇ 2 ♣	1 ♠ ?	♠A986 ♡8753 ◇Q83 ♣94
17.	1 ♣ 2 ♠	1 ♠ ?	♠Q965 ♡AK3 ◇A432 ♣87
18.	1 ♡ 2 ♣	1 ♠ ?	♠KQ865 ♡84 ◇AJ65 ♣97
19.	1 ◇ 2 NT	1 ♠ ?	♠A1085 ♡Q63 ◇Q73 ♣985
20.	1 ♡ 3 ♣	2 ♣ ?	♠KQ3 ♡74 ◇865 ♣AKJ74
21.	1 ◇ 1 NT	1 ♠ ?	♠KQ865 ♡KJ3 ◇32 ♣AJ7
22.	1 ◇ 1 ♠	1 ♡ ?	♠Q1086 ♡A10975 ◇J83 ♣2
23.	1 ♣ 4 ♡	1 ♡ ?	♠32 ♡5432 ◇AQ3 ♣J1064
24.	1 ♣ 3 NT	1 ♠ ?	♠Q10865 ♡A63 ◇74 ♣432
25.	1 ◇ 2 ♣	1 ♡ ?	♠A865 ♡AQ865 ◇74 ♣32
26.	1 ◇ 3 ◇	1 ♠ ?	♠KJ107 ♡A83 ◇64 ♣J654
27.	1 ♣ 1 ♠	1 ◇ ?	♠AJ4 ♡Q543 ◇KQ83 ♣106
28.	1 ♣ 2 ♣	1 ♡ ?	♠863 ♡AQ10653 ◇653 ♣3
29.	1 ♡ 2 ♠	1 ♠ ?	♠Q8653 ♡QJ1032 ◇A76 ♣---
30.	1 ◇ 2 ◇	1 ♠ ?	♠AK10976 ♡AQ3 ◇87 ♣103

SOLUTIONS

	POINTS	BID	
1.	16	3 ♡	Jump raise partner's major with 13–16 points. Raising partner's major takes priority over bidding a new major suit—or anything else, for that matter.
2.	8	1 NT	Do not rebid hearts; partner may not have support. Your hand is relatively balanced.
3.	9	Pass	There is no chance for game.
4.	12	2 NT	Invite game with 12 points and a relatively balanced hand. There is no point in bidding spades, as partner would have rebid 1 ♠ with four or more. Do *not* count a PROMOTED Length Point in diamonds for notrump. Your suit is not *good*.
5.	13	3 NT	You have relatively balanced suit distribution and stoppers in all unbid suits.
6.	8 (in notrump) 9 (in suit)	3 ♡	You want partner to raise to 4 ♡ with three-card support. You will pass if he rebids 3 NT.
7.	12	2 NT	You have balanced suit distribution and stoppers in all unbid suits.
8.	13	3 ♠	After PROMOTING your heart singleton, your hand is just worth the double raise.
9.	6 (in notrump) 7 (in suit)	2 ◇	Although game is unlikely, do not pass 1 NT with such an unbalanced hand. You do plan to pass anything partner now bids; hopefully he will

	POINTS	BID	
			pass 2 ◇ * (or convert to 2 ♡ if he prefers hearts to diamonds).
10.	12	3 ♣	Raising partner's minor takes priority over rebidding your own suit. You may not bid notrump with only 9 HCP (you do not count your Distribution Points when bidding notrump, and 11 points are required for a 2 NT bid).
11.	8	4 ♡	Partner's bid shows 17–19 points, which means that your partnership total is 25–27 (be sure to PROMOTE by adding one point for a supported five-card suit). You would like to bid 3 and ½ ♡ so that partner could pass with only 17 points, but this is quite against the rules of bridge. Thus, you must make the decision, and since either 18 or 19 points in partner's hand will produce game, you should bid it.
12.	7	Pass	Game is impossible. Do not rebid the five-card suit, as partner could have only a doubleton.
13.	10	1 ♠	Show the new major suit at the one-level.
14.	8	Pass	Game is impossible and you have no useful bid to make.
15.	10	2 ♠	Your hand meets all the requirements for the single major raise.
16.	7	2 ◇	You know that diamonds will make a better trump suit than clubs. The

---

* In the Roth Method (Part II), 2 ◇ in this sequence is a one-round force.

POINTS	BID	
		simple preference to 2 ◇ does *not* show any better a hand than a pass of 2 ♣, so partner will not get unduly excited.
17. 14	4 ♠	Game is definite—bid it! (There is no chance for slam.)
18. 10	2 ◇	Since you can show the new minor suit without reversing, do so.
19. 8	3 NT	Your 8 points plus partner's minimum of 19 more than reach the magic 26 point total, and your hand is ideally suited for playing in notrump.
20. 14 (in notrump) 15 (in suit)	3 ♠	Show partner that you have spades stopped so that he can bid 3 NT with diamonds stopped. Though your hand is worth *1* point more for suit purposes, game in a minor requires 3 more points than game in notrump. If a partner of rather dubious ability raises to 4 ♠, you had better go back to 5 ♣, since he's obviously missed the point!
21. 15	3 NT	Game is definite and you have balanced suit distribution.
22. 10	2 ♠	Raising partner's major takes priority over supporting his minor or rebidding your own suit.
23. 8	Pass	There is no chance for slam. Do not worry about the quality of your heart suit; partner must have four for his raise, and they are probably good ones since his hand is strong.
24. 6	Pass	There is no chance for slam and

	POINTS	BID	
			your hand is relatively balanced. Partner could have only two spades.
25.	10	2 ♡	You may not reverse (bid 2 ♠) with less than 13 points.
26.	9	3 NT	Partner has at least 17 points for the jump in his own suit, and therefore game is definite. With balanced suit distribution and stoppers in the un-bid suits, suggest that the game be played in notrump.
27.	12	2 NT	You have balanced suit distribution and a stopper in the unbid suit.
28.	7	2 ♡	Here you may insist on your own suit, as you have every reason to believe that it will be as good as or better than clubs.
29.	14	4 ♥	Your hand is worth 14 points in hearts (9 HCP and 5 points for the PROMOTED void) but only 13 points in spades (9 HCP, 3 for the void, and 1 for the supported five-card suit). A bid of 4 ♠ would not be terrible, but the Roth Point Count shows that the heart game should be easier to make. (An original raise to 4 ♡ would be preferable. We give this sequence to show the futility of bidding spades—your hand will always evaluate best in hearts.)
30.	14	3 ♠	With 13 or more points, jump to tell partner that you have a good hand.

CHAPTER

6

Advanced Point-Count Principles

The Roth Point Count that you have learned in the preceding chapters will give you a definite advantage over players using traditional standard methods. Regardless of the system of bidding you and your partner use, and regardless of whether or not your *partner* uses the Roth Point Count, you now have the skill to arrive at better contracts.

This chapter will deal with a few advanced point-count principles. *Do not attempt this chapter until you feel quite secure in the use of the basic mechanics of the Roth Point Count.*

The Principle of Self-Promotion

The new concept that will occupy us in this chapter is that some hands promote and demote *themselves.* Just as the bids your partner makes affect your point count because you and your partner are working together, *the cards in your own hand* are all on the same team and will work together to take tricks for your side. Thus, there are some instances when you will PROMOTE or DE-MOTE your hand simply because of the nature of the cards that you hold—you will promote when your cards are working well together and demote when your cards are not cooperating with one another.

PROMOTING FOR ALL FOUR ACES

If you hold all four aces, PROMOTE by adding one point. It is advantageous to hold all the aces, partly because aces are really worth slightly more than four points and partly because it is an advantage to be sure of taking the first trick (called "having control") regardless of the contract, which you are sure to do with all the aces (except in the unlikely event that the opening lead is ruffed by the enemy).

DEMOTING FOR NO ACES

One of the primary purposes of an opening bid is to show defensive strength. *For defensive purposes,* your other honors are not working at peak efficiency if you hold no aces at all. Therefore, *when considering an opening bid* (ONLY), SUBTRACT one HCP if you hold no aces. Note that this subtraction applies *only to point-counting for purposes of the opening bid.*

RELIABLE SUITS AND SELF-SUFFICIENT SUITS

When you hold a very good suit, your cards cooperate well regardless of the bids your partner makes. You can be quite sure that a reasonable trump suit exists and that your side has "ruffability" simply because your own suit is so good. Thus, when you hold a suit that you are willing to insist on as the trump suit with no support from partner (let's call such suits "reliable suits"), do *not* DEMOTE your Distribution Points regardless of the bids your partner makes—your cards can take care of themselves!

For example, if you hold

♠ AKQ8643   ♡ 85   ◇ J82   ♣ 2

your hand is worth 15 points before partner acts (10 HCP, 3 Distribution Points, and 2 points for a seven-card major suit). If partner opens **one heart**, *do not* DEMOTE your Distribution Points. Your hand is still worth 15 points because you have a RELIABLE suit and can therefore take care of yourself.

How good must a suit be to qualify as RELIABLE? It would be easy enough to answer this question by listing all the RELIABLE suits, or all the different conditions a suit could satisfy to be RELIABLE, but that would simply take up a lot of space.

Instead, we will give you examples of *minimum strength* RELIABLE suits, and let you use your judgment on others by comparing them with the minimum standard. Thus, for a *six*-card suit to be RELIABLE, it must be at least as strong as K Q 10 9 x x; for a *seven*-card suit to be RELIABLE, it must be at least as strong as K Q x x x x x.

Within the category of RELIABLE suits are the "self-sufficient suits." A suit is SELF-SUFFICIENT if you expect to lose no more than one trick in the suit even if partner provides no support. Examples of SELF-SUFFICIENT suits of *minimum strength* are: K Q J 10 x x; K Q J x x x x.

Obviously, the possession of a SELF-SUFFICIENT suit provides its owner with a source of many sure tricks. Therefore, when you hold a SELF-SUFFICIENT suit, not only should you not demote your Distribution Points according to partner's response, but you should automatically *double your Length Points* in the long suit.[*]

For example (moving the jack from diamonds to spades in the previous example), if you hold:

♠ AKQJ643   ♡ 85   ◇ 832   ♣ 2

your hand is worth 17 points before partner acts (10 HCP, 3 Distribution Points, 4 Length Points—double value). If partner opens

---

[*] If you have doubled your Length Points you should make no further PROMOTION for length, even if partner shows support.

with **one heart,** you will *not* demote your Distribution Points. (Any SELF-SUFFICIENT suit is, *a fortiori*, RELIABLE.)

UNGUARDED HONORS

Often, when you hold singleton or doubleton honors, your honor cards and small cards are not working together in an efficient manner. If, for example, you hold a singleton king, an opponent can render this card valueless if he has the ace and plays it. Had you held a small card along with the king, you would of course play your small card instead, and your king would be a winner on the next round.

For purposes of playing in notrump, there is *no* change in the usual counting procedure. Thus, if you hold

$$\spadesuit KJ84 \quad \heartsuit A863 \quad \diamondsuit K \quad \clubsuit QJ52$$

and partner opens **one diamond,** you respond **one heart,** and partner rebids **one notrump.** You do not count your Distribution Points for notrump purposes, so your hand is worth 14 Roth Points (and a raise to 3 NT). It is only when you are considering a *suit contract* that the values change, as follows:

DEMOTE one High Card Point in any suit with one of the following holdings:

Singletons: K; Q; J

Doubletons: KQ; KJ; QJ; Qx; Jx

For any other doubleton honor, or a singleton ace, count HCP as usual.

The following examples will show how the Advanced Point-Count Principles work in action:

1. Partner bids 1 ◊. You hold:

$$\spadesuit Q \quad \heartsuit KJ876 \quad \diamondsuit A83 \quad \clubsuit 6432$$

This hand is worth 11 Roth Points: 3 points in spades (adjusted HCP plus 2 Distribution Points) and 8 HCP elsewhere. (Bid 1 ♡.)

2. Partner bids 1 ♠. You hold:

$$\spadesuit 8765 \quad \heartsuit K \quad \diamondsuit AJ10643 \quad \clubsuit 32$$

Here your hand is worth 12 Roth Points: 5 points in hearts (2 adjusted HCP plus 3 for the PROMOTED singleton), 5 HCP in diamonds, and 2 points for the PROMOTED club doubleton. PROMOTE a singleton (or doubleton) when PROMOTION is called for. After all, with

♠ 8765   ♡ 2   ◇ AJ10643   ♣ 32

you would PROMOTE by adding 1 point for the heart singleton, and a singleton king certainly can't be *worse* than a small singleton! (Bid 2 ◇ or 4 ♠.)

3. Partner bids 1 ♡. You hold:

♠ A   ♡ QJ106   ◇ 987654   ♣ QJ

Your hand is worth 14 Roth Points: 9 adjusted HCP, 3 Distribution Points, one point PROMOTION for the singleton spade and one point PROMOTION for the doubleton club. (Bid 3 ♡.)

4. As dealer you hold:

♠ KQ432   ♡ K7542   ◇ K2   ♣ 2

Your hand is worth only 13 Roth Points: 10 HCP (including a subtraction of 1 point for holding no aces *for an opening bid*) and 3 Distribution Points. (Pass.) For your later bids, the subtraction for no aces does not apply and you would have *11* HCP.

5. Partner bids 1 ♣. You hold:

♠ AQJ1043   ♡ 32   ◇ 7532   ♣ 6

This hand is worth 12 Roth Points: 7 HCP, 3 Distribution Points, (*not* demoted because you have a RELIABLE suit), and 2 Length Points (double the usual value because your suit is SELF-SUFFICIENT). Notice how the presence of the ten of spades—indeed a valuable card—affects the valuation of the hand. This factor is not taken into account in traditional point count (or other less popular counting methods). (Bid 1 ♠.)

Capsule Summary: Advanced Point-count Principles

1. ACES ADJUSTMENT: PROMOTE by adding 1 point for all four aces.

DEMOTE by deducting 1 point with no aces *for purposes of the opening bid (only)*.

2. RELIABLE AND SELF-SUFFICIENT SUITS: With a RELIABLE suit (KQ109 x x, KQ x x x x x or better), do *not* DEMOTE any Distribution Points regardless of partner's bids.

With a SELF-SUFFICIENT suit (KQJ10 x x, KQJ x x x x or better), double the count for Length Points in that suit (in addition to not DEMOTING Distribution Points). When you double your Length Points, make no further PROMOTIONS for Length.

3. UNGUARDED HONORS: For purposes of suit contracts, DEMOTE one HCP for each of the following holdings: K; Q; J; KQ; KJ; QJ; Qx; Jx.

PROMOTE these singletons and doubletons (when holding a good fit for partner's suit) just as you would any other singleton or doubleton.

For notrump purposes, do not DEMOTE for unguarded honors.

REVIEW QUIZ FOR CHAPTER 6

In each case, count your Roth Points. Be sure to check for the three adjustments—"aces," "RELIABLE and SELF-SUFFICIENT suits," and "unguarded honors." If you would like further bidding practice, you may also state your bid, as the correct bid will also be given in the solutions. By the way, with the tools for point counting given up to and including this chapter, your hand evaluation technique will be on the expert level. So if you can pass this quiz you have quite a lot to be proud of.

	Partner bids	You bid	You hold:			
1.	1 ◇	?	♠ Q10865	♡ K	◇ KJ	♣ 98765
2.	1 ♣	1 ♠	♠ A987	♡ A83	◇ A96	♣ A43
	2 ♠	?				

3.	1 ♡	?	♠ Q ♡ QJ7 ◇ A9654 ♣ K843
4.	1 ♠	?	♠ K7 ♡ A ◇ QJ1065 ♣ QJ1065
5.	1 ♣	?	♠ AQ ♡ K87654 ◇ J7 ♣ J85
6.	1 ◇	1 ♡	♠ K765 ♡ KJ102 ◇ Q3 ♣ 987
	1 ♠	?	
7.	1 ◇	?	♠ 32 ♡ AKQJ97 ◇ 54 ♣ AJ10

SOLUTIONS

1. *7 points.* You have 7 adjusted HCP. With only two diamonds, your Distribution Points are demoted to zero. (Bid 1 ♠.)

2. *17 points.* 16 HCP, and 1 point for all four aces. (Do *not* bid 4 ♠—slam is possible if partner holds 16 points. See Chapter 9 on slam bidding.)

3. *13 points.* 11 adjusted HCP plus 2 Distribution Points. (Bid 2 ◇—not 3 ♡ as you lack four-card support.)

4. *13 points.* Nothing unusual here; just DEMOTE your Distribution Points with a doubleton in partner's suit. (Bid 2 ◇.)

5. *13 points.* 10 HCP (adjusted), 2 Distribution Points and 1 Length Point for the six-card major suit. (Bid 1 ♡.)

6. *10 points.* 8 HCP (adjusted) plus 2 Distribution Points (PRO-MOTED doubleton). (Bid 2 ♠.)

7. *19 points.* 15 HCP, 2 Distribution Points (not demoted because of the RELIABLE suit) and 2 Length Points in hearts (double the usual value because of the SELF-SUFFICIENT suit). (Bid 2 ♡.)

A complete chart of the ROTH POINT COUNT will be found on p. 512.

CHAPTER

7

Notrump Bidding

An opening notrump bid conveys a clear and specific message. As we saw in Chapter Two, the opening 1 NT bid requires 16–18 HCP, balanced suit distribution (4–3–3–3, 4–4–3–2, or 5–3–3–2), and high-card points in at least three of the four suits. Since this bid is *limited*, responder is in an excellent position to decide on game prospects; and since the distribution of the notrump bidder's hand is also relatively limited, responder also has a good idea where to play the hand.

On occasion, opener will have a hand suitable for a more powerful opening notrump bid: an opening bid of 2 NT or 3 NT. To open 2 NT, you must have 22–24* HCP; to open 3 NT, you must have 25–27 HCP. As was the case with the 1 NT opening, you also must balanced suit distribution. Thus, with

♠ AKJ6   ♡ KQ8   ◇ KQJ5   ♣ K7

open 2 NT; you have 22 HCP and balanced suit distribution. With

---

* In the Roth method (Part II), this range is 21–23 points.

♠ AKJ6   ♡ AKQ   ◇ KQJ5   ♣ K7

open 3 NT. However, with

♠ AKJ6   ♡ K87   ◇ KQJ5   ♣ K7

you may not open with a notrump bid. With 20 HCP, you are too strong to open 1 NT and not strong enough to open 2 NT. Therefore, you must open with one of a suit—in this case, 1 ◇. Since you are bidding a suit, you count your Distribution Points; with the club doubleton, your hand is worth 21 points. (But remember not to count Distribution Points *for purposes of bidding notrump!* If your hand does not qualify for a notrump bid and you must bid a suit, then and then only count your Distribution Points.)

Responding to 1 NT Openings

When partner opens 1 NT, you should do two things: first, decide whether game is definite, possible, or impossible, using the fact that partner must have 16–18 Roth Points to make your decision. Second, you should decide whether you wish to play in notrump or whether you should try for or, in some cases, insist on a suit contract.

PLAYING IN NOTRUMP

If game is impossible, you should pass partner's 1 NT opening with *any balanced hand.* If your points added to partner's maximum of 18 do not result in 26, you have no reasonable chance for game; and if your hand is balanced, notrump is likely to be as good a contract as anything else and there is no reason to confuse the issue by bidding further. Thus, with

♠ Q83   ♡ 74   ◇ A1064   ♣ 8732

you would *pass* partner's opening 1 NT bid, as your 6 Roth Points plus partner's maximum of 18 add up to 24—not enough for game. Since you have balanced suit distribution, take the simple route and pass.

If game is possible or definite, you should plan to play in notrump if you have balanced suit distribution *and* no four-card or longer *major* suit. If game is possible, invite by raising to 2 NT; if game is definite, simply bid 3 NT. Before bidding 3 NT, however, count your points to check on slam possibilities. If the partnership total may add up to 33 or more points, you are potentially in the slam range. If slam is possible, be kind to partner and let him know by bidding *4 NT**; while if slam is definite, make things simple and bid it yourself—jump to 6 NT.

The following examples will help clarify the above rules. In each case, partner opens the bidding with 1 NT.

1. ♠J876 ♡J83 ◇8743 ♣A2: *Pass.* When game is impossible, pass with *any* balanced hand (6 Roth Points)

2. ♠Q83 ♡Q107 ◇A1086 ♣1032: *Bid 2 NT.* You have 8 Roth Points, so game is possible if partner has his maximum of 18. If he goes on with only 17 points, your three tens may make up for the "missing" point.

3. ♠KJ8 ♡AQ6 ◇K973 ♣865: *Bid 3 NT.* You have 13 Roth Points, so game is definite even if partner has his minimum of 16. However, there is no chance for slam, as partner's maximum of 18 will produce a total of only 31 points.

4. ♠KJ8 ♡AQ6 ◇K973 ♣K75: *Bid 4 NT.* Your 16 Roth Points make game definite, but do not just bid 3 NT as you are in the slam range. If partner has 17 or 18 points, you will reach the total of 33 Roth Points needed for slam. Therefore, slam is possible, and you should indicate this to partner by bidding 4 NT.

5. ♠KJ8 ♡AQ6 ◇K973 ♣A107: *Bid 6 NT.* With 17 points, you will reach the 33 point total needed for slam even if partner has his minimum of 16. *Slam* is definite—so bid it!

6. ♠J1074 ♡K3 ◇A1085 ♣432: *Do not bid notrump.* Game is possible since you have 8 Roth Points, and you should not bid notrump when you have a four-card or longer *major* suit and game is possible or definite.

---

* A jump to four notrump is a notrump raise (not a conventional bid) when made directly over partner's notrump bid.

7. ♠ AQ865   ♡3   ◇9865   ♣432: *Do not pass.* Though game is unlikely, your hand is *not* balanced.

8. ♠3   ♡AKJ107   ◇A83   ♣Q764: *Do not bid notrump* when game is definite and you hold a four-card or longer major suit; also, your hand is *not* balanced.

Capsule Summary: Raising Notrump After a 1 NT Opening Bid

CHANCES FOR GAME	YOUR DISTRIBUTION	YOUR ACTION
NONE	*Any* balanced hand	Pass.
POSSIBLE	Balanced hand; no four-card or longer *major* suit	Raise to 2 NT.
DEFINITE; SLAM IMPOSSIBLE	Balanced hand; no four-card or longer major suit	Raise to 3 NT.
DEFINITE; SLAM POSSIBLE	Balanced hand; no four-card or longer major suit	Raise to 4 NT.
SLAM IS DEFINITE	Balanced hand; no four-card or longer major suit	Raise to 6 NT.

QUIZ

In each case, partner opens the bidding with 1 NT. First, count your Roth Points for notrump; then decide on your action.

1. ♠AJ876   ♡873   ◇7432   ♣3
2. ♠K83   ♡Q108   ◇KJ64   ♣A103
3. ♠876   ♡32   ◇J653   ♣8742
4. ♠KQ8   ♡QJ9   ◇AKQ86   ♣98
5. ♠87   ♡KJ3   ◇AJ864   ♣432
6. ♠K9   ♡AQ6   ◇A1064   ♣K865

7. ♠ Q832 ♡ A62 ◇ 87 ♣ J765
8. ♠ KJ87 ♡ 63 ◇ Q83 ♣ A743
9. ♠ Q106 ♡ AJ3 ◇ K854 ♣ 432

SOLUTIONS

1. *Do not pass.* Game is unlikely,* but you should not pass the 1 NT opening bid with an unbalanced hand. (5 points for notrump).

2. *Bid 3 NT.* With 13 Roth Points, game is definite and slam is impossible, and you have balanced suit distribution and no four-card or longer major suit.

3. *Pass.* You have but one lonely point. With balanced suit distribution, pass.

4. *Bid 6 NT.* Your 18 Roth Points (diamonds are "supported" and the suit is *good*) plus partner's minimum of 16 guarantee that the 33 point total needed for slam is present.

5. *Bid 2 NT.* You have 9 Roth Points (here the diamonds are *not good*) and game is possible if partner has 17 or 18 points.

6. *Bid 4 NT.* With 16 points, slam is possible if partner holds 17 or 18 points, but not if he has his minimum of 16.

7. *Pass.* Game is impossible since you have only 7 Roth Points, and your hand is balanced.

8. *Do not bid notrump.* When game is possible or definite, do not bid notrump when you hold a four-card or longer *major* suit. (10 points)

9. *Bid 3 NT.* Your 10 Roth Points make game definite.

---

* It will be noted that we do not say game is "impossible." The reader may wonder why, since this responding hand contains only 5 Roth Points for notrump (the spade suit is not GOOD, so the PROMOTED Length Point does not count for notrump). But observe what happens if opener can freely support spades (with 3 or more spades). The hand now contains 8 Roth Points (5 HCP, 2 Distribution Points because of the 8-card fit, and 1 PROMOTED Length Point in spades) for play *in spades.* Thus, game is really possible after all. But it is *unlikely* since opener must have 3-card spade support *and* a maximum. The theme of a possible game in one denomination but not another will be developed more fully later in this chapter.

GETTING OUT OF NOTRUMP

When your hand does not meet the requirements discussed in the previous section, you should consider the merits of playing in a suit contract. The correct procedure will depend on your chances for game.

When game is impossible, and you cannot pass because your hand is unbalanced, you simply "escape" into your best suit. However, you must have at least five cards in your suit; otherwise your "escape" is likely to be from the frying pan into the fire! Thus, with

♠ AJ876 ♡ 873 ◇ 7432 ♣ 3

bid 2 ♠ over partner's 1 NT opening. Aside from getting out of a potentially poor notrump contract, the 2 ♠ bid also tells partner (politely!) to keep quiet; *partner is not expected to bid again*. Similarly, with

♠ 3 ♡ K87654 ◇ 8743 ♣ 32

escape to 2 ♡. You need not worry that partner will get excited and push the bidding to too high a level, because *he is required to pass your bid unless he has a maximum with a good fit for your suit.* (So, if he does raise, you will not be in trouble.)

There is one exception to this rule: *you may not bid 2 ♣ as an "escape."* As we will see later, a very special meaning is reserved for the bid of 2 ♣ over partner's 1 NT opening: Therefore, while you may always escape by bidding 2 ♠, 2 ♡, or 2 ◇, you must not bid 2 ♣ for escape purposes. With a hand such as

♠ Q83 ♡ 3 ◇ 8632 ♣ A7653

just pass, since you may not bid 2 ♣. With a *very* "club-oriented" hand, such as

♠ 8 ♡ 62 ◇ 8754 ♣ AJ9654

bid 3 ♣. Since 2 ♣ is reserved for special purposes, the bid of 3 ♣ carries the "escape" message,* and partner is required to pass. Thus,

---

* Some players prefer to use a response of three clubs as a strong bid. They "escape" into clubs by using the Stayman Convention (described later)—a forcing response of two clubs—and *then* bidding three clubs. There is little to choose between the two methods. The one presented has, if nothing else, the advantage of simplicity.

simply remember not to "escape" in clubs unless under extreme provocation, and in such cases bid 3 ♣.

When game is definite, and you hold a five-card or longer major suit, jump in the major suit. Thus, with

$$♠ AQ1065 \quad ♡ 87 \quad ◇ 863 \quad ♣ AJ2$$

jump to 3 ♠ over partner's 1 NT opening. You may not bid only 2 ♠, as that suggests a pass to partner—a message you most certainly do *not* want to convey, since you know game is definite! When you jump to 3 ♠, announcing that your side has game, *partner may not pass*. With three or more cards in spades, he will raise to 4 ♠, as your bid promises at least five cards in spades. With only two spades, partner will rebid 3 NT, which you should pass. (Partner cannot have a singleton spade, as he would not have opened 1 NT with a singleton or void in any suit.) If you hold

$$♠ AJ10654 \quad ♡ 87 \quad ◇ 86 \quad ♣ A93$$

you may bid 4 ♠ directly over the 1 NT opening. Since partner must have at least a doubleton spade, you are sure that an eight-card holding for an adequate trump suit is present, and your point count is more than adequate. (14 points).

With a five-card or longer *minor* suit, raise notrump (unless your hand is especially unbalanced). It is usually much easier to make 3 NT, which requires 26 Roth Points, than to make 5 ♣ or 5 ◇, which require 29 Roth Points. Thus, if you hold

$$♠ 73 \quad ♡ 98 \quad ◇ AQ10653 \quad ♣ Q76$$

raise partner's 1 NT opening to 3 NT. With

$$♠ J \quad ♡ 876 \quad ◇ A9865 \quad ♣ K973$$

raise to 2 NT. With a very unbalanced hand, such as

$$♠ \text{---} \quad ♡ 7 \quad ◇ AQ9876 \quad ♣ KJ7653$$

jump to 3 ◇ (the higher-ranking suit with equal length), then bid your clubs later.

THE STAYMAN CONVENTION*

Suppose partner opens 1 NT and you hold:

♠ KJ87   ♡ A3   ◇ K864   ♣ 432

Game is definite, as your 11 Roth Points plus partner's minimum of 16 add up to 27—one more than the minimum needed for game. But you should *not* simply bid 3 NT, as you hold a four-card major suit. Experience has shown that if both partners hold four cards in a major suit, so that an eight-card trump fit is present, it is usually better to play in four of the major than in three notrump. You may bid spades yourself, as that would promise at least *five* cards in the suit. *How can you find out if partner has four cards in spades?*

Again, suppose partner opens 1 NT, and you hold:

♠ AJ1065   ♡ 43   ◇ K83   ♣ 432

Game is possible, since you hold 9 Roth Points in spades, or 8 for notrump (remember the PROMOTION point for "supported" spades) but you would like to try for game in spades in case partner holds three (or four!) cards in that suit. Yet a raise to 2 NT would say nothing about the spade suit, a bid of 2 ♠ would request partner to pass, and a bid of 3 ♠ would convey the message that game is definite. *How can you logically investigate game prospects?*

In order to solve these (and other) problems, virtually all experts make use of the "Stayman Convention." This convention is essential for good notrump bidding, and is not at all difficult to learn. Here's how it works:

Over partner's opening bid of 1 NT, *a response of 2 ♣ is con-*

---

* The convention described in this section is often called "nonforcing Stayman," for technical reasons to be discussed later in the book (Chapter 22). This is the more popular of the two standard methods of treating the Stayman Convention. The Roth Method (Part II) requires the use of forcing Stayman, so the reader will be exposed to both methods and can choose for himself. In the text of this chapter we make one compromise between the two methods. Many practitioners of the nonforcing variation treat a response of 2 ♡ or 2 ♠ as an *absolute command* that opener pass. We allow opener to bid again with a maximum *and* a fit.

ventional and says nothing at all about your holding in clubs. It promises *at least 8 Roth Points.* Opener is not permitted to pass, since you are not promising anything in the way of a good club suit. Instead, the 2 ♣ bid asks partner if he holds a four-card major suit. Opener answers the question as follows:

1. Wtih a four-card (or five-card) major suit, he bids that major suit at the two-level.

2. With no four-card (or longer) major, partner bids 2 ◇. This does not promise a biddable diamond suit, but simply says "I do not have a four-card major suit."

Here is how the Stayman Convention conveniently resolves the two difficulties mentioned previously. With

♠ KJ87　♡ A3　◇ K864　♣ 432

bid 2 ♣ over partner's 1 NT opening, to find out whether or not he has a four-card spade suit. If partner bids 2 ♠, jump to 4 ♠, as game is definite. You have 13 Roth Points.* If partner instead bids 2 ♡ or 2 ◇, simply bid 3 NT. Game in notrump is definite, and since partner does not have four spades you are quite willing to accept a notrump contract. With a weaker hand:

♠ KJ87　♡ A3　◇ K864　♣ 432

you would again bid 2 ♣ over partner's 1 NT opening. However, game is not definite, since you have only 8 Roth Points; partner must have his maximum of 18 for the 26 point total to be reached. Therefore, if partner responds 2 ♡ or 2 ◇, you rebid only 2 NT (asking partner to go to 3 NT if he has a maximum). If partner bids 2 ♠, you can raise to four (10 Roth Points).

If you hold

♠ AJ1065　♡ 43　◇ K83　♣ 432

you may not bid spades directly over partner's 1 NT opener, because 2 ♠ would request partner to pass and 3 ♠ would force him to bid.

---

* This hand is counted as if partner had bid spades—for he has, *and an 8-card fit has been established.* Thus, there are 11 HCP plus 2 Distribution Points.

(179)

Neither of these messages is appropriate, since game is only possible. You would really like to bid 2–1/2 ♠, and you can do this using the Stayman Convention! Bid 2 ♣ over the 1 NT opening. If partner bids 2 ◇ or 2 ♡, bid 2 ♠. Partner knows that you are not just trying to escape from notrump, as the Stayman 2 ♣ bid promises at least 8 Roth Points. Thus, he will know that you are *inviting* game. Furthermore, he knows you have at least five spades, since you are still interested in the suit even though he did not show four of them. Therefore, he can pass if game is impossible; bid 2 NT if he wishes to continue trying for game but has only two spades; bid 3 ♠ (or even 4 ♠) with a maximum point-count and three-card spade support, or jump to 3 NT with a maximum point-count and two-card spade support.

If partner responds 2 ♠ to your Stayman bid, your hand is now worth 10 points (8 HCP, 2 Distribution Points). Partner must have at least 16 points, so game is definite, and you should jump directly to 4 (spades).

Here are some examples of the Stayman Convention in action:

	PARTNER	YOU	YOU HOLD			
1.	1 NT	?	♠ 87	♡ K864	◇ A1065	♣ Q97

Bid 2 ♣. You have the necessary 8 points (in fact, you have 9 Roth Points) and would like to know if partner has a four-card heart suit. If partner bids 2 ◇ or 2 ♠ in response to your Stayman bid, rebid 2 NT. Game is possible, but partner should be permitted to pass short of game if he has only 16 points. However, if partner bids 2 ♡, you add 2 Distribution Points. With 11 Roth Points, game is definite, so you should jump to 4 ♡. Notice how in one case the Roth Point Count told you to *invite* game, in the other case to *bid* game. Why? Because your hand is better when partner has four hearts! And the point count tells you this.

2.	1 NT	?	♠ K9765	♡ 74	◇ AJ3	♣ 642

Bid 2 ♣. If partner now responds 2 ◇ or 2 ♡, bid 2 ♠; your hand is worth 8 Roth Points in notrump and game is *possible*. If partner bids

2 ♠ (over 2 ♣), however, your hand is worth 10 Roth Points (8 HCP, 2 Distribution Points), and game is *definite,* so bid 4 ♠. In these examples, note how the Roth Point Count clearly shows you that your hand is worth more points when partner bids the suit you like! While many players use the Stayman Convention, they must rely on special rules or intuition so that they will make the correct decision after partner's bid—or they use the traditional standard point-count and sometimes arrive at the wrong contract. Using the Roth Point Count, you know how much your hand is worth as a result of partner's bids, and can act accordingly!

3.	1 NT	?	♠K965 ♡AQJ65 ◇643 ♣2

Bid 2 ♣. Game is definite as you have 10 HCP. You would like to know if partner has a four-card spade suit, in which case spades will be a fine contract, or if he has *three*-card (or longer) heart support, in which case you would like to play the hand in hearts. Using the Stayman Convention, you can have your cake and eat it too. If partner bids 2 ♠ or 2 ♡ over your Stayman response, raise to four. You have found a good trump fit, and there is no bonus for finding another one. If partner bids 2 ◇, denying a four-card or longer major suit, *jump to 3 ♡.* Your jump tells partner that game is definite, and therefore he must not pass. Also, your 3 ♡ bid informs partner that you have a five-card suit—even though he denied having four of them by bidding 2 ◇, you are still interested and therefore must have (at least) five hearts. Thus, partner will raise to 4 ♡ with three-card support or bid 3 NT with a doubleton, either of which you will pass. If game were only possible, i.e. if you held

♠ K965   ♡ AJ765   ◇ 643   ♣ 2

and partner responded 2 ♦, you would bid only 2 ♥ and leave the rest up to him. (Your hand is worth a raise to game if opener shows a four-card major suit, but worth only a game invitation when he does not.)

4.	---	1 NT	♠8765 ♡K3 ◇AQJ7 ♣AQ6
	2 ♣	?	

Here we have shifted across the table to see how the bidding appears to the opening notrump bidder. In this situation, you should bid 2 ♠. Your hand is worth 16 Roth Points (you do not know if partner has spades or not, so do not count Distribution Points). If partner now bids 2 NT, you should pass, as you have only the minimum 16 Roth Points required to open 1 NT. If partner bids 3 ♡, you should also pass. Partner is showing the "2–1/2 ♡" hand—too strong to "sign off" at 2 ♡, but too weak to state that game is definite by jumping directly to 3 ♡ over 1 NT. With your minimum 16 points and poor support for hearts, you should pass. However, if partner raises to 3 ♠, your hand is worth 17 Roth Points (you count a Distribution Point for the doubleton heart now that a good trump fit has been found). This means you must use your judgment as to whether you have a minimum or a maximum. With weak spades conservatism is in order, so you should pass 3 ♠.

| 5. | --- | 1 NT | ♠Q765 ♡K3 ◇AQJ7 ♣AQ6 |
| | 2 ♣ | ? | |

Once again, you should bid 2 ♠—show your four-card major suit. If partner bids 2 NT, go on to 3 NT. You have 18 Roth Points and partner must have at least 8 points to use the Stayman Convention, so game is definite. If partner bids 3 ♡, bid 3 NT. You do not like hearts with only a doubleton, but game is still definite. Finally, if partner bids 3 ♠, continue to 4 ♠ with your maximum values.

| 6. | --- | 1 NT | ♠AQ8 ♡AKQ ◇653 ♣J1065 |
| | 2 ♣ | ? | |

With no four-card major, you must respond 2 ◇. If partner rebids 2 ♡, 2 ♠, or 2 NT, you should pass with your minimum 16 Roth Points.

As you can see, the Stayman Convention requires no complex rules to memorize. All you need to remember is that a 2 ♣ response asks opener to bid a four-card major suit and promises at least 8 Roth Points. Opener complies if he can, and otherwise bids 2 ◇. Upon hearing the answer to his question, the Stayman bidder bids

an indicated game if game is definite, or invites game by bidding
2 NT, raising a major suit with four-card or longer support, or bidding a new major suit if game is only possible.

Capsule Summary: Getting Out of Notrump

CHANCES FOR GAME	YOUR DISTRIBUTION	YOUR ACTION
NONE (or SLIGHT)	Five-card or longer spade, heart or diamond suit	Bid your five-card or longer suit. (Partner will pass unless he has a maximum and a fit for the bid suit.)
	Six-card or longer club suit	Bid 3 ♣. (Partner must pass.)
POSSIBLE	One or two four-card major suits	Bid 2 ♣ (the Stayman Convention). *Then:* If partner bids your four-card major, re-count your Roth Points. If game is still possible, raise to three; if game is now definite, raise to four. If partner does not bid your four-card major suit, bid 2 NT.
	One five-card major suit	Bid 2 ♣ (the Stayman Convention). If partner does not bid your five-card suit, bid it yourself. If he does bid your suit, raise to three if game is still only possible, and

CHANCES FOR GAME	YOUR DISTRIBUTION	YOUR ACTION
		raise to four if game is now definite.
	One five-card major suit and one four-card major suit	Bid 2 ♣ (the Stayman Convention). If partner bids 2 ◊, bid your five-card major suit. If partner bids a major, raise to three if game is still only possible and raise to four if game is now definite.
DEFINITE (NO SLAM)	Five-card major suit	Jump to three of major suit. Pass if partner re-bids 3 NT.
	Six-card major suit	Jump to four of major suit.
	One or two four-card major suits	Bid 2 ♣ (the Stayman Convention). If partner now bids your major suit, raise to four; otherwise jump to 3 NT.
	One five-card major suit and one four-card major suit	Bid 2 ♣ (the Stayman Convention). If partner bids a major suit, raise to four. If he bids 2 ◊, *jump* to three of your five-card suit.

- -

QUIZ

In this quiz, we will deal only with the possible actions of the responder to the 1 NT opening. For each hand, first count your

Roth Points (making any adjustments required by partner's bidding); then decide your action.

	PARTNER	YOU	YOU HOLD			
1.	1 NT	?	♠ 87	♡ A1086	◇ 432	♣ J875
2.	1 NT	?	♠ 9	♡ A10965	◇ 654	♣ 9765
3.	1 NT	?	♠ KQ86	♡ AQ86	◇ 754	♣ 62
4.	1 NT	?	♠ 8	♡ Q10965	◇ AQ86	♣ 432
5.	1 NT	?	♠ AQ1064	♡ A73	◇ 432	♣ 32
6.	1 NT	?	♠ 8	♡ QJ10875	◇ AQ8	♣ 753
7.	1 NT	2 ♣	♠ KJ65	♡ AJ43	◇ 653	♣ 32
	2 ◇	?				
8.	1 NT	2 ♣	♠ Q1076	♡ 64	◇ AQ8	♣ J764
	2 ♠	?				
9.	1 NT	2 ♣	♠ K8765	♡ A83	◇ J85	♣ 32
	2 ♡	?				
10.	1 NT	2 ♣	♠ KJ76	♡ 865	◇ AQ106	♣ K5
	2 ♡	?				

SOLUTIONS

1. *Pass.* Your hand is relatively balanced, and game is impossible. You should not use the Stayman Convention with fewer than 8 HCP, and you have no five-card suit to bid. (5 points)

2. *Bid 2 ♡.* Game is virtually impossible and your hand is unbalanced. Bid your five-card suit; partner is asked to pass. (5 points in hearts including 1 Length Point for "supported" hearts, but no Distribution Points since no 8-card fit is assumed.)

3. *Bid 2 ♣.* You would like to know if partner has a four-card major suit. Partner will not pass your Stayman bid. (11 points; you cannot count a Distribution Point as there may be no 8-card fit).

4. *Bid 2 ♣.* You are too strong to bid 2 ♡ (signoff) and to weak to bid 3 ♡ (which would insist on game). The Stayman Convention solves the problem: You will bid 2 ♡ over a 2 ◇ re-

sponse, 3 ♡ over a 2 ♠ response, and raise a 2 ♡ response to 4 ♡. (9 points in hearts; 11 points if partner bids 2 ♡—you should count as though you are suporting partner's suit: 8 HCP, 3 Distribution Points.)

5. *Bid 3 ♠*. You have 11 points, so game is definite. You will pass next whether partner bids 3 NT or 4 ♠.

6. *Bid 4 ♡*. Game is definite as you have 14 Roth Points in hearts (9 HCP, 2 Distribution Points—hearts must be at least an 8-card fit and 3 Length Points). Partner must have at least two hearts as he may not open 1 NT with a void or singleton in any suit.

7. *Bid 2 NT*. You have 9 Roth Points and game is possible only if partner has a maximum.

8. *Bid 4 ♠*. You have 11 Roth Points, counting 2 points for the doubleton, so game is definite.

9. *Bid 2 ♠*. You have 9 Roth Points in spades (1 PROMOTED Length Point) so game is possible.

10. *Bid 3 NT*. With 13 Roth Points, game is definite. Do *not* bid only 2 NT (which partner can pass).

Rebids by the 1 NT Opener

The 1 NT opener's job on the second round of bidding is simply to follow orders. As we saw in the previous section, the responder's bid conveys clear instructions about what opener is expected to do. Therefore, whether you are the opening 1 NT bidder or the responder, you must know the meanings of the various bids responder can make, so that you and your partner will be "talking the same language" and your messages will be clearly understood.

If you open 1 NT and partner responds 2 ◊, 2 ♡, 2 ♠, or 3 ♣, you should almost always pass. Responder is telling you that unless you have 18 points and a fit in a major suit game is impossible; and furthermore, that he wishes to "sign off" and play in the suit he has bid. Therefore, follow orders and pass, unless you have that exceptional hand.*

If you open 1 NT and partner raises to 3 NT, you also must pass. Partner is saying that game is definite, slam is impossible, and that notrump will be a fine contract.

If partner raises your 1 NT opening to 2 NT, he is informing you that game is possible. If you have 17 or 18 points, go on to 3 NT; otherwise pass. You would really like to bid 3 NT with 18 points, bid 2½ NT with 17 points, and pass with 16 points, but the rules of the game must be respected. Since a bid of 2½ NT is not allowed, you must make a decision one way or the other with 17 points, and it will be better in the long run to go on to game in this situation.

When partner raises your 1 NT opening to 4 NT, he is asking you if slam is possible. Pass with 16 points; go directly to 6 NT with 17–18 points.

If partner jumps to 3 ♡ or 3 ♠ over your 1 NT opening, he is announcing that game is definite. Therefore, you must not pass. Why didn't partner simply bid 3 NT if game is definite? The answer is that he has five cards in his major suit, and would like to play the game in the major-suit contract if you have three-card or four-card support. Thus, with three or four cards in the suit partner has bid, raise to four; with only a doubleton, bid 3 NT. If partner jumps all the way to 4 ♡ or 4 ♠, you must pass. Partner has at least six cards in the major suit and your side will be in a playable trump suit regardless of your holding. (Remember that you may not open 1 NT with a void or singleton in any suit.)

Finally, if partner bids 2 ♣, (the Stayman Convention), asking you to bid a four-card major suit, your job is to follow orders and bid a four-card major suit if you can. If you have no four-card (or longer) major suit, bid 2 ◊. If partner then returns to 2 NT, raises your major suit to three, or bids a new major suit at the two-level, he is stating that game is possible, and you should act accordingly

---

* Even with the exceptional hand, raise only to three of partner's major suit. Partner may have virtually no points at all and *any* bid by you (when asked to pass) shows a "super-duper" hand.

(continue towards game with 17 or 18 points; pass with 16 or 17 points). You may raise a new major suit shown by partner at the two-level with three-card support, as he must have five cards in the suit for his bid. Remember that partner must have at least one four-card (or longer) major suit for his Stayman bid, so if you have two major suits and partner does not like the first one, he is sure to be happy to hear about the other. Thus, if you hold

♠ KJ87   ♡ AQ65   ◇ AQ3   ♣ 32

and the bidding goes 1 NT--2 ♣--2 ♠--2 NT, bid 3 ♡. With a maximum hand, such as

♠ AQ87   ♡ AQ65   ◇ AQ3   ♣ 32

jump to 4 ♡. Game is definite, as partner must have at least 8 points for his Stayman 2 ♣ bid; so do not bid only 3 ♡ which partner could pass.

Thus, as long as you are fully familiar with the meanings of responder's bids, you will have no trouble whatsoever rebidding after the 1 NT opening bid. Partner is in charge; follow his orders!

Capsule Summary: Rebids by the 1 NT Opener

RESPONDER'S BID	YOUR ACTION
2 ◇, 2 ♡, 2 ♠, 3 ♣ 3 NT, 4 ♡, 4 ♠	Pass. (over 2 ♡ or 2 ♠, raise to 3 with an exceptional hand.)
2 NT	Bid 3 NT with a maximum (17–18 points). Pass with a minimum (16 points).
4 NT	Bid 6 NT with a maximum. Pass with a minimum.
2 ♣ (Stayman Convention)	Bid a four-card major suit.
	Bid 2 ◇ with no four-card or longer major suit.
	Note: You may then pass any *non-jump* notrump or major-suit bid by partner, but *must* bid if he *jumps* to three of a

RESPONDER'S BID	YOUR ACTION
	suit. You should insist on game with a maximum regardless of partner's action.
3 ♡, 3 ♠	Raise to four with three-card or longer support.
	Otherwise bid 3 NT.

— —

QUIZ

In this quiz, you are the opening 1 NT bidder and the bidding proceeds as indicated. Count your Roth Points and decide on your action.

	YOU	PARTNER	YOU HOLD
1.	1 NT ?	2 NT	♠ KQ107 ♡ AQ85 ◇ AK8 ♣ 32
2.	1 NT ?	3 ♠	♠ Q65 ♡ AK107 ◇ QJ83 ♣ A7
3.	1 NT ?	2 ♡	♠ KQ107 ♡ 32 ◇ AKQ7 ♣ K42
4.	1 NT ?	2 ♣	♠ K86 ♡ AQ5 ◇ J64 ♣ AQ104
5.	1 NT ?	4 ♡	♠ AJ76 ♡ 87 ◇ KQ107 ♣ AK6
6.	1 NT ?	3 NT	♠ AKQ ♡ AJ7 ◇ Q1086 ♣ Q86
7.	1 NT 2 ◇ ?	2 ♣ 2 ♡	♠ KJ7 ♡ AQ6 ◇ AK73 ♣ J105
8.	1 NT 2 ♠ ?	2 ♣ 2 NT	♠ KJ65 ♡ Q1064 ◇ AK10 ♣ A8
9.	1 NT 2 ◇ ?	2 ♣ 3 ♡	♠ KQ8 ♡ K7 ◇ AK1065 ♣ J62

	YOU	PARTNER	YOU HOLD
10.	1 NT ?	4 NT	♠ AQ6 ♡ AJ73 ◇ KJ7 ♣ K62
11.	1 NT ?	3 ♡	♠ KJ86 ♡ 75 ◇ AQ10 ♣ AQ72
12.	1 NT ?	2 NT	♠ 865 ♡ AQ8 ◇ KJ7 ♣ KQJ3
13.	1 NT 2 ♡ ?	2 ♣ 2 NT	♠ J54 ♡ 8643 ◇ AKQ ♣ AQ3
14.	1 NT 2 ♠ ?	2 ♣ 3 ♠	♠ K1076 ♡ 85 ◇ AQJ7 ♣ AQJ
15.	1 NT 2 ♠ ?	2 ♣ 3 ♡	♠ AQ65 ♡ 94 ◇ KQ3 ♣ AJ42

SOLUTIONS

1. *Bid 3 NT.* Partner is inviting game and you have the maximum 18 points.

2. *Bid 4 ♠.* Partner has announced that game is definite and asks you to raise to four with three-card or longer spade support, and otherwise bid 3 NT. (17 points, including the standard one point for the doubleton with three-card support.)

3. *Pass.* You should usually pass a response of 2 ♡ or 2 ♠.

4. *Bid 2 ◇.* This bid simply says, "I do not have a four-card (or longer) major suit." (16 points)

5. *Pass.* Partner must have at least six hearts for this bid, and his bid requires you to pass. (17 points)

6. *Pass.* You should always pass a raise to 3 NT. Partner would not bid 3 NT if there is any chance for slam, so there is no reason for you to bid further. (18 points)

7. *Bid 4 ♡.* Game is definite whenever you have a maximum and partner uses the Stayman Convention. His second bid promises

a five-card heart suit, so three-card support is sufficient for the raise. (18 points)

8. *Bid 4 ♡.* If partner uses the Stayman Convention and does not like spades, he must like hearts. With 19 points, counting 2 Distribution Points for the PROMOTED doubleton club with four-card support (for hearts!), game is definite—bid it! This example shows that point count isn't everything—clear thinking helps.

9. *Bid 3 NT.* You may not pass when partner *jumps* in a new suit. You do not like hearts, so bid game in notrump. (16 points)

10. *Bid 6 NT.* You have a maximum 18 points.

11. *Bid 3 NT.* You are under orders to raise to four with three-card or longer support and bid 3 NT otherwise. (16 points)

12. *Pass.* You have only the minimum 16 points.

13. *Pass.* You have only the minimum 16 points.

14. *Bid 4 ♠.* Counting one Distribution Point for the heart doubleton (an 8-card spade fit is assured) you have 18 points. Note that *partner is supporting you,* so you do not PROMOTE the doubleton.

15. *Pass.* Partner did not *jump,* so you are permitted to pass— and should do so with the minimum 16 points. Had partner wanted to force you to bid game, he would have jumped to 3 ♡ directly over the 1 NT opening bid.

Bidding After 2 NT and 3 NT Openings

When partner opens the bidding with 2 NT, showing 22–24 HCP, your choices are relatively few. You first must decide on your chances for game and slam by the usual process of adding your points to partner's minimum and maximum and thereby deciding the possible point range for your side. For example, if you hold 7 Roth Points, the total for your side is 29 to 31 points—game definite, no slam.

If game is impossible (which will admittedly require a pretty poor hand on your part!), *you must pass.* When partner opens the bidding with 2 NT, *any* bid that you make carries the message that game is definite; so if game is hopelessly out of the question, you are forced to pass regardless of your holding.

If game is possible or definite, you should proceed as though it were definite. Partner has opened the bidding at such a high level that it is impossible to untangle these two possibilities, since any bid that you make will lead to a contract at the game level. Therefore, do not worry about this, and just assume that game is there for your side.

With a balanced hand with no four-card or longer major suit and no chance for slam, just raise to 3 NT. The weakest hand with which you are likely to make this bid is a hand such as

♠ K106   ♡ 432   ◇ 9843   ♣ 432

(3 Roth Points); the strongest is

♠ K106   ♡ A43   ◇ J843   ♣ 432

(8 Roth Points). In each case, you can tell that the partnership is likely to have the 26 points needed for game, but cannot have the 33 points required for slam. If slam is possible and you have a balanced hand with no four-card or longer major suit, bid 4 NT; if slam is definite, go directly to 6 NT.

Just as over 1 NT opening bids, you should bid a five-card major suit if game is definite. Thus, with

♠ Q10865   ♡ A43   ◇ 32   ♣ 432

bid 3 ♠ over partner's 2 NT opening, planning to pass if he rebids 3 NT (or raises to 4 ♠). With a six-card major suit and a definite game, bid three (and then four) of the major. However, remember to *pass* if game is impossible, for example if you hold:

♠ 96543   ♡ 543   ◇ 42   ♣ 983

Over partner's 2 NT opening bid, *3 ♣ is the Stayman Convention.* You should use this convention any time game is definite and you have at least one four-card major suit. For example, if you hold

♠ K1063   ♡ A43   ◇ 9873   ♣ 72

bid 3 ♣ over partner's 2 NT opening. You will rebid 3 NT if partner bids 3 ◊ (showing no four-card major suit) or 3 ♡, but will raise a 3 ♠ response to 4 ♠. The convention works much the same as over 1 NT, except that the responses are one level higher *and* your partnership is committed to a game contract.

If partner opens the bidding with 3 NT, showing 25–27 HCP, you are certainly overjoyed to learn of his extremely powerful holding. However, the auction is at so high a level that your choices are quite restricted. If slam is impossible, you should bid a strong five-card or longer major suit, planning to play the hand at four of the major; otherwise pass (unless your hand is very unbalanced). Once again, a raise to 4 NT shows balanced suit distribution and conveys the message that slam is possible, while a 6 NT bid ensures that the partnership holds at least 33 points (and that your hand is balanced). You may wish to use 4 ♣ as the Stayman Convention so as to be able to locate four-card major suits in partner's hand, but you had better not do so unless you have discussed this with your partner beforehand. Not all players agree that 4 ♣ over 3 NT should be used as Stayman, and partner may misread your message. So be sure you are on the same wavelength before trotting out this particular bid!

Here is a short quiz to test your comprehension of bidding over 2 NT and 3 NT openings. In each case, count your Roth Points and decide on your action.

	PARTNER OPENS:	YOU HOLD:
1.	2 NT	♠ 108432 ♡ 432 ◊ 96 ♣ 962
2.	2 NT	♠ K83 ♡ Q76 ◊ K87 ♣ 8642
3.	2 NT	♠ A106 ♡ K85 ◊ Q865 ♣ J63
4.	2 NT	♠ K643 ♡ A842 ◊ 863 ♣ 32
5.	2 NT	♠ 3 ♡ K10965 ◊ A642 ♣ 763
6.	2 NT	♠ K83 ♡ AQ6 ◊ Q8765 ♣ 102
7.	2 NT	♠ K109654 ♡ 763 ◊ 642 ♣ 2
8.	3 NT	♠ 10976 ♡ 763 ◊ 642 ♣ 432
9.	3 NT	♠ A83 ♡ 642 ◊ 109765 ♣ 73
10.	3 NT	♠ K83 ♡ A62 ◊ Q854 ♣ 863

(193)

SOLUTIONS

1. *Pass.* When game is out of the question and partner has opened 2 NT, you must pass. (6 points)

2. *Bid 3 NT.* You have 8 Roth Points. Slam is out of the question, as partner cannot have more than 24 points, making the maximum for your side 32. Yet game is definite—your side must have at least 30 points.

3. *Bid 4 NT.* You have 10 Roth Points, so slam is possible if partner has a maximum.

4. *Bid 3 ♣.* An ideal hand for the Stayman Convention. Game is definite, as your 7 Roth Points plus partner's minimum of 22 add up to 29—more than enough for game. You will raise 3 ♡ to 4 ♡, raise 3 ♠ to 4 ♠, or convert 3 ◊ to 3 NT.

5. *Bid 3 ♡.* Game is definite, so show your five-card major suit. Partner will raise to four with three-card or better support, and otherwise will bid 3 NT (which you will pass). (8 points; 7 points for notrump).

6. *Bid 6 NT.* Even if partner has only 22 points, slam is definite, as your holding of 11 points (the diamonds are not GOOD) ensures that a total of 33 will be present. With a balanced hand, bid the slam in notrump.

7. *Bid 3 ♠.* Game is definite. With a six-card major, bid three and then four in the major. (8 points)

8. *Pass.* You cannot *reduce* the level of bidding and bid (much as you would like to!) Hope for the best. (0 points)

9. *Pass.* Game is definite, and your hand is relatively balanced. There is no reason to bid a minor suit unless under extreme provocation, since game in a minor requires 29 Roth Points. (4 points)

10. *Bid 6 NT.* Your 9 Roth Points plus partner's minimum of 25 ensures that the total of 33 needed for slam is present—in fact, you have one point to spare.

Capsule Summary: Notrump Bidding

1. OPENING NOTRUMP BIDS

BID	MEANING	
1 NT	16–18 points	balanced suit distribution and
2 NT	22–24 points	HCP in at least three suits.
3 NT	25–27 points	

2. RESPONDING TO 1 NT

A. PLAYING IN NOTRUMP

   BID   MEANING

   PASS   Game impossible; any balanced hand or unbalanced hand with no convenient bid to make.

   2 NT   Game possible; balanced hand; no four-card or longer *major* suit.

   3 NT   Game definite; slam impossible; balanced hand; no four-card or longer *major* suit.

   4 NT   Slam possible; balanced hand, no four-card or longer *major* suit.

   6 NT   Slam definite; balanced hand, no four-card or longer *major* suit.

B. GETTING OUT OF NOTRUMP: NON-CONVENTIONAL BIDS

   BID   MEANING

   2 ◊, 2 ♡,

   2 ♠, 3 ♣   Game unlikely; five-card (or longer) suit; opener should usually pass.

   3 NT   Game definite; slam impossible; opener must pass.

   3 ♡, 3 ♠   Game definite; five-card major suit; opener should raise to four with three-card (or longer) support or bid 3 NT otherwise.

C. GETTING OUT OF NOTRUMP: THE STAYMAN CONVENTION

   2 ♣ = Stayman Convention, shows at least 8 HCP and asks partner to bid a four-card major suit

   Opener's Rebids: Bid a four-card (or longer) major; bid 2 ♠ with two four-card majors.

Bid 2 ◇ with no four-card (or longer) major.

Responder's Rebids:

GAME POSSIBLE: Raise a major to three with four-card (or longer) support.

Bid a new five-card major suit at the two-level.

Bid 2 NT.

GAME DEFINITE: Bid the indicated game (four of major or 3 NT).

Jump in a new five-card major suit.

3. RESPONDING TO 2 NT

GAME CHANCES	BID
IMPOSSIBLE	Pass.
POSSIBLE or DEFINITE	Bid a five-card or longer major suit at the three-level (facing).
	Bid 3 ♣ (Stayman Convention) with four-card major suit(s).
(NO SLAM)	Bid 3 NT with balanced suit distribution and no four-card or longer major suit.
DEFINITE, POSSIBLE SLAM	Bid 4 NT with balanced suit distribution and no four-card or longer major suit.
DEFINITE SLAM	Bid 6 NT with balanced suit distribution and no four-card or longer major suit.

4. RESPONDING TO 3 NT

SLAM CHANCES	BID
IMPOSSIBLE	Bid a six-card or longer major suit.
	Pass with relatively balanced hand.
POSSIBLE	Bid 4 NT with balanced suit distribution.
DEFINITE	Bid 6 NT with balanced suit distribution.

FOR HANDS IN THE SLAM RANGE WHICH DO NOT MEET THE ABOVE REQUIREMENTS, SEE CHAPTER 9 ON SLAM BIDDING.

REVIEW QUIZ FOR CHAPTER 7

In each case, count your Roth Points and decide on your action. Part 1 of this quiz deals with bids made by responder; Part 2 will cover rebids made by the opening notrump bidder.

Part 1

	PARTNER	YOU	YOU HOLD
1.	1 NT	?	♠ K86 ♡ AQ3 ◇ KJ107 ♣ 763
2.	1 NT	?	♠ 86 ♡ J742 ◇ AK8 ♣ 10432
3.	1 NT	?	♠ A876 ♡ 43 ◇ Q1063 ♣ 742
4.	1 NT	?	♠ K765 ♡ AJ1083 ◇ 642 ♣ 7
5.	1 NT	?	♠ Q9765 ♡ A42 ◇ 6432 ♣ 7
6.	1 NT	?	♠ K10876 ♡ 73 ◇ A98 ♣ 1062
7.	1 NT	?	♠ Q108 ♡ 432 ◇ AQJ ♣ 7532
8.	1 NT 2 ◇	2 ♣ ?	♠ K853 ♡ A764 ◇ J83 ♣ 32
9.	2 NT	?	♠ 109765 ♡ 843 ◇ 762 ♣ 105
10.	1 NT	?	♠ AQ3 ♡ KJ6 ◇ KQ5 ♣ J762
11.	1 NT	?	♠ 75 ♡ AQ876 ◇ 983 ♣ 643
12.	1 NT 2 ♡	2 ♣ ?	♠ KQ85 ♡ A63 ◇ Q842 ♣ 74
13.	1 NT	?	♠ AQ10654 ♡ K63 ◇ 842 ♣ 2
14.	1 NT	?	♠ AQ7 ♡ KJ6 ◇ AJ74 ♣ Q107
15.	2 NT	?	♠ K8765 ♡ A43 ◇ 9654 ♣ 2
16.	1 NT	?	♠ 8 ♡ KQJ64 ◇ AJ7 ♣ J874
17.	1 NT 2 ♡	2 ♣ ?	♠ 87 ♡ AJ65 ◇ A742 ♣ 763
18.	1 NT	?	♠ Q86 ♡ Q1075 ◇ K76 ♣ 432
19.	1 NT 2 ◇	2 ♣ ?	♠ A765 ♡ KQ1086 ◇ Q83 ♣ 2
20.	1 NT	?	♠ A86 ♡ Q103 ◇ 864 ♣ A1076
21.	2 NT	?	♠ K83 ♡ Q76 ◇ 98765 ♣ 42
22.	1 NT 2 ♠	2 ♣ ?	♠ QJ65 ♡ A32 ◇ 987 ♣ Q62
23.	2 NT	?	♠ K876 ♡ A3 ◇ 109876 ♣ 42
24.	3 NT	?	♠ 8765 ♡ J87 ◇ 986 ♣ K106
25.	3 NT	?	♠ 86 ♡ A8765 ◇ 8763 ♣ 107

Part 2

	YOU	PARTNER	YOU HOLD
26.	1 NT ?	2 ♣	♠ KQ106 ♡ AQ85 ◇ AQ8 ♣ 98
27.	1 NT ?	2 NT	♠ KQJ8 ♡ 98 ◇ AQ106 ♣ AJ10
28.	1 NT ?	2 ♣	♠ K83 ♡ AQ64 ◇ 32 ♣ AKJ7
29.	1 NT ?	4 NT	♠ AQ106 ♡ KJ7 ◇ AQ3 ♣ Q83
30.	1 NT ?	3 ♡	♠ QJ32 ♡ A3 ◇ AQ7 ♣ K643
31.	1 NT 2 ◇ ?	2 ♣ 3 ♠	♠ J85 ♡ 32 ◇ AKJ7 ♣ AK106
32.	1 NT ?	2 NT	♠ QJ5 ♡ QJ2 ◇ AK76 ♣ K63
33.	1 NT 2 ♡ ?	2 ♣ 2 NT	♠ 865 ♡ AQJ7 ◇ K106 ♣ AQ2
34.	1 NT ?	2 ♡	♠ AQ ♡ KQ87 ◇ AJ63 ♣ Q102
35.	1 NT ?	3 ♠	♠ K107 ♡ AJ65 ◇ AQ8 ♣ Q105
36.	1 NT ?	4 NT	♠ K987 ♡ AJ3 ◇ KJ8 ♣ A76
37.	1 NT 2 ♠ ?	2 ♣ 2 NT	♠ K1086 ♡ AQ3 ◇ AJ65 ♣ A8
38.	2 NT 3 ♠ ?	3 ♣ 3 NT	♠ AKJ6 ♡ AQ7 ◇ KQ85 ♣ A8
39.	1 NT 2 ♠ ?	2 ♣ 2 NT	♠ K865 ♡ J765 ◇ AKQ ♣ A7
40.	2 NT ?	3 ♡	♠ AK87 ♡ Q106 ◇ AKQ7 ♣ A3

SOLUTIONS

	POINTS	BID	
1.	13	3 NT	Game is definite, slam impossible, and your hand is balanced with no four-card or longer major suit.
2.	8	2 ♣	If partner bids 2 ♡, you will raise to 3 ♡; otherwise you plan to rebid 2 NT, since game is only possible.
3.	6	Pass	Game is impossible and your hand is balanced. You must have 8 HCP to use the Stayman Convention.
4.	9 (in hearts) 8 (in notrump)	2 ♣	If partner bids a major suit, your hand goes up, so your raise to *four*. If partner bids 2 ◇, denying a four-card major suit, you will rebid 2 ♡ since with 9 points game is only possible. Note how the Roth Point Count keeps you instantly attuned to the game chances for your side!
5.	7 (in spades)	2 ♠	Game is unlikely. "Sign off" in your five-card suit.
6.	8 (in spades) 7 (in notrump)	2 ♣	You are too strong to "sign off" in 2 ♠ since game is possible, but too weak to insist on game by bidding 3 ♠. When you bid 2 ♣ followed by a 2 ♠ rebid (over a 2 ◇ or 2 ♡ response), you convey the "2½ ♠" message—that game in spades is *possible*. If partner responds 2 ♠, raise to 3 ♠.
7.	9	2 NT	Game is possible if partner has 17 or 18 points.*

---

* If partner has 17 points he must use his judgment, but you can't have a bid for every point count.

	POINTS	BID	
8.	8	2 NT	Game is possible if partner has 18 points.
9.	0 (in notrump)	Pass	You must pass a 2 NT opening bid if game is impossible.
10.	16	4 NT	*Slam* is possible if partner holds 17 or 18 points.
11.	7	2 ♡	Game is doubtful, so escape to your good five-card major suit. (*Pass* is also an acceptable solution since the hand is balanced.)
12.	11	3 NT	Game is definite. Do not bid only 2 NT, as partner would pass with a minimum.
13.	14	4 ♠	Game is definite, so bid game in your six-card major suit.
14.	17	6 NT	Slam is definite even if partner has his minimum of 16 points.
15.	8 (in spades)	3 ♠	Game is definite, so show your five-card major suit. You will pass if partner rebids 3 NT (or 4 ♠).
16.	13	3 ♡	Game is definite, so jump in your five-card major suit, and let partner decide whether to play the game in 3 NT or in 4 ♡.
17.	11	4 ♡	Remember to PROMOTE your spade doubleton.
18.	7	Pass	Game is impossible. (*Don't* DEMOTE for no aces—you are not opening the bidding.)
19.	12	3 ♡	Game is definite. Partner does not have a four-card major, but might have three-card heart support. When you jump to tell him he must bid again, he will raise to 4 ♡ with three-card support and bid 3 NT otherwise.

	POINTS	BID	
20.	10	3 NT	Game is definite even if partner has a minimum.
21.	5	3 NT	The total for your side must be at least 26 points.
22.	9	3 ♠	Game is possible if partner has 17 or 18 points.
23.	7	3 ♣	The Stayman Convention. If partner bids 3 ♠, you will raise to 4 ♠; otherwise you will rebid 3 NT.
24.	4	Pass	Slam is out of the question.
25.	4 (in notrump)	Pass	Slam is out of the question; game may or may not be easier to make in your five-card major suit—as you can't tell, pass.

Part 2

26.	17	2 ♠	Show a four-card major.
27.	17	3 NT	You have more than a minimum; accept partner's game try. (Note the two ten-spots, indicating a "good" 17-point hand.)
28.	17	2 ♡	Partner has asked you to show a four-card major suit; follow orders.
29.	18	6 NT	You have a maximum and should go straight to slam.
30.	16	3 NT	You must bid, as partner has announced that game is definite. With only a doubleton heart, bid the no-trump game.
31.	17	4 ♠	Regardless of your point count, you must bid, as partner has jumped the bidding. He has asked you to bid 4 ♠ with three-card support and bid 3 NT otherwise. Since a good trump fit has been found, you count your Distribu-

POINTS	BID	

tion Points (as usual, KEEP with 3-card support).

32. 16 — Pass — You have a minimum holding.

33. 16 — Pass — You have a minimum holding.

34. 20 (in hearts) — 3 ♡ — The exception that "proves the rule." Usually you would pass a response of 2 ♡.

35. 16 — 4 ♠ — Partner has asked you to raise with three-card or longer support (and to bid 3 NT with only a doubleton spade). You may not pass partner's jump.

36. 16 — Pass — You have a minimum holding and should not accept partner's slam try. You would like to go back to 3 NT, but bridge laws are quite explicit in this regard! (But don't worry. Partner has 15-16 points, so 4 NT should be made.)

37. 18 — 3 NT — With a maximum, proceed to game. Partner must have at least 8 points for his Stayman bid.

38. 23 — Pass — Partner was apparently looking for a four-card heart suit; when he did not find it, he now says that the hand should play in game at notrump.

39. 19 (in hearts) — 4 ♡ — Partner must have at least one four-card major suit to use the Stayman Convention. Since you know a good heart trump suit exists, count your Distribution Points; with 19 points, insist on game.

40. 23 — 4 ♡ — Partner's bid promises a five-card suit, so you should raise with three-card or longer support (or return to 3 NT with only a doubleton heart).

CHAPTER
8

Unusual Openings and Responses

Once in a while, you will have a hand that justifies a suit opening bid *above the one-level.* Such hands may conveniently be divided into two main categories: First, strong two-bids, which tell partner that your hand is so strong that he *must* respond regardless of the number of points that he holds; and second, preemptive bids, which are made at the three-level or higher and are primarily designed to make life miserable for the opponents. Since these two categories of bids are quite different in meaning and are made with totally different kinds of hands, we will consider them separately.

Strong Two-Bids*

When fortune favors you with a hand so strong that game is virtually certain even if partner holds no points at all, a special kind

---

* Although strong two-bids are almost an anachronism in expert circles (only about 10% of all experts use them) the *requirements* are still used in modern bidding, in which all "powerhouse" hands are opened *two clubs*. More on this in Part II.

of bid is needed to convey this information to partner. For example, you might hold

♠ AKQJ765   ♡ A83   ◇ A2   ♣ A

and need no help at all from partner to make game. You have the awesome total of 30 Roth Points: 22 HCP, one point for all four aces, three Distribution Points, and four Length Points for your spade suit (double the usual number of Length Points with a SELF-SUFFICIENT suit). Even with a somewhat weaker hand, such as

♠ AKQJ765   ♡ A83   ◇ A2   ♣ 2

special measures are required. Nothing more than a club stopper (perhaps only a lot of small clubs) will guarantee three notrump, yet partner will pass an opening 1 ♠ bid if he has less than the six Roth Points required for a response. He has no way of knowing that your hand is so good—25 Roth Points, in this case—unless you take unusual measures to let him know!

While such hands admittedly do not come along every day, it would obviously be a shame to miss a cold game (or slam) when they do appear on the horizon. The solution is to open with a *strong two-bid;* with each of the above examples, you would open the bidding with 2 ♠. When you make a strong two-bid, *partner is not allowed to pass,* no matter how few his points or how bad his distribution.

If you are going to compel partner to respond, you need quite a strong hand. Players using traditional standard point count must learn various additions and adjustments in order to correctly decide whether a hand qualifies for a strong two-bid. However, using the Roth Point Count, the procedure is straightforward. The value of your hand has been built into the point count by various processes of counting points including, as is often the case with strong two-bids, doubling your Length Points when you hold a SELF-SUFFI-CIENT suit. Simply open with a strong two-bid (bid two of your longest suit, or the higher ranking of equally long suits) any time you hold *25 or more Roth Points and your hand is unsuitable for a notrump opening bid.* All of the following hands would be opened with a strong two-bid:

1. ♠AKQ63 ♡AJ7 ◇KQ106 ♣A: 25 Roth Points; distribution unbalanced so you may not open in notrump. Open 2 ♠.

2. ♠7 ♡AKJ10643 ◇AKJ ♣A6: 27 Roth Points; unbalanced distribution prohibits a notrump bid. Open 2 ♡.

3. ♠AK7 ♡AKQ ◇AKQ85 ♣K9: 28 Roth Points; distribution is balanced but you are too strong to open 3 NT. Open 2 ◇.

4. ♠AKJ1093 ♡AKQ842 ◇7 ♣---: You have 26 Roth Points (17 HCP, 5 Distribution Points, and 4 Length Points, doubling *all* Length Points with a SELF-SUFFICIENT suit. Open 2 ♠ (the higher-ranking suit with equal length).

Remember to open in notrump when you meet the requirements for the bid. Thus, with

♠AK7 ♡KQ6 ◇AKQ65 ♣A3

open 3 NT. You have 25 HCP and balanced suit distribution.

Astute readers may ask at this point, "why not just open with game—4 ♡, 4 ♠, and so on—and be done with it?" The answer is threefold: first, you may not know which game to play. In the third example above, you have no idea whether to play in notrump, diamonds, or possibly even a major suit (partner is still on the team and may have a fine major suit to contribute to the partnership holding). Second, an opening bid at such a high level uses up so much room that it becomes too difficult to investigate *slam* in an intelligent manner. Surely, when you have such a powerful hand, you are interested not only in game but in slam possibilities—why not make the most of a good thing?—and there is no point in getting in your own way by opening the bidding at a very high level and ruining your chances to do some intelligent detective work regarding the likelihood of slam. Third, openings such as 4 ♡ and 4 ♠ have a better use—to be described later in this chapter.

RESPONDING TO STRONG TWO-BIDS

If it happens to be your partner's lucky day and he is the one to open with a strong two-bid, the most important thing to remember is that *you must not pass*. While it may admittedly take some courage to make a bid with some ungodly mess such as

♠ 8643   ♡ 82   ◇ 9743 ♣ 762

you have no choice; partner has insisted that you bid. It is said that friendships (and even marriages!) have broken up as a result of the failure to respond to a strong two-bid. Such stories may be apocryphal, but it is clearly disturbing, to say the least, for a player to sit with game in his own hand and hear his partner pass his two-bid! So remember that you must respond any time partner opens the bidding with a strong two-bid, and thereby maintain civility in your partnership.

As to what to respond, your action is relatively straightforward. Bid 2 NT with 7 Roth Points or less regardless of your distribution, and make any other response (usually a bid in a good new suit of your own) with 8 Roth Points or more. Thus, if partner opens 2 ♠, respond 2 NT with

♠ 863   ♡ J742 ◇ J63 ♣ 842 (2 Roth Points) or

♠ 3   ♡ 98765 ◇ 87432 ♣ 62 (0 Roth Points); but bid 3 ♡ with

♠ 87   ♡ KQ865 ◇ K63 ♣ 852 (8 Roth Points); bid 3 ◇ with

♠ 863   ♡ 42 ◇ AQJ65 ♣ Q83 (10 Roth Points), and raise to 3 ♠ with

♠ Q732   ♡ 6 ◇ A643 ♣ 7432 (9 Roth Points, counting three points for a PROMOTED singleton with four cards in partner's suit). When you have 8 or more Roth Points and can make a "positive response" (that is, a bid other than 2 NT), let logic rather than a complex list of rules be your guide. Raise partner's suit with good support; bid a good new suit of your own that you think partner might like to hear about. When you are able to make a positive response, *slam* is often definite and always at least possible; so discussion of further bids with these hands will be deferred to the chapter on slam bidding, (See Chapter 9.)

If you respond 2 NT and opener rebids his own suit without jump-

ing, you should pass with *no* Distribution Points and 1 Roth Point
or less.* There is no reason to get to game and go down one if
opener holds

♠ AKQJ765   ♡ A   ◇ A83   ♣ 32

and responder is unfortunate enough to hold

♠ 43   ♡ 5432   ◇ 6542   ♣ 862

However, you should bid game at the slightest excuse, as even one
stray queen or the ruffing value provided by a side-suit doubleton
and three-card trump support may be all partner needs to make
game. As a corollary, opener must not rebid his own suit over a 2 NT
response if he holds a definite game in his own hand. Thus, with

♠ AKQJ765   ♡ A   ◇ A83   ♣ A2

he should bid 3 NT or 4 ♠ over 2 NT. If opener does anything but
rebid his first suit—for example, if he bids a new suit—you *must*
continue bidding until *game* is reached. A bid in a new suit after an
opening strong two-bid also conveys the message that game is
definite no matter how terrible your hand is, so you must cooperate
by continuing to bid until game is reached.

Preemptive Bidding

An opening suit bid at the three-level or higher is called a "preemptive" bid. It has two main purposes: to irritate and annoy the
opponents by preventing them from using the usual bidding machinery (such as opening the bidding at the one-level), and to inform partner that your hand is suitable only for play in your own
suit and that your hand is sufficiently weak so that your main purpose in life (for this hand, at least) is to get on the enemy's nerves.

When preemptive opening bids are made on hands that are too
weak, the opponents have a most effective rebuttal. One of them
says "double," the other one says "pass," and the one keeping score

---

* Originally, strong two-bids were *forcing to game*. Nowadays, however, most
players using this method allow the bidding to die if opener can do no more
than rebid his original suit and responder is completely "broke."

writes down a large number above the line on his side of the score sheet when the hand is over. When this happens, it is partner rather than the opponents who becomes irritated and annoyed. To prevent this unfortunate occurrence, it is best to follow these rules:

1. Always have at least a *reliable* seven-card suit.

2. When vulnerable, be within two tricks of your bid. For example, to open 3 ♠, you must have a seven-trick hand.

3. When not vulnerable, be within three tricks of your bid. Thus, to open 3 ♠, you need a six-trick hand; to open 4 ♠, a seven-trick hand.

Finally, an opening preemptive bid shows *at most 9 HCP*. With more, you will usually satisfy the requirements for an opening *one-*bid.

The following examples will help clarify these rules:

1.   ♠ KQ1096542   ♡ 83   ◊ 964   ♣ ---: You should open 3 ♠ vulnerable and 4 ♠ not vulnerable. You must lose a spade trick to the trump ace (assume that the opponents hold any missing high trump honors for purposes of evaluating your hand), so you have seven spade winners. Thus, you will be within two tricks of your contract if you open 3 ♠ if vulnerable, and within three tricks of your contract if you open 4 ♠ not vulnerable. What about that missing jack of spades? The modern style is to *evaluate aggressively*, so assume that the jack of spades will drop under your high honors.

2.   ♠ 8   ♡ AQ109654   ◊ 863   ♣ 42: You should assume that you will lose a trump trick to the king of hearts, but evaluate aggressively and do not worry about the heart jack. Thus, your hand is worth six tricks, and you should open 3 ♡ if not vulnerable. If you are vulnerable, you should *pass*. To be within two tricks of your contract, you would have to open 2 ♡, but that is a strong bid showing 25 or more Roth Points!

3.   ♠ Q876543   ♡ K65   ◊ 8   ♣ 32: Pass, regardless of vulnerability. Do not preempt with such a poor suit; you may have anywhere from three to five trump losers depending on how badly the spades are situated, and you have nowhere near the six-trick hand needed to preempt 3 ♠.

4. ♠AK107654 ♡K63 ◇85 ♣2: Open 1 ♠. You may not preempt with more than 9 HCP. You satisfy all the requirements for an opening one-bid: You have 10 HCP and 15 Roth Points (counting two Length Points for the seven-card major suit).

5. ♠8 ♡62 ◇KQJ87654 ♣32: This hand is worth seven tricks, so you should open 3 ◇ if vulnerable and 4 ◇ if not vulnerable. The highest preempts you should ever make are 5 ◇, 5 ♣, 4 ♠, and 4 ♡—that is, game. Thus, with

♠8 ♡6 ◇AKQ987654 ♣32

open 5 ◇ vulnerable or not vulnerable.

RESPONDING TO PREEMPTIVE BIDS

The most important rule for responding to preemptive bids is that you must resist the temptation to trot out a suit of your own. Partner is showing a good long suit, and it is usually best to play the hand in his suit, even if you have poor support. Thus, if partner opens 3 ◇, *pass* with a hand such as

♠AQ7 ♡KQ1065 ◇4 ♣KJ42

In general, you should not bid without *certain* side tricks (i.e., aces) *unless you have a fit with partner's suit*. Why not bid notrump? If partner has his most likely hand—such as

♠65 ♡432 ◇KQJ8652 ♣3

you have no way to reach dummy and will be unable to take any diamond tricks at all in a notrump contract!

With a fit, you should simply add your *tricks* to partner's known total and take the appropriate action. If for example you hold

♠865 ♡AJ3 ◇A1064 ♣A63

and partner opens 3 ♡, you should pass if your side is not vulnerable. Partner has only six tricks, and your three aces will raise the total to nine—one short of game. However, if your side is vulnerable, you should raise to 4 ♡. Partner must have a seven-trick hand to make a vulnerable three-level preempt, and your additional three tricks should produce the ten tricks needed for game.

If partner opens with 3 ♣ or 3 ◊ *and* you have a good fit for partner's suit, you may bid 3 NT if you have stoppers in all unbid suits and can count nine tricks (assuming that partner has a seven-card suit). For example, over partner's 3 ◊ opening, bid 3 NT with

♠ AJ8 ♡ QJ62 ◊ A83 ♣ AQ5

You may reasonably expect to take seven diamond tricks and two aces (partner is most likely to have the king, and probably the king and queen, of diamonds), and your stoppers in all unbid suits ensure that you can prevent the opponents from running enough tricks to set you in a side suit before you can obtain the lead.

With a weak hand *and* a good fit with partner, you should keep the ball rolling by increasing the level of bidding *if* you are not vulnerable. Thus, with

♠ 6 ♡ K854 ◊ 98765 ♣ 643

raise partner's 3 ♡ preempt to 4 ♡ and raise a 3 ◊ preempt to 5 ◊ You do not expect to make either contract, but can afford to continue to plague the opponents with such a good fit with partner. You know it is to your advantage to do so, since partner has at most 9 HCP (and probably less), so the opponents must be able to make something if given the opportunity. However, be sure you are not vulnerable! The penalties for going down doubled *when you are vulnerable* are too severe to risk such tactics. With the same hand, you should pass a spade or club preempt, as you do *not* have a good fit with partner.

REBIDDING BY THE PREEMPTIVE BIDDER

The rules for rebidding by the preemptive bidder can be expressed in one word: don't! While there are few if any "always" or "never" rules in bridge, it is safe to say that you should *almost always* pass after having opened the bidding with a preemptive bid. You have told your whole story with your opening preempt, and partner is fully capable of deciding what action to take. Don't get in his way by trying to tell the same story twice! The following sad tale happens all too often when players violate this rule:

SOUTH (you)	WEST	NORTH	EAST
3 ♡	Pass	4 ♡	4 ♠
5 ♡ (?)	Double		

North was "loaded" in spades and fully prepared to make a punishing penalty double; East was under great pressure as a result of your preemptive tactics and guessed wrong. When you bid again, you let the opponents escape—and also expose yourself to danger, as you have no reason to believe you can make 5 ♡. It would have been better to pass and leave matters in the hands of partner, who knows just what you have—he heard you open 3 ♡! If he passes and allows the opponents to play 4 ♠, you can be quite sure that that is the best outcome for your side.

So, don't "mastermind" just because you have a long suit—you told partner that when you opened with a preempt. Pass and leave the decision to partner.

Capsule Summary: Unusual Openings and Responses

1. STRONG TWO-BIDS

OPENING REQUIREMENTS:	25 or more Roth points; hand unsuitable for an opening no-trump bid.
RESPONSES:	
0–7 Roth Points:	Bid 2 NT. (You must not pass!) If partner rebids his suit, you may pass with no distribution points and 1 Roth Point or less; otherwise continue to game. If partner rebids anything else, you *must* continue to bid until game is reached.

8 or more Roth Points:	Raise partner's suit with good support.
	Bid a good new suit of your own.
2. PREEMPTIVE BIDS:	SHOW NO MORE THAN 9 HCP AND AT LEAST A *RELIABLE* SEVEN-CARD SUIT
OPENING:	SHOWS:
Three-bid	Six tricks not vulnerable; seven tricks vulnerable.
Four-bid	Seven tricks not vulnerable; eight tricks vulnerable.
5 ♣, 5 ◇	Eight tricks not vulnerable, nine tricks vulnerable.

RESPONSES:

WITHOUT A FIT, you should usually pass.

WITH A FIT, count the tricks for your side and take the appropriate action (usually a raise of partner's suit; occasionally 3 NT over a 3 ♣ or 3 ◇ preempt with nine tricks—assuming a seven-card suit in partner's hand—and stoppers in all unbid suits)

OPENER'S REBIDS: *Pass!*

_____

REVIEW QUIZ FOR CHAPTER 8

In each case, decide on your action. Remember to count *tricks* when preemptive situations are involved.

Part 1: You are Opener

	YOU	PART-NER	YOU HOLD	VULNER-ABILITY
1.	?		♠ --- ♡ AKQJ876 ◇ AKJ ♣ 432	None
2.	?		♠ KQJ10765 ♡ 863 ◇ 432 ♣ ---	None
3.	?		♠ AKQ65 ♡ AKQ4 ◇ A1062 ♣ ---	None

	YOU	PART-NER	YOU HOLD	VULNER-ABILITY
4.	?		♠3 ♡J9876543 ◇864 ♣2	None
5.	?		♠6 ♡32 ◇KQJ10743 ♣543	You
6.	?		♠8 ♡943 ◇--- ♣KQ10765432	You
7.	?		♠3 ♡KQJ9763 ◇A104 ♣72	You
8.	?		♠AKJ7 ♡AKQ ◇KQ106 ♣A6	None
9.	?		♠AKJ107643 ♡32 ◇84 ♣7	You
10.	?		♠3 ♡KQ1096543 ◇3 ♣643	You
11.	2♠ ?	2 NT	♠AKQ10654 ♡A63 ◇AK ♣2	You
12.	2♡ ?	2 NT	♠3 ♡AKQJ1065 ◇A83 ♣A2	You
13.	3◇ ?	3 NT	♠6 ♡--- ◇KQJ97643 ♣7642	You

Part 2: You are Responder

	YOU	PART-NER	YOU HOLD	VULNER-ABILITY
14.	2♠	?	♠3 ♡8763 ◇9642 ♣10872	You
15.	2♣	?	♠K8652 ♡62 ◇Q83 ♣J62	None
16.	2♠	?	♠863 ♡AQ1065 ◇864 ♣K2	You
17.	2♠	?	♠J865 ♡743 ◇AQ102 ♣32	You
18.	2♡	?	♠AKJ32 ♡2 ◇65432 ♣32	None
19.	3♠	?	♠6 ♡AQ1065 ◇KJ2 ♣Q1062	None
20.	3♠	?	♠983 ♡A1065 ◇A763 ♣A2	You
21.	3◇	?	♠KJ7 ♡KJ65 ◇3 ♣AJ532	You
22.	4♡	?	♠A1065 ♡432 ◇A73 ♣A42	You
23.	4◇	?	♠AK7 ♡A1063 ◇8742 ♣A3	None
24.	3♣	?	♠A87 ♡AJ6 ◇KJ65 ♣A107	You
25.	3♡	?	♠A106 ♡432 ◇AJ65 ♣A73	None

SOLUTIONS

1. *Open* 2 ♡. You have 25 Roth Points (18 HCP, 3 Distribution Points, and 4 Length Points after doubling the points for your SELF-SUFFICIENT suit).

2. *Open 3 ♠*. You have six tricks and will therefore be within three tricks of your non-vulnerable bid.

3. *Open 2 ♠*. You have 25 Roth Points (22 HCP and 3 Distribution Points).

4. *Pass*. Your suit is very poor and you have far too few tricks to preempt.

5. *Pass*. Vulnerable, you must be within two tricks of your bid; but 2 ◇ would be a strong two bid. With six tricks, you must therefore pass. Not vulnerable, you would open 3 ◇.

6. *Open 4 ♣*. Count your hand as worth eight tricks. When vulnerable, you must be within two tricks of your bid.

7. *Open 1 ♡*. You have 10 HCP and 15 Roth Points.

8. *Open 3 NT*. Do not use a strong two-bid when you meet the requirements for a notrump opening.

9. *Open 4 ♠*. Evaluating aggressively, this hand is worth eight tricks.

10. *Open 3 ♡*. Evaluating aggressively, this hand is worth seven tricks.

11. *Bid 4 ♠*. You have ten tricks in your own hand (barring a very unlikely distribution in spades). Partner could pass a 3 ♠ bid.

12. *Bid 3 ♡*. If partner is forced to pass, you will be high enough!

13. *Pass*. This is no problem—you should almost always pass after having opened the bidding with a preempt. Partner must have a diamond fit to bid 3 NT.

14. *Bid 2 NT*. You must bid 2 NT in response to a strong two-bid with 7 Roth Points or less.

15. *Bid 2 NT*. You have less than the 8 Roth Points needed for a positive response.

16. *Bid 3 ♡*. You have 10 Roth Points and should make a positive response. A raise to 3 ♠ on the three-card support would not be horribly wrong, but it is better to show the fine values in hearts first.

17. *Bid 3 ♠*. You have 9 Roth Points, counting a PROMOTED Distribution Point in clubs. With such fine support for partner, prefer the raise. Partner will not pass your positive response, as

game and probably slam are definite; so you will have time to show the values in diamonds.

18. *Bid 2 ♠.* You have 8 Roth Points, so show your good spade suit.

19. *Pass.* You have no fit with partner and no reason to believe your side can take ten tricks.

20. *Bid 4 ♠.* Partner must have seven tricks for his vulnerable 3 ♠ bid, and your three should produce the ten needed for game. Also, the ruffing value in clubs may come in handly in an emergency.

21. *Pass.* You have no fit with partner and no reason to bid.

22. *Pass.* Partner promises eight tricks for his vulnerable 4 ♡ bid; your three should ensure game—but there is no slam.

23. *Bid 5 ◇.* Partner has promised seven tricks and you have four. The total of eleven spells game in diamonds.

24. *Bid 3 NT.* You are most likely to take nine tricks.

25. *Pass.* Partner shows six tricks for his non-vulnerable 3 ♡ bid. Your three raises the total to only nine—not enough for game.

CHAPTER
9

Slam Bidding

The bridge scoring table affords highly lucrative bonuses for those fortunate enough to bid and make slam contracts. This is only fair, since bidding a slam entails a certain amount of risk. It may seem at first glance that a slam that is bid but not made costs only a small amount; unless your bidding is grossly in need of repairs, you will usually go down not more than one or two tricks. However, the actual cost is much greater. When a slam goes down, you have almost certainly lost the opportunity to cash in on the *game* that you could have made by stopping short of slam. As games are "gold" to the bridge player in his quest for victory, this is quite a serious loss indeed! Thus, it is necessary to be judicious in your slam investigations, so as not to lose the game that is rightfully yours should slam turn out to be a poor risk.

There are two different sorts of circumstances under which slams should be bid. The first is the holding of sheer *power:* If your side is *known* to hold at least 33 HCP, slam should be bid. For example, if partner opens the bidding with 1 NT, you should go straight to 6 NT with

♠ KJ8   ♡ AQ6   ◇ KQ107   ♣ Q105

Your 17 points plus partner's minimum of 16 ensures that the minimum total of 33 HCP needed for slam is present. Similarly, if you open 1 ♠ on

♠ AK1076   ♡ AQ3   ◇ AK8   ♣ 32

and partner bids 2 NT, showing 13–15 points, you should proceed directly to 6 NT, as your 20 points guarantees that the 33 points required for slam will be present even if partner has only 13 points. *When considering the bidding of a "power" slam, you may rely on point count as an extremely accurate guide.*

The second situation in which slam should be bid is when your side holds *a good trump fit. In this area of bidding—bidding slams in suits—point count bidding is at its worst. Even the Roth Point Count cannot properly evaluate (though it may suggest) suit slams in all cases.* Here, the points need not necessarily all be HCP, as the presence of a trump fit indicates that "ruffability" will be present. Thus, suppose you open 1 ♡ on

♠ A83   ♡ AK1097   ◇ AQ86   ♣ 3

and partner raises to 3 ♡, showing 13 to 15 Roth Points. Your hand is worth 20 Roth Points—17 HCP, two Distribution Points for the singleton club, and one point for a supported five-card major suit —so the minimum total of 33 needed for slam is at hand even if partner has only 13 points. With this hand, you would be justified in proceeding directly to 6 ♡.

Thus, you may not try for slam unless there is a chance to make it on *power*—the chance that 33 HCP are present—or a chance to make it on *ruffability*, which will require 33 points of any kind *and* a trump fit. *Do not rely too heavily on point count in suit-slam bidding.**

---

* This is one of the reasons that traditional slam bidding is so atrocious, and one reason the United States has such a poor record in international competition. Some modern slam methods will be presented in Part II.

Slams on Power

Usually, slams on power will be played in notrump and will follow the rules for notrump bidding described in previous chapters. For example, if partner opens the bidding with 1 NT, you simply raise to 3 NT with a hand such as

♠ AQ6　♡ KJ7　◇ K1062　♣ 763

Your 13 Roth Points plus partner's maximum of 18 will leave you short of the 33 needed for slam, so there is no chance for a power slam. With

♠ AQ6　♡ KJ7　◇ AQ62　♣ 763

you raise to 4 NT. You have 16 points, so slam is possible if partner has 17 or 18. Therefore, you *invite* slam by bidding 4 NT. Finally, with a hand such as

♠ AQ6　♡ AQ7　◇ AJ106　♣ 1063

you go straight to 6 NT, as your 17 points are enough to guarantee that the 33 points needed for slam are safely in your grasp.

Over notrump responses, follow the same procedure. For example, we saw in Chapter Four that holding

♠ KQJ2　♡ AJ103　◇ KQ42　♣ 2

and having opened the bidding with 1 ◇, you should not pass partner's 3 NT response. You have 16 Roth Points, and since partner's bid shows 16–18 points you are in the slam range. Slam is possible if partner has 17 or 18 points, so you should *invite* slam by raising to 4 NT. Had you held a slightly stronger hand, such as

♠ AQJ2　♡ AJ103　◇ KQ42　♣ 2

you could go straight to 6 NT with your 17 Roth Points. Had partner responded 2 NT, showing 13–15 points, you would know that slam was impossible with either of the above two hands and would content yourself with stopping in game. Slam would be possible over a 2 NT response if you hold a strong hand such as

♠ AKJ3　♡ AKJ2　◇ K83　♣ 72

Since you may not open 1 NT with 19 HCP, you open 1 ◇ and partner responds 2 NT. Slam is possible if he holds 14 or 15 points, so raise to 4 NT. With

♠ AKJ ♡ AKJ2 ◇ K83 ♣ Q65

or 21 Roth Points, your side must hold at least 34 points—one more than the minimum needed for slam—so you may quite comfortably go straight to 6 NT.

The logic is quite the same over notrump rebids by opener. Suppose you hold

♠ AJ97 ♡ 53 ◇ KQ86 ♣ AJ4

Partner opens 1 ♡, you respond 1 ♠, and partner rebids 2 NT, showing 19–20 points. Even if partner has only 19 points, your 15 give you enough for slam with one point to spare. Simply bid 6 NT. If you hold

♠ AJ97 ♡ 53 ◇ Q1086 ♣ AQ4

13 Roth Points, slam is possible if partner has his maximum of 20, so you should *invite* slam by raising to 4 NT. With a hand with no slam possibilities, such as

♠ AJ97 ♡ 53 ◇ Q1076 ♣ A86

you would terminate the proceedings by raising to 3 NT.

Slams on Ruffability

When you bid a slam on power, you do not have to worry about the gruesome possibility of the opponents taking the first two tricks. Since your side holds at least 33 HCP, the opponents cannot have two aces unless you are using a deck of cards left behind by the previous evening's pinochle addicts. It is true that when you hold the absolute minimum of 33 HCP, the opponents *might* have an ace and king in the same suit and quickly take them, but such pessimism is most definitely not the route to winning bridge! Most often, the opponents' share of the points will consist largely of scattered queens and jacks that will not make life unduly difficult in your slam contract; and partner will often have more than the minimum points for his bid, making it impossible for the opponents to hold so much as an ace and a king.

When you are considering a slam based on ruffability, however, the possibility that the opponents will take the first two tricks is greatly increased. Not all your points are HCP; some are Distribution Points (very likely including PROMOTED points for a good trump fit) and perhaps some are Length Points. Thus, there are more HCP outstanding for the opponents to have, and it is more likely that the opponents will be able to take the first two tricks and defeat your contract before you can even get started.

Therefore, when you do have a trump fit and 33 points, you still must ask yourself if you are in danger of losing the first two tricks. *If you cannot lose the first two tricks in any one suit* but are afraid that the opponents may have two aces to take, you may use the Blackwood Convention. This convention is used *only* when you have an agreed-on trump suit, a definite 33 points, and you cannot possibly lose *the first two tricks in the same suit*. To put the convention into operation, *bid 4 NT*. Partner responds as follows:

    5 ♣ = 0 or 4 aces
    5 ♢ = 1 ace
    5 ♡ = 2 aces
    5 ♠ = 3 aces

Then, you bid a slam if your side has at least three aces, and "sign off" in five of your suit (or pass if partner's Blackwood response is in your suit) if your side has only two aces.

Here are a few examples of the Blackwood Convention in action:

OPENER	RE-SPONDER				
1. 1 ♡	3 ♡	♠6	♡AQ10976	◇KQ3	♣KQ3
4 NT					

Opener has 21 Roth Points: 16 HCP, two Distribution Points, one Length Point for a six-card major suit, and two PROMOTION points for a supported six-card suit. Since partner must have 13 to 15 points to bid 3 ♡, your hand satisfies the three requirements: you have an agreed-on trump suit (hearts); your side holds at least 33 points; and you cannot possibly lose the first two tricks in any suit (barring a most unlikely ruff by the opponents). If partner bids 5 ♢ (only one ace) you will stop in 5 ♡; if the response is 5 ♡ (two aces), you will bid 6 ♡.

2.   1 ♣   1 ♡   ♠ K76 ♡ KJ1032 ♢ A87 ♣ K4
     3 ♡   4 NT

Responder has 16 Roth Points: 14 HCP, one Distribution Point, and one point for a supported suit of five cards. Since opener's bid shows 17 to 19 points, the total for your side must be 33 points; you have an agreed-on trump suit; and the opponents cannot take the first two tricks in any one suit.

3.   1 ♡   3 ♡   ♠ 6 ♡ AQ10976 ♢ Q83 ♣ AKJ
     ?

Do not use Blackwood. You fail to satisfy a very important requirement: the opponents could take the first two tricks in diamonds.

4.   1 NT   ?   Regardless of your hand, 4 NT is
     1 ♢   2 NT   *never* the Blackwood Convention
     ?   when partner's last bid was in no-
     1 ♣   1 ♡   trump!
     2 NT   ?
5.   1 ♡   2 ♢   ♠ AK8 ♡ AK1065 ♢ 4 ♣ AKJ3
     ?

Do not use Blackwood. You do not have an agreed-on trump suit.

Possibly because of its simplicity, the Blackwood Convention is one of the most overused bids in bridge. Remember *not* to use it unless you satisfy the three requirements: an agreed-on trump fit; at least 33 points; and no possibility of losing the first two tricks in the same suit.

When your side does have 33 points but you are worried about the possibility of losing the first two tricks in a particular suit, your best procedure is to *cue-bid* a new suit which you can take good care of and wait to hear if partner can bid the suit you are worried about. Thus, with the example hand given earlier,

♠6   ♡AQ10976   ◇Q83   ♣AKJ

you open 1 ♡ and partner raises to 3 ♡. Your 20 points plus partner's minimum of 13 spells slam *if* the opponents cannot strike first and take the first two tricks. *Cue-bid 4 ♣.* This shows you have "control" (ace or void) in clubs. If partner now bids 4 ◇, promising to take care of the diamond problem, you can go straight to 6 ♡. If partner bids 4 ♠, you are still unsure of the diamond situation but can clearly convey this information to partner simply by cuebidding 5 ♣, giving partner a second chance to mention that troublesome diamond suit. What if partner passes any of these cuebids? Get a new partner! *It is not permitted to pass a new suit when there is a firmly established and agreed-on trump suit.*

Here is another way of bringing a gap in your hand to partner's attention. Suppose you hold

♠Q83   ♡AQ10976   ◇6   ♣AKJ

and the bidding once again proceeds 1 ♡—3 ♡. You correctly cuebid 4 ♣, and partner bids 4 ◇. If you now *jump to 5 ♡*, that tells partner that everything is under control except the unbid suit— spades—and to go on to slam if he can take care of the spade suit— i.e., has a void, singleton, ace, or king. Similarly, if the bidding proceeds 1 ◇—1 ♡—1 ♠—3 ♠—5 ♠, opener is stating that slam is definite if responder can prevent those troublesome opponents from taking the first two tricks in the unbid suit—clubs.

So, if you are worried about the possibility of losing the first two tricks in a given suit, simply bid everything else. Partner should get the message and go on to slam if he can prevent the opponents from taking the first two tricks in the unbid suit.

When your side has an agreed-on trump fit and may or may not have 33 points, slam is only *possible.* Once again, it is a good idea to cue-bid, but here you must listen for signs of encouragement

(222)

from partner. In the previous examples, you didn't much care whether or not partner liked the idea of slam, because you knew that the 33 needed points were present and it was only a question of not losing the first two tricks. However, if partner raises you from 1 ♡ to 3 ♡ and you have a hand such as

♠873   ♡AQ10976 ◇6 ♣AKJ

you have 18 Roth Points, so slam will be present only if partner has his maximum of 15. Once again, cue-bid 4 ♣, showing your ability to take good care of the club suit and your interest in slam. However, if partner now goes back to 4 ♡, indicating that he is pessimistic about slam chances, you should pass. Even if partner cue-bids 4 ◇, indicating an interest in slam, you should bid only 4 ♡, as you have nothing to add to your original message. Partner knows you must have at least 18 points to be interested in slam at all (otherwise the total of 33 could not possibly be reached, since his maximum is 15), so unless he now bids slam himself you are willing to stop in game. Thus, if you are not sure whether or not you have the 33 required points, cue-bid and cooperate. Remember that each new cue-bid is indicative of still further interest in slam, while a return to your agreed-on trump suit conveys a pessimistic "not interested" message.

Finally, if you have no agreed-on trump suit, you may *not* make a slam try. It is a matter of first things first, and until you locate a suitable trump suit you have no business worrying about slam possibilities!

Capsule Summary: Slam Bidding

1. SLAMS ON POWER

PARTNERSHIP POINTS	YOUR ACTION
33 or more	Slam definite: Bid it (usually in notrump).
Possible 33	Slam possible: Invite it (usually in notrump).
Less than 33	No chance for slam. Play in game; do not make a slam try.

2. SLAMS ON RUFFABILITY

PARTNERSHIP POINTS	SUIT HOLDINGS	YOUR ACTION
33 or more	Agreed-on trump fit No chance of losing the first two tricks in any one suit Possibility of opponents having two aces	Blackwood Convention: Bid 4 NT. Partner's Responses: 5 ♣ = 0 or 4 aces 5 ◊ = 1 ace 5 ♡ = 2 aces 5 ♠ = 3 aces. 4 NT Bidder's Rebid: Bid slam if partnership holds 3 or 4 aces; play in five of agreed-on trump suit with only two aces. DO NOT USE BLACKWOOD UNLESS YOU SATISFY *ALL THREE* REQUIREMENTS
33 or more	Agreed-on trump fit Possibility of losing first two tricks in one suit	Cue-bid other suits. Bid slam if partner cue-bids suit you are worried about; otherwise play in five of your agreed-on trump suit.
Possible 33	Agreed-on trump fit	Cue-bid and cooperate. Do not tell the same story twice; remember each new cue-bid shows additional interest in slam.

WITH NO AGREED-ON TRUMP FIT, YOU MAY NOT MAKE A SLAM TRY.

REVIEW QUIZ FOR CHAPTER 9

In each case, count your Roth Points and decide your action. Once you have learned the few basic rules, such as when and when not to use the Blackwood Convention, let logic and common sense be your guide.

Part 1: You are Opener

	YOU	PARTNER	YOU HOLD
1.	1 ♠ ?	3 ♠	♠ AKJ65 ♡ AKQ4 ◇ 2 ♣ 432
2.	1 ♡ ?	3 ♡	♠ A3 ♡ KQ1076 ◇ A32 ♣ K82
3.	1 ◇ ?	2 NT	♠ KQ8 ♡ KJ3 ◇ AJ72 ♣ 653
4.	1 ♠ ?	3 ♠	♠ KQ10765 ♡ A93 ◇ K2 ♣ K3
5.	1 ♡ ?	3 ♡	♠ 432 ♡ AKQ65 ◇ KQJ2 ♣ A
6.	1 ♠ ?	3 ♠	♠ AJ1065 ♡ AK8 ◇ K3 ♣ A87
7.	1 ♡ ?	3 NT	♠ 86 ♡ KQJ63 ◇ AK3 ♣ KJ10
8.	1 ♣ ?	2 NT	♠ KQ7 ♡ AQ8 ◇ KQ6 ♣ K1085
9.	1 ♡ 4 ♣ 5 ♣ ?	3 ♡ 4 ♠ 5 ♠	♠ 86 ♡ AKQ85 ◇ Q63 ♣ AKQ
10.	1 ♠ 4 ♡ ?	3 ♠ 4 ♠	♠ AK9876 ♡ A83 ◇ 87 ♣ K7

Part 2: You are Responder

	PARTNER	YOU	YOU HOLD
11.	1 ♣	1 ◇	♠87 ♡AK86 ◇KQJ8 ♣Q105
	1 ♡	3 ♡	
	5 ♡	?	
12.	1 ♠	3 ♠	♠K1086 ♡63 ◇AQ87 ♣Q72
	4 ♡	?	
13.	1 ♠	3 ♠	♠QJ103 ♡AK43 ◇K83 ♣32
	4 NT	5 ◇	
	5 ♠	?	
14.	1 ◇	2 NT	♠KQ3 ♡AQ7 ◇653 ♣Q863
	4 NT	?	
15.	1 ♡	3 ♡	♠Q86 ♡KQ106 ◇A874 ♣32
	4 ♣	4 ♡	
	4 ♠	?	
16.	1 ♠	3 ♠	♠AQ96 ♡AK7 ◇8632 ♣74
	4 ♣	4 ♡	
	4 ♠	?	
17.	1 ♠	3 ♠	♠A9865 ♡A987 ◇K83 ♣2
	4 ◇	?	
18.	1 ♣	1 ◇	♠AQ3 ♡873 ◇KQJ32 ♣32
	2 NT	?	
19.	1 ◇	1 ♡	♠86 ♡KQ107 ◇A1064 ♣KJ7
	3 NT	?	
20.	1 ◇	1 ♡	♠3 ♡KQ10965 ◇AJ874 ♣2
	3 ♡	?	

SOLUTIONS

	POINTS	BID	
1.	20	4 ♡	With 17 HCP, two Distribution Points, and one point for a supported five-card suit, your side must total at least 33 points. However, you may not bid slam directly, as the op-

POINTS	BID	

ponents could take the first two tricks in clubs. If partner now cue-bids 5 ♣, you will jump to 6 ♠; if partner returns to 4 ♠, you should now bid 5 ◇ to call his attention to the club suit and urge him to bid slam if he has an ace, king, void, or singleton in clubs.

2.	18	3 ♠	Partner's bid shows 13–15 points, so slam is possible if he holds a maximum or near-maximum.
3.	14	3 NT	There is no chance for slam as partner has 13 to 15 points.
4.	20	4 NT	A good hand for the Blackwood Convention: Your side has an agreed-on trump suit, 33 points, and you are sure that you cannot lose the first two tricks in any side suit. If partner responds 5 ♡ or 5 ♠, bid 6 ♠; otherwise "sign off" at 5 ♠. If partner's response is 5 ♣, you should have a quiet word with him about his bidding after the hand is over!
5.	22	4 ♣	You have a tremendous hand, but must be sure that the opponents cannot take the first two tricks in spades. If partner bids 4 ♡, cue-bid 5 ◇; he will then know to go on to slam if he can take care of the spade suit. If partner cue-bids 4 ♠, you may confidently go to 6 ♡ (or even try for seven).
6.	21	6 ♠	You have an agreed-on trump suit and at least 34 points and cannot possibly be off two aces or the first two tricks in any side suit. Since you need no additional information from partner, bid the slam!
7.	17	6 NT	Partner must have at least 16 points, so slam on power is definite.
8.	19	4 NT	Slam is possible if partner has 14 or 15 points, but not if he has 13. Your 4 NT bid

POINTS	BID

is *not* the Blackwood Convention (since partner's last bid was in notrump) but simply an invitation to bid slam in notrump.

9.   22   Pass   If you trust partner's bidding, you must pass. He has steadfastly refused to cue-bid diamonds, so you must conclude that the opponents can take the first two diamond tricks. Partner's hand:

♠ AKQJ   ♡ J1065   ◇ J843   ♣ 2

10.   19   5 ♣   Partner is unlikely to make the pessimistic response of 4 ♠ if he holds the maximum 15 points, but slam is still possible if he has 14 points. Therefore, make one more try, calling partner's attention to the diamond problem in the process.

Part 2

11.   17   Pass   Partner has asked you to bid a slam if you can take care of the unbid suit, spades. Since you cannot, you must pass; the opponents can take the first two spade tricks.

12.   13   4 ♠   You have an absolute minimum and should indicate a definite lack of interest in slam.

13.   15   Pass   Once again, you must trust partner's bidding. When he "signs off" in 5 ♠ after a Blackwood bid, he is indicating that the opponents hold two aces.

14.   13   Pass   You have the minimum holding for your 2 NT response.

15.   13   5 ◇   You indicated a lack of slam interest by bidding 4 ♡ over partner's 4 ♣ cue-bid, but partner is still interested in slam, so he must have quite a good hand. Show your ability to control diamonds.

	POINTS	BID	
16.	15	5 ♠	You have a maximum and would like partner to go on to slam if he can take care of the unbid diamond suit.
17.	15	6 ♠	After PROMOTING your club singleton with five-card support for partner, you have a maximum, and no worries about losing the first two tricks in any suit. A Blackwood bid would not be so bad, but it is unnecessary; partner should have the diamond ace for his cue-bid. (4 ♡ would also be correct, intending to bid six later.)
18.	12	3 NT	Slam is impossible even if partner has the maximum 20 points.
19.	13	6 NT	Your 13 HCP plus partner's 21 ensure that slam on power is present.
20.	17	4 NT	You have an agreed-on trump suit and a minimum of 34 points, and no worries about losing the first two tricks in any one suit. Slam will be a good bet provided the opponents do not hold two aces, so this is a good hand for the Blackwood Convention.

CHAPTER
10

Defensive Bidding

Up to now, you have had things pretty much your own way. In previous chapters, fortune has blessed your partnership with a wealth of points of all kinds, so that either you or your partner has been able to open the bidding for your side. However, you cannot always expect to be this lucky. It is sad but true that the opponents figure to get their share of the points in the long run, and sometimes they will be the ones to make the opening bid. Therefore, it is most desirable to be familiar with the basic rules of *defensive bidding*— what to do after the opponents have opened.

Since the opening bidder has indicated more than the average quota of points, you must be reasonably cautious, as the opponents are likely to hold more points than your side. However, excess caution is a losing strategy; you must get in there and fight when you have the strength to do so. It may be that the hand really does "belong" to your side even though the opponents opened; and it is also possible that your entering the bidding will interfere with their normal procedures and make it harder for them to reach the correct contract. Thus, while entering the bidding with insufficient firepower is likely to lead to disaster, staying out of the bidding when you actually do have sufficient strength to compete is also undesirable. In this chapter, we will be concerned with three of the most common methods of defensive bidding: the takeout double; the overcall in a suit; and the 1 NT overcall. The correct use of each of these techniques will ensure that you get into the auction when you have sufficient strength, and also that you pass quietly when your hand is so weak that competitive action is highly dangerous.

The Takeout Double

One of the most frequently used methods for striking back after the opponents have opened the bidding is the *takeout double*. This is a double which is *not* an attempt to set the opponents, but instead a request to partner to bid his best suit. A double of an opening suit bid is a takeout double.

In order to make a takeout double at the one-level, your hand must meet the requirements for an opening bid (14 Roth Points and at least 10 HCP), *and* you must have at least three cards in the three unbid suits.* For example, if your right-hand opponent opens 1 ♡, make a takeout double with

    ♠ KJ86 ♡2 ♢ A1074 ♣ A864 or
    ♠ Q1065 ♡3 ♢ AK987 ♣ AJ6 or
    ♠ J987 ♡32 ♢ AKQ6 ♣ K64

Count all Distribution Points, just as you would for purposes of opening the bidding. However, do *not* make a takeout double of 1 ♡ with

    ♠ KJ86 ♡32 ♢ A107 ♣ A864 (only 13 Roth Points) or
    ♠ 65 ♡743 ♢ AKQ2 ♣ AK76 (only two cards in spades, and you must have at least three cards in all unbid suits).

---

* With a very strong hand (19 or more Roth Points) you may make a takeout double without three or more cards in each unbid suit *if you have a "reliable"* (See Chapter 6) *suit of your own.*

If the opponents open the bidding at a higher level, it is still possible to make a takeout double; but since you are forcing your partner to respond at a higher level you must have a better hand. As we will see later, some players use an opening two-bid as a weak preempt, and *not* the usual forcing two-bid showing 25 points. When a two-bid is weak, you should make a takeout double with 15 or more points and at least three cards in all unbid suits. (The opponents are required by the laws of bridge to tell you whether their opening two-bids are weak or strong, so you can plan your strategy in advance.) If the opponents open at the three-level, which is virtually always a weak preempt, you should have at least 16 points and at least three cards in all unbid suits to make a takeout double.

The following examples will help illustrate when and when not to use the takeout double. In general, you should make a takeout double when you have the necessary points and support (at least three cards) for all other suits.

RIGHT-HAND
OPPONENT
OPENS: YOU HOLD:

1. 1 ◇   ♠ Q1086 ♡ K974 ◇ 32 ♣ AKJ

Double. You have 14 Roth Points and support for all unbid suits.

2. 1 ♠   ♠ 3 ♡ AK76 ◇ AJ105 ♣ 5432

Double. Once again, you have 14 Roth Points and support for all unbid suits.

3. 1 ♣   ♠ AJ876 ♡ KQ102 ◇ A83 ♣ 7

Double. You have 16 Roth Points and support for all unbid suits.

4. 1 ◇   ♠ 32 ♡ KQ107 ◇ 654 ♣ AKQ2

Do not double. You have only two cards in spades, an unbid suit.

5. 1 ♡   ♠ KQ86 ♡ 32 ◇ A975 ♣ J106

Do not double. You have too few points—only 11 Roth Points, and you need 14.

6. 2 ♡ ("weak") ♠ KJ107 ♡ 65 ◇ AKJ7 ♣ Q103

Double. You have the necessary 15 Roth Points and support for all unbid suits.

7. 2 ♡ (strong)   ♠ KJ107   ♡ 65   ◇ AKJ7   ♣ Q103

Pass. It is admittedly puzzling that the opening bidder should have a strong two-bid when your hand is this good, but you must believe his claim. Since he holds almost all of the missing points, it is too dangerous to enter the bidding. Don't make takeout doubles over *strong* two-bids—there is very little to gain since the opponents hold so many points.

8. 3 ♡   ♠ AK76   ♡ 3   ◇ A1064   ♣ K1072

Double. You have just enough points, 16, to double a three-level bid, and you have fine support for all unbid suits.

Capsule Summary: Takeout Doubles

AT ONE-LEVEL:	14 Roth Points (including at least 10 HCP) and at least three cards in each unbid suit (or 19 or more Roth Points and a reliable suit).
AT TWO-LEVEL: (over *weak* two-bids only)	15 Roth Points, 10 HCP, and at least three cards in all unbid suits.
AT THREE-LEVEL:	16 Roth Points, 10 HCP, and at least three cards in all unbid suits.

QUIZ

Here is a short quiz to check your understanding of takeout doubles. In each case, count your Roth Points, and decide whether or not the hand qualifies for a takeout double.

RIGHT-HAND OPPONENT OPENS:	YOU HOLD:
1. 3 ◇	♠ K1086 ♡ K1072 ◇ 72 ♣ AK5
2. 1 ♡	♠ 8643 ♡ 7 ◇ AK109 ♣ AJ72
3. 1 ◇	♠ K1097 ♡ 84 ◇ A63 ♣ AK62

4.	1 ◇		♠ AK76	♡ AK3	◇ 32	♣ K843
5.	1 ♡		♠ K186	♡ 7	◇ A763	♣ Q965
6.	1 ♣		♠ AQ86	♡ AQ86	◇ 863	♣ K2
7.	2 ♠	("weak")	♠ 86	♡ AK109	◇ KQ86	♣ K107
8.	1 ♠		♠ AK8	♡ K7	◇ A109654	♣ 32
9.	1 ♠		♠ AKJ10765	♡ 86	◇ 74	♣ 32

SOLUTIONS

1. *Pass*. Your distribution is fine, but you need 16 Roth Points to make a takeout double at the three-level and have only 14.

2. *Double*. You have 14 Roth Points and support for all unbid suits.

3. *Pass*. You may not make a takeout double with only a doubleton in the unbid heart suit. (15 points)

4. *Double*. You meet all the requirements. (18 points)

5. *Pass*. You have only 11 Roth Points and need 14 to make a takeout double.

6. *Double*. You meet all the requirements. (16 points)

7. *Double*. With 16 Roth Points, you have one to spare for the two-level takeout double and you have support for all unbid suits.

8. *Do not double*. You have no support for the unbid heart and club suits. As we will see later, you are too strong to pass and should make an overcall of 2 ◇. (16 points)

9. *Pass*. You would like to play 1 ♠ doubled, but the double is a request for partner to bid! (13 points)

RESPONDING TO TAKEOUT DOUBLES

If it is your partner who makes the takeout double, remember that you *must* bid no matter how weak your hand. Partner is *not* trying to set the opponents; he promises that he can support any (other) suit that you bid, so a bid will be reasonably safe even with a poor hand. For example, suppose that you hold

♠ 8643   ♡ 743   ◇ 10965   ♣ 32

your left-hand opponent opens the bidding with 1 ♡, partner doubles, and the next player passes. *Bid 1 ♠*. You must bid, and so select your best suit (such as it is). It is true that the diamonds are equally long, but there are two reasons for bidding spades instead: First, *always prefer a four-card major suit to a four-card (or even a five-card) minor suit*. Game in a major is much easier to make than game in a minor, so the bidding of major suits in response to a take-out double is given top priority. Second, with such a weak hand, you certainly don't want to bid at the two-level unless you have to!

Since you may have a zero-point hand for your response to partner's bid, it is especially important to let him know when your hand is actually pretty good, so that he can take appropriate action. To do this, just bid according to the following table:

YOUR HOLDING	YOUR ACTION
0–8 points	Bid new suit without jumping.
9–11 points	*Jump* in a new suit.
12 or more points	Cue-bid* the enemy's suit; then bid your best suit. Partner *must* make another bid over your cue-bid.
7–10 points, *stopper* in opponent's suit, balanced suit distribution with *no* four-card or longer major suit	Respond 1 NT.
11–12 points, *stopper* in opponent's suit, balanced suit distribution with *no* four-card or longer major suit.	Respond 2 NT.

On rare occasions, you will want to try to set the opponents in their one-level contract. However, you must be extremely careful about making such a decision! One-level contracts are quite easy to make, and you will need a very powerful trump holding to be

---

* This cue-bid does *not* show a "control" in the enemy suit, since it is not a slam try.

sure of defeating the contract. Therefore, do not try to set the opponents unless you have at least a five-card trump suit headed by four honors (AKQJ, AKQ10, KQJ10, or, in a pinch, QJ109). Thus, if partner makes a takeout double of a 1 ◇ opening bid, you may pass with

♠ 643   ♡ 7   ◇ AKQ1065   ♣ 843

but *not* with a hand such as

♠ 643   ♡ 7   ◇ AJ9765   ♣ 843

as your diamonds are not good enough. Is the pass a violation of the previously mentioned rule that you must bid in response to partner's takeout double? Not at all! In this unusual situation, the pass is a positive statement to the effect that you wish to try to defeat the opponents, and is made only with a very strong trump suit. In effect, it turns partner's takeout double into a penalty double. Thus, it is in fact a positive procedure, and *is* in agreement with the rule that you *must* take some "positive action" over partner's takeout double—you may *not* pass simply because you don't like your hand or have no good suit to bid.

Here are some examples to show how the above rules work in action. In each case, you are South.

	WEST	NORTH	EAST	SOUTH	YOU (SOUTH) HOLD:
1.	1 ♡	Double	Pass	?	♠ 10986 ♡ 3 ◇ 10865 ♣ 5432

Bid 1 ♠. Prefer the four-card major suit.

2.	1 ♡	Double	Pass	?	♠ AQ106 ♡ 743 ◇ 8432 ♣ K8

Bid 2 ♠. Jump in your best suit with 9–11 Roth Points. (9 points; you cannot count a Distribution Point since no 8-card fit is certain.)

3.	1 ◇	Double	Pass	?	♠ KJ1065 ♡ AQ3 ◇ 863 ♣ 87

Bid 2 ◇. This hand is worth 12 Roth Points: 10 HCP, one Distribution Point (spades must provide an 8-card fit), and one Length Point for the *supported* five-card suit. Did I hear you ask "what support?" Partner's takeout double promises support for *any* new suit that you bid, so you don't have to wait to hear him *raise* spades to know that he can support spades! Partner has, in fact, supported your suit before you bid it. With 12 Roth Points, you are too strong for a simple jump and should cue-bid the opponent's suit. Partner must bid, and you will bid spades on the next round. If partner should happen to bid 2 ♠, you will just raise to 3 ♠, since you have the minimum 12 points for your cue-bid.

4.	1 ♡	Double	Pass	?

♠ K86 ♡ KJ7
◇ 8643 ♣ Q108

Bid 1 NT. You have a stopper in hearts, 9 Roth Points, and balanced suit distribution.

5.	1 ♡	Double	Pass	?

♠ 432 ♡ 98765
◇ 863 ♣ 32

Bid 1 ♠. Occasionally you get a nightmare like this: no suit, no points or stopper to justify a notrump bid, and too poor a trump suit to pass and convert partner's takeout double into a penalty double. In such cases, grit your teeth and bid your best suit, keeping the bidding as low as reasonably possible. (However, be sure to grit your teeth silently. It is unethical to make it obvious to partner that you have a problem and don't like the bid you are making.)

6.	1 ♣	Double	Pass	?

♠ 653 ♡ 72
◇ 1063 ♣ AQ865

Bid 1 NT. Your club suit is too weak to pass and play for a penalty, and you can't bid clubs yourself, as that would be a forcing cue-bid. Don't bid a three-card suit if you can possibly avoid it, even if you have to "lie" by one point and bid 1 NT on only 6 HCP.

7.	2 ♡ (weak)	Double	Pass	?	

♠ KQ87 ♡ 63
◇ 10987 ♣ 653

Bid 2 ♠. As was the case with a one-level takeout double, you simply bid a new suit with 0–8 Roth Points; here you have five points.

    8. 2 ◇ (weak) Double Pass ?   ♠ K83 ♡ AQ96
                                            ◇ 86 ♣ 9842

Bid 3 ♡. Your 9 points are worth a jump even though the takeout double was made at the three-level; you should still jump with 9–11 points and cue-bid with 12 or more. Since partner must have at least 15 Roth Points to make a takeout double at the two-level, your side is likely to have a game, and the jump conveys this message to partner. Remember, you would bid 2 ♡ on a hand as bad as

             ♠ 983   ♡ 9876   ◇ 86   ♣ 9842,

so you can't make the same bid on this hand.

    9. 3 ♠   Double   Pass   ?   ♠ 86 ♡ KJ1086
                                          ◇ A83 ♣ 642

Bid 4 ♡. Though you have 10 Roth Points (counting one point for the five-card suit since you know partner must be able to support it), it would be silly to jump, as 4 ♡ is a game bid. Had the opening bid been 3 ◇, you would then jump to 4 ♡, as a simple bid of 3 ♡ would not put you in game and might be passed by partner.

Capsule Summary: Responding to a Takeout Double

BID	MESSAGE
New suit	0–8 points
Jump in new suit	9–11 points; at least four cards in suit bid
Cue-bid	12 or more points. Doubler *must* bid again; game definite
1 NT	7–10 points; balanced distribution; stopper in opponents' suit
2 NT	11–12 points; balanced distribution; stopper(s) in opponents' suit

Pass	At least five cards headed by four honors in opponents' suit
REMEMBER:	Add 1 point for any five-card or longer suit (it has been "supported")
	Bid a four-card (or longer) major rather than a four- or five-card minor or notrump

----

QUIZ

In each of the problems below, the bidding is shown; count your Roth points and decide on your action. You are South.

	WEST	NORTH	EAST	SOUTH	YOU (SOUTH) HOLD:
1.	1 ♠	Double	Pass	?	♠ 8643 ♡ Q42 ◇ AJ85 ♣ 32
2.	1 ♣	Double	Pass	?	♠ KQJ6 ♡ 83 ◇ K10875 ♣ 42
3.	1 ◇	Double	Pass	?	♠ A1085 ♡ K1085 ◇ Q32 ♣ 86
4.	1 ♡	Double	Pass	?	♠ AK1065 ♡ 8743 ◇ A83 ♣ 2
5.	1 ◇	Double	Pass	?	♠ K86 ♡ 432 ◇ AQ9 ♣ 5432
6.	1 ♣	Double	Pass	?	♠ 874 ♡ 32 ◇ 73 ♣ KQJ1094
7.	1 ♡	Double	Pass	?	♠ KJ3 ♡ AQ74 ◇ J102 ♣ Q103
8.	1 ◇	Double	Pass	?	♠ J86 ♡ 743 ◇ AK954 ♣ 102
9.	1 ♣	Double	Pass	?	♠ 1065 ♡ J43 ◇ 862 ♣ 8765
10.	3 ♡	Double	Pass	?	♠ AQ86 ♡ 8654 ◇ A83 ♣ 32

SOLUTIONS

1. *Bid 2* ◇. You have 7 Roth Points—two short of a jump. You should not bid notrump with no spade stopper.

2. *Bid 2* ♠. Jump with 10 Roth Points (9 HCP, 1 PROMOTED Length Point in diamonds), and prefer a four-card or longer major suit to a four- or five-card minor suit. An eight-card spade fit is not assured. Do not count any Distribution Points.

3. *Bid 2* ♠. Jump with 9 Roth Points; pick the higher-ranking major suit with equal length.

4. *Bid 2* ♡. You have 14 Roth Points (11 HCP, 2 Distribution Points, and one point for the "supported" five-card suit) and are too strong for a simple jump. You will bid spades next time; or, if partner happens to bid 2 ♠ over your cue-bid, raise to 4 ♠. You are stronger than the minimum 12-point cue bid.

5. *Bid 1 NT.* You have 9 Roth Points, diamonds stopped, and balanced suit distribution.

6. *Pass.* You may pass since you have a six-card club suit headed by four honors.

7. *Bid 3 NT.* You have 13 Roth Points, balanced suit distribution, and hearts well stopped. You are too strong to bid only 2 NT.

8. *Bid 1 NT.* Your diamond suit is too weak to pass partner's double and you should not bid a three-card suit except under extreme provocation. With 8 Roth Points, relatively balanced distribution, and diamonds stopped, bid 1 NT.

9. *Bid 1* ◇. A horrible situation! However, you *must* bid. Since you will have to bid a three-card suit in any event, you may as well keep the bidding as low as possible.

10. *Bid 4* ♠. Simply a matter of logic: Partner must have at least 16 points and support for all unbid suits to double a three-level bid; you have 10 points, so game is definite. Since partner must have spade "support," bid the major suit game. With a weaker hand, such as

♠ A875   ♡ 8654   ◇ K83   ♣ 32, you would simply bid 3 ♠,

since you have no reason to believe that game is definite.

REBIDS BY THE TAKEOUT DOUBLER

After partner responds to your takeout double, the *first* thing to do is to determine how many points your partnership holds. Then, you simply pass if game is impossible, invite game if game is possible, and bid game yourself or make a bid that cannot be passed if game is definite.

By following this procedure, you will find it easy to avoid one of the most common errors in bridge: overbidding by the takeout doubler. For example, if you hold ♠K1086 ♡7 ◇A8753 ♣AJ3 and your right-hand opponent opens the bidding with 1 ♡, you have a very fine takeout double—14 Roth Points and support for all unbid suits. Now suppose partner responds 1 ♠. You know that he has from zero to eight points. Since you have four cards in partner's suit, you PROMOTE your singleton; your hand is now worth 15 Roth Points.* Nevertheless, game is still impossible; even with 17 points, partner's maximum of eight will not provide the 26 points needed for game. Therefore, you should *pass*.

When game is impossible, there is no reason to bid further. All you can accomplish is to please the opponents by getting to too high a contract and going down, and your purpose in life is certainly not to make the opponents happy. Since you must be in a playable contract, just pass.

If game is possible, invite it and leave the rest to partner. If you hold

♠K1086 ♡7 ◇A10753 ♣AJ6

make a takeout double of a 1 ♡ opening bid, and partner responds 2 ♠, you should raise to 3 ♠. Your hand is now worth 15 points, so game is possible if partner has his maximum of 11. Similarly, if you hold

♠KJ97 ♡63 ◇AQJ2 ♣AQ6

---

* Actually it is worth somewhat more because your honors are favorably located behind the opening bidder.

and partner responds 1 NT to your takeout double of 1 ♡, raise to 2 NT. You have 17 Roth Points, so game should be bid if partner has 9 or 10 points. You need not worry about a heart stopper, as partner must have one (or more) to bid notrump in response to your takeout double. With

♠ AQ97   ♡ 63   ◊ AQJ2   ♣ AQ6,

game would be definite, and you would jump straight to 3 NT.

Over a suit response, any bid you make is at least invitational to game, since you would pass if game were impossible. Thus, with

♠ KJ97   ♡ 53   ◊ AQJ2   ♣ AQ6

suppose partner responds 1 ♠ to your takeout double of 1 ♡ You have 19 Roth Points, so game should be bid if partner holds 7–8 points but not if he holds 0–6 points. Just raise to 2 ♠. If this seems timid to you, remember that you would not bid at all unless you held at least 18 points, since partner cannot have more than 8 for his 1 ♠ response. You are only one point above minimum for your game try, and there is no reason to get excited. Another way of looking at it is that partner must have a maximum—7 or 8 points— for there to be any chance for game. To *jump* raise to 3 ♠, you would need a hand such as

♠ AQ106   ♡ 7   ◊ AQJ2   ♣ KQJ5;

your 22 Roth Points require only 4 or more from partner to make game.

If partner cue-bids the opponents' suit in response to your takeout double, he is conveying the message that game is definite, so you may not pass until game has been bid. Over the cue-bid, just bid your best suit and await developments; partner will let you know what *his* best suit is on his next turn to bid. Since you both know that game is definite, you and your partner should proceed slowly in your search for the best game contract without worrying that the other will gum up the works by passing short of game.

Capsule Summary: Rebids by the Takeout Doubler

FIRST: DETERMINE YOUR CHANCES FOR GAME.

CHANCES FOR GAME	YOUR ACTION
IMPOSSIBLE	*Pass.*
POSSIBLE	*Invite game,* usually by raising partner's suit or notrump bid.
DEFINITE	Jump to an indicated game
	Make a bid that partner cannot pass: if partner has cue-bid, game is definite, so *no* below-game bid can be passed.

QUIZ

In each case you are South. First count your Roth Points; next decide if game is impossible, possible, or definite; then select your action.

	EAST	SOUTH (you)	WEST	NORTH	YOU HOLD:
1.	1 ◇ Pass	Double ?	Pass	1 ♡	♠ AJ76 ♡ AK76 ◇ 32 ♣ Q85
2.	1 ◇ Pass	Double ?	Pass	1 ♠	♠ K1086 ♡ AQ965 ◇ 3 ♣ AK6
3.	1 ♠ Pass	Double ?	Pass	1 NT	♠ 8 ♡ KQJ6 ◇ AQ105 ♣ AKJ7
4.	1 ◇ Pass Pass	Double 2 ♡ ?	Pass Pass	2 ◇ 2 ♠	♠ K108 ♡ AQJ6 ◇ 32 ♣ K1084
5.	1 ♣ Pass	Double ?	Pass	2 ♠	♠ K86 ♡ 8643 ◇ AKQJ ♣ 42
6.	1 ♡ Pass	Double ?	Pass	2 NT	♠ QJ86 ♡ 3 ◇ AQ3 ♣ KQ1053

＃ (243)

	EAST	SOUTH (you)	WEST	NORTH	YOU HOLD:
7.	1 ♣	Double	Pass	2 ♡	♠ K1086 ♡ AQ105
	Pass	?			♢ A83 ♣ 32
8.	1 ♢	Double	Pass	1 NT	♠ AJ1065 ♡ KQ108
	Pass	?			♢ 3 ♣ Q82
9.	1 ♣	Double	Pass	2 ♡	♠ AJ8 ♡ AJ106
	Pass	?			♢ KQ83 ♣ 62
10.	1 ♠	Double	Pass	2 ♡	♠ 8 ♡ KJ107
	Pass	?			♢ A863 ♣ A862

SOLUTIONS

1. *Pass.* Even after PROMOTING for your doubleton diamond with four cards in partner's suit, your total is only 16 Roth Points; so even if partner has his maximum of 8, you cannot possibly have game.

2. *Bid 2 ♠.* You have 19 Roth Points, so game should be bid if partner has a maximum of 7 or 8 points.

3. *Bid 3 NT.* With 20 points (for notrump), game is definite as partner must have at least 7 points to respond 1 NT to your take-out double.

4. *Bid 3 ♣.* (A 3 ♠ bid is also acceptable.) The important thing is that you must not pass, since partner's previous 2 ♢ cue-bid guarantees that game is definite. It would also be wrong to bid notrump with no stopper in the opponents' suit. Since you have a minimum for your takeout double, there is no reason to jump the bidding.

5. *Pass.* With your 13 points, game is impossible even if partner has his maximum of 11. You may not count the Distribution Point since no eight-card fit is assured.

6. *Bid 3 NT.* Partner's bid shows 11 to 12 points. It is true that if he has only 11, your 14 HCP will leave you one short of game, but there is no way to find this out; and when faced with a decision

such as this, it is far better to take the aggressive action and bid game.

7. *Bid 3 ♡.* You have 15 Roth Points, so game should be bid if partner has his maximum of 11.

8. *Pass.* You hold only 12 Roth Points, so there is no chance for game.

9. *Bid 4 ♡.* After PROMOTING, you have 17 Roth Points, which with partner's minimum of 9 must add up to the magic 26-point total. Note that if partner had responded 2 ♠, you would *not* promote—having only three-card support—and your hand would be worth only 16 Roth Points, and only a raise to 3 ♠. Using the Roth Point Count, the more *trumps*—the more *points!* The value of your hand is built right into the point count, where it belongs!

10. *Pass.* You have 15 Roth Points but partner, who did not jump, cannot have more than 8. Therefore, game is impossible and you should pass.

Overcalling in a Suit

When you hold a hand with a particularly good suit, you can best convey this information to partner by simply overcalling in your suit. However, be sure that your suit is a good one! Having a good suit is even more important than the total number of points that you hold. The opponents have already announced a goodly share of the points by opening the bidding, and if in addition they are fortified with a powerful holding in your suit, the result is likely to be disastrous for your side. Thus, if the opponents open the bidding with 1 ♠, you would be more than happy to overcall 2 ♣ (non-vulnerable) on

♠ 643   ♡ 82   ◇ 76   ♣ AKJ865

(11 Roth Points, counting one Length Point for the good six-card minor), but would be better off passing with

♠ A83   ♡ A2   ◇ 763   ♣ Q5432

(also 11 Roth Points, but a poor club suit).

A second consideration in overcalling is whether you can do so at the one-level or at the two-level. A one-level overcall, such as 1 ♠ over an opposing 1 ♡ opening, does not require as strong a hand as a two-level bid.

These two rules—the need for a good suit plus the need for a stronger hand for a two-level overcall—can be conveniently summarized as follows:

1. AT THE ONE-LEVEL: You need 10 Roth Points plus at least a strong five-card suit to overcall. Bid your longest suit, choosing the higher-ranking in case of ties.

2. AT THE TWO-LEVEL: You need *either:* (1) 11 Roth Points *and* a strong six-card suit; (2) 14 Roth Points *and* a strong five-card or longer suit. Bid your longest suit, choosing the higher-ranking in case of ties.*

Returning to the previous examples, it is therefore permissible to overcall a 1 ♠ opening bid with 2 ♣ on

♠ 643   ♡ 82   ◇ 76   ♣ AKJ865

as you have 11 Roth Points *and* a good six-card suit. However, you would pass with

♠ A83   ♡ A2   ◇ 763   ♣ Q5432

as your suit is not strong.

Do not, however, let rules prevent you from exercising sound bridge judgment. Bridge would not be much of a game if it could conveniently be reduced to a list of "dos" and "don'ts"! In borderline situations, let the quality of your suit decide your action. With a poor suit, tend to pass; with a very good suit, tend to bid. Thus, with

---

* With very strong hands, Standard American methods recommend a *jump* overcall. The requirements for this bid, however, are vague, and it will be omitted for the sake of simplicity. A superior use of the *jump* overcall will be discussed in Part II.

♠ 98765　♡ AQ3　◇ K83　♣ 32

where your right-hand opponent opens 1 ♡, you may overcall if
you wish (you have 10 Roth Points and a five-card suit), but your
suit is poor and you have only the minimum 10 Roth Points needed
to overcall, and we would recommend a pass. On the other hand,
with

♠ AKJ106　♡ 863　◇ 832　♣ 72

you have only 9 Roth Points, but your suit is excellent. Here we
would overcall 1 ♠. What is the purpose of this explanation? We
wish to be sure that you clearly understand that the above rules for
overcalls are *guidelines*, and not moral commandments. With a
borderline hand, it is the *quality of your suit*, and not the presence
or absence of a stray jack to provide one necessary point, that should
guide your decision.

Above all, remember that you must have a *reason* to overcall: to
get to game, to find a sacrifice, or to suggest a lead. An overcall is a
dangerous action—too dangerous to be taken just to hear yourself
speak.

RESPONDING TO OVERCALLS IN A SUIT

The responses to partner's overcall in a suit are quite straightforward. Make a *single raise* just as you would over an opening bid
—with 7 to 10 Roth Points and at least three-card support (partner
must have at least five cards in the suit to overcall, so three-card
support is sufficient). If partner overcalls with *one of a major*, raise
to three with 11–12 Roth Points and at least three-card support. The
jump raise to three shows a hand too strong for just a single raise
and invites game, but the overcaller can and should pass if game is
impossible. With 13 to 15 Roth Points and at least three-card support, raise directly to four of the major.

In general, you should tend not to bid without a good fit for
partner's suit unless you have a very good reason. Thus, if partner
overcalls an opening 1 ♣ bid with 1 ♡, you should pass with

♠ Q8765　♡ 32　◇ K85　♣ 432

Your hand is weak, so your team is not going anywhere; and you have no reason to believe spades will prove a superior trump suit to hearts. (In fact, they will probably be worse. Partner did not make a takeout double, so he is unlikely to have support for spades; and he should have a respectable suit of his own for his overcall.) However, with a very good suit of your own, you should bid it. With

♠ AK10965   ♡3   ◇ 863   ♣Q82,

you would be quite correct to bid 1 ♠ over partner's 1 ♡ overcall.

Thus, be sure to pass when you have no truly good reason for bidding. Good opponents get rich on hands where you have one suit, partner has another, and you "fight" each other by refusing to give in and pass until the contract is at so high a level that the opponents can double and collect a lucrative penalty.

If your hand is very strong, say 14 Roth Points or more, but you have no idea what game to bid, you may cue-bid the opponents' suit. Just as over a takeout double, this promises a strong hand and suggests that game is highly probable or definite, but in this case also conveys the message that you are not sure *which* game to bid. Partner should cooperate by rebidding his suit if it is very strong, bidding notrump with the enemy's suit stopped, or bidding a new suit; you and partner will continue to cooperate until a satisfactory decision concerning game can be reached.

Finally, it is occasionally proper to bid notrump after an over-call by partner. Since an overcall promises less strength than a takeout double, you need a stronger hand. Bid 1 NT with 9–11 HCP and at least one (preferably two) stoppers in the opponent's suit; bid 2 NT with 12–13 HCP and two stoppers in the opponent's suit.

The 1 NT Overcall

The 1 NT overcall is a rigidly limited bid, made only when you meet the requirements for an opening 1 NT bid *and* have two stoppers in the opponent's suit. For example, overcall a 1 ◇ opening with 1 NT on

♠K86   ♡K103   ◇AQ8   ♣KQ72

you have 17 HCP, balanced suit distribution, and two stoppers in diamonds.

The responses to a 1 NT overcall should be made exactly the same as to an opening 1 NT, provided the opponent after the 1 NT overcaller does not get in the way by making a bid. If the opponent passes, the bid of a new suit without jumping is still a request to pass; 2 ♣ is still the Stayman Convention; notrump raises still convey the usual meanings; and a jump to three of a major is still a request to go on to four with three-card or longer support and bid 3 NT otherwise.

Capsule Summary: The Overcall

1. OVERCALLING IN A SUIT

LEVEL OF BIDDING	REQUIREMENTS FOR OVERCALL
ONE-LEVEL	10 or more Roth Points *and* at least a strong five-card suit.
TWO-LEVEL	11 or more Roth Points *and* at least a strong six-card suit.
	14 or more Roth Points *and* a strong five-card or longer suit.
	WITH MINIMUM AND NEAR-MINIMUM HOLDINGS, LET THE QUALITY OF YOUR SUIT GUIDE YOUR DECISION.

RESPONDING TO SUIT OVERCALLS

OVERCALL	BID	REQUIREMENTS
One of a major	Raise to two	7–10 Roth Points and at least three-card support.
	Raise to three	11–12 Roth Points and at least three-card support.
	Raise to four	13–15 Roth Points and at least three-card support.

2 ♡ over 1 ♠	Raise to 3 ♡	6–9 Roth Points and at least three-card support.
	Raise to 4 ♡	10 or more Roth Points and at least three-card support.
Any	1 NT	9–11 HCP; balanced suit distribution; one (preferably two) stoppers in opponents' suit.
	2 NT	12–13 HCP; balanced suit distribution; two stoppers in opponents' suit.
	Cue-bid	Strong hand (14 or more points).

2. THE NOTRUMP OVERCALL

OVERCALL: Same as 1 NT opening, but two stoppers in opponent's bid suit.

RESPONSES: Same as over 1 NT opening (provided opponent after 1 NT overcaller passes).

QUIZ

In each problem, you are South. What call do you make?

	WEST	NORTH	EAST	SOUTH	YOU (SOUTH) HOLD:
1.	---	---	1 ♡	?	♠ K86 ♡ 743 ◇ 32 ♣ AQ865
2.	---	---	1 ◇	?	♠ KQ865 ♡ A43 ◇ 8642 ♣ 2
3.	---	---	1 ♣	?	♠ KJ106 ♡ AQ1065 ◇ K83 ♣ 7
4.	---	---	1 ◇	?	♠ AQ865 ♡ AQ865 ◇ 86 ♣ 2
5.	---	---	1 ♣	?	♠ AK86 ♡ AK3 ◇ K83 ♣ 432

(250)

	WEST	NORTH	EAST	SOUTH	YOU (SOUTH) HOLD:
6.	1 ♠	2 ♡	Pass	?	♠ 863 ♡ 32 ◇ AQ1065 ♣ 432
7.	1 ◇	1 ♠	Pass	?	♠ K1084 ♡ 643 ◇ 32 ♣ AJ87
8.	1 ♣	1 ♡	Pass	?	♠ AJ654 ♡ KQ103 ◇ J83 ♣ 2
9.	1 ◇	1 NT	Pass	?	♠ KQ103 ♡ AJ86 ◇ 62 ♣ 863
10.	1 ♣	1 ♡	Pass	?	♠ 862 ♡ 8 ◇ AKJ1065 ♣ 432

SOLUTIONS

1. *Pass.* To overcall at the two-level, you must have either 14 Roth Points, or 11 Roth Points and a very good suit. You have only 10 points and your suit is motheaten, so you are not even close to an overcall.

2. *Bid 1 ♠.* You have 11 Roth Points and a good five-card suit.

3. *Double.* With 15 points and support for all unbid suits, you have an ideal hand for a takeout double.

4. *Bid 1 ♠.* With equal length, bid the higher-ranking suit. You should not make a takeout double with a singleton in the unbid club suit.

5. *Double.* Do not overcall 1 NT without a club stopper.

6. *Pass.* You have nothing constructive to say. Do not fight with partner by bidding diamonds—the only winners in such battles are the opponents.

7. *Bid 3 ♠.* You have 11 Roth Points and four-card support.

8. *Bid 4 ♡.* You have 14 Roth Points and four-card support.

9. *Bid 2 ♣.* Use the Stayman Convention to try to locate a four-card major suit. If you fail, you can still bid 3 NT next time.

10. *Bid 2* ♢. With such a good suit and such poor support for partner, you are justified in trying to improve the contract.

Capsule Summary: Defensive Bidding

1. THE TAKEOUT DOUBLE

    AT ONE-LEVEL: 14 or more Roth Points, at least 10 HCP, and at least three cards in each unbid suit.

    AT TWO-LEVEL: Same as one-level but need 15 or more Roth Points.

    AT THREE-LEVEL: Same as one-level but need 16 or more Roth Points.

    RESPONSES:

    0–8 points: Bid a new suit.

    9–11 points: *Jump* in new suit.

    13–15 points: *Cue-bid* opponents' suit.

    7–10 points, balanced distribution, stopper in opponents' suit: Bid 1 NT.

    11–12 points, balanced distribution, stopper in opponents' suit: Bid 2 NT.

    Four honors and at least five cards in opponents' suit, no good suit of your own to bid: Pass for penalties.

    REBIDS:

    Game impossible: Pass.

    Game possible: Invite game (raise partner's bid).

    Game definite: Bid indicated game or make bid partner cannot pass (Neither partner may pass below game if responder has cue-bid).

2. OVERCALLS IN A SUIT

    AT ONE-LEVEL: 10 or more Roth Points; at least a good five-card suit.

    AT TWO-LEVEL: 11 or more Roth Points *and* a good six-card suit *or* 14 or more Roth points *and* at least a good five-card suit.

    RESPONSES:

    Single major raise: 6–9 Roth Points; at least three-card support.

Double major raise: 10–12 Roth Points; at least three-card support.

Triple major raise: 13–15 Roth Points; at least three-card

1 NT: 9–11 HCP; Balanced distribution; stopper in opponents' suit.

2 NT: 12–13 HCP; Balanced distribution; stopper in opponents' suit.

Cue-bid: Strong hand (14 or more points).

Other single raise: 6–9 Roth Points; at least three-card support.

3. 1 NT OVERCALL

OVERCALL: Same as 1 NT opening (16–18 HCP; balanced suit distribution) with two stoppers in opponent's suit.

RESPONSES: Same as over 1 NT opening.

_____

REVIEW QUIZ FOR CHAPTER 10

In each of the following problems, you are South. First, count your Roth points; then decide on your action.

	WEST	NORTH	EAST	SOUTH	YOU (SOUTH) HOLD:	POINTS	BID
1.	---	---	1 ◇	?	♠ 8743 ♡ AQ86 ◇ 2 ♣ AQ105	___	___
2.	1 ♣	Double	Pass	?	♠ KJ96 ♡ 3 ◇ 87654 ♣ Q32	___	___
3.	Pass	Pass	1 ◇	?	♠ AQ1065 ♡ K843 ◇ 2 ♣ 863	___	___

(253)

	WEST	NORTH	EAST	SOUTH	YOU (SOUTH) HOLD:	POINTS	BID
4.	1 ◊	Double	Pass	?	♠ 763 ♡ Q842 ◊ 6432 ♣ 97	___	___
5.	---	---	1 ♡	?	♠ AJ76 ♡ 6 ◊ K843 ♣ J976	___	___
6.	1 ◊	1 ♠	Pass	?	♠ Q108 ♡ A9765 ◊ 32 ♣ 853	___	___
7.	---	---	1 ♠	?	♠ 863 ♡ AJ3 ◊ 62 ♣ AJ765	___	___
8.	--- Pass	--- 1 ♠	1 ◊ Pass	Double ?	♠ AK76 ♡ K1085 ◊ 32 ♣ AJ7	___	___
9.	---	---	1 ♡	?	♠ K83 ♡ 643 ◊ A2 ♣ AQ1096	___	___
10.	1 ♡	Double	Pass	?	♠ K83 ♡ AJ92 ◊ 854 ♣ 543	___	___
11.	Pass	Pass	1 ◊	?	♠ Q10865 ♡ AKJ3 ◊ 2 ♣ K85	___	___

	WEST	NORTH	EAST	SOUTH	YOU (SOUTH) HOLD:	POINTS	BID
12.	1 ♣	Double	Pass	?	♠ AK1065 ♡ K83 ◇ 8432 ♣ 2	___	___
13.	---	---	1 ♣	?	♠ AKJ106 ♡ 863 ◇ 942 ♣ 32	___	___
14.	1 ♠	1 ♡	Pass	?	♠ K10865 ♡ 32 ◇ Q106 ♣ 432	___	___
15.	---	---	1 ◇	?	♠ 32 ♡ AKJ6 ◇ 863 ♣ AJ42	___	___
16.	1 ◇	1 ♠	Pass	?	♠ K1086 ♡ AQ7 ◇ 32 ♣ 10954	___	___
17.	1 ♠	Double	Pass	?	♠ 863 ♡ K1087 ◇ AQ64 ♣ 32	___	___
18.	--- Pass	--- 1 ♠	1 ♡ Pass	Double ?	♠ KJ106 ♡ 32 ◇ AKJ7 ♣ AQ5	___	___
19.	---	---	3 ♡	?	♠ AQ76 ♡ 32 ◇ AK107 ♣ K83	___	___

	WEST	NORTH	EAST	SOUTH	YOU (SOUTH) HOLD:	POINTS	BID
20.	---	---	1 ♡	?	♠ J87 ♡ AQ106 ◇ AQ ♣ KJ86	___	___
21.	1 ♣ Pass	Double 2 ♠	Pass Pass	1 ♠ ?	♠ K986 ♡ A107 ◇ 32 ♣ 10543	___	___
22.	1 ♡	Double	Pass	?	♠ J65 ♡ Q9765 ◇ 983 ♣ 32	___	___
23.	1 ◇	1 ♡	Pass	?	♠ Q106 ♡ J7 ◇ AQ96 ♣ J1042	___	___
24.	--- Pass	--- 3 ♠	1 ◇ Pass	1 ♠ ?	♠ AK9765 ♡ 8 ◇ 983 ♣ AJ9	___	___
25.	---	---	1 ♣	?	♠ K103 ♡ AQJ106 ◇ 863 ♣ K2	___	___

SOLUTIONS

	POINTS	BID	
1.	14	Double	You have the required 14 Roth Points and support for all unbid suits.
2.	6	1 ♠	Prefer to respond to the double in the four-card major rather than a four-card or five-card minor.

	POINTS	BID	
3.	11	1 ♠	You do not have the 14 Roth Points required for a takeout double, but do meet the requirements for a one-level overcall in your five-card suit.
4.	2	1 ♡	Though you would like to ask for a new deal, you must respond to partner's takeout double.
5.	11	Pass	You are too weak to make a takeout double, and may not overcall without a five-card (or longer) suit.
6.	7	2 ♠	Raise partner's overcall with 6 to 9 Roth Points and at least three-card support.
7.	11	Pass	To overcall at the two-level, you need either 14 Roth Points and a five-card or longer suit *or* 11 Roth Points and a strong six-card suit. Your club suit is definitely too weak!
8.	17	Pass	Even after PROMOTING your doubleton, game is impossible; partner can have 8 points at most.
9.	14	2 ♣	You have just enough points for the two-level overcall.
10.	8	1 NT	You have balanced suit distribution, 8 HCP, and hearts well stopped—an ideal 1 NT response.
11.	15	Double	Be sure to make a takeout double when you meet the requirements for the bid. Your major suits are both very good and you will be happy whichever one partner bids; but if you were to overcall, you might guess the wrong suit.
12.	13	2 ♣	With 13 Roth Points, counting one point for the "supported" five-card suit, you are too strong merely to jump in spades. Game is definite, so let partner know by cue-bidding. You will bid spades the next time.

	POINTS	BID	

13. 9 1 ♠ — Theoretically, a pass could not be criticized, as you are one point short of the minimum 10 needed to overcall. In practice, however, a very good suit such as your spade suit is worth a bid at the one-level. In close situations, let the quality of your suit decide the issue.

14. 5 Pass — You have a poor hand and nothing constructive to say. There is no reason to believe that spades will be a better trump suit than hearts.

15. 14 Pass — You may not make a takeout double with only a doubleton in the unbid spade suit, and you may not overcall without a five-card or longer suit.

16. 11 3 ♠ — After PROMOTING your doubleton with four cards in partner's suit, you are just worth the double raise, which shows 11–12 points.

17. 9 3 ♡ — With 9–11 points, you must jump in response to partner's takeout double. Since game in a major suit is much easier to make than game in a minor suit, bid your four-card major.

18. 20 2 ♠ — Though you have a fine hand, partner will need a maximum or near-maximum (6 to 8 points) for game to be definite. Partner should bid again after your 2 ♠ bid with 6 or more points, allowing you to reach game.

19. 17 Double — You have the required 16 Roth Points for a double at the three-level and support for all unbid suits.

20. 17 1 NT — Your hand meets the requirements for a 1 NT opening bid and you have two stoppers in the enemy's suit.

	POINTS	BID	
21.	8	4 ♠	Partner has invited game and you have the maximum possible number of points for your 1 ♠ response (with 9 to 11 you would have jumped to 2 ♠). Therefore, accept his invitation and go directly to game. With a somewhat weaker hand, such as

♠ J1086   ♡ A107   ◊ 432   ♣ 1054 (5 Roth Points),

you would raise to 3 ♠ and leave the decision to partner.

22.	3	1 ♠	A gruesome situation. You certainly cannot pass as your hearts are far too weak, and you are far below the 7 points needed to respond 1 NT. Thus, the least of evils is to bid your "longest" suit and hope for the best.
23.	10	1 NT	You have 10 HCP, balanced suit distribution, and diamonds well stopped.
24.	17	4 ♠	Counting one Length Point for the six-card major suit and two PROMOTION points when the suit is supported, your hand is worth 17 Roth Points. Since partner's bid shows 10 to 12 points, game is definite—bid it! With

♠ A109765   ♡ 8   ◊ 983   ♣ A83,

only 13 Roth Points, game would be impossible so you would *pass*.

25.	14	1 ♡	A takeout double would not be very bad, but you have quite a strong preference for the heart suit.

CHAPTER
11

Overcoming Interference

The techniques discussed in the previous chapter enable you to make life difficult for the opponents when it is safe to do so. The opponents would certainly prefer to have the auction all to themselves so that they may investigate game and slam possibilities in a leisurely and undisturbed fashion. However, when your side can safely enter the auction and contest the issue with a takeout double or an overcall, the opponents know they have a fight on their hands. Their normal bidding processes are disrupted by your entry into the auction, and they will have to bid quite well in order to reach an appropriate contract.

Since the job of the opponents is to make *your* life difficult, they will try to disrupt your bidding by chiming in with takeout doubles and overcalls and making thorough nuisances of themselves. Therefore, you must know how to overcome such interference by the opponents—how to reach your best contract in spite of the fact that the opponents are trying to confuse the issue. Also, since you will often encounter opponents who are not familiar with the guidelines described in the previous chapter and who will therefore "step out of line" and enter the auction when they don't really belong there, you will at times find it advantageous to punish the enemy with a penalty double. In this chapter, we will discuss ways and means of overcoming interference by the opponents and keeping the bidding on the straight and narrow path towards the proper contract. The discussion will be divided into two main parts: bidding after an interfering takeout double, and bidding after an interfering overcall.

Bidding Over a Takeout Double

If your partner opens the bidding with one of a suit and the next player makes a takeout double, your very first call will convey important information regarding the number of points that you hold. With 10 or more HCP, you should *redouble*. Thus, *any* other bid—whether it is a pass, a simple bid in a new suit, a notrump bid, or even a jump in a suit—carries the message that you have fewer than 10 HCP, since you did not redouble. For example, if partner opens 1 ♠ and the next player doubles, you should redouble with

♠ 86   ♡ AKJ96   ◊ Q103   ♣ 432 (10 HCP)
♠ QJ106   ♡ AK76   ◊ 8632   ♣ 2

(13 Roth Points, counting three points for the PROMOTED club singleton and 10 HCP), or

♠ AJ6   ♡ AK106   ◊ AQ6   ♣ 432

(18 Roth Points; 18 HCP). In other words, *any* hand with 10 HCP or more calls for a redouble.

When you have fewer than 10 HCP, you still have numerous weapons at your disposal. With a bad hand, just pass. The single raise of partner's suit retains exactly the same meaning as it would without the takeout double: 7 to 10 Roth Points and support for opener's suit. Also, a 1 NT response still shows 6 to 10 Roth Points and it also shows relatively balanced suit distribution; and bids in a new suit at the one-level are made just as they would be without the takeout double. As examples, consider the following illustrations:

(261)

	WEST	NORTH	EAST	SOUTH	YOU (SOUTH) HOLD:
1.	---	1 ♠	Double	?	♠ 987 ♡ Q63 ◊ J83 ♣ J432
2.	---	1 ◊	Double	?	♠ K1086 ♡ 432 ◊ 86 ♣ A432
3.	---	1 ♡	Double	?	♠ Q83 ♡ A763 ◊ 86 ♣ 7654
4.	---	1 ◊	Double	?	♠ KJ6 ♡ Q103 ◊ 864 ♣ K1097

In the first example, you should pass. You would have passed in any case since you have less than the 6 Roth Points needed for a response, and there is no reason to change your mind just because East has made a takeout double. In the second case, you should bid 1 ♠, just as you would have without the double, since your 7 HCP leaves you short of the minimum needed to redouble.* With the third hand, worth 8 Roth Points, raise to 2 ♡, just as you would have without the double; and with the fourth hand, you should make your normal 1 NT response.

Since any bid other than a redouble shows fewer than 10 HCP, several bids that you can make will have new meanings as a result of the enemy's takeout double.

The double raise of partner's suit, for example from 1 ♡ to 3 ♡, cannot show 13 to 15 points over a takeout double (as you must redouble with 10 or more HCP). Therefore, *over a takeout double,* the double raise is *preemptive.* It promises at least five-card (or very good four-card) support and shows a hand with relatively few HCP (roughly 5 or less). For example, if partner opens 1 ♡ and the next player doubles, raise to 3 ♡ on

♠ 8 ♡ QJ1076 ◊ 98 ♣ 65432

(9 Roth Points, counting four for the PROMOTED singleton spade

---

* The traditional method uses a new-suit bid over a double as an "escape." While this technique is still used by a majority, it seems to be on the way out.

with five-card support for partner and two for the PROMOTED doubleton diamond). This bid conveys the message that your hand is weak in HCP and will be worthwhile only for purposes of playing the hand in partner's suit. Since your hand is valuable only in hearts, the preemptive raise to three also has the advantage of interfering with the opponents as much as possible and making it harder for them to determine the proper contract.

The triple major raise, from 1 ♡ to 4 ♡ or 1 ♠ to 4 ♠, also has a preemptive meaning after a takeout double. Once again, you cannot possibly have 10 HCP or you would have redoubled. To raise to four, you should have very good support for partner and roughly 6–8 HCP. Thus, with

♠8   ♡QJ1076   ◇K8   ♣65432

suppose partner opens 1 ♡ and the next player doubles. Your hand is worth 12 Roth Points, but you lack the 10 HCP needed for a redouble. Simply jump to 4 ♡.

Bids of a new suit at the two-level no longer require 11 Roth Points, since if you had 11 Roth Points you would probably be able to redouble. Thus, if partner opens 1 ♠ and the next player doubles, it is quite proper to respond 2 ♣ on

♠86   ♡432   ◇62   ♣AK10965

(8 Roth Points, DEMOTING your Distribution Points with only two cards in partner's suit but counting one Length Point for the good six-card minor suit). However, you must have a powerful suit for this bid. After the same auction, you would bid 1 NT, not 2 ♣, on

♠86   ♡AJ3   ◇632   ♣Q5432

the club suit is quite poor and you have no reason to be proud of it.

Jumps in a new suit also have a new meaning after a takeout double, since if you held 18 points you would of course redouble. Over a takeout double, a jump in a new suit has a special meaning: it is *preemptive,* and tells partner very quickly that your hand is likely to be valueless unless it is played in your suit. For example, if partner opens 1 ♡ and the next player doubles, jump to 2 ♠ on

♠QJ109876   ♡43   ◇2   ♣763

Your hand will be practically worthless unless you can play in a spade contract; and the jump in a new suit over a takeout double conveys this message to partner in one bid. However, do not jump to 2 ♠ on a hand such as

♠ A109876   ♡ K83   ◊ 643   ♣ 2

you have three-card support for partner's heart suit and will be quite content to play the hand in hearts. With 9 Roth Points, just raise to 2 ♡. (It is acceptable to bid *one* spade, intending to bid hearts later.)

Upon hearing the responder's message, the opening bidder is in a good position to evaluate the partnership prospects. If responder redoubles, and the next opponent passes, opener should usually pass. With a minimum of 24 points in the partnership (opener's 14 plus redoubler's 10), there should be no trouble making the re-doubled contract if the opponents decide not to bid. More important, however, is the fact that with so many points, you have a good chance to double the opponents and punish them for their temerity in entering the bidding; unless the opponents have a good trump suit, they are likely to be in trouble. Thus, if either you or your partner has a good holding in the suit the opponents bid—at least four cards *and* a probable two or more tricks, such as KJ95— you should double. It is important to remember that if neither you nor your partner is able to double, *you must not pass!* With a minimum of 24 points, you are close to game; so if you cannot double, just proceed with your investigation of game chances. For example, suppose you hold

♠ AQ1065   ♡ 863   ◊ AK3   ♣ 32

and open 1 ♠. The next player doubles, partner redoubles, and the player on your right passes. You pass, since you expect to have no trouble making one spade redoubled if necessary. Even if partner has inferior spade support, your side has so many points that taking seven tricks should present no trouble; and one spade redoubled *is game,* so there is no point in bidding. Now let us suppose that the opponent on your left bids 2 ♡, which is passed back to you. Your hearts are not nearly good enough to double, so you should just bid

2 ♠, and cooperate with partner from then on. Thus, if partner bids 3 ♠, showing spade support, go on to 4 ♠; if he bids 2 NT, promising balanced distribution and a heart stopper, *pass*. With just 13 HCP, you do not expect to make game if partner has a minimum of 10, 11, or 12 points, and he should not bid only 2 NT if he is stronger. As part of the partnership cooperation, if either partner knows that game is definite he should bid it (or make a bid that cannot be passed, such as a bid in a new suit), just as he would in any other situation. Suppose you hold

♠97   ♡AQ6   ◇A1065   ♣KJ102

and partner opens 1 ♠, next player doubles, and you redouble. This is passed back to the takeout doubler, who escapes to 2 ♡. You should not double with only three cards in hearts, so you pass and await developments, secure in the knowledge that your partner may not pass the hand out since you have redoubled originally. Partner rebids 2 ♠. Since you have 14 HCP, game is definite, and you should jump to 3 NT with your balanced suit distribution and two heart stoppers.

Thus, bidding after a redouble is logical and cooperative. You try to punish the opponents with a double if you can; if you cannot, you simply proceed with your partnership bidding, inviting game if it is only possible and bidding game if it is definite.

If responder does not redouble, opener proceeds as usual. Over a limited response, he determines game chances and bids accordingly. For example, suppose you are first to speak and hold

♠86   ♡AK1075   ◇AQ3   ♣643

You open 1 ♡, the next player makes a takeout double, and partner raises to 2 ♡, showing 7 to 10 Roth Points and at least three-card heart support. Since you have only 15 Roth Points (PROMOTING one point for the supported five-card suit), game is impossible, and you should pass. With

♠86   ♡AQ1075   ◇AQ3   ♣K63

or 17 Roth Points, game is possible if partner has 9 or 10 points, so you should invite game by bidding 3 ♡; and with a still stronger hand, such as

♠ 86　♡ AK1075　◇ AQ3　♣ KQ3

(20 points), game is definite and you would proceed directly to 4 ♡.

If responder makes a different limited response, such as a new suit at the two-level, opener again evaluates game chances and proceeds accordingly. Thus, with

♠ K10976　♡ A83　◇ 32　♣ AQ2

after the auction 1 ♠—Double—2 ♣—Pass, opener should pass. With only 14 Roth Points, game is out of the question, as responder must have fewer than 10 points (otherwise he would have redoubled). Since the contract is a playable one, pass.

Finally, if responder makes an unlimited bid, namely a new suit at the one-level, opener proceeds the same way as over any unlimited response: he makes the most informative possible bid. With

♠ K1086　♡ 32　◇ AQ82　♣ A76

after the auction 1 ◇—Double—1 ♠—Pass, opener raises to 2 ♠, just as he would without the takeout double; after the auction 1 ◇—Double—1 ♡—Pass, opener bids 1 ♠. The usual priorities concerning responding to an unlimited bid still apply; the takeout double has not changed anything in this regard.

Bidding Over an Overcall

When the opponents overcall in a suit, you should make your usual bid if possible. However, there is no need to join the bidding with a skimpy 6- or 7-point hand, since partner will have a second chance to act. The only change is that you may not bid notrump without at least one stopper in the opponents' suit. For example, consider the following hands:

	WEST	NORTH	EAST	SOUTH	YOU (SOUTH) HOLD:	
1.	---	1 ◇	1 ♡	?	♠ K10863　♡ Q4 ◇ A1073　♣ 43	*Bid 1 ♠.*
2.	---	1 ♡	2 ♣	?	♠ K83　♡ AQ106 ◇ K843　♣ 32	*Bid 3 ♡.*

3.	---	1 ♠	2 ◇	?	♠ 83 ♡ A10862	*Pass.*
					◇ Q653 ♣ 32	
4.	---	1 ♡	1 ♠	?	♠ AQ3 ♡ Q106	*Bid 2 ♡.*
					◇ 65432 ♣ 82	
5.	---	1 ◇	1 ♠	?	♠ AJ9 ♡ K83	*Bid 1 NT.*
					◇ 432 ♣ J1043	

In examples 1 and 2, you make exactly the same response as you would have without the overcall. In example 3, however, you would ordinarily have responded 1 NT; you may not bid at the two-level without 11 Roth Points. Since it is illegal to bid 1 NT over a 2 ◇ overcall, the only remaining possibility is a pass. In example 4, you make your normal raise of partner's suit, while in the fifth example, you may make your usual 1 NT response since you have a stopper in the enemy's spade suit.

Thus, if you are fully familiar with the rules for responding, you should have no trouble as a result of an enemy overcall, since your actions are much the same. Sometimes you will be prevented from making your normal bid, as in the third example above, and may have to pass; but in many cases your procedure will be identical to what you would have done without the overcall.

There is one additional weapon in your arsenal to combat the opponents' overcall, and that is the *penalty double*. Brash opponents can at times be punished for their intrusion into the auction by a judicious penalty double. However, it is necessary to be cautious, as the opponents will reap substantial bonuses if they make their doubled contract. Thus, you should not double unless you fulfill *all* of the following conditions:

1. 11 or more Roth Points;

2. No more than two cards in partner's suit;

3. At least four cards in the opponents' suit *and* a likely two (or more) tricks, e.g. Q1092 or better;

4. No good suit of your own to bid.

For example, if partner opens 1 ♡ and the next player overcalls 1 ♠, bid 1 NT with

♠ K1086 ♡ 64 ◇ A1073 ♣ Q32

as you are short of the 11 Roth Points needed for a double. If, however, partner opens 1 ♡ and the next player overcalls 2 ♣, a double would be quite in order with ♠ A83   ♡2   ◊ K10865   ♣KJ92. You have 11 Roth Points, shortness in partner's suit, a fine holding in the opponents' suit, and no powerful suit of your own. The 11 Roth Points and the good trump holding make it likely that you will be able to set the opponents (possibly by a substantial amount), and the shortness in partner's suit and absence of any very fine suit of your own ensure that you are not missing bigger and better contracts of your own (such as a good game or slam).

The double is *not* a unilateral command to opener to pass, and if opener has a clearly indicated rebid he should make it. Holding

♠AQ9765   ♡AQ976   ◊32   ♣---

you open 1 ♠, next player bids 2 ♣, and partner doubles. You should rebid 2 ♡ with this highly distributional hand. However, do *not* bid just to hear the sound of your own voice! With a hand such as

♠AK987   ♡A83   ◊K63   ♣72

pass. You have excellent potential for taking tricks with all your aces and kings, and nothing more to say with your relatively balanced hand. Remember, partner's double says he is *short* in your suit—spades.

Capsule Summary: Overcoming Interference

1. BIDDING AFTER A TAKEOUT DOUBLE

With 10 or more HCP, *redouble*.

Otherwise, the following bids still have the usual meaning:

1. Single raise of partner's suit (6–9 Roth Points plus support).
2. 1 NT response (6–10 Roth Points).
3. Pass (inability to respond—5 Roth Points or less).
4. New suit at the one-level (shows four cards or more, but less than 10 HCP since you did not redouble).

The following bids have *new meanings:*

1. Double raise of partner's suit: Preemptive; very good support; 5 HCP or less.

2. Triple major raise: Preemptive; at least five-card support; 6–8 HCP.

3. New suit at the two-level: Good suit but less than 10 HCP (since you did not redouble).

4. Jump in a new suit: Preemptive; shows bad hand and good suit; less than 10 Roth Points.

Rebids:

1. After a redouble, both partners are committed to bid further if it is not profitable to double the opponents.

2. Over other bids, opener determines game chances and bids accordingly.

2. BIDDING OVER OVERCALLS

1. All responses retain their usual meanings. If you would be forced into a "violation" by the overcall (e.g., bidding at the two-level with less than 11 points, or bidding 1 NT without a stopper in the opponent's suit), pass.

2. You should double with: (1) 11 or more Roth Points; (2) no more than two cards in partner's suit; (3) at least four cards and two tricks in the opponents' suit; (4) No good suit of your own.

REVIEW QUIZ FOR CHAPTER 11

As usual, count your Roth Points and decide on your action. In each case, you are South.

	West	North	East	South	You (South) Hold:		Points	Bid
1.	---	1 ◇	Double	?	♠ K1076 ♡ A83 ◇ 6543 ♣ 32		___	___
2.	---	1 ♡	1 ♠	?	♠ QJ65 ♡ 87 ◇ AJ72 ♣ 1043		___	___
3.	---	1 ◇	Double	R'dbl	♠ K86 ♡ AQ1065			
	2 ♣	Pass	Pass	?	◇ Q83 ♣ 32		___	___

	West	North	East	South	You (South) Hold:	Points	Bid
4.	---	1 ♠	2 ◇	?	♠86 ♡AQ865 ◇863 ♣1074	___	___
5.	---	1 ♡	2 ◇	?	♠K86 ♡Q1065 ◇86 ♣Q764	___	___
6.	---	1 ♠	2 ♣	?	♠AJ76 ♡63 ◇AK43 ♣863	___	___
7.	---	1 ♡	1 ♠	?	♠863 ♡KQ107 ◇A9876 ♣2	___	___
8.	---	1 ♡	Double	?	♠865 ♡72 ◇K8 ♣AJ10765	___	___
9.	---	1 ◇	Double	?	♠986 ♡AJ8 ◇643 ♣K432	___	___
10.	---	1 ♣	Double	?	♠KQ106 ♡A83 ◇A83 ♣432	___	___
11.	---	1 ♠	2 ◇	?	♠KJ7 ♡63 ◇KJ97 ♣A432	___	___
12.	---	1 ◇	2 ♣	?	♠A832 ♡K76 ◇32 ♣KQ106	___	___
13.	---	---	---	1 ♡	♠8 ♡AQ1096 ◇AJ965 ♣32	___	___
	Double	2 ♠	Pass	?			
14.	---	1 ♡	Double	?	♠109876 ♡Q10432 ◇--- ♣1096	___	___
15.	---	---	---	1 ♡	♠86 ♡KQ1096 ◇AKQ7 ♣K2	___	___
	1 ♠	2 ♡	Pass	?			

SOLUTIONS

	POINTS	BID	
1.	9	1 ♠	Show your four-card major suit, just as you would have without the dou-

POINTS	BID

ble. PROMOTE your doubleton with four cards in partner's suit.

2. 8   1 NT

The opponents' 1 ♠ overcall has prevented you from making your normal 1 ♠ response, but you can still bid 1 NT, showing 8–10 Roth Points and a stopper in the opponents' suit.

3. 12   2 ♡

Partner's main reason for passing was to give you a chance to double 2 ♣. You must not pass, since game is definite (unless partner has had to DEMOTE from his original 14 Roth Points needed to open the bidding). Show your good heart suit.

4. 6   Pass

You need 11 Roth Points to bid a new suit at the two-level.

5. 9   2 ♡

Make your normal heart raise.

6. 14   3 ♠

Once again, do not let the overcall deter you from your standard raise.

7. 12   2 ◇

You are too strong to raise to 2 ♡ and too weak to raise to 3 ♡. Temporize by bidding 2 ◇, just as you would have without the overcall.

8. 8   2 ♣

You are not worth a redouble. You should, however, show your good club suit. You may bid at the two-level since any bid over a takeout double other than a redouble shows less than 10 HCP.

9. 8   1 NT

You have an ideal hand for the 1 NT response.

10. 13   Redouble

You must redouble with 10 or more HCP.

11. 13   3 ♠

Do not make a penalty double with good support for partner.

(271)

	POINTS	BID	
12.	12	Double	You meet all four requirements for the penalty double.
13.	11	Pass	Partner is stating that the hand will play well only in spades. You must trust him.
14.	7	3 ♡	A good hand for a preemptive raise: Less than 5 HCP and five-card support for partner.
15.	20	4 ♡	Partner's bid shows 7 to 10 Roth Points, so game is definite. Bid it!

CHAPTER

12

Advanced Bidding Techniques

In any detailed presentation of recommended bidding procedures, it must be recognized that too close an examination of the trees will render the forest invisible. It is desirable and necessary to become fully familiar with various rules of bidding, such as the point-count range for the most common bids and the priorities that make clear which bids are most informative and should be given precedence over other alternatives. However, too much attention to detail runs the risk that the general strategies of bidding, such as the determination of game chances based on the bids made by partner and your point count, will be overlooked.

In the preceding chapters, we have attempted to give equal stress to both the general and specific aspects of bridge bidding, since both are essential for success. For example, knowing that the single raise in a major suit shows 7 to 10 Roth Points is unlikely to be especially helpful if you do not know how to use this information to evaluate your game chances and select the appropriate action; conversely, knowing how to evaluate game chances will not solve your problems if you do not remember how many points partner's bid shows. By now—whether or not you remember specific point ranges—you should have a good understanding of both the general and the specific aspects of partnership bidding, and it is therefore time to turn to a discussion of certain more advanced procedures that will increase the accuracy of your bidding by providing you with additional weapons for your bridge arsenal.

Bidding by a Passed Hand

When you have the chance to open the bidding and fail to do so, you convey the message to partner that you have less than 14 Roth Points; your opening pass *limits* your hand. If your partner then opens the bidding, some of your responses will have new meanings because you are a "passed hand."

The most important thing to keep in mind when you are a passed hand is that partner is permitted to pass any bid that you make. Your original pass has put a damper on the proceedings by placing a limitation on the maximum number of points that partner can expect to find in your hand, and he is fully justified in passing if he sees that game is impossible. Therefore, it is especially important to make the most informative bid possible.

Many bids still have the same meaning as before: a 1 NT response still shows 6 to 10 Roth Points; a single raise of partner's suit still shows 7 to 10 Roth Points and support for the suit (at least three cards if a major suit; at least four cards if a minor suit), and a bid of a new suit at the two-level still requires 11 Roth Points. However, the following bids now have new meanings:

The double major raise does not now show 13 to 15 Roth Points, as with such a good hand you would probably have opened the bidding. This bid is needed to handle the following situation: suppose you hold

♠ A83   ♡ Q1062   ◇ 3   ♣ Q10865

As dealer, you pass, since you have only 10 Roth Points. Partner opens 1 ♡, so you PROMOTE your singleton diamond, making your hand worth 11 Roth Points; you are too strong to raise to 2 ♡ and too weak to raise to 3 ♡, according to the usual rules for responding. If you were not a passed hand, this would be no problem; you would temporize with 2 ♣. Partner would be required to bid again, and you would support hearts the next time, showing the "2½ ♡" raise. However, when you are a passed hand *partner might pass* 2 ♣. You certainly do not want to play in clubs when you have a very fine heart fit; it would be highly embarrassing to play in 2 ♣ only to find that you were cold for 4 ♡! Yet game in hearts is not definite; your 11 points will not be enough for game if partner has less than 15.

Therefore, *as a passed hand*, it is essential to support partner's suit whenever you can do so; and the double major raise is therefore given on 10 to 11 Roth Points. With a stronger hand (12 or more Roth Points) such as

♠ A83   ♡ Q1062   ◇ 3   ♣ K10865

you may raise directly to 4 ♡, as partner must have at least 14 Roth Points, giving the partnership the total of 26 needed for game.

The jump to 2 NT may be made on only 11 to 12 HCP, since partner is permitted to pass. Thus, as a passed hand, bid 2 NT over partner's 1 ♡ opening with

♠ AQ6   ♡ 107   ◇ KJ107   ♣ Q1082

The opening bidder evaluates game prospects and bids as usual, keeping in mind the important fact that responder cannot have 14 or more Roth Points since he did not open the bidding. Thus, while most of opener's actions remain unchanged, he is permitted to pass any response.

The Double Minor-Suit Raise

Responder should not be overly eager to support opener's minor suit, since game in a minor is much more difficult to make than game in a major or in notrump. However, you will occasionally run into a hand that qualifies for a double minor-suit raise: a hand with 13 to 15 Roth Points which is unable to make any of the high priority bids (bidding a new major suit or bidding notrump). The double raise usually shows five-card support for partner's minor, since opener may have only a three-card suit. For example, if partner opens 1 ◇, raise to 3 ◇ on

♠ 32   ♡ A86   ◇ AJ1065   ♣ K83

(14 Roth Points).

After the double minor raise, your partnership should try for game in notrump by bidding suits that it has stopped. If opener now bids 3 ♠, for example, this does not indicate that he wishes to try for a spade contract, but merely shows that he has spades stopped. Responder should therefore rebid 3 NT with the above hand. If instead opener bids 3 ♡, responder should not bid 3 NT (as spades may very well be unstopped) and so should return to 4 ◇.

The Double Raise after a Strong Two-Bid

There is a very convenient bid used by experts to convey a specific message after a strong two-bid. If, for example partner opens 2 ♡, the raise to 4 ♡ shows at least four good trumps and *no* outside ace, king, void, or singleton. Thus, raise to 4 ♡ with

♠ 86   ♡ Q10862   ◇ Q83   ♣ 875

or

♠ 653   ♡ KQ32   ◇ 5432   ♣ 32

The purpose of this bid is to let partner know right away that even though he has a strong hand, you have so little that he should not try for slam unless he can expect to make it with no help outside the trump suit.

Bidding a New Suit as a Game Try

Suppose you hold:

♠86 ♡AK1075 ◇K1083 ♣A2

You open 1 ♡ and partner raises to 2 ♡. You have 17 Roth Points (14 HCP, two Distribution Points, and one point for a supported five-card suit), so game is possible if partner has 9 or 10 points but not if he has only 7 or 8. Thus, a game try is in order. A bid of 3 ♡ would not be bad, as it would convey the proper message to partner (to bid game with a maximum and pass with a minimum). However, why not call attention to *where* you would like partner's high cards to be? A game try of **three diamonds** is certainly more informative. You would like to be in game if partner can help you out in your side suit, for example, with a hand such as

♠975 ♡QJ3 ◇QJ54 ♣K83

but will not be very happy about game prospects if partner's hand is

♠QJ54 ♡QJ3 ◇975 ♣K83

Both hands count 9 Roth Points, so partner is likely to go on to game over a 3 ♡ bid. The 3 ◇ game try, on the other hand, lets him know *where* you will most appreciate his high-card points, and makes it easy for him to go on to 4 ♡ with the first hand but to downrate the second hand with its very poor diamonds (and stop at only 3 ♡).

Additional Slam Conventions

In the chapter on slam bidding, the Blackwood 4 NT Convention was discussed. It is also possible to use this convention to ask for kings, as follows: *after* a Blackwood 4 NT bid has been made and responded to, a 5 NT bid asks for the number of kings held by partner. The responses are:

5 ♣ = 0 or 4 kings
5 ◇ = 1 king
5 ♡ = 3 kings
5 ♠ = 3 kings

In order to use the Blackwood 5 NT bid, you must be sure that your side has all the aces. The 5 NT bid is used primarily to try for grand slams, and you will not be very successful in your attempt to make all the tricks if the opponents have an ace!

The *Gerber Convention* is similar in purpose to the Blackwood Convention, but is designed for use *over notrump openings*. You cannot use Blackwood over a notrump opening, since a bid of 4 NT over an opening of 1 NT or 2 NT is simply a notrump raise, inviting opener to bid slam in notrump with a maximum number of points. The Gerber Convention, therefore, is needed in order to be able to ask for aces and kings after a notrump opening bid. The convention works quite simply: a bid of *4 ♣* asks for aces, and the responses are as follows:

```
4 ◇  = 0 or 4 aces
4 ♡  = 1 ace
4 ♠  = 2 aces
4 NT = 3 aces
```

After hearing the response, the Gerber bidder may ask for kings by bidding 5 ♣. He should do so, however, only if his side holds all the aces, just as in the Blackwood Convention. The responses to the 5 ♣ bid are as follows:

```
5 ◇  = 0 or 4 kings
5 ♡  = 1 king
5 ♠  = 2 kings
5 NT = 3 kings
```

A typical hand which would justify the use of the Gerber Convention is

♠8   ♡KQJ109876   ◇KQ8   ♣3

where partner opens 1 NT. You confidently expect to make a grand slam if partner holds all the aces; a small slam if he holds any three aces; and game if he holds fewer than three aces. If partner bids 4 ♡, showing only one ace, just pass. (You can verify for yourself that partner cannot possibly have *no* aces and still have enough points to open 1 NT when your hand is as above.)

The Forcing Pass

Suppose the bidding proceeds as follows:

NORTH	EAST	SOUTH (you)	WEST
2 ♡	Pass	3 ♡	5 ◇
Pass	Pass	?	

What call do you make?

While this is not an easy problem—especially as you haven't been shown a hand!—one thing is certain: *you cannot pass!* Partner's strong two-bid has guaranteed *game* for your side, and you cannot allow the opponents to steal the hand. Partner has passed for one reason: to give you a chance to make a penalty double of 5 ◇. He is unsure whether the partnership's best course is to double the opponents or bid on. You might have quite a good diamond holding. If your hand is

♠ 643   ♡ A653   ◇ QJ102   ♣ 32

doubling the opponents offers the best chance for a good score.

Any time your side clearly has the balance of power and the opponents are competing, it would be illogical to allow the enemy to steal the hand, and a pass under such circumstances should therefore be considered *forcing*. For example, consider the following auction:

NORTH	EAST	SOUTH (you)	WEST
1 ♠	Pass	3 ♠	4 ♣
4 ♠	5 ♣	*Pass*	

Partner's opening bid promised at least 14 Roth Points; your raise to 3 ♠ shows 13 to 15 Roth Points. Since your side owns the majority of the outstanding points, it cannot be correct to allow the opponents to play quietly in 5 ♣ undoubled. Therefore, your pass is forcing. It states that you do not wish to double 5 ♣, and are uncertain as to whether or not 5 ♠ can be made, and are therefore leaving the decision to partner. A typical hand would be

♠ Q1086   ♡ AK7   ◇ Q1086   ♣ 32;

you have the minimum 13 Roth Points for your double raise and should not double 5 ♣ with such weak clubs. If partner has an above-minimum hand with good offensive possibilities, such as

♠ AKJ97   ♡ 86   ◇ AK3   ♣ 865

(worth 17 Roth Points) he should proceed on to 5 ♠. With a minimum hand and/or good clubs, he should double. Thus, with a hand such as

♠ AKJ97   ♡ 86   ◇ Q83   ♣ QJ2

worth only 15 Roth Points, opener has no reason to expect that 5 ♠ can be made, and should collect the maximum possible score by doubling the 5 ♣ bid.

The Immediate Cue-Bid

On certain rare but happy occasions, you will hold a hand that is too strong for a takeout double. For example, suppose your right-hand opponent opens the bidding with 1 ◇ and you hold

♠ AK1096   ♡ AKQJ   ◇ ---   ♣ KQJ3

You have the remarkable total of 26 points, and a mere takeout double would not do justice to such a powerful hand. There is a bid designed to show such a hand: a direct overcall of 2 ◇, a *cue-bid* in the enemy's suit. This bid indicates that game is virtually certain even if partner holds no points at all, and that slam is possible even if partner's hand is only medium. Partner should bid his best suit, just as he would in response to a takeout double, keeping in mind that even an apparently bad hand may nevertheless be just what the cue-bidder needs for slam purposes. Opposite the example hand given above, you certainly want to be in game even if responder's hand is as bad as

♠ 873   ♡ 976   ◇ 865   ♣ 10873

and *slam* will be laydown opposite

♠ QJ85   ♡ 863   ◇ 874   ♣ 1075

It will certainly take violent action to convince partner that slam is possible with so few points, and the cue-bid is designed to meet this purpose.

Part Two

The second half of this book is unusual in that we suggest that you unlearn (or perhaps *relearn*) some of the material in the first half. In particular, we hope to demonstrate some of the deficiencies of Standard American bidding and present a modern approach, that of Alvin Roth, which eliminates the shortcomings of standard methods.

The Roth Point Count, of course, will be retained, but, with few exceptions there will be no further discussion of *how* to count points. It will be assumed that the reader is familiar with the various techniques of counting presented in Part One. The reader is cautioned not to proceed with Part Two until he has mastered the principles of point counting and the fundamentals of standard bidding given in Part One.

A summary of the differing objectives of the two halves of the book will be found in the Introduction.

CHAPTER
13

The Roth Approach to Bidding

Now that you have learned the Roth Point Count, you already have an advantage over most opponents you are likely to meet at the bridge table. The majority of your adversaries—including some experts—will be using the more rigid, traditional point count. You, on the other hand, will be watching the value of your hand automatically correcting itself as the result of bids you and your partner make, and getting to better contracts as a result. Remember, you can use the Roth Point Count no matter what your system is. Try it with the system you now play.

The Roth Point Count is one unique and important departure from "run-of-the-mill" works on bidding. Now let's introduce another innovation. Most books on bidding assume that the reader is unable to use expert bidding tools. Often, the authors of such books preach one thing and do another. The teach traditional Standard American (which they wouldn't be "caught dead" playing!) and employ a widely different approach at the bridge table. If these experts are queried about this apparent inconsistency, they reply that beginners and average players just can't cope with high-level bidding procedures, so why confuse them?

Some authors devote their books to new bidding systems they have developed. These books, however, are rarely if ever oriented towards the beginner. They usually assume a thorough grounding in standard bidding methods. All too often, these authors are among those who believe that the typical player is incapable of using expert methods.

This book has adopted a different philosophy. We feel not only that the average bridge player can employ expert evaluation techniques (which we have tried to teach in Part One of this book) *but also that he can successfully use expert bidding methods*. We don't expect to be able to turn every reader into an expert overnight, but we are confident that players at all levels of skill will be able to improve their results by employing more accurate bidding methods than those found in ordinary texts.

In order to fully understand the reasons for the departures from standard methods we will present, it may be helpful to know some bridge history. This will be presented from the point of view of one of the authors, Alvin Roth, who is primarily responsible for the innovations in bidding technique to be presented here.

When Al first learned how to play bridge, he, along with everyone else, used traditional Standard American bidding. Although this was back in 1937, Standard American bidding at that time was almost identical with what it is today, save for its name (it was then called the Culbertson system). The Culbertson system was, in fact, an excellent system. It was far superior to any of its competitors and years, perhaps decades, ahead of its time. It had sounder principles than any other method then known. Further, it clarified literally hundreds of situations for the average player and thus helped him avoid partnership confusion. In the late 1930s, however, the public began to catch up with the system. When interest in bridge revived after the Second World War, it was "last year's system," but still not out of date. By the 1950s, however, the public was clearly ready for bigger and better things; the Culbertson system had become out of date. Yet it was still used by a majority of players! The trouble with American bidding today is not the Culbertson system; it is that the same system has been used, essentially unimproved, for more than twenty years after outliving its usefulness.

But back in 1937 there was no other guide to bidding. When Al went to his first national tournament he took along his Culbertson Gold Book, his bridge bible. But gradually, he discovered the inadequacies of the method. He found himself unable to communicate with his partner in many instances. After much frustration, he began to drop some of the old-fashioned (but in fashion then, and, unfortunately, still very much in fashion today) bids and replace them with more useful and more descriptive bids, which had as their purpose more effective bidding, more winning, and more fun out of bridge.

Violent arguments at the bridge table—then and now—are usually over the bidding. Yet both partners are very often right! Al observed this phenomenon back in the 1930s. He drew the obvious conclusion that *the system must be at fault*. Disasters occurred because both partners—whether experts or beginners—were handicapped by the bidding methods that had been handed down to them. They were unable to describe hands that had been dealt to them because they lacked the proper tools. And yet, they still refuse to change! Some players, including experts, boast that they play with a minimum of conventions. Yet, without definitive bids, it is impossible to bid well; and without bidding well it is impossible to play decent bridge. And there is no reason why definitive bids, so necessary to good bridge, should be used only by experts. Not all of us can play like experts, but all of us, from beginner on up, are entitled to the tools of the expert. *What is good for the expert can also be good for the average player, and this book is an attempt to preach what experts practice.*

Everyone can be equipped with the proper tools for successful bidding. Unlike some of our pessimistic brethren, we believe that you *can* learn modern expert techniques—that you can discard the outmoded framework of traditional Standard American bidding and use, for example, the more precise Roth method of hand evaluation within a modern streamlined framework—and that you *should*. The Roth Point Count will unquestionably give you an edge at the bridge table regardless of the system that you use, but using it with Standard American bidding methods is akin to using a high-powered jet engine in a Model T Ford. Up to now, we have used the context of traditional Standard American to enable you to learn Roth Point Count in a familiar setting. Now that you have done this, it is time to discard the Model T; time to shift into high gear and really learn how to *bid!*

In the remainder of this book, we will teach you new meanings for old bids. Here, having learned traditional Standard American will serve an extra purpose. By knowing the old-fashioned, meanings of bids, you will be better equipped to understand the reasons for changing these meanings. Since you now know Standard American, you can still play with a partner using this method (remember, you can use Roth Point Count even if your partner does not), at least until you can persuade him to change to the experts' approach. Once you have combined the Roth Point Count and the Roth approach to bidding, you will be in full possession of all the tricks of the expert bidding trade; your jet engine will be housed in a sleek and powerful aircraft, and you will leave the Standard American players far behind.

As before, the chapters in this section will contain capsule summaries and quizzes to assist you along the road to expert bidding. May we remind you once again *not* to attempt to rush through large chunks of the material in a single evening; don't be like some "pesudo-experts" we know who have a smattering of knowledge about this and that but who don't really understand what they are doing. The expert not only *uses* the techniques we will describe, but *understands* why as well. Just as you did with the Roth Point Count, make the Roth approach to bidding work for you by learning the material in each chapter thoroughly before going on to the next one.

CHAPTER
14

The Trouble with "Standard American"

So-called "Standard American bidding" is a myth, passed down (under various names) from the days of Culbertson and seldom used by our top-ranking players. During the past 20 years there have been many players throughout the world who *thought* they were using Standard American bidding, but this supposed system is so badly defined that it would be difficult to find more than a few players among the world's bridge players who were all using exactly the same variation.

The only part of Standard American bidding which has survived and is universally known is a list of several general principles, their basic applications, and some of the exceptions to the basic applications, and a few of the exceptions to the exceptions to the exceptions . . . Unfortunately for bridge players all over the globe, what has survived is horribly unsound, both in theory and in practice.

Perhaps it has never occurred to you that a great deal is wrong with many of the bids advocated by traditional Standard American theorists. Concerned with improving your bridge game, you try to seek out errors in order to prevent their recurrence. This is well and good. Often, however, even correct use of Standard American will lead to inferior results. Good contracts will be missed because Standard American does not have the necessary machinery to reach them; opponents will have an easy time reaching *their* best contract because Standard American does not have the right tools to interfere with enemy bidding processes. Thus, when a bad result obtains, Standard American itself is frequently the culprit; yet players who have learned this method either blame themselves for bidding poorly or do not even realize that an avoidable disaster has occurred *because* their bidding was "straight from the book."

In this chapter, we will list many areas in which Standard American bidding methods are deficient; this will serve to introduce the various topics and provide a summary for ready reference. Subsequent chapters will be devoted to a more detailed discussion of these flaws and how they can be corrected.

1 / Why Can't You Raise Partner's Major Suit?

In Chapter Three, we saw that in Standard American the proper response to partner's **one-heart** opening, holding

♠ A63   ♡ K842   ◇ 62   ♣ Q1098

was **two clubs.** With 11 Roth Points, you are too strong for a raise to two hearts and too weak for a (forcing) raise to three hearts.

Now this is a pretty sad state of affairs. The main feature of this hand is *not* the four-card club suit; *it is the fine support for partner's major suit.* The most natural and straightforward thing to do is to raise hearts; yet this is impossible because of the peculiar point ranges for major-suit raises used by Standard American. Eleven- and twelve-point hands with good support for partner's major suit occur frequently, yet Standard American handles such hands in a roundabout manner that can lead to serious ambiguity.

Perhaps nothing bad will happen if you respond two clubs and support hearts later, but we wouldn't want to bet on it. Suppose partner rebids **two hearts** and you raise to **three hearts**. *You* know that you have good heart support, but does your partner know it? You would bid the same way with

$$\spadesuit A2 \quad \heartsuit A3 \quad \diamondsuit 983 \quad \clubsuit A98643$$

or

$$\spadesuit A2 \quad \heartsuit K83 \quad \diamondsuit 983 \quad \clubsuit A8643$$

When you bid the hand in the manner prescribed by Standard American, the opening bidder has no idea whether you have two-, three-, four-, or even *five*-card support for his major suit! Since the strength of partner's hand is affected by the quality of your heart support, this is quite a serious disadvantage that can severely hinder you in your quest for game. For example, partner might stop at three with a reasonable hand because his trump suit is weak and he is uncertain of the quality of your support.

Thus, Standard American methods for raising major-suit opening bids lead to complications *because you cannot make your most natural response*, a heart raise, on your first turn to bid. Using the Roth approach, however, you do raise hearts directly with

$$\spadesuit A63 \quad \heartsuit K842 \quad \diamondsuit 62 \quad \clubsuit Q1098$$

or

$$\spadesuit A2 \quad \heartsuit K83 \quad \diamondsuit 983 \quad \clubsuit A8643$$

but *not* with

$$\spadesuit A2 \quad \heartsuit A3 \quad \diamondsuit 983 \quad \clubsuit A98643$$

2 / Wasting Your Own Bidding Room with the Forcing Major Raise

Standard American players are taught that the raise from one heart to three hearts (or from one spade to three spades) shows 13 to 15 points and good support for partner's suit. This has become so deeply ingrained that some players would regard a change in the meaning of this bid as near sacrilege. Yet this bid, too, is a potential source of trouble. When responder's hand is strong enough to justify the double major raise, your side may have a slam. Unfortunately, the double major raise takes up so much room that there are very few bids available to you in your search for slam. You certainly don't want to play the hand any higher than the four-level if there is no slam, yet a precise investigation of slam prospects may force you up to the five-level before it becomes clear that slam is out of the question. Going down one trick in a five-heart or five-spade contract is one of the most ignominious fates that can befall a bridge player, but stopping in game when slam is cold—because neither partner wished to risk being stuck at the five-level—is just as costly. The Roth approach, as you will see, creates the *extra bidding space* needed for careful slam investigation.

3 / Had Any Strong Two-Bids Lately?

If a professor of logic with some knowledge of bridge examined the structure of Standard American bidding methods, he would be forced to conclude that strong two-bids were one of life's more frequent occurrences. After all, *four* opening bids—two clubs, two diamonds, two hearts, and two spades—are reserved for such hands. Unless your luck is much better than ours, you will probably have difficulty remembering the last three times your hand justified opening with a strong two-bid. What a waste to use *four* opening bids for such an infrequent hand!

Furthermore, such bids also waste room. (In fact, Standard American would seem to have been designed by a misguided theorist who believed that there are fifteen or sixteen levels of bidding instead of only seven.) If responder holds a weak hand, he must respond two notrump, and the bidding is at the three-level before it has hardly begun. Furthermore, if the hand is to be played at notrump, the strong hand will become dummy. Those wily defenders will thus see exactly what they have to contend with, and their defense will be annoyingly good.

A third problem with strong two-bids is not immediately obvious, but is equally important. Many hands which are not good enough for a preemptive opening bid at the three-level could be opened safely with a limited *two-level* bid. In the review quiz for Chapter Eight, we saw that

♠ 6   ♡ 32   ◊ KQJ10765   ♣ Q43

was too weak for a vulnerable three-diamond opening. A preemptive-type yet constructive two-diamond bid would be just what the doctor ordered, but in Standard American this opening is forcing to game. Similarly, a hand such as

♠ KQJ943   ♡ 643   ◊ Q32   ♣ 6

does not qualify for either a vulnerable or nonvulnerable three-spade opening, but a preemptive two-spade opening is safe and likely to be most annoying to the opponents, who would very much like to have you pass so that they can proceed with their usual one-level opening bids. Such hands occur far more frequently than strong two-bids.

As we will see, the Roth approach is to use opening bids of two diamonds, two hearts, and two spades as limit-type preemptive bids, and use the two-club opening for any really strong two-bid (regardless of suit). This, in effect, enables you to have your cake and eat it too, for you can bid your strong hands effectively while *adding a new limit bid*—one which shows a hand in-between a one-opening and a preemptive opening.

4 / Confusing your own Bidding with the Strong Single-Jump Overcall

In Standard American, a single-jump overcall over an opponent's opening bid of one of a suit is a strong bid. Thus, if your right-hand opponent opens **one diamond**, a **two heart** overcall would presumably show a hand such as

♠ 6   ♡ AKJ976   ◊ AQ3   ♣ Q62.

Our objections to this treatment can be briefly summarized:

(a) It practically never occurs.

(b) Even when it does occur, partner rarely knows what if anything to bid in response.

(c) It prevents the use of an effective method of interfering with the opponents' bidding. The best time to interfere with enemy lines of communication is when you have a weak hand with a long suit.

(d) Hands of this type can be bid effectively with other methods.

Examining Standard American, our professor of logic would certainly be forced to conclude that our side holds most of the cards, what with the plethora of strong two-bids, strong jump overcalls, and so forth. The fact of the matter is that extremely good hands occur very rarely. Hands similar to those calling for a preemptive two-bid

(e.g. ♠KQJ943   ♡643   ◇Q32   ♣6)

are far more frequent. The modern expert approach to bidding stresses getting in one's opponent's way when it is safe to do so, and a two spade overcall on this weak hand is certain to prove most annoying to your left-hand opponent, while running little risk. Also, partner has an excellent idea of what you have (a good suit without much on the side) and can bid accordingly. One of the distinguishing features of the expert bidder is that he makes use of the many bids available to him, while lesser players wait patiently throughout the years for hands which will meet the exacting requirements for such unlikely bids as strong single-jump overcalls.

Furthermore, the use of strong jump overcalls makes the *simple overcall* very ambiguous. Everyone is tempted to take some action with a long, strong suit. It is unreasonable to expect someone to pass an opposing bid of **one club** holding:

♠KQJ943   ♡643   ◇Q32   ♣6

But if the strong jump overcall is being employed, the only possible call on this hand is one spade (*three* spades is not justified by the playing strength held). If we are forced to overcall one spade with hands of this type, it is clear that we cannot use the simple overcall to show significant values to our partner.

However, if *weak* (preemptive) jump overcalls are being used, we can differentiate clearly between overcalls of varying quality. On the above hand we can jump to **two spades** over the opening bid of one club. This both hinders the opposition and gives partner an excellent picture of our hand. Furthermore, on those occasions when we overcall only *one* spade, partner will know we have extra values in either high cards or distribution. *For if we held nothing more than a long strong suit we would have made a jump overcall.*

It is time to do away with the strong jump overcall.

5 / More Useless Bids: High-Level Notrump Openings

Another good example of a wasted bid is the three-notrump opening bid, which promises 25–27 points and balanced suit distribution. Not only is this bid highly infrequent, but the hand it describes can be taken care of equally well by the catch-all two-club opening used to describe a strong two-bid in any suit (open two clubs, rebid three notrump). Therefore, you can add another weapon to your arsenal by abandoning the useless Standard American meaning for this bid and substituting a preemptive meaning that we will discuss later on.

The two-notrump opening is unquestionably a useful call, but the Standard American point range is too high. Since the two-club opening bid, as we will see, can easily describe any hand of 24 or more points, the Standard American point range for this bid (22 to 24 points) is no longer necessary. Therefore, you can use a range of 21 to 23 points. This seems like a minor change, but has several advantages. Since 21-point hands are far more frequent than 24-point hands, you will get to open two notrump more often, and describe your hand in a single bid more frequently. Also, recall that partner is required to pass an opening bid of one of a suit with five points or less. In Chapter 3 we said that you should not mind missing games when one partner has 21 points and the other has 5 points because the unbalanced distribution of points makes games hard to play. Such games are hard to play, but the expert is expected to make difficult contracts. Therefore, the expert will be quite satisfied if he opens two notrump on 21 points and partner raises to three notrump with 5 points—a game that would be missed using the Standard American point range for the two-notrump opening bid.

6 / Still More Useless Bids: The Powerhouse Jump Shift

In the same category as the strong two-bid and strong jump overcall is the powerhouse jump shift. When you meet the Standard American requirement of 18 points, it is temporarily satisfying to jump shift over partner's opening bid and let him know, so that both of you can glow happily and the opponents can wallow in gloom. But there is little true gain, for you are almost certainly on your way to slam in any event. The expert does not see any advantage in using bids that may come up five or six times a year if he plays every day. Since there are other ways to handle very strong hands, jump shifts can be used to solve a particularly vexing problem that occurs much more often than 18-point responses. Consider the following two hands:

1. ♠ Q109843   ♡ 543   ◇ 2   ♣ 863
2. ♠ KJ10642   ♡ A53   ◇ Q2   ♣ 32

Partner opens **one diamond**. On the first hand, you are not strong enough to respond, and must pass. This is enough to turn the stomach of any strong bridge player. Diamonds may turn out to be a disaster, yet your nice spade suit must go unmentioned; and the opponents, who clearly have a fair share of the points and are likely to want to enter the bidding, have only a puny one-diamond bid to contend with. Yet there is good reason for the pass in Standard American: since a response promises 6 points, partner may jump to game (such as three notrump) over a one-spade response, and fail to make it because you cannot come up with the points that you have promised.

On the second hand, you can and should bid **one spade** on your first turn. Suppose partner now bids **two clubs** or **two diamonds**. You are not strong enough to jump to three spades, which is forcing to game; yet a two-spade bid would indicate a distinct lack of interest in the proceedings (you would make this bid without the ace of hearts).

In the Roth system, problems such as this are easily handled by scrapping the useless powerhouse jump shift. A jump shift now has a new meaning: a weak hand with a long suit. Thus, on hand 1, respond **two spades.** This immediately tells partner that you have a bad hand, gets you to what is likely to be your best suit, and makes life difficult for the opponents (who now must bid at the three-level if they wish to enter the auction). On the second hand, you can respond **one spade** and follow with a **two-spade** rebid. This is now constructive, since with a weak hand you would have jumped to two spades on the first round.

So let the losing players wait for powerhouse jump shifts that rarely occur, and solve your more practical problems by using weak jump-shift responses. Take advantage of your opportunities to make life difficult for your opponents when you can do so safely.

7 / The Days of Huge Sets are Gone: The Negative Double

Every bridge player dreams of the following situation: Partner opens the bidding (say with **one spade**), the next player overcalls **two clubs,** and you hold four or five trump tricks (say a hand such as

♠3   ♡A84   ◊543   ♣KQ10987).

We agree this is a nice dream, but it's rather impractical. These days bridge players just don't overcall on really bad suits. In addition, more and more players are preempting the bidding, presenting problems such as the following:

You hold:	PARTNER	OPPONENT	YOU
♠ 86	1 ♡	2 ♠ (weak)	?
♡ 72		or	
◇ AQ106	1 ♠	2 ♡	?
♣ KJ632			

Even if you don't like weak jump overcalls (an attitude we expect to change before this book is over), other people do, and you're likely to be faced with the situation shown in the first auction above. How nice it would be to make a takeout double, asking partner to select one of the unbid suits! However, every bridge player knows that a takeout double is made over an opponent's opening bid, and never over an overcall. It is time for a change. Many experts* are now using the "negative double" that Roth and Tobias Stone popularized some years ago. This double *is* for takeout; in the auctions above, it would show length in the two unbid suits—clubs and diamonds. The Standard American player must pass; a three-club bid would show a much stronger hand and would get things overboard very quickly. Using the Roth approach, you make a negative double, immediately informing partner about your strength and distribution. And the possibility of setting the opponents who are overbidding is still there, as we will see later.

8 / That Ghastly Three-Notrump Response

The misguided theorist I mentioned a while back who thought that there were fifteen or sixteen levels of bidding must have loved the three-notrump response over an opening of one of a suit. Standard American teaches that this bid shows 16–18 points and a balanced hand. Since partner must have at least 14 points for his opening bid, slam is very likely when responder has a hand worth a three-notrump response. So look what Standard American does.

---

* In fact, a majority, according to a recent survey conducted by Bridge World magazine.

it requires responder to jump all the way from one of a suit to three notrump, using up vast amounts of bidding room that could profitably be devoted to slam investigation.

To take just one example, suppose that you hold

♠ KJ96   ♡ 2   ◇ A1064   ♣ AQ32

You open **one diamond** and partner responds **three notrump.** What now? In notrump, your hand is worth only 14 Roth Points and slam is out of the question. But if partner has four cards in spades, diamonds, or clubs, you will have a playable trump suit and can count two Distribution Points for your singleton heart. With 16 points, slam is now very possible. Yet what can you bid? Any bid at the four-level runs the risk of getting your side too high when there is no slam. Also, a four-club bid at this point might imply a five-card diamond suit, and partner might bid diamonds with only three-card support. And it may be difficult to sign off later. It would have been much nicer if partner had responded at a lower level, giving you a chance to explore possible suit fits; but Standard American required that horrible three-notrump response.

In subsequent chapters, we will show that it is possible to handle such hands *without* resorting to a three-notrump response. In fact, most experts think so little of this response that we will suggest using it as Blackwood!

9 / Handling Interference over Blackwood

It is not difficult to memorize the responses to the Blackwood four-notrump bid. However, do you know how to handle this situation?

PARTNER	OPPONENT	YOU	OPPONENT
1 ♠	2 ◇	3 ♠	4 ◇
4 NT	5 ◇	?	

Obviously, some change is necessary, as you can no longer make use of your normal five-club and five-diamond responses. Very few partnerships have discussed the use of Blackwood over opponents' interference. Yet even experts go wrong. It has happened in the world championships! Particularly as modern players have learned to "bid a lot with a little," a firm partnership agreement to handle this situation is clearly necessary, and we will propose suitable methods for dealing with this problem.

10 / "How I Wish I Could Make a Takeout Double!"

Suppose that your right-hand opponent opens the bidding with **one club** and you hold

♠ K543   ♡ A862   ◇ QJ63   ♣ 2

According to proponents of Standard American, this hand is too weak to make a takeout double. If you double, partner will expect a stronger hand, and your side is likely to get into trouble. Yet it is criminal to pass with such fine support for the three unbid suits. Your hand, which is now worth 12 Roth Points, will go up in value to 13 points when partner responds to a takeout double; whatever suit he holds, you have four-card support and can PROMOTE for your singleton club. Your hand is well oriented for competing with the opponents, yet Standard American suggests a meek pass! Wouldn't you like to make a takeout double if your partner is aware that you may be "light"?

The solution to this problem is to make use of another wasted bid. In Standard American, the cue-bid of the suit opened by the opponents shows a powerful hand and is forcing to game. Once again, we can only ask: Have you had any lately? These cue-bids are so rare that one can go for months or years without running into one. You, however, will not allow your partnership to waste bids by waiting for hands that come up once in a blue moon. By using the cue-bid to show a very strong takeout double, and allowing the double to show a hand such as the example hand above, partner will not be misled as to your strength (provided you have discussed this with him beforehand!) and you will be able to enter the auction safely in *both* situations.

11 / Who Knows How to Respond to Notrump Openings?

An examination of Standard American bidding practices would suggest that the answer to the above question is "Nobody." For example, suppose you hold

♠ AK10964   ♡ 653   ◇ 543   ♣ 2

Partner opens **one notrump,** showing 16–18 points, and your 12 Roth Points indicate that game is definite. In Standard American, you bid **four spades.** As a result, the opening notrump hand becomes dummy. As we mentioned in the discussion of strong two-bids, it is a great advantage to the defenders to see what the strong hand has. Your hand is no mystery; you must have a long and strong spade suit for your four-spade bid. The opening notrumper's hand, however, is not nearly so well determined, and the opponents will be most eager to see it. In addition, it is an advantage to have the lead come up to the strong hand rather than through it. The notrump bidder is likely to hold one or more tenaces, such as AQ or KJ. You would certainly rather have the opponents lead into such holdings rather than through them. Therefore, we will recommend the use of "transfer" bids that allow the opening notrump bidder to become the declarer.

Further confusions arise in the use of the Stayman convention for slam purposes. Most players who use this convention have a fairly good idea of how to handle it when the only questions are whether or not to bid game and where to play the hand. When a slam appears on the horizon, however, confusion runs rampant. In this book, we will present the first consistent notrump structure that will be effective in all cases—whether you are bidding part scores, games, or slams.

Summary

Old-fashioned Standard American bidding methods would be useful if 20-point hands were an everyday occurrence and if there were many more than seven levels of bidding permitted by the rules. Since this is not the case, it is necessary for the expert to change the meanings of those bids which otherwise occur only rarely, or which take up too much bidding space. It is perhaps trite to point out that the only permissible words in the bidding process are one, two, three, four, five, six, seven, notrump, spade(s), heart(s), diamond(s), club(s), double, redouble, and pass, but Standard American appears to have ignored this severe limitation to the exchange of information during the bidding.

To the expert, any bid that occurs rarely is a waste, and experts look for new meanings for bids that will give them more practical value. It is certainly valuable to have a precision device such as the Roth Point Count at your disposal; but why limit its effectiveness by having to pass too often because you don't have the large number of points needed to justify some bids in Standard American methods? Using the Roth approach to bidding, you will have far more possible bids at your disposal than the Standard American player. You will reach better contracts and make your opponents' bidding life far more difficult. What more can any bridge player ask?

CHAPTER
15

The Single Major Raise and The Forcing One-Notrump Response

In Part One of this book we explained that an opening bid in a major suit should be based on a suit of at least five cards. The reason we introduced this rule in the section on standard bidding was not that it was standard (it is not—many players still open four-card majors) but because it greatly simplifies the rules for determining which suit to open.

However, we believe this rule is not only simple but effective. By knowing your partner has five or more cards in his major suit, you are often able to locate an eight-card fit immediately and bid accordingly. We will continue the use of this convention (not to open four-card major suits) in Part Two. In particular, the material in this chapter depends very strongly on the assumption that an opening bid in a major suit indicates at least five cards.

As the first step in providing a remedy to the numerous deficiencies inherent in old-fashioned Standard American bidding methods, let us consider the problem of the single raise of partner's opening of one of a major.* In the previous chapter, we saw that if you must respond **two clubs** to partner's **one-heart** opening and support hearts on the next round with both

♠ A63   ♡ K842   ◇ 62   ♣ Q1098

and

♠ A2   ♡ A3   ◇ 983   ♣ A98643

partner has no idea how good your heart support is. If his heart suit is weak, he cannot tell whether you can provide help or whether the opponents possess substantial numbers of trump tricks that will make his life difficult in a heart contract. He also does not know if your heart support is good enough to provide the "ruffability" necessary to take care of his side-suit losers.

The Roth approach solves this problem by allowing you to raise directly to two of partner's major on hands with 10 to 12 points and at least three-card support for partner's suit. This means that a different procedure will have to be used for hands with 6 to 9 points and support for partner's major, but we will see that this presents no great difficulty.

The Single Major Raise

When partner opens one in a major suit, the requirements for the single major raise in the Roth method are straightforward: 10 to 12 points and three or more trumps. The following examples should help to make this clear:

1. ♠ A63   ♡ K842   ◇ 62   ♣ Q1098   Partner opens 1 ♡

You hold four-card heart support and have 11 Roth Points. Raise to 2 ♡.

---

* A discussion of the double major raise will be postponed until Chapter 25. The triple major raise will retain the same meaning (preemptive) as before.

2.   ♠ 1083 ♡ AKJ75 ◇ 85 ♣ K43   Partner opens 1 ♠

Your hand is worth 12 Roth Points and you have three-card spade support. Raise to 2 ♠. Do not help the opponents defend by bidding hearts; there is no bonus for finding a second trump suit. Too many bids spoil the broth.

3.   ♠ 863 ♡ KJ42 ◇ 62 ♣ A1085   Partner opens 1 ♡

After PROMOTING your diamond doubleton, your hand is worth 10 Roth Points. Raise 2 ♡.

4.   ♠ A2 ♡ A3 ◇ 983 ♣ A98643   Partner opens 1 ♡

After DEMOTING your Distribution Points with a doubleton in partner's suit, your hand is worth 12 Roth Points, but you may not raise with only a doubleton heart.

5.   ♠ K843 ♡ A82 ◇ K8543 ♣ 2   Partner opens 1 ♠

After PROMOTION, your hand is worth 13 Roth Points, and is *too strong* for a single major raise.

As you can see, the new requirements for the single major raise are simple and easy to learn. Now let us see how to handle hands with only 6 to 9 points and support for partner's major.

The Forcing One-Notrump Response

In order to inform partner that you hold a minimum response with support for his major suit, you will keep the basic idea of making a single major raise, but will do so in a different way. Simply bid one notrump at your first turn to speak, and then return to two of the major on the next round.

No doubt you are tempted to ask, "What if partner passes my one-notrump response?" The answer is that using the Roth approach to bidding, *partner is not permitted to pass the 1 NT response to a major suit;* this bid is forcing for one round.

Here are a few examples of the forcing 1 NT response in action:

(304)

1. ♠85   ♡9654   ◊A84   ♣Q832   Partners opens 1 ♡

Bid 1 NT. You will have a chance to show your heart support since partner must bid again; the 1 NT response to an opening bid of one of a major is forcing for one round. If partner rebids 2 ♣ or 2 ◊, now bid 2 ♡. The fact that you have bid 1 NT first will alert partner to the fact that you have 6–9 points.* If partner rebids 2 ♡, showing a minimum opening, just pass; you are not going anywhere. (8 Roth Points; count your PROMOTED Distribution Points since you are merely using the 1 NT bid as a vehicle to raise to two of partner's major.)

2. ♠863   ♡7   ◊Q853   ♣A9742   Partner opens 1 ♠

Bid 1 NT. You are not strong enough to bid a new suit at the two-level or raise o 2 ♠. (8 Roth Points)

3. ♠K753   ♡A842   ◊65   ♣432   Partner opens 1 ♡

Bid 1 NT. Once again, you are too weak to raise to 2 ♡. Do not respond 1 ♠; you should not bid a new suit when you meet the requirements for the raise of partner's major. (The fact that you are using the forcing 1 NT response as the vehicle to raise partner's major is no excuse for violating our established rule of priority that a raise of partner's major takes precedence over bidding a new suit.) (9 Roth Points)

4. ♠853   ♡42   ◊Q1086   ♣Q432   Partner opens 1 ♠

Pass. You are too weak to respond. (5 Roth Points)

5. ♠K942   ♡65   ◊A843   ♣643   Partner opens 1 ♡

Bid 1 ♠. You should not plan to support hearts with only a doubleton, so do not respond 1 NT for that purpose. Since you are unable to raise partner's major, follow the next highest priority and show the new major suit. (7 Roth Points; DEMOTE your Distribubution Points with a doubleton in partner's suit.)

---

* In fact, on occasion you will be able to rebid *three* hearts, to show a maximum hand. Partner will know you have 9 points, rather than 10 or 11, because your original response was one notrump (not two hearts).

Other Uses of the Forcing Notrump Response

Even if the only advantage of the forcing notrump response were to make the raising partner's major suit clearer, the bid would be well worth using. However, the forcing notrump response is useful on many other hands as well.* Standard American players have a terrible time trying to cope with hands such as the following:

1. ♠8 ♡62 ◇AQ876 ♣Q5432   Partner opens 1 ♡ (8 Roth Points)
2. ♠63 ♡AQJ94 ◇864 ♣432   Partner opens 1 ♠ (7 Roth Points)
3. ♠86 ♡86 ◇762 ♣AQ10943   Partner opens 1 ♡ (7 Roth Points)

Since none of the above hands is strong enough for a two-over-one response, the Standard American player must bid one notrump and hope for the best. If partner passes, they are likely to be in a terrible contract. Using the Roth approach, you can bid one notrump with confidence, since partner must bid again. As we will see in the next section, partner's responses to the forcing notrump response are designed in such a way that you will have no trouble getting to the right contract with the above hands, and many similar ones. Since you cannot bid at the two-level without 11 points, you will sometimes be forced to bid one notrump (in standard bidding) with a wholly unsuitable hand. *If the bid is forcing, however, you need not worry.*

The rules for using the forcing one-notrump response are quite simple:

1. You must have 6 to 11 Roth Points. With 12 points, you are strong enough to bid at the two-level; with fewer than 6 points you

---

* When you know opener has a five-card major suit for his opening bid, it is unlikely that one notrump is the best contract. If responder has 3 (or more) cards in opener's suit, an 8-card (or better) fit is present; if responder has 2 cards in opener's suit, *at worst* a 5–2 fit can be played and often a better one is found along the way; if responder has 0 or 1 card(s) in opener's suit there must be a better spot than notrump.

are not strong enough to respond. Also, if you have 10–11 points, you must have no more than a doubleton in partner's suit, since with three-card or longer support and 10–12 points you raise to two of partner's major.

2. If partner has opened **one heart** and you have 6–9 Roth Points, four or more spades, and three or fewer hearts, bid **one spade.** In all other cases, with 6–9 points, respond **one notrump.** With 10–11 points and no more than two cards in partner's major suit, bid a four-card or longer spade suit over partner's 1 ♡ opening. Otherwise respond 1 NT.

Thus, holding 6–11 Roth Points, your first duty is to support partner's major; your next task is to show a spade suit at the one-level; and if you cannot do either of these, you respond one notrump. What could be simpler?

Capsule Summary: The Single Major Raise

If partner opens 1 ♡ or 1 ♠ :

YOU HOLD	YOUR ACTION
10–12 points and at least three-card support	Raise to two of the major.
6–9 points and at least three-card support	Raise "indirectly" by responding 1 NT. Partner must bid again, so you will have a chance to show your support. BUT: With four or more spades and exactly three hearts, bid 1 ♠ over partner's opening 1 ♡.
6–11 points and two-card support or less	If partner has opened 1 ♡ and you have four or more spades, bid 1 ♠. Otherwise, respond 1 NT.

(307)

REMEMBER THAT THE 1 NT RESPONSE IS FORCING *ONLY* OVER A *MAJOR*-SUIT OPENING BID.

QUIZ

In each case, count your Roth Points and decide your action.

	PARTNER OPENS	YOU HOLD
1.	1 ♡	♠ A864 ♡ Q85 ◇ 6432 ♣ 74
2.	1 ♡	♠ K83 ♡ J1042 ◇ 2 ♣ AJ654
3.	1 ♠	♠ A843 ♡ 643 ◇ 853 ♣ J42
4.	1 ♠	♠ 74 ♡ AJ1076 ◇ Q83 ♣ 852
5.	1 ♡	♠ 85 ♡ AJ75 ◇ Q106 ♣ J1098
6.	1 ♠	♠ K8432 ♡ AJ5 ◇ J1042 ♣ 2
7.	1 ♠	♠ 543 ♡ AQ87 ◇ 653 ♣ 1072
8.	1 ♡	♠ AJ942 ♡ 64 ◇ K1043 ♣ 43
9.	1 ♠	♠ KQ8 ♡ 86 ◇ AQ1042 ♣ 432
10.	1 ♠	♠ 64 ♡ 7 ◇ A987 ♣ Q108432

SOLUTIONS

1. *Bid 1 ♠.* You have 7 Roth Points and three-card heart support. You will show your heart support next time (or pass if partner rebids 2 ♡ or 2 ♠).

2. *Bid 2 ♡.* After PROMOTION, you have 12 Roth Points. Using the Roth approach, hands with 10–12 points and support for partner's major raise directly; there is no roundabout bidding and no confusion.

3. *Pass.* You may not respond with only five Roth Points.

4. *Bid 1 NT.* With any 6 to 11 point hand that cannot support partner's major suit or show a new spade suit at the one-level, respond 1 NT. (7 Roth Points)

5. *Bid 2 ♡.* After PROMOTION, you have 10 Roth Points.

6. Be careful! After PROMOTING by adding two points for a singleton with five-card support for partner's suit, this hand is worth 13 Roth Points, and is too strong for a single raise to 2 ♠. In Chapter 25, we will discuss the treatment of such hands.

7. *Bid 1 NT.* You will show your spade support next time. (6 Roth Points)

8. *Bid 1 ♠.* You may not plan to support hearts with only a doubleton. Bid your new major suit. (8 Roth Points)

9. *Bid 2 ♠.* With 12 Roth Points, do not bid a new suit; raise partner's major directly. Do not bid diamonds and help the opponents defend.

10. *Bid 1 NT.* The proper bid with a 6 to 11 point hand that cannot support partner's major suit or show a new spade suit at the one-level. (6 Roth Points)

As you can see, the forcing notrump response may seem a bit unusual at first glance but becomes quite easy to use with a little practice. You may wonder why we were so critical of the roundabout old-fashioned American procedures for raising major suits, yet advocate the "indirect" single major raise via the one notrump response on 6 to 9 point hands with support for partner's suit. The answer is simple. The 10 to 12 point hands are far more likely to lead to game; since games are "gold" to the bridge player, these are the hands which cry out for the direct, simple major suit raise. On the weaker hands, where game is not that likely, the indirect method of raising is acceptable.

Furthermore, as you saw on hands 4 and 10 of the last quiz, the forcing notrump response makes hands that give impossible problems to Standard American players quite easy to bid. In order to obtain a fuller understanding of this aspect of the Roth approach to bidding, let us shift across the table and consider what opener should do at his second turn to bid.

Opener's Rebid after a Single Raise

When responder raises directly to two hearts or two spades, you know he holds 10 to 12 Roth Points and support for your major suit.

Your action is the same as it would be over any limited bid by responder: if game is definite (and slam is out of the question), jump to four of the major; if game is possible, invite it by rebidding three of the major. The following examples should make this clear:

YOU	PARTNER	YOU HOLD
1. 1 ♠	2 ♠	♠KQ10865 ♡AQ43 ◇32 ♣2

Your hand was originally worth 15 Roth Points (counting one Length Point for the six-card major suit). When partner raises, you PROMOTE by adding two points for the supported six-card suit, and your hand is now worth 17 Roth Points. Since partner must have at least ten points to raise to 2 ♠, the total for your side is at least 27 points, and game is definite. Jump to **four spades.**

2. 1 ♡	2 ♡	♠A83 ♡KQ865 ◇863 ♣A2

After PROMOTING, your hand is worth 15 Roth Points. Game is possible if partner has 11 or 12 points, so invite game by bidding **three hearts.**

We cannot present a hand with which you should pass the single major raise because it is mathematically impossible. Since you must have at least 15 points (the minimum of 14 needed to open plus one point for a supported suit of five cards or more), game is always at least possible. Thus, the immediate single raise is, in effect, *forcing.**
This need not confuse you, however; you cannot possibly make a mistake if you understand how to act after a limited response by your partner. (See Chapter 4B).

Opener's Rebid after a 1 NT Response

In rebidding over the forcing notrump response, opener must keep in mind that responder can have almost any distribution. As we saw in hands 4 and 10 of the last quiz, responder is not necessarily

---

* The partnership will not be forced overboard, however, for responder needs at least 10 points for this raise. Opener's 14 + 10 = 24 (minimum), so the three-level is safe.

going to support your major suit! Therefore, DEMOTE your Distribution Points until a suit fit is found (but keep your Length Points).
The rebids over the 1 NT response, however, are easy to learn and
are designed to take all possibilities into account. First, let us deal
with certain strong hands that opener may happen to hold.

1. With 19 or more points and an unbalanced hand, *jump* to game
in your major suit if it is strong and six or more cards in length or
jump in your longest side suit if your major is only five cards in
length (the side suit must be at least four cards in length if your
hand is unbalanced).

2A. With 19 HCP and a balanced hand, raise to 2 NT.

2B. With 20 or more HCP and a balanced hand, raise to 3 NT.

Here are a few examples to illustrate these rules:

	YOU	PARTNER	YOU HOLD
1.	1 ♠	1 NT	♠ KQ854 ♡ AQ3 ◇ AQ2 ♣ K8
	?		

Bid 3 NT. You have 20 HCP and a balanced hand.

2.	1 ♡	1 NT	♠ 8 ♡ AQJ1065 ◇ AK3 ♣ AJ2
	?		

Bid 4 ♡. You have 19 HCP, but should not raise notrump with
unbalanced distribution. Jump to game in your six-card major suit.

3.	1 ♡	1 NT	♠ -- ♡ AQ1096 ◇ AK532 ♣ AQ3
	?		

Bid 3 ◇. You may not bid 3 NT with unbalanced distribution or
jump rebid in a five-card major suit. Jump in your longest side suit.

4.	1 ♠	1 NT	♠ AQ965 ♡ KJ3 ◇ AK3 ♣ K7
	?		

Bid 2 NT. You have 19 HCP and balanced suit distribution.

More often than not, opener's hand will not be suitable for any
of these strong bids. If so, opener simply rebids as follows:

1. Rebid a six-card or longer major suit. (You must not rebid a
suit of only five cards, for if partner is not planning to support your

major suit he will have *at most* a doubleton. If he does plan to support your suit, you will find out about it on his next turn to bid.) If you have a good hand with a six-card suit, but are not strong enough to jump in your major (same requirements as in Standard) you can "temporize" with a new-suit bid, as in (2.) below.

2. If your major suit is only five cards in length, bid your longest lower-ranking new suit even if it is only 3 cards long! With suits of equal length, bid the *lower-ranking.**

Here's how these rules work in practice:

	YOU	PARTNER	YOU HOLD
1.	1 ♠	1 NT	♠ KQ8654 ♡ A83 ◇ K2 ♣ 32
	?		

Bid 2 ♠. Rebid your six-card major suit. (13 Roth Points)

	YOU	PARTNER	YOU HOLD
2.	1 ♠	1 NT	♠ KQ865 ♡ A83 ◇ K842 ♣ 2
	?		

Bid 2 ◇. Bid your longest (lower-ranking) new suit. Do not rebid a five-card major. (12 Roth Points)

	YOU	PARTNER	YOU HOLD
3.	1 ♠	1 NT	♠ AJ1054 ♡ 63 ◇ AKQ ♣ 432
	?		

Bid 2 ♣. With lower-ranking new suits of equal length, bid the lower. (14 Roth Points)

	YOU	PARTNER	YOU HOLD
4.	1 ♡	1 NT	♠ K83 ♡ QJ1065 ◇ AK3 ♣ 32
	?		

Bid 2 ◇. Bid the longest lower-ranking new suit. (13 Roth Points)

---

* It is still possible to show a *relatively* balanced hand with which you want to invite game. However, this must be done one round later. For example:

Opener	Responder
1 ♡	1 NT
2 ◇	2 ♡
2 NT	

shows about 18 points and probably 2–5–4–2 distribution. (With 3–5–3–2 and 18 points, the opening bid would be one notrump.)

5. 1 ♡   1 NT   ♠863 ♡AK765 ◇AQ53 ♣2
    ?

Bid 2 ◇. Bid the longest lower-ranking new suit. (13 Roth Points)

6. 1 ♡   1 NT   ♠8 ♡KQ10532 ◇J432 ♣A2
    ?

Bid 2 ♡. Rebid your six-card major suit since your hand is minimum. With a better hand (but not enough to rebid three hearts) you could bid two diamonds. (11 Roth Points)

7. 1 ♡   1 NT   ♠K843 ♡AQJ65 ◇K83 ♣2
    ?

Bid 2 ◇. Did you bid 2 ♠ because it was your longest new suit? If so, you have forgotten that the bid of the spade suit (which is higher-ranking than your heart suit) at the two-level is a reverse and promises at least 18 points. Since you have only 13 Roth Points, you may not reverse, and must look elsewhere for a new suit.

8. 1 ♡   1 NT   ♠K843 ♡AQJ65 ◇K3 ♣32
    ?

Once again, you may not reverse (only 13 Roth Points). Since a bid of a two-card suit is distinctly unappetizing and can have serious consequences, rebid 2 ♡ as the least of evils. *This is the only time a rebid of a five-card major suit is permitted,* except when your five-card suit is so strong (e.g.: AKQJ10) you are willing to treat it as a six-card suit.

Capsule Summary: Opener's Rebid after a Single Major Raise or Forcing 1 NT Response

AFTER A SINGLE MAJOR RAISE

Add your points to partner's 10 to 12 point total. If game is definite and slam is impossible, bid game in the major; if game is possible, invite game by raising to three of the major.

AFTER A FORCING 1 NT RESPONSE

YOUR HOLDING	YOUR ACTION

19 or more HCP *and:*

A balanced hand — Raise to 2 NT (19 points) or 3 NT (20 or more points).

A six-card (or longer) major suit — Jump to game in your major suit.

A five-card major suit and an unbalanced hand — Jump in your longest side suit.

If your hand does not qualify for any of the above, then:

1. Six-card (or longer) major suit — Rebid your major suit.

2. Five-card major suit — Bid your longest lower-ranking new suit.

With lower-ranking suits of equal length, bid the lower suit.

Do not reverse (rebid 2 ♠ after a 1 ♡ opening) unless you have at least 18 points. If necessary, bid a three-card minor suit; with 4–5–2–2 distribution, rebid 2 ♡.

QUIZ

For each of the following problems, count your Roth Points and decide on your action. Remember to adjust your point count depending on partner's response.

	YOU	PARTNER	YOU HOLD
1.	1 ♠ ?	1 NT	♠ AK654 ♡ AJ6 ◊ 62 ♣ J85

	YOU	PARTNER	YOU HOLD
2.	1 ♡	1 NT	♠ A ♡ AKJ542 ◇ AK8 ♣ 432
	?		
3.	1 ♡	1 NT	♠ AKQ6 ♡ KJ1065 ◇ 43 ♣ 43
	?		
4.	1 ♠	2 ♠	♠ J10965 ♡ AQ5 ◇ K83 ♣ K6
	?		
5.	1 ♡	1 NT	♠ KQ3 ♡ AQ1065 ◇ KJ8 ♣ 74
	?		
6.	1 ♡	1 NT	♠ 82 ♡ AQ10965 ◇ AQ7 ♣ 32
	?		
7.	1 ♠	1 NT	♠ AQJ95 ♡ AQ3 ◇ 74 ♣ AQ10
	?		
8.	1 ♡	2 ♡	♠ K8 ♡ QJ1065 ◇ AK842 ♣ 7
	?		
9.	1 ♠	1 NT	♠ AKJ87 ♡ K8 ◇ AKJ87 ♣ 2
	?		
10.	1 ♡	1 NT	♠ 6 ♡ AQ654 ◇ K873 ♣ AQ2
	?		
11.	1 ♠	1 NT	♠ AQ1086 ♡ KQ7 ◇ K103 ♣ AQ
	?		
12.	1 ♠	2 ♠	♠ AQ10976 ♡ A ◇ AQ87 ♣ 32
	?		
13.	1 ♠	1 NT	♠ KJ765 ♡ AQ102 ◇ K83 ♣ 10
	?		
14.	1 ♡	1 NT	♠ QJ102 ♡ A7642 ◇ AQ5 ♣ 3
	?		
15.	1 ♡	1 NT	♠ KQJ2 ♡ AKQ76 ◇ A73 ♣ 10
	?		

SOLUTIONS

	POINTS	BID	
1.	13	2 ♣	Bid your lower-ranking three-card suit.
2.	20	4 ♡	With 19 HCP (and one Length Point)

POINTS	BID	

and a six-card major, you should jump directly to game. With an unbalanced hand, bid game in your six-card major suit.

3. 13 — 2 ♡ — Least of evils. You may not reverse with fewer than 18 points and should never bid a two-card suit.

4. 15 — 3 ♠ — Game is possible if partner has 11 or 12 points, so invite it by bidding 3 ♠.

5. 15 — 2 ♦ — With suits of equal length, bid the lower-ranking.

6. 15 — 2 ♡ — Rebidding a six-card major suit takes priority over other calls. Remember to KEEP your Distribution Points with a RELIABLE suit.

7. 19 — 2 NT — With 19 HCP and balanced suit distribution, raise to 2 NT.

8. 17 — 4 ♡ — Game is definite, but slam is impossible even if partner has a maximum 12 points. Do not bid diamonds; there is no bonus for finding a second fit. Why tell the opponents how to defend?

9. 19 — 3 ♦ — With 19 or more HCP, unbalanced suit distribution, and only a five-card major suit, jump in your longest suit.

10. 15 — 2 ♦ — Bid your longest new suit, since no reverse is involved.

11. 20 — 3 NT — With 20 or more HCP and balanced suit distribution, raise to 3 NT.

12. 22 — 3 ♦ — A trick question to keep you on your toes. Slam is likely; if partner has 11 or 12 points, your side will reach the necessary total of 33. Therefore, you cannot simply jump to 4 ♠ (which partner must pass). If you recall the

POINTS	BID	

chapter on slam bidding (Chapter 9), this slam will be based on "ruffability," so you must be certain not to be off the first two tricks in any suit. By bidding diamonds, hearts, and then returning to spades, you will alert partner to the club problem. (Take an extra point if you solved this problem correctly. However, deduct an extra point if you bid a Blackwood 4 NT, as you cannot possibly know what to do if partner shows no aces; for example, he *could* have ♣ KQ *or* ♣ 65.)

	POINTS	BID	
13.	13	2 ♡	Bid your longest new suit.
14.	13	2 ♢	You may not reverse with less than 18 points, so a 2 ♠ bid is out. Bid your three-card minor suit.
15.	19	2 ♠	With 18 points or more, you may reverse, so bid your longest new suit.

Further Rebids After the 1 NT Response

After making a forcing notrump response and hearing partner's reply, responder usually has very little difficulty in selecting his next call. Let us suppose first that opener rebids two of a minor suit, his most frequent action. If your plan at the outset was to use the forcing 1 NT response to show 6 to 9 points and support for partner's suit, now is the time to bid two of partner's major and let him know. If, on the other hand, you have poor support for partner's suit and a suit of your own, you may now bid *your* suit; the original 1 NT response will serve as a warning to partner that your hand is not very good. For example, if partner opens 1 ♠ and you hold

♠ 63 ♡ AQJ94 ◇ 864 ♣ 432

we saw earlier that your correct response is **one notrump**. If partner rebids **two clubs** or **two diamonds**, you should bid **two hearts**. (Old-fashioned American players, who cannot bid the heart suit because they are too weak to respond **two hearts** originally and **one notrump** is not forcing, often miss their best contract on hands like this.)

It may be that you hold a void or singleton in partner's suit and no particularly good suit of your own. As an example, suppose partner opens **one spade** and you hold

♠6   ♡Q85   ◇10987   ♣A5432

You respond **one notrump** and partner bids **two diamonds**. *Pass* and stay out of trouble. The clubs are not good enough to bid at the three-level, and opener must have at least three diamonds (he may not bid a two-card suit). (Do not count any Distribution Points for your spade singleton; partner is following orders and may well have only a three-card diamond suit. In effect, partner is "supporting" your suit.) If you think for a moment, you will realize that opener must have more diamonds than clubs, since with suits of equal length he would bid the lower-ranking one, and there is therefore no need to bid clubs at all.

Naturally, if partner rebid two clubs, you would also pass. (Since partner must have at least three clubs, PROMOTE by adding one point for a supported five-card suit.) You should have at least three (usually four) cards in the minor suit bid by partner and no more than a singleton in his major to pass the minor suit rebid. With a maximum (9–10 HCP), four-card or longer support for partner's minor suit, and no more than a doubleton in his major suit, raise to three of partner's minor. Thus, with

♠8   ♡9832   ◇AK103   ♣Q1092 (9 Roth Points)

respond **one notrump** to partner's **one-spade** opening; if he rebids either **two clubs** or **two diamonds**, raise to three.

One of the most important aspects of the forcing 1 NT response is that you may return to two of partner's major with only a doubleton in support. Suppose you hold

♠85   ♡654   ◇K83   ♣A7432

Partner opens **one spade,** and with 7 Roth Points you are far short of a two-level response and make the correct bid of **one no-trump.** Partner rebids **two diamonds.** The clubs are too weak to bid at the three level and partner may have only three diamonds. Since partner *must have at least five spades,* return to **two spades.** If you have doubleton support for partner's major suit, you should return to two of partner's major unless you have a very good five-card or good six-card or longer suit of your own to bid.

The rules for bidding over a rebid of two of a minor can be summarized simply as follows:

1. If you had an original plan (such as supporting partner's major to show 6–9 points, or bidding a good suit of your own), carry it out. (With 9 points and three-card or better support you may jump to three of the major suit.) Sometimes you can raise partner from two to three with a doubleton (since he showed a six-card suit)—but be sure to have your points in aces and kings when you do so.

2. With a void or singleton in partner's major and at least three (usually four) cards in his minor, and no good suit of your own to bid, pass with a minimum (6 to 8 points) and raise to three with 9 or 10 points. On occasion, your hand may PROMOTE to 11 or more points in support of the minor suit. To show this super-maximum, make an "impossible" bid, e.g.: 1 ♠–1 NT–2 ♣–3 ♡ (strong club hand); 1 ♡–1 NT–2 ◇–2 ♠ (strong diamond hand).

3. Bid 2 NT with 10–11 HCP and stoppers in the unbid suits.

4. If you cannot make any of the above bids but have a doubleton in partner's major, return to two of his major suit.

If opener rebids two of his major suit over the forcing 1 NT response, act as follows:

1. Raise to three with 9–10 points and two or more trumps, or 8 points and three or more trumps.

2. Bid 2 NT with 10–11 HCP and stoppers in all three unbid suits.

3. Bid a strong six-card or longer suit at the three-level.

4. If you cannot make any of these bids, *pass.*

If opener makes one of the less frequent rebids over the forcing

1 NT response, your next action will still be straightforward. Over a raise to 3 NT, it is usually correct to pass, though you should bid a good six-card or longer heart suit if you have one. If partner instead raises to 2 NT, showing 19 points, bid game with 7 or more points. Of course, you should show support for his major suit if you have it. Finally, if opener jumps in a new suit, guaranteeing 19 or more HCP, you must continue to bid until game is reached. Make the bid that best describes your hand.

Here are some examples to clarify the above discussion:

	PARTNER	YOU	YOU HOLD
1.	1 ♠	1 NT	♠ 8 ♡ K63 ◇ 87654 ♣ A1065
	2 ♣	?	

Pass. With four cards in partner's minor, you may safely pass (although you would return to 2 ♠ if you held a doubleton spade). The diamonds are far too weak to bid; besides, you aren't going anywhere (7 Roth Points). Do not count Distribution Points; partner could have only three clubs, so an eight-card fit is not definite.)

2.	1 ♡	1 NT	♠ 86 ♡ Q6 ◇ AJ632 ♣ 9832
	2 ♣	?	

Bid 2 ♡. With four cards in partner's minor and a strong doubleton in support of his major, you should usually return to the major suit. The diamond suit is too weak to bid. (6 Roth Points)

3.	1 ♠	1 NT	♠ J86 ♡ 85 ◇ AJ876 ♣ 432
	2 ◇	?	

Bid 2 ♠. You planned this all along to show 7 points and spade support. Don't change horses in mid-stream just because partner bid your five-card minor—spades is still the proper denomination.

4.	1 ♡	1 NT	♠ 863 ♡ 7 ◇ 863 ♣ AKJ986
	2 ◇	?	

Bid 3 ♣. A very strong six-card suit may be bid at the three-level. You may not support partner's major with a singleton or pass 2 ◇

with only three-card support—and who would want to, looking at that wonderful club suit? (9 Roth Points).

5.	1 ♠	1 NT	♠ 86	♡ QJ107	◇ AQ86	♣ J32
	2 ♣	?			

Bid 2 NT. You have 10 HCP and the unbid suits well stopped.

6.	1 ♠	1 NT	♠ 86	♡ QJ107	◇ AQ86	♣ 432
	2 ◇	?			

Bid 3 ◇. You may not bid 2 NT with the club suit unstopped, but can and should raise partner's minor with 9 HCP and four-card support. (9 Roth Points)

7.	1 ♡	1 NT	♠ Q63	♡ 86	◇ 9853	♣ AJ72
	2 ♡	?			

Pass. With 7 Roth Points, you are not going anywhere. Partner's bid shows a six-card suit, so you are in a playable contract. But you should also pass with ♠ Q63 ♡ 8 ◇ 98532 ♣ AJ72—why look for trouble?

8.	1 ♠	1 NT	♠ Q63	♡ 86	◇ 9853	♣ AJ72
	2 ♠	?			

Raise to 3 ♠. A minimum raise: 8 Roth Points and three-card support.

9.	1 ♡	1 NT	♠ K63	♡ 52	◇ A10976	♣ 842
	2 NT	?			

Bid 3 NT. Partner has 19 points and you have 7, so game is definite. There is no reason to show the diamond suit. (Remember that game in a minor requires 29 Roth Points.)

10.	1 ♠	1 NT	♠ 86	♡ 3	◇ AQ9643	♣ J864
	2 ♣	?			

Bid 2 ◇. It is better to show a strong six-card suit than to pass 2 ♣ with four-card support or return to 2 ♠ with only a doubleton spade. Remember, the bidding is not yet over. (8 Roth Points)

- -

Capsule Summary: Rebids by the 1 NT Bidder

IF OPENER REBIDS 2 ♣ or 2 ◊ (or 2 ♡ having opened one spade):

1. Support partner's major at the two-level if this is what you planned all along (to show 6 to 9 points in support).
2. Bid a new six-card suit (or very good five-card suit).
3. With a singleton or void in partner's original major and at least four-card support for his second suit, pass (with 6–8 Roth Points) or raise the second suit to three (with 9–10 Roth Points). With 11 or more points in support, make an "impossible" bid.
4. Bid 2 NT with 10–11 HCP and the unbid suits stopped.
5. If unable to do any of the above, return to two of partner's major if you have at least a doubleton in support, or jump to three of his major with 9 points and three or more trumps.

IF OPENER REBIDS TWO OF HIS MAJOR:

1. Raise to three with 9–10 points and two or more trumps or 8 points and three or more trumps.
2. Bid a good six-card or longer suit.
3. Bid 2 NT with 10–11 HCP, no more than a doubleton in partner's major, and something in all three unbid suits.
4. Otherwise pass.

IF OPENER MAKES A STRONG REBID:

1. Over a raise to 3 NT, it is usually best to pass. However, if you have a good heart suit of six or more cards, correct to four hearts.
2. Over a raise to 2 NT (showing 19 HCP), evaluate game prospects as you would over any limited bid and act accordingly. If game is definite, 3 NT is often the best spot.
3. If partner jumps in a new suit, you must find some rebid as his bid is forcing to game. Make the most descriptive bid: support his major; support his second suit; show a good new suit of your own; bid notrump with all unbid suits stopped and no particularly good support for either of partner's suits.

QUIZ

For each problem, count your Roth Points and decide your action.

	PARTNER	YOU	YOU HOLD
1.	1 ♡	1 NT	♠ Q86 ♡ 7 ◇ J865 ♣ A8432
	2 ♡	?	
2.	1 ♠	1 NT	♠ J865 ♡ AJ965 ◇ 432 ♣ 3
	2 ♣	?	
3.	1 ♠	1 NT	♠ 85 ♡ A1065 ◇ Q865 ♣ 432
	2 NT	?	
4.	1 ♡	1 NT	♠ 986 ♡ K7 ◇ A632 ♣ 10643
	2 ♣	?	
5.	1 ♠	1 NT	♠ 8 ♡ KQ9864 ◇ 864 ♣ J53
	2 ◇	?	
8.	1 ♠	1 NT	♠ 10876 ♡ AQ3 ◇ 743 ♣ J72
	3 ◇	?	
9.	1 ♠	1 NT	♠ K8 ♡ 8654 ◇ AK97 ♣ 983
	2 ♠	?	
10.	1 ♠	1 NT	♠ 8 ♡ KQJ109 ◇ Q832 ♣ 642
	2 ♣	?	
	2 ◇	?	
11.	1 ♠	1 NT	♠ 7 ♡ 1065 ◇ Q83 ♣ KQJ943
12.	1 ♠	1 NT	♠ 7 ♡ Q1065 ◇ A1065 ♣ 8654
	2 ◇	?	
13.	1 ♡	1 NT	♠ 75 ♡ 98 ◇ AQ65 ♣ A10965
	2 ♡	?	
14.	1 ♠	1 NT	♠ 8 ♡ Q6543 ◇ A87 ♣ 10654
	2 ◇	?	
15.	1 ♡	1 NT	♠ K83 ♡ 8 ◇ 109643 ♣ AJ107
	2 ◇	?	

SOLUTIONS

	POINTS	BID	
1.	7	Pass	There is no chance for game, and you have no constructive action to take. Partner has at least a six-card heart suit, so you can afford to stay put.
2.	9	3 ♠	Stay with your original plan of showing 6 to 9 points and spade support. Remember to PROMOTE your singleton with four-card support for partner's suit. This gives you the maximum of 9 points and you are therefore justified in jumping to three spades.
3.	6	Pass	Even with partner's 19 points, game is out of the question. Your hand is balanced and thus suited for play in notrump.
4.	7	2 ♡	Prefer supporting partner's major with a strong doubleton to passing with four cards in his minor.
5.	7	2 ♡	Bid your strong six-card suit.
6.	6	Pass	No choice; the diamonds are too weak to bid.
7.	10	2 NT	You have 10 HCP and all unbid suits well stopped.
8.	7	3 ♠	Partner's jump in a new suit shows a very powerful hand, but your first duty is still to inform him of your support for his major suit.
9.	10	3 ♠	Raising with two trumps is indeed a bit unsettling, but partner has shown a six-card suit and with ten excellent points you have little choice.
10.	8	2 ♡	Bid your strong major suit.
11.	11	3 ♣	You may force the hand to the three-level with such a good club suit.

	POINTS	BID	
12.	6	Pass	There is little chance for game. Why bid on?
13.	10	3 ♡	Here your trump support is even worse than in problem 9, but with 10 good points you must raise.
14.	6	Pass	Least of evils. The heart suit is far too weak to bid and you may not support spades with a singleton.
15.	11	3 ◊	With a maximum, you should raise partner's minor suit to indicate that you are interested in game. PROMOTE by adding one point for a "supported" five-card suit, and KEEP your Distribution Points since an eight-card fit has been found.

If you have worked your way carefully up to this point, you should have no difficulty putting the forcing notrump response and the strong single major raise into practice. We have not covered every possible situation; such a treatment would be hopelessly tedious and boring. If you understand what you are doing, you should have no problem even with auctions we have not discussed. For example, if you hold

♠ 86   ♡ 863   ◊ AQ107   ♣ Q865

and the auction proceeds 1 ♠ –1 NT–2 ♡, simply return to **two spades**. With

♠ 8   ♡ 863   ◊ AJ976   ♣ Q864

after 1 ♠ –1 NT–2 ♡ **pass** and hope for the best, as you are not strong enough to bid 2 NT and the diamond suit is not good enough to bid at the three-level. If partner opens **one heart**, you respond **one notrump** with

♠ 863   ♡ 86   ◊ AQ106   ♣ Q1097

and partner reverses with **two spades** promising at least 18 points, bid **two notrump** to show that you have all the unbid suits well stopped. You do not need the usual 10–11 points to bid two notrump as partner has points to spare. With

♠ 82   ♡ 86   ◇ AQ10965   ♣ 643

and after the auction 1 ♠ –1 NT–2 ♡, bid **three diamonds**; your suit is good enough to show at the three-level. As you can see, a careful application of the principles discussed in previous sections will lead you to the correct response in just about every possible auction.

Major-Suit Raises after Interference

There is one situation, however, that requires discussion before we can successfully conclude this chapter: what to do if the opponents overcall partner's opening major-suit bid. If, for example, partner opens **one spade** and your right-hand opponent bids **two clubs,** *you can no longer bid one notrump.* If this happens, your responses should be the following:

With 6 to 9 points and support for partner's major, do not raise. You can no longer bid one notrump followed by a preference for partner's major at the two-level. The single raise still shows 10–12 points and at least three-card support; the double raise shows 13–15 points and at least four-card support; the triple raise is pre-emptive.

If the opponents are using weak single jump overcalls, a treatment we recommended in the previous chapter and will discuss in detail later on, you may find them using up even more of your bidding room. For example, suppose partner opens **one spade** and your right-hand opponent overcalls with a weak **three-heart** bid. (The laws of bridge compel the opponents to inform you if they are using the jump overcall as a weak or strong bid.) Your actions are as follows:

1. With 6 to 8 points and support for partner's major, do not raise. You are still unable to use the forcing notrump response.

2. With 9 to 10 points and at least three-card support for partner's suit, support his suit at the three-level. Since you are not

making a *jump* response but bidding at the three-level only under duress, your bid shows only 9–10 Roth Points.

3. With 11 to 15 points and at least three-card support for partner's suit, jump to game in partner's major. *Over a jump overcall,* this shows a strong hand and is *not* preemptive.

These considerations also play a part in later stages in competitive auctions. Consider the following situations:

	PARTNER	OPPONENT	YOU	OPPONENT
1.	1 ♠	Pass	4 ♠	5 ♣
	Pass	Pass	?	
2.	1 ♠	3 ♡	4 ♠	5 ♡
	Pass	Pass	?	
3.	1 ♠	2 ♢	2 ♠	3 ♢
	4 ♠	5 ♢	?	

In the first situation, you are under no compulsion to bid and may pass if you wish. You have made a preemptive raise to four spades, and partner has indicated a distinct lack of interest in the proceedings by passing over the five-club bid.

In the second auction, however, it would be most illogical to pass. Your four-spade bid showed 11 to 15 points and spade support, and indicated that your side has a definite game. You cannot allow the opponents to play in an undoubled five-heart contract and pay only a small penalty when your side has game in a spade contract. If partner knew this, why did he pass? The answer is that he does not know whether to bid five spades or double the opponents for penalties, and would like you to make the decision. With an "offensive" hand such as

♠ K1095   ♡ 2   ♢ AK1087   ♣ Q85

bid **five spades.** You have a maximum (15 points), good spade support, and heart "ruffability." However, you should **double** with

♠ Q86   ♡ KJ8   ♢ AQ85   ♣ 1062

You have a near minimum hand with no "ruffability" and have no reason to believe you can make five spades. But with 26 points your side should have no trouble defeating the opponents' heart contract soundly.

In the third case, you have shown 10 to 12 Roth Points, and partner might like to know whether you have a maximum or minimum. You can tell him by doubling with a minimum and passing with a maximum. After this auction, you rarely have many tricks in the opponents' suit, so it is more important to use the double to show a minimum and warn partner against going on. As in the second example, partner must bid again if you pass since you are in a forcing situation.

Capsule Summary: The Single Major Raise and Forcing Notrump Response

I. THE FIRST RESPONSE: Partner opens one of a major suit, and:

YOU HOLD	YOUR ACTION
1. 10 to 12 points and at least three-card support	Raise to two of major.
2. 6 to 9 points and at least three-card support	Bid 1 NT; support partner's major at the two-level on the next round. But with four or more spades and exactly three hearts bid 1 ♠ over partner's 1 ♡ opening.
3. 6 to 11 points and at most two cards in support	Bid a four-card or longer spade suit over a 1 ♡ opening; otherwise respond 1 NT.

II. OPENER'S REBID

1. Over a single major raise, opener simply adds his points to responder's. If game is definite (and slam impossible) bid game in the major; if game is possible, invite it by raising to three.
2. Over the forcing 1 NT response, rebid as follows:

(1) 19 or more HCP	Balanced hand: bid 2 NT (19 points) or 3 NT (20 or more points).

YOU HOLD	YOUR ACTION
	Six-card major: Jump in major. Five-card major, unbalanced hand: Jump in new suit.
(2) Six-card major suit; less than 19 HCP	Rebid six-card major (jump with 17–18 HCP).
(3) Five-card major suit; less than 19 HCP	Bid your longest new suit; with suits of equal length, bid the lower-ranking. Do not *reverse* unless you have at least 18 points.

III. RESPONDER'S REBID

1. Over a rebid of 2 ♣ or 2 ♢ (or 2 ♡ after an original one-spade opening) by opener:

(1) A hand as in I-2	Bid two of partner's major as planned.
(2) A strong six-card suit	Bid the suit. (A very strong five-card suit may be bid at the two-level).
(3) Singleton or void in opener's original major; at least four cards in his second suit	Raise (with 9–10 Roth Points*). Pass (with 6–8 Roth Points).
(4) 10–11 HCP, all unbid suits stopped	Bid 2 NT.
(5) Doubleton in partner's major; unable to make any of the above bids	Return to two of partner's major.
(6) Anything else	Pass.

2. If opener rebids two of his original major:

(1) 9–10 points and at	Raise to three of the major.

---

* With a stronger hand in support of opener's minor suit, a special bid is needed. Such bids were introduced in the text and will be discussed in detail later.

YOU HOLD	YOUR ACTION
least two-card support *or* 8 points and at least three-card support	
(2) Unable to raise major; good new six-card suit	Bid new suit.
(3) Unable to do (1) or (2) above; 10–11 HCP, no more than a doubleton in partner's major, all unbid suits stopped	Bid 2 NT.
(4) Anything else	Pass.

3. If opener bids 3 NT, it is usually best to pass (or support his original major suit if you always intended to do so).

4. If opener raises to 2 NT, bid as you would over any limited bid; add your points to partner's, determine game chances, and bid accordingly.

5. If partner jumps in a new suit, you are forced to bid until game is reached. Support partner's major; support his second suit; show a good suit of your own; or bid notrump with all unbid suits stopped.

IV. COMPETITIVE AUCTIONS

1. After a simple overcall (e.g. 1 ♠ —2 ♣):

(1) 6–9 points and support for partner's major	Do *not* raise.
(2) 10–12 points and at least three-card support	Raise partner's major to two.
(3) 13–15 points and at least four-card support	Raise partner's major to three (as before).

YOU HOLD	YOUR ACTION

2. After a weak jump overcall (e.g. 1 ♠—3 ♡):

(1) 6–8 points and support for partner's major — Do *not* raise.

(2) 9–10 points and at least three-card support — Bid three of partner's major.

(3) 11–15 points and at least three-card support — Jump to four of partner's major.

— —

REVIEW QUIZ FOR CHAPTER 15

On each of the hands below, count your Roth Points and decide on your action.

Part I: You are Opener

	YOU	PARTNER	YOU HOLD
1.	1 ♡ ?	1 NT	♠8 ♡K109865 ◇AQ3 ♣A32
2.	1 ♠ ?	1 NT	♠AQ765 ♡KQ3 ◇A4 ♣432
3.	1 ♠ ?	1 NT	♠AK9765 ♡AKJ ◇A103 ♣7
4.	1 ♡ ?	1 NT	♠AQ ♡KJ1085 ◇AQ3 ♣KJ7
5.	1 ♠ ?	2 ♠	♠K8765 ♡A83 ◇AK7 ♣42
6.	1 ♡ ?	1 NT	♠8 ♡AJ1093 ◇KQ87 ♣A82
7.	1 ♠ ?	1 NT	♠AKJ85 ♡A9865 ◇K83 ♣---
8.	1 ♡ ?	1 NT	♠AK43 ♡AK865 ◇432 ♣2

	YOU	PARTNER	YOU HOLD			
9.	1 ♡ ?	1 NT	♠K8	♡KQ1065	◇A42	♣Q42
10.	1 ♡ ?	2 ♡	♠86	♡A10876	◇KQ3	♣A32

Part II: You are Responder

	PARTNER	YOU	YOU HOLD			
11.	1 ♠	?	♠Q87	♡6	◇AJ10985	♣K104
12.	1 ♡	?	♠964	♡843	◇AQJ7	♣432
13.	1 ♠	?	♠8	♡863	◇AK10954	♣743
14.	1 ♡	?	♠8	♡K86	◇1098765	♣432
15.	1 ♡ 2 ♡	1 NT ?	♠987	♡6	◇Q875	♣AQ986
16.	1 ♠ 2 ♣	1 NT ?	♠85	♡963	◇AK72	♣J865
17.	1 ♡ 3 ♡	2 ♡ ?	♠K654	♡AQ85	◇107	♣864
18.	1 ♠ 2 ◇	1 NT ?	♠7	♡KJ10965	◇863	♣Q85
19.	1 ♡ 2 ♡	1 NT ?	♠J85	♡K106	◇A8543	♣32
20.	1 ♠ 2 ◇	1 NT ?	♠85	♡KJ107	◇A106	♣Q1098
21.	1 ♠ 2 ♣	1 NT ?	♠2	♡AQ64	◇76543	♣972
22.	1 ♡ 2 ♣	1 NT ?	♠KQ8	♡72	◇8543	♣A1086
23.	1 ♠ 2 ♡	1 NT	♠7	♡AQ85	◇A1064	♣7643

	PTNR	OPP	YOU	YOU HOLD			
24.	1 ♠	2 ♣	?	♠J86	♡7	◇A10865	♣8642
25.	1 ♡	2 ♠*	?	♠85	♡J1087	◇AKQ5	♣1072
		*(weak)					

SOLUTIONS

Part I

	POINTS	BID	
1.	14	2 ♡	Rebid your six-card major.
2.	15	2 ♣	With lower-ranking suits of equal length, bid the lower.
3.	20	4 ♠ (or 3 ◇)	You should have a play for game opposite even a minimum response. While four spades is acceptable, the expert bid is three diamonds—just in case partner has diamonds (or hearts).
4.	20	3 NT	With balanced suit distribution and 20 HCP, bid the notrump game.
5.	16	4 ♠	Partner must have at least ten points, so game is definite. Bid it!
6.	14	2 ◇	Bid your longest lower-ranking new suit.
7.	15	2 ♡	Not quite strong enough for a jump to 3 ♡, and you may not raise notrump with an unbalanced hand.
8.	14	2 ◇	You are not strong enough to "reverse," and thus cannot bid 2 ♠. Bid your three-card minor suit.
9.	14	2 ♣	Bid your lower-ranking new suit.
10.	15	3 ♡	Game is possible if partner has 11 or 12 points; invite it by bidding 3 ♡.

Part II

11.	12	2 ♠	A maximum single raise. Do not bother to mention diamonds. ("Too many bids spoil the broth.")

	POINTS	BID	
12.	7	1 NT	You will support hearts next time around, or pass if partner rebids 2 ♡. Note that the diamond suit is *reliable*.
13.	10 (in ◊) 8 (in NT)	1 NT	The only possible response. You need 11 points to respond at the two-level.
14.	5	Pass	You need six Roth Points to respond.
15.	8	Pass	You have nowhere to go. Partner should not be too miserable as he has at least a six-card heart suit.
16.	8	2 ♠	Support partner's major with a doubleton and only four cards in his minor.
17.	11	4 ♡	Partner must have at least 15 Roth Points (14 needed to open plus one additional point for his supported five-card major), so game is definite.
18.	7	2 ♡	A good example of the effectiveness of the forcing 1 NT response. Standard American players are likely to lose the heart suit.
19.	9	3 ♡	A clear-cut raise; with 9 Roth Points you would raise even with only a doubleton heart, since partner's bid shows a six-card suit.
20.	10	2 NT	With all unbid suits stopped and 10 HCP, you may rebid 2 NT. A bid of 2 ♠ would follow the rule of supporting partner's major with a doubleton rather than passing his minor with only four-card support,

(334)

	POINTS	BID	
			but the notrump bid is more descriptive.
21.	6	Pass	And hope for the best. You may not bid the pitifully weak diamond suit, or the four-card heart suit, or support spades with a singleton.
22.	9	3 ♣	Raise partner's minor with 9 or 10 points and at least four-card support. Do not count Distribution Points as partner may be bidding a three-card suit.
23.	13	4 ♡	An imaginative but entirely proper call that you should find if you did not answer too quickly. Partner must have at least four hearts to bid the suit,* so a playable trump suit has been found and you may count your Distribution Points. With 13 Roth Points, game is definite, so bid it! (Don't give partner a chance to pass—he doesn't know you have a super-maximum, a hand that now is actually too good for your 1 NT response!)
24.	7	Do not raise	2 ♠ would show 10–12 points.
25.	12	4 ♡	Raising as cheaply as possible over the competition shows only 9–10 Roth Points. A 4 ♡ bid shows 11 to 15 points.

* This is not necessarily true if the rebid is in a *minor*, but a *heart* rebid always shows four or more. The reader is invited to prove this to his own satisfaction.

CHAPTER
16

The Weak Two-Bid

Your right-hand opponent has dealt the cards, and you hold

♠ J43   ♡ AQ875   ◇ AQ8   ♣ 86

Your 14 Roth Points clearly warrant an opening bid of **one heart**, so you look forward to the bidding with confidence. To your horror, your right-hand opponent opens with a **two-spade** bid, which his partnership plays as "weak." Suddenly, instead of confidence, you are skating on thin ice. Your heart suit is too shaky to risk a bid at the three-level; a three heart overcall could be doubled and severely penalized. Your points and support for the unbid suits are not good enough to justify a takeout double that would force partner to bid at the three-level. On the other hand, a pass risks missing a makeable game or part score. Regardless of what action you decide to take, your auction has been plunged into a state of confusion by the opponents' preemptive tactics. Modern expert technique favors interfering with the opponents' auction when it is safe to do so, and the weak two-bid is ideally suited to this purpose.

Do you lose anything by abandoning the old-fashioned American strong two-bid? On the contrary, you gain a considerable advantage, because strong two-bids are wasteful and useless. Strong two-bids occur so rarely that it is criminal to reserve four opening bids—two clubs, two diamonds, two hearts, and two spades—for such hands. There is little point in having weapons in your bidding arsenal that are almost never used. Also, strong two-bids waste valuable bidding room. If partner, as is likely, has a weak hand, he must respond two notrump, and the auction is at the three-level before you have a chance to begin.

Therefore, as long as a satisfactory method is available for handling hands worth a strong two opening, you should be quite happy to abandon the archaic Standard American treatment and switch to weak two-bids. They will occur much more often and will make your opponents' bidding life far more difficult. Instead of being able to open peacefully at the one-level and bid according to familiar methods, they will be faced with difficult decisions at a higher level and will have a much greater chance to go wrong. If there is anything more pleasant than bidding accurately to your own best contract, it is undermining the enemy's bidding and watching them flounder in a sea of confusion, often missing good games and part scores (and even slams).

First, we will consider the meaning and use of weak-two bids. Subsequently, we will treat the problem of how to handle hands that would ordinarily qualify for a strong two-bid, since you may be lucky enough to get one of these once in a while.

The Weak Two-Bid

To open with a weak two-bid, you must first consider the vulnerability, just as you would with any other preemptive-type bid. If you are not vulnerable, you should have:

1. A good six- (or seven-) card suit (or very strong five-card suit).

2. 7–10 HCP including one defensive trick, most of which are in your long suit, *but less than 14 total Roth Points.*

3. Usually no side four-card (or longer) major suit.

4. *In close cases,* avoid opening a weak two-bid if you have a side singleton.*

If you are vulnerable, you should have 9–11 HCP, and should not bid a five-card suit unless it is absolutely solid. The other requirements remain the same.

It is very important to note that only two spades, two hearts, and two diamonds are weak two-bids. A special meaning is reserved for the opening bid of two clubs, as we will see later.

Here are some examples of the "do's" and "don'ts" of weak two-bids:

1. ♠86 ♡KQ10965 ◇K83 ♣32   Not Vulnerable

Open 2 ♡. An ideal hand for a weak two bid: a good six-card suit; 8 HCP, mostly in your long suit, and no side four-card major. Vulnerable, you would need one more HCP to open 2 ♡ (as you must have 9–11 HCP).

2. ♠86 ♡K83 ◇32 ♣KQ10965   Not Vulnerable

Pass. You may not open 2 ♣ because a special meaning is reserved for this opening; it is *not* a weak two-bid.

3. ♠AQJ965 ♡8 ◇643 ♣432   Not Vulneräble

Open 2 ♠. While you would prefer not to have a singleton, all the other signs are right: all of your 7 HCP are concentrated in your fine six-card suit.

4. ♠AQ8 ♡K7 ◇1086432 ♣32   Not Vulnerable

Pass. Never open with a weak two-bid when the majority of your points are outside your six-card suit. Also, your diamond suit is too weak.

5. ♠8 ♡AQJ843 ◇A107 ♣432

Open 1 ♡ whether you are vulnerable or not. Do not make a weak

---

* Very often, when you have a singleton your hand has too much potential playing strength to open with a weak two-bid.

two-bid when you meet the requirements for an opening bid of one, which you do since you have 14 Roth Points (with 11 HCP).

6.　♠ KQ8742　♡ Q83　◇ 32　♣ 32　Vulnerable

Pass. You must have at least 9 HCP for a vulnerable weak two-bid; also, your spade suit is moth-eaten—♠ KQ10987 would be more suitable.

7.　♠ 86　♡ Q83　◇ AK10965　♣ 32　Vulnerable

Open 2 ◇. You have the minimum required 9 HCP; your hand is not strong enough to open 1 ◇; and you have a good six-card suit with most of your points concentrated in your long suit.

Responses and Rebids

After the weak two-bid, responder is in charge of the auction. Opener has defined his hand within narrow limits, and it is up to responder to decide where your side is going. As responder, you have the following weapons at your disposal:

1. If you raise partner's suit to *any* level, he must pass. Thus, if partner opens two spades, he must pass if you raise to three spades, four spades, or for that matter *any* number of spades.

2. Partner must also pass if you make any game bid. For example, if partner opens two hearts, he must pass if you bid three notrump or four spades.

3. Similarly, partner is required to pass if you jump in a new suit (e.g., he opens two hearts and you bid three spades).

4. If you bid two notrump, or a new suit, partner must bid again.

The following examples will illustrate the reasons for these rules. In each case, partner has opened with a weak **two-heart** bid; you are not vulnerable and the opponents are.

1.　♠ 743　♡ K8　◇ AK107　♣ AK96

Bid 4 ♡. You expect to make it, but give yourself an extra chance by not telling the opponents what to lead. Since partner should have a six-card suit, two-card support is adequate.

2.　♠85　♡A1083　◇6　♣KJ9765

Bid 4 ♡. The opponents probably have a game in spades (partner is not supposed to have more than three spades) or even a slam. Thus, you should make it as difficult as possible for them to enter the auction. You may make your contract, but even if you do not you will have an excellent result if the opponents are so hindered by your preemptive tactics that they cannot reach their proper contract. Compare this to the first example and note that the opponents may have a great deal of trouble trying to figure out whether your raise to 4 ♡ is preemptive or strong. If they guess wrong, they are headed for disaster! You, on the other hand, couldn't care less; partner must pass your 4 ♡ response and you will be most happy to play in 4 ♡ with either of the above example hands.

3.　♠KQJ10865　♡86　◇K2　♣32

Bid 3 ♠. Remember that partner must pass this bid, so it is safe to make a preempt of your own. The opponents are likely to have game, and the spade jump will certainly prove bothersome to them.

4.　♠75　♡J8　◇A1065　♣A9765

Bid 3 ♡. Make it more difficult for the opponents to compete. They have no idea what your hand is, so the pressure is on them. Since partner should have a six-card heart suit and since he must pass this bid, you are in no real danger.

5.　♠K1087　♡3　◇A654　♣A1097

Pass. You are not going anywhere.

6.　♠KJ8　♡A87　◇A1083　♣KJ2

Bid 3 NT. A bid of 4 ♡ could not be severely criticized, but it may be easier to win nine tricks than ten when your hand is balanced and all unbid suits are securely stopped.

7. ♠ KQ8   ♡ A87   ◇ KQ109   ♣ KJ10

Bid 3 NT. Though much stronger than the hand in problem 6, there is still no chance for slam, as partner has a maximum of 10 HCP.

In the above hands, you required no cooperation from partner. There will be times when you have a strong hand and would like to know how good partner's hand is before reaching a decision concerning game prospects. When this is the case, you simply make use of your forcing two-notrump response *or* a simple bid in a new suit (invitational). Opener's action is straightforward:

1. With a minimum, he rebids his suit (or passes in responder's suit).

2. With a maximum, he bids the best suit that he has below the level of his original suit.

3. If you have bid a new major suit, he may show three-card support by raising.

4. With a maximum and a near-solid suit, he rebids three no-trump.

As responder, you would make use of these ideas on the following hands: (again, partner opens **two hearts,** non-vulnerable against vulnerable)

1.   ♠ AJ10643   ♡ 7   ◇ A105   ♣ AQ6

Bid 2 ♠. If partner rebids 3 ♠, which shows three-card support (he should not have four or more), bid 4 ♠. Over any other rebid, try again by bidding 3 ♠. If partner passes 2 ♠ or 3 ♠, you have no game.

2.   ♠ K8   ♡ J97   ◇ AJ65   ♣ A1052

Bid 2 NT. This is not an attempt to play in notrump, but rather an inquiry as to the strength of partner's hand. If he rebids 3 ♣ or 3 ◇, showing a maximum, jump to 4 ♡. If he rebids 3 ♡, showing a minimum, accept his decision and pass. You need not worry about being abandoned in your notrump bid as partner is required to bid again.

Now let's look at this from the other side of the table. Once again, you are not vulnerable.

	YOU	PARTNER	YOU HOLD
1.	2 ♡	2 NT	♠K86 ♡A108654 ◇32 ♣85
	?		

Bid 3 ♡. You have a minimum hand (7 HCP).

	YOU	PARTNER	YOU HOLD
2.	2 ♠	2 NT	♠AK10965 ♡86 ◇Q83 ♣64
	?		

Bid 3 ◇. With a maximum (9–10 HCP), bid your best suit that ranks below the level of your original suit.

	YOU	PARTNER	YOU HOLD
3.	2 ♡	2 NT	♠Q86 ♡AK10965 ◇105 ♣62
	?		

Bid 3 NT. You have a maximum and a powerful suit.

	YOU	PARTNER	YOU HOLD
4.	2 ♡	2 ♠	♠864 ♡AK10765 ◇J83 ♣3
	?		

Bid 3 ♠. Your first duty is to show your three-card support for partner's major, and the raise carries this message. As you can see, a weak two-bid is acceptable with a singleton when all strength is concentrated in a strong six-card suit.

Subsequent Bidding

Though things may seem a bit strange at first glance, bidding after the weak two-bid is not at all difficult so long as you remember that responder is in charge and opener must follow orders. (Compare with the discussion of limit bids, Chapter 3, Chapter 4B). Opener simply determines whether or not he is permitted to bid. If he must pass, he does so. If he is allowed to bid, he determines if he has a maximum or minimum (remembering that the non-vulnerable weak two-bid shows 7–10 HCP and the vulnerable weak two-bid shows 9–11 HCP) and bids accordingly.

There are a few additional situations that we need to consider before moving on:

	PTNR	OPP.	YOU	YOU HOLD			
1.	2 ♡	2 ♠	?	♠ KQ1087	♡ 64	◇ Q64	♣ 532

Pass. At the moment, you have the opponents in their worst contract (they must be able to do better in diamonds or clubs). If you double, the opponents are certain to run out to a different suit, so pass and hope that they stay in spades. Do not double unless you are prepared to double *all* other contracts.

	PTNR	OPP.	YOU	YOU HOLD			
2.	2 ♡	2 ♠	?	♠ K1086	♡ 7	◇ AQ108	♣ AQ92

Double. The opponents have guessed wrong; the pressure applied by partner's weak two-bid has led them into a losing decision. If the opponents run out into a new suit, you will double again. Partner is not permitted to bid again, so you need not worry that he will get in your way.

	YOU	PARTNER	YOU HOLD			
3.	2 ♡	2 NT	♠ 86	♡ KQJ962	◇ 53	♣ Q63
	3 ♣	3 ♡				
	?					

Pass. You have shown your feature; accept partner's decision. He was hoping that your side values would be in a different suit, and held

$$\text{♠ AK7} \quad \text{♡ A53} \quad \text{◇ AJ102} \quad \text{♣ 754}$$

Game is practically hopeless, but switch your diamonds and club holdings and you would respond 3 ◇, partner would jump to 4 ♡, and you would have reached the good game contract.

(343)

When Responder is a Passed Hand

If responder has passed originally, he cannot hold a strong hand, so the meanings of some bids over a weak two-bid change. Two notrump is not forcing. A new suit bid should be passed whether a jump or not (remember that if responder held a good hand, he would have opened the bidding). A raise to three is now invitational. A few examples:

	YOU	PARTNER	YOU HOLD
1.	Pass	2 ◇	♠ A107 ♡ A83 ◇ 1085 ♣ A764
	?		Vulnerable

Bid 2 NT. You may be able to run nine tricks in notrump if partner has a solid (or near-solid) six-card suit.

	PARTNER	YOU	YOU HOLD
2.	Pass	2 ♡	♠ 76 ♡ AQ10865 ◇ K109 ♣ 32
	3 ♡	?	Not Vulnerable

Bid 4 ♡. When partner is a passed hand, his 3 ♡ raise is invitational.

The Strong 2 ♣ Bid

With the two-diamond, two-heart, and two-spade openings reserved for the weak two-bid, a method is needed for taking care of the occasional strong two-bid that may come along. The strong two-club bid, which shows at least 24 Roth Points and is forcing to game, is reserved for this purpose. It shows *either* a strong two bid in *any* suit, or a very strong balanced hand. The following are good examples of opening two-club bids:

♠ A ♡ AKQ10865 ◇ 7 ♣ AK86: open 2 ♣. You will bid hearts next time.

♠ AQ8 ♡ AKJ ◇ AK86 ♣ KQ6: open 2 ♣. You will rebid 2 NT to show 24–26 HCP.

♠AKQJ875　♡A8　◇AQ8　♣2: open 2 ♣; rebid in spades.

You should open two notrump directly with 21–23 HCP and balanced suit distribution. Therefore, a two-club opening bid followered by a two-notrump rebid shows a stronger hand of 24–26 HCP (and balanced suit distribution). If you should ever happen to hold 27–29 HCP and balanced suit distribution, open two clubs and rebid three notrump. Finally, with the strong suit two-bids, open two clubs and show your suit on your next turn to bid.

Since the two-club bid is forcing to game (remember, the bid has no relation to clubs), responder is not allowed to pass. With more than six points of good quality (such as an ace and a king) he should make the *positive response of two diamonds** (regardless of his distribution) to announce a good hand. With other hands, responder has several options:

1. Bid a good five-card or longer suit (2 ♠, 3 ♣, 3 ◇ or 3 ♡). With diamonds, responder must bid 3 ◇, as 2 ◇ would say nothing about the diamond suit, only show 7 points or more.

2. Bid 2 NT (or 3 NT) to show a balanced hand with 7–8 (or 9–10) points but lacking quality.

3. Bid 2 ♡ to show a very weak hand.

Here's how the rules work:

You are dealer. What call do you make?

1.　♠A6　♡AKJ765　◇KJ3　♣32

Bid 1 ♡. This is a good hand, but much too weak to force to game by bidding 2 ♣. You have 19 Roth Points and need 24 to open with a forcing 2 ♣ bid.

2.　♠AKQJ86　♡AK8　◇AJ8　♣2

Bid 2 ♣. You have 26 Roth Points (doubling your Length Points with a self-sufficient suit) and practically have game in your own

---

* Most players who use two clubs as an artificial strong opening use two diamonds as the *negative* response. The trouble with this treatment is that a suit must be shown to make a positive response—and sometimes no suit of sufficient strength is available. By making two diamonds a "general positive" response rather than a "general negative" this problem is avoided.

hand; just a red queen or a club stopper in partner's hand will produce game.

      3.   ♠ KQ8 ♡ AK97 ◇ AKQ ♣ A108

Bid 2 ♣. You will rebid 2 NT to show 24–26 HCP and balanced
suit distribution.

Partner open 2 ♣. What is your response?

      1.   ♠ 5432 ♡ 432 ◇ 432 ♣ 432

Bid 2 ♡. This is a dreadful hand, but you are not permitted to
pass; partner may well have game in his own hand. The two-heart
response shows a bad hand and no good suit and this mess certainly
qualifies!

      2.   ♠ Q85 ♡ Q85 ◇ J865 ♣ Q62

Bid 2 NT. With 7 "junky" Roth Points or more, you must respond
2 NT.

      3.   ♠ Q85 ♡ K85 ◇ 86 ♣ KJ942

Bid 2 ◇. You will show your clubs later.

      4.   ♠ 8 ♡ 875 ◇ 9654 ♣ KJ976

Bid 3 ♣. The most descriptive bid at this point: weak hand, good
clubs.

You open 2 ♣ and partner responds 2 ♡. What call do you make?

      1.   ♠ AK7 ♡ AQ8 ◇ KQ96 ♣ AK7

Bid 2 NT. This shows 24–26 HCP and a balanced hand.

      2.   ♠ A ♡ AKJ876 ◇ AQJ1095 ♣ ---

Bid 3 ♡. There is no reason to rush the bidding; the 2 ♣ opening
is forcing to game.

      3.   ♠ AQ ♡ A ◇ AKQ876 ♣ AK87

Bid 3 ◇. Once again, do not get carried away; the 2 ♣ opening
is forcing to game.

Suppose you hold:

      ♠ AKJ ♡ AK8 ◇ AJ96 ♣ AJ6

With 26 Roth Points (including one point for all four aces) you open **two clubs,** and to your surprise and gratification partner responds **two diamonds,** showing 7 or more points. Even if he has only 7 points, your side has the necessary total of 33 and slam should be bid. Jump to **three notrump** to show extra strength. With a minimum, such as

♠ AK8   ♡ AK8   ◇ AJ96   ♣ KQ6

just bid **two notrump** to show 24–26 points. Partner will continue on to slam with a maximum.

As you can see, you can have your cake and eat it too. The forcing two-club opening allows you to handle all strong-two bid hands, freeing the two-diamond, two-heart, and two-spade bids for weak two-bid duty. Also, by using the two-club opening bid to take care of balanced hands with 24 or more HCP, you may now open 2 NT with 21–23 HCP (and a balanced hand). This may seem like a small change from the Standard American 22–24 point range, but in fact we have substituted 21-point hands for 24-point hands, and the former occur much more often. Thus, you will get to open 2 NT more frequently, which leads to better bidding since 2 NT describes your hand completely in just one bid.

The Gambling 3 NT Opening

Now that we handle the Standard American 3 NT opening by first opening with the forcing two club bid and rebidding two notrump (and rebidding three notrump with 27–29 points), the opening three notrump bid is free to assume a new meaning. Remember that the expert tries not to let any bid go to waste! Therefore, when you are using the forcing two club opening, the opening three notrump bid may be used as a preempt. This bid shows a special kind of hand: one with a seven-card minor suit headed by the AKQ and an outside king or ace. (The hand may contain a singleton, but no void.) For example, open a "gambling" **three–notrump** bid with

♠ K8   ♡ 6   ◇ AKQJ865   ♣ 876

However, never open a gambling three notrump with a long *major* suit; open with one or four of the major as your hand and the vulnerability indicate.

The purpose of the gambling three notrump is to try to "steal" game by running nine tricks in a notrump contract. Since game in a minor requires 11 tricks (and 29 Roth Points), three notrump is often the only chance for game. The gambling three notrump opening puts the opponents under pressure. If they pass, they often must find just the right lead if three notrump is not cold. If they bid, they must enter the auction at the four-level. However, as with all of the other conventional treatments we are recommending, be sure your partner is playing the same system. If he thinks you have about 25 HCP and a balanced hand, you may achieve a most unenviable result!

Since the gambling three notrump opener's hand is clearly defined, responder has no difficulty in bidding over it. If for example partner opens a gambling **three notrump,** the next player doubles, and you hold a very bad hand, such as

♠ 865   ♡ Q8632   ◊ 432   ♣ 32

run out to **four clubs.** Partner is required to correct to **four diamonds** if that is his long suit and to pass if clubs is his long suit. A three notrump contract could be severely penalized, but the minor-suit contract is safe; even if the opponents double and set you, they probably could have scored even more by playing in a game or slam of their own. If partner opens **three notrump** and you hold

♠ 8652   ♡ A86   ◊ A86   ♣ 543

you should **pass** whether the opponents double or not. Since you have the ace of diamonds, you know that partner has seven solid clubs (he must have a seven-card minor head by AKQ). If he has the ace or king of spades, three notrump is laydown. If he has a red king instead, it is still worth the risk that the opponents will lead the wrong suit, or will not be able to run enough spade tricks to defeat the contract. Finally, with

♠ AK52   ♡ A86   ◊ AJ5   ♣ 543

raise to **six notrump.** Partner must have seven solid clubs and a red-suit king, so you can count 12 tricks. Note that the gambling three notrump, in addition to severely hampering the opponents' bidding, often enables you to reach a game or slam that would be most difficult to bid using standard methods. If used carefully and strictly in accordance with the rules, this bid will be a useful addition to you repertoire of expert bidding techniques.

Capsule Summary: The Weak Two-Bid and Related Openings

I. OPENING BIDS

BID	REQUIREMENTS
2 ♦, 2 ♥, or 2 ♠	Good six-card or longer suit (or very strong five-card suit).
	(Usually) No side four-card (or longer) major suit.
	Non-vulnerable: 7–10 HCP; Vulnerable: 9–11 HCP; points concentrated in your long suit; one defensive trick.
2 ♣	24 or more Roth Points.
2 NT	21–23 HCP and balanced suit distribution.
3 NT	Seven-card minor suit headed by AKQ. One outside ace or king.

II. BIDDING AFTER A WEAK TWO-BID WHEN RESPONDER IS NOT A PASSED HAND

RESPONSE	MEANING
Raise of opener's suit to any level	Opener must pass. Responder may either have a strong hand or be preempting.
Any game bid	Opener must pass.
Jump in a new suit	Preemptive. Opener must pass.
2 NT	"Is opener maximum or minimum?" With a maximum, opener rebids his best new suit or three notrump with a near

RESPONSE	MEANING
	solid suit. With a minimum, opener rebids his suit
New suit	Forcing. Opener may raise with three-card support. Otherwise, opener bids as if responder had bid two notrump.

III. BIDDING AFTER A WEAK TWO-BID WHEN RESPONDER IS A PASSED HAND

RESPONSE	MEANING
Two notrump	Invitational but not forcing.
Single raise	Invitational.
Anything else	Opener should usually pass.

IV. BIDDING AFTER A 2 ♣ OPENING

RESPONSE	MEANING
2 ◇	Seven "quality" points or more, any distribution.
2 ♠, 3 ♣, 3 ◇,	Good five-card or longer suit and at most 6 points.
2 NT, (3 NT)	Balanced hand; 7–8 (9–10) scattered points.
2 ♡	Less than 6 points, no good suit.

OPENER'S REBID	MEANING
Opener rebids a suit without jumping	Opener has a strong two-bid in the suit he has bid.
2 NT	24–26 HCP and balanced suit distribution.
3 NT	27–29 HCP and balanced suit distribution.

V. BIDDING AFTER A 3 NT OPENING

Responder knows that opener has a solid seven-card minor and an outside king or ace and can bid accordingly. If responder bids any number of clubs, opener must pass if clubs is his suit and correct to diamonds at the same level if diamonds is his suit. Other bids are natural.

REVIEW QUIZ FOR CHAPTER 16

For each problem, count your Roth Points and decide on your action.

Part I: You are Dealer
You are the dealer and first to speak. What call do you make?

	VUL.	YOU HOLD
1.	None	♠1098765 ♡A1043 ◇K7 ♣2
2.	None	♠AK10865 ♡AKQ ◇AK3 ♣2
3.	None	♠KQ85 ♡AJ7 ◇AQ8 ♣AJ10
4.	None	♠AQJ865 ♡873 ◇32 ♣32
5.	Both	♠8 ♡AQ10965 ◇864 ♣AJ7
6.	Both	♠AK8 ♡KQJ7 ◇AK10 ♣A108
7.	Opp.	♠K83 ♡7 ◇AKQ9765 ♣86
8.	Both	♠86 ♡K73 ◇64 ♣AQ10764
9.	You	♠85 ♡AKJ864 ◇Q83 ♣32
10.	Both	♠74 ♡854 ◇AJ10965 ♣Q83

Part II: You are Responder

	VUL.	PART-NER	YOU	YOU HOLD
11.	Opp.	2 ♠	?	♠KJ108 ♡7 ◇A10965 ♣843
12.	You	2 ♡	?	♠863 ♡983 ◇A632 ♣A53
13.	Both	2 ♣	?	♠J83 ♡76532 ◇2 ♣10643
14.	Opp.	2 ♡	?	♠A7 ♡Q105 ◇A1084 ♣K976
15.	None	2 ♣	?	♠J65 ♡AQ1086 ◇86 ♣763
16.	Opp.	2 ◇	?	♠KJ97 ♡AQ6 ◇A83 ♣KJ9
17.	Opp.	2 ♠	?	♠K8 ♡AK97 ◇K1087 ♣A83
18.	Opp.	2 ♡	?	♠863 ♡107 ◇A1086 ♣AJ97
19.	You	2 ♣	?	♠AJ8 ♡10864 ◇K108 ♣987
20.	Opp.	3 NT	?	♠K1098 ♡AK109 ◇432 ♣32

(351)

	VUL.	PART-NER	YOU	YOU HOLD
21.	Both	2 ♣	?	♠82 ♡KQJ1086 ◇863 ♣85
22.	Opp.	2 ♡	?	♠QJ96 ♡7 ◇A1094 ♣QJ97

Part III: You are Opener

	VUL.	YOU	PART-NER	YOU HOLD
23.	Opp.	2 ♡ ?	4 ♡	♠K83 ♡AQ9876 ◇432 ♣2
24.	Both	2 ♣ ?	2 ♡	♠KQ8 ♡AK9 ◇AKQ8 ♣A109
25.	None	2 ♠ ?	2 NT	♠AK10965 ♡863 ◇Q83 ♣2
26.	You	2 ♠ ?	2 NT	♠AK10965 ♡863 ◇Q83 ♣2
27.	None	2 ♡ ?	2 ♠	♠642 ♡KJ10965 ◇A2 ♣32
28.	Both	3 NT ?	4 ♣	♠86 ♡A85 ◇AKQJ763 ♣2
29.	Both	2 ♣ ?	2 ♡	♠86 ♡AKQJ1098 ◇AK ♣A7
30.	None	2 ♡ ?	2 ♠	♠98 ♡AQ8642 ◇J43 ♣64

SOLUTIONS

POINTS	BID	

Part I

1.	11	Pass	A terrible hand for a weak two-bid. All your points are outside your long suit; you have an outside four-card major; and your long suit is very weak.

	POINTS	BID	
2.	26	2 ♣	Make the forcing 2 ♣ opening; you will show your spades on your next turn.
3.	21	2 NT	Open 2 NT with 21–23 HCP and balanced suit distribution.
4.	10	2 ♠	An ideal non-vulnerable weak two-bid: 7 HCP, all in your good six-card suit. Vulnerable, you should pass, as you would need 9 HCP to open with a weak two-bid.
5.	14	1 ♡	Do not open with a weak two-bid when you meet the requirements for an opening bid of one of a suit.
6.	24	2 ♣	You will rebid 2 NT to show 24–26 HCP and a balanced hand.
7.	(19)	3 NT	The "gambling" 3 NT: a solid seven-card minor and an outside king or ace. Point requirements are not too relevant for this opening bid, but remember to double your Length Points with a self-sufficient suit.
8.	12	Pass	You may not make a weak two-bid in clubs. An opening 2 ♣ bid is forcing to game.
9.	13	2 ♡	You meet all the requirements for the vulnerable weak two-bid.
10.	8	Pass	You must have 9–11 HCP for a vulnerable weak two-bid.

Part II

11.	11	4 ♠	The vulnerability dictates a preemptive raise. Let the opponents guess whether your hand is weak or strong. Partner does not care as he is required to pass.
12.	8	Pass	The opponents may have a game, but the vulnerability is against you. If you bid on, the opponents will be able to gain more

POINTS	BID	
		by doubling and setting you than by bidding a non-vulnerable game.
13. 1	2 ♡	You must respond, and with 6 points or less and no suit you must bid 2 ♡.
14. 14	2 NT	You will jump to 4 ♡ if partner shows a maximum by bidding a new suit but pass a minimum rebid of 3 ♡.
15. 7	2 ◇	Your hand qualifies for a positive response.
16. 18	3 NT	Partner has at most 10 HCP, so there is no chance for slam. 3 NT should be easy to make.
17. 17	4 ♠	You expect to make 4 ♠, and if the opponents think you are preempting and enter the auction, you will be able to double and obtain a sizable penalty.
18. 9	3 ♡	With favorable vulnerability, step up the pressure on the opponents. Partner must pass. (A *pass* is acceptable).
19. 8	2 ◇	A positive response.
20. 10	Pass	There is little chance for slam and no reason to bid. Maybe an unfavorable opening lead will set you, but such pessimism is a losing tactic. The opponents are under pressure and likely to guess wrong on the opening lead.
21. 10	4 ♡	The 14 ♡ bid shows a solid suit missing the ace. Partner will greatly appreciate this information. (Partner will interpret this bid correctly if he remembers that with a strong hand you would bid 2 ◇).
22. 10	Pass	Your offensive prospects are nil. Let the opponents bid and get into trouble.

Part III

23. 14	Pass	You must follow orders. You are not permitted to bid.

	POINTS	BID	
24.	25	2 NT	Show your 25 HCP and balanced suit distribution.
25.	12*	3 ◇	With 9 HCP, you have a near-maximum non-vulnerable weak two-bid. Bid your best new suit that is lower-ranking than your first suit.
26.	12*	3 ♠	9 HCP is a minimum for a vulnerable weak two-bid. To show a minimum, rebid your suit.
27.	10	3 ♠	Show your three-card support for partner's major suit. When raising partner's suit, do *not* count any Length Points for side suits.
28.	(21)	4 ◇	You are under orders to pass if clubs is your long suit or correct to diamonds if that is your suit. Partner is simply trying to get out of 3 NT and may have nothing in clubs.
29.	28	3 ♡	Show your suit. Since the opening 2 ♣ bid is forcing to game, partner must bid again.
30.	8	Pass	You have a minimum; there is no reason to think any other contract will be better; the 2 ♠ response is not forcing.

---

* Since partner's two-notrump bid is not a true attempt to play in notrump (more likely a game invitation in support of your suit—remember, a raise would be preemptive) do *not* DEMOTE your distribution points.

CHAPTER

17

The Preemptive Jump
Overcall

As your next step down the road to making your own bidding more accurate and your opponents' lives more uncomfortable, we strongly recommend that you drop the Standard American strong jump overcall and replace it with the preemptive (weak) jump overcall. When used correctly, preemptive bids have tremendous advantages. They can cause the enemy to miss a game or slam, get to the wrong game or slam and go down, or walk into a trap and suffer a large penalty. Also, your own bidding is simplified, since after only one bid your partner has an excellent picture of your entire hand. Players not using weak two-bids and weak jump overcalls often have to pass, leaving their partners in the dark as to their holdings and permitting their opponents a leisurely and uninterrupted auction.

We have seen that the weak two-bid is a very effective preemptive device as well as an accurate limit bid for constructive purposes. Sometimes, however, the opponents will scuttle your plans by opening the bidding with one of a suit before your turn to bid comes around. While they have escaped the fangs of the weak two-bid, you can nevertheless confound them with another of your modern expert bidding weapons: the weak jump overcall. This device will also be an aid in your own constructive bidding, for a simple overcall will show a reasonably good hand (often enabling the overcaller's partner to make a penalty double).

Before turning to a discussion of this bid, it is important to repeat a basic principle of preemptive bidding. *After a preempt, the partner of the preemptive bidder is in charge of the auction.* Unless a forcing bid is made (such as 2 NT by partner over your weak two-bid), the preemptive bidder must accept his partner's decision. If you make *any* preempt—an opening bid of three or four of a suit, a weak two-bid, or a weak jump overcall—remember that partner is in command. Do not be concerned if he doubles the opponents in a suit in which you are void, or jumps to a game contract; and do not be tempted to bid again if he passes. You have told your story and partner knows your hand; let him decide what to do and accept his decision.

The Preemptive Jump Overcall

Standard American uses the strong jump overcall to show a good hand (approximately 19 points or more) and a good suit. Aside from the fact that this bid rarely comes up, it usually confuses rather than helps matters; partner almost always as a very poor hand and rarely knows what he is expected to do. You, however, will not be using this wasted bid, for you will be playing the weak jump overcall. Here's how the bid works:

1. If you are not vulnerable, you should have a fairly strong six-card suit, a maximum of 9 HCP, mostly in your long suit, and a reasonable expectation of winning within four tricks of your bid. You will usually *not* have a solid suit, and you are warning partner against taking any further action except at his own risk.

2. If you are vulnerable, you should have a *very* strong six-card suit; a maximum of 11 HCP, mostly in your long suit; and a reasonable expectation of winning within three tricks of your preemptive

contract if the opponents are also vulnerable. If the opponents are not vulnerable, they are more likely to double you than to try for a contract of their own, so you should be within two tricks of your preemptive contract.

Let's look at some examples:

OPP.	YOU	YOU HOLD
1. 1 ♡	?	♠8 ♡65 ◇QJ10965 ♣A1095
(Opponents Vul.)		

Bid 3 ◇. An ideal non-vulnerable weak jump overcall. You have very little defense against a major-suit contract and may get the opponents into the wrong contract by crowding the bidding. Furthermore, your bid simultaneously warns partner that your hand is not of prime quality and gives him the opportunity to participate in further destructive action against the opponents.

2. 1 ◇	?	♠AQ10965 ♡9876 ◇3 ♣32
(Opponents Vul.)		

Bid 2 ♠. With favorable vulnerability and a reasonable six-card suit, the preemptive jump overcall is indicated. In addition to obstructing the opponents, it also acts as a warning to partner.

3. 1 ♣	?	♠3 ♡AK10864 ◇Q1054 ♣72
(None Vul.)		

Bid 1 ♡. This hand is too strong for a weak jump overcall. Hands with 6–4–2–1 distribution often produce game if partner has a few key cards, and you do have some defensive values.

4. 1 ♡	?	♠AQ1065 ♡8643 ◇83 ♣92
(Opp. Vul.)		

Pass. This hand is too weak for an overcall of any kind. Also, it is especially dangerous to overcall with length in the opponents' suit. If your left-hand opponent is less likely to have cards in his partner's suit, he is more likely to have cards in your suit (and thus more likely to double).

(358)

5.   1 ♡   ?   ♠86   ♡45   ◇A86   ♣J108642
(Opp. Vul.)

Pass. You are too weak for a simple overcall and have too much defense for a weak jump overcall. Just like a weak two-bid, a weak jump overcall should be made only when most of the strength is concentrated in your long suit.

6.   1 ◇   ?   ♠AKJ865   ♡963   ◇853   ♣2
(Both Vul.)

Bid 2 ♠. Your hand is good enough for a vulnerable weak jump overcall and you have little in the way of outside defensive values.

7.   1 ♣   ?   ♠8   ♡AKQJ86   ◇432   ♣J104
(Opp. Vul.)

Bid 1 ♡. With a solid suit, you do not wish to convey the message to partner that your offensive prospects look poor, and that is what a nonvulnerable weak jump overcall would mean. However, if you are vulnerable, you may overcall 2 ♡ even if the opponents are not vulnerable as you are within two tricks of your preemptive bid. A vulnerable weak jump overcall may be made on a very good suit.

8.   1 ♡   ?   ♠KQJ1042   ♡863   ◇753   ♣2
(Both Vul.)

Bid 2 ♠. You are within three tricks of your preemptive bid and have your strength concentrated in your six-card suit.

9.   1 ♡   ?   ♠KQJ1042   ♡863   ◇753   ♣2
(You Vul.)

Pass. If you are vulnerable and the opponents are not, you must be within two tricks of your contract.

10.   1 ◇   ?   ♠83   ♡Q87654   ◇863   ♣86
(None Vul.)

Pass. You must assume at least three heart losers and are not within four tricks of your contract.

Responding to Weak Jump Overcalls

Since the preemptive bidder's hand is defined within narrow limits, responder usually has a good idea of what action to take. Responder is in complete charge of the auction and can double the opponents, bid game, pass, or bid a new suit without fear of intervention by partner. The only forcing bid responder can make is a cue-bid of the opponents' suit. The weak jump overcaller can and usually should pass any other bid. In general, you are likely to have little difficulty handling the subsequent auction because partner's hand is very well defined.

Let's try a little experiment. Without any further discussion of the responses to weak jump overcalls or a Capsule Summary of any kind, try the following short quiz. With logic as your guide, you should be able to determine most of the correct answers.

	OPP	PTNR	OPP	YOU	VUL	YOU HOLD	
1.	1 ◇	2 ♠	Pass	?	None	♠ 8	♡ AQ965
						◇ Q83	♣ K843
2.	1 ♠	3 ◇	Pass	?	None	♠ QJ3	♡ AKQ
						◇ AK5	♣ Q1092
3.	1 ♣	2 ♠	Pass	?	Opp.	♠ K1096	♡ 86
						◇ AJ876	♣ 32
4.	1 ♡	3 ♣	Pass	?	Opp.	♠ K63	♡ AJ6
						◇ K865	♣ Q32
5.	1 ♡	1 ♠	4 ♡	?	You	♠ KQ83	♡ 8
						◇ 10642	♣ A742

On both the first and fourth hands, you should pass. Partner's non-vulnerable weak jump overcall announces a relatively poor hand with a broken suit and warns you against bidding further. You have no reason to disregard his warning and should pass before you get into trouble.

On the second hand, a 3 NT response is correct. Partner has at least a six-card diamond suit and you can count nine tricks.

On the third hand, raise to 4 ♠. The opponents probably have a vulnerable game in hearts or clubs, so you will show a profit even if 4 ♠ is doubled and set a trick or two. Furthermore, the opponents have to guess what to do if they bid on and may well wind up in the wrong contract.

On the last hand, you may be tempted to pass because you have only 11 Roth Points and partner merely overcalled at the one-level. However, you have a valuable clue at your disposal: partner did *not* make a weak jump overcall! This must be because his hand is too strong for such a bid. Therefore, you should bid 4 ♠. Note how the weak jump overcall gives you an extra advantage: you can place more confidence in partner's simple overcalls and bid (or double) accordingly. Since partner's overcall shows true values, this is probably "your hand." Don't let the opponents talk you out of it.

Capsule Summary: The Weak Jump Overcall

VULNERABILITY	REQUIREMENTS FOR WEAK JUMP OVERCALL
You are not vulnerable	Fairly good (but not solid) six-card suit. Maximum of 9 HCP; points concentrated in your long suit. Within four tricks of your contract.
You and the opponents are both vulnerable	Good six-card suit (may be solid). Maximum of 11 HCP; points concentrated in your long suit. Within three tricks of your contract.
You are vulnerable, opponents are not	Good six-card suit (may be solid). Maximum of 11 HCP; points concentrated in your long suit. Within two tricks of your contract.

SUBSEQUENT BIDS

Responder is in charge of the auction and opener must accept his decision. Responder bases his action on his knowledge of partner's hand and the vulnerability, remembering that a non-vulnerable weak jump overcall is a warning to pass.

REVIEW QUIZ FOR CHAPTER 17

Since weak jump overcalls are based on HCP, suits, and playing strength, you need not count your Roth Points (though it is always a good idea to do so, if only for practice). In each of the following problems, what call do you make?

Part I

	OPP.	YOU	VUL.	YOU HOLD
1.	1 ◇	?	You	♠ KQ10965 ♡ 863 ◇ 863 ♣ 2
2.	1 ♣	?	Opp.	♠ 8 ♡ QJ10965 ◇ Q83 ♣ 865
3.	1 ♠	?	None	♠ 8 ♡ AK10875 ♡ A864 ♣ 32
4.	1 ♡	?	Both	♠ KQ10842 ♡ 73 ◇ Q105 ♣ 32
5.	1 ♣	?	You	♠ 86 ♡ KQJ1098 ◇ K108 ♣ 74
6.	1 ◇	?	Opp.	♠ Q86432 ♡ AJ7 ◇ Q108 ♣ 3
7.	1 ♡	?	Opp.	♠ 9 ♡ 86 ◇ KJ10864 ♣ Q1054
8.	1 ♠	?	Both	♠ 86 ♡ KQJ954 ◇ AJ10 ♣ 54
9.	1 ♠	?	You	♠ 8 ♡ AK10432 ◇ KQ9 ♣ 653
10.	1 ♣	?	Opp.	♠ QJ10874 ♡ Q86 ◇ 43 ♣ 32

Part II

	OPP.	PART.	OPP.	YOU	VUL.	YOU HOLD
11.	1 ◇	2 ♡	Pass	?	None	♠ KQ8 ♡ AJ8 ◇ AQ10 ♣ KJ87
12.	1 ♣	2 ♠	Pass	?	Opp.	♠ 65 ♡ KJ987 ◇ AQ865 ♣ 3
13.	1 ◇	2 ♠	Pass	?	Both	♠ KJ96 ♡ 9 ◇ 643 ♣ AQJ65

	OPP.	PART.	OPP.	YOU	VUL.	YOU HOLD
14.	1 ♠	3 ♦	Pass	?	Opp.	♠KJ865 ♡AQ73 ♦--- ♣K1084
15.	1 ♡	2 ♠	4 ♡	?	Opp.	♠8 ♡AQ65 ♦8642 ♣K832
16.	1 ♡	2 ♠	4 ♡	?	Both	♠8 ♡AQ65 ♦A832 ♣KQ85
17.	1 ♠	3 ♡	3 ♠	?	Both	♠KQ1086 ♡8 ♦Q83 ♣9876
18.	1 ♠	3 ♡	4 ♣	?	Opp.	♠QJ102 ♡AK98 ♦6432 ♣3
19.	---	---	1 ♡	2 ♠	Opp.	♠KJ10964 ♡--- ♦8643 ♣532
	3 ♡	Dbl	Pass	?		
20.	---	---	1 ♠	3 ♡	Opp.	♠--- ♡KQ9864 ♦862 ♣J864
	4 ♠	Pass	Pass	?		

S O L U T I O N S

Part I

BID

1. Pass — If you are vulnerable and the opponents are not, you must be within two tricks of your contract. You can be reasonably sure of only five tricks, three short of a 2 ♠ contract. (8 Roth Points)

2. 2 ♡ — An ideal nonvulnerable weak jump overcall. (8)

3. 2 ♡ — With 11 HCP, you are too strong for a nonvulnerable weak jump overcall. Even vulnerable, you should prefer a 2 ♡ overcall with your two aces, a king, and 6–4–2–1 distribution. (15)

4. 2 ♠ — You have a reasonable expectation of taking at least five tricks. (10)

BID
—

5. 2 ♡   You have a reasonable expectation of taking six tricks. (Compare with the first problem.) (13)

6. Pass   Never make a weak jump overcall when the majority of your strength is outside your long suit. A 1 ♠ bid is not horrendous but you should have a better suit for this call. (12)

7. 3 ♦   A fine hand for the weak jump overcall: little defense, and most of your HCP in your long suits. (9)

8. 2 ♡   You have too much offensive potential to flash the stop sign to partner. Your heart suit is good enough for a vulnerable overcall at the two-level. (14)

9. 2 ♡   With 12 HCP, you are too strong for a weak jump overcall. (15)

10. 2 ♠   A good weak jump overcall. Standard American players would have to pass—you can annoy the opponents with safety. (8)

Part II

11. 3 NT   With a balanced hand and plenty of stoppers in all suits, nine tricks will be easier than ten. A 4 ♡ bid is not bad, but 3 NT figures to make more often. (20)

12. Pass   Partner's nonvulnerable weak jump overcall is a warning against bidding on. With broken suits, only 10 HCP, and no fit for his suit, you have every reason to heed his warning. (10)

13. 4 ♠   You might make 4 ♠, but even if you don't it may be a good save against the opponents' possible heart game. The opening bidder must have a good hand with diamonds and hearts, and his partner was not quite good enough to come in at the three-level. There is an excellent chance that the opponents will never find the heart suit at all. (14)

14. Pass   Bidding can only make things worse. (13)

BID
---

15. Pass   Despite your good heart holding, 4 ♡ is odds on to make. Partner has a poor hand for his weak jump overcall, and you should not even be tempted to double. A save is not to be considered; with such a poor fit for partner's suit, the penalty will surely be excessive. (9)

16. Double   The opponents have guessed wrong, and you must exact punishment. Opener undoubtedly has a very light hand, and responder stretched to jump to game since a simple 3 ♡ raise would show minimal values. Partner may even contribute a trick on defense, as he has made a *vulnerable* weak jump overcall. (15)

17. Pass   The opponents have found the only denomination you can defeat. If you don't tell them by doubling, they may stay there. (7)

18. 5 ♡   A save will not be excessively penalized because of your good fit with partner. Hopefully, the opponents will wind up in 5 ♠ (which you will *not* double). This is a "premature save," designed to force the opponents to guess. (13)

19. Pass   Partner knows you have a bad hand. Follow orders. (8)

20. Pass   You have no choice and should not even think about bidding. The opponents may have missed a slam or may be in the wrong suit; but even if 4 ♠ is the right contract, you must pass as you are not permitted to bid again. Remember that the *partner* of the preemptive bidder is in charge of the auction! (10)

CHAPTER
18

The Weak Jump Response

Let us return to a problem we posed back in chapter 14. Your partner opens **one diamond,** and you must decide what to respond with each of the following hands:

      1.   ♠ Q109843   ♡ 543   ◊ 2   ♣ 863
      2.   ♠ KJ10642   ♡ A53   ◊ Q2   ♣ 32

If you are playing Standard American, you are in trouble. With the first hand, you must pass; you have only three points and are not strong enough to respond. You are unable to bid your best suit; and the opponents, who are most likely to have their fair share of the points and be most interested in entering the auction, have only a feeble one-diamond bid to contend with. Faced with this dreary situation, perhaps you will decide to "cheat" and respond one spade, but this is equally unsatisfactory. Since you do not have the values for a one-level response, your side is quite likely to get overboard. Partner would be fully within his rights to drive to game over your one-spade response with ♠ 76 ♡ AK8 ◊ AKJ9 ♣ AJ72. He will be quite upset to find that your hand will not produce a single trick in three notrump and will go down two or three tricks for a most unsatisfactory result. Nor is a four-spade contract much better.

With the second hand, you have no problem at your first turn to bid and make the obvious response of **one spade.** What do you do if partner rebids **two clubs?** A two-spade bid would indicate a minimum response and a three-spade bid would be forcing. Neither message is warranted.

The reason for this problem is that Standard American uses the jump response over partner's opening bid of one of a suit as a powerhouse bid, promising at least 19 points. Such hands do come up, but are relatively infrequent. More important, scientific bidding has reached a point where it is relatively easy to bid very strong hands without using the strong jump response. There is plenty of bidding room, since slam is all but certain. Consequently, the strong jump response accomplishes nothing whatsoever.

As we have noted in previous chapters, one of the important characteristics of modern expert bidding is that no bid is allowed to be wasted. Let the losing traditional Standard American players use the worthless strong jump shift response. You will use the jump response as a weak bid, which will effectively and easily solve the problems described at the beginning of this chapter.

The Weak Jump Response

Provided you are not a passed hand, the requirements for the weak jump response over partner's opening bid of one of a suit are as follows:

1. A maximum of 6 HCP.

2. A six-card or longer suit. If your jump response is made at the two-level, a fairly good five-card suit is acceptable. If your response is made at the three-level, you should have a *strong* six-card suit.

3. Inability to support partner's major suit. (Remember that if partner opens one heart or one spade, showing a five-card suit, three-card support is sufficient.)

Here are some examples:

PARTNER	YOU	YOU HOLD
1. 1 ◇	?	♠ QJ9765 ♡ 863 ◇ 1092 ♣ 4

Bid 2 ♠. This is no problem when you are using weak jump responses. The 2 ♠ bid warns partner that you are very weak, immediately gets you to what is most likely to be your partnership's best suit, and forces the opponents to enter the auction at the three-level if they wish to compete.

2. 1 ♡	?	♠ 1098432 ♡ 86 ◇ 42 ♣ QJ8

Bid 2 ♠. The weak jump shift response was created for hands such as this. Note that you do *not* need a *strong* six-card suit to make a weak jump response.

3. 1 ♣	?	♠ KQJ98 ♡ 743 ◇ 643 ♣ 32

Bid 2 ♠. It is permissible to have a *strong* five-card suit when your bid is at the two-level, so long as you meet all the other requirements for the weak jump response.

4. 1 ◇	?	♠ 86 ♡ 743 ◇ 32 ♣ J98765

Pass. Too weak for a jump to the three-level.

5. 1 ◇	?	♠ 86 ♡ J42 ◇ 27 ♣ QJ10984

Bid 3 ♣. This is a minimum for the jump *to the three-level.* A slight amount of risk is involved, but you are unlikely to play 3 ♣ doubled, as the opponents will probably bid. Make it as difficult as possible for them to reach the best contract by using the weak jump response.

6. 1 ♣	?	♠ AJ9765 ♡ Q103 ◇ Q4 ♣ 32

Bid 1 ♠. You are too strong for the weak jump response, which shows a maximum of 6 HCP. When you later rebid 2 ♠ partner will know you have at least 7 HCP *because you did not jump originally.*

A second important thing to note is that a jump response is always preemptive over an intervening call by right-hand opponent. In each of the following auctions, the last bid is a weak jump response:

	PARTNER	OPPONENT	YOU	OPPONENT
(1)	1 ♣	1 ♦	2 ♠	
(2)	1 ♦	Double	2 ♡	
(3)	Pass	Pass	1 ♡	1 ♠
	3 ♣			
(4)	Pass	Pass	1 ♦	Double
	2 ♠			

A jump response is *not* weak only when you are a passed hand *and* there is no interference by the opponents. In this case, the bid shows a maximum pass and is strongly invitational. For example:

	YOU	OPP.	PART.	OPP.	YOU HOLD
1.	Pass	Pass	1 ♦	Pass	♠ QJ10965 ♡ AK8
	?				♦ 643 ♣ 2

With 13 Roth Points, you were only one point short of an opening and had to pass (you had too much in the way of outside values to open with a weak two-bid). Show your maximum pass by jumping to 2 ♠, which strongly invites partner to continue. Since you are a passed hand and the opponents have been silent, this is *not* a weak jump response.

	YOU	OPP.	PART.	OPP.	
2.	Pass	Pass	1 ♦	1 ♡	♠ QJ10965 ♡ AK8
	?				♦ 643 ♣ 2

Bid 1 ♠. A 2 ♠ bid would be a weak jump response since your right-hand opponent has entered the auction; your hand is much too good for such a bid.

So, remember that a jump response is weak *except* when you have passed originally *and* the opponents are silent. If you are not a passed hand, or if your right-hand opponent has bid, the jump response is weak.

Bidding after a Weak Jump Response

It is essential for opener to keep in mind that responder's hand is very weak. Even a hand that looks like a powerhouse may have trouble producing a game opposite a weak jump response. Responder is flashing the red light, and opener must proceed with extreme caution (if he proceeds at all). Opener has the following options available:

1. A single raise of responder's suit is invitational. Responder should proceed to game if he has a maximum weak jump response.

2. A bid of 2 NT is forcing for one round. Responder must bid again and is allowed to bid 3 NT or a new suit. The 2 NT bid usually denies three or more cards in partner's suit.

3. A bid in a new suit or a jump in a new suit is highly invitational (but not forcing) and warns responder that opener does not like his suit.

4. Any other bid must be passed.

Some illustrations:

	YOU	OPP.	PART.	OPP.		
1.	1 ◇	Pass	2 ♡	Pass	♠ KJ10 ♡ 7	
	?				◇ AK654 ♣ A1064	

Pass. There is no chance for game and it is too risky to look for a better spot.

	YOU	OPP.	PART.	OPP.		
2.	1 ♣	Pass	2 ♠	Pass	♠ Q1064 ♡ 8	
	?				◇ AQ7 ♣ AK765	

Bid 4 ♠. You hope to make it, perhaps losing only one spade, one heart and one diamond.

	YOU	OPP.	PART.	OPP.			
3.	1 ♣	Pass	2 ♡	Pass	♠ A86	♡ 7	◇ K3
	?				♣ KQJ8642		

Bid 3 ♣. Since you have not raised partner's suit or bid a new suit, partner is required to pass, so there is no danger. The opponents may take over from this point, but at least they are forced to start at the three-level.

	YOU	OPP.	PART.	OPP.	
4.	1 ◇	Pass	2 ♠	Pass	♠ AK96 ♡ A8
	?				◇ AK10642 ♣ 3

Bid 6 ♠. You can set up the diamond suit for discards. Even if partner has only six small spades, the odds favor bringing home the trumps without a loser.

	YOU	OPP.	PART.	OPP.	
5.	1 ◇	Pass	2 ♡	Pass	♠ A7 ♡ KJ
	?				◇ AK9765 ♣ AJ5

Bid 3 ♡. Invite partner to bid game with a maximum weak jump response. If he passes, don't be astonished if he has difficulty making 3 ♡.

	YOU	OPP.	PART.	OPP.	
6.	1 ◇	Pass	2 ♡	Pass	♠ AJ64 ♡ 7
	?				◇ AQ109 ♣ AQJ7

Pass. And pass quickly! You aren't going anywhere opposite a weak jump response. If you pass fast enough, the opponents may enter the auction and get demolished.

	YOU	OPP.	PART.	OPP.	
7.	1 ◇	Pass	2 ♡	Pass	♠ A765 ♡ K
	?				◇ AK87 ♣ AKJ8

Bid 4 ♡. As you can see, you need quite a good hand to have a play for game opposite a weak jump response. Do not bid notrump;

you will have great difficulty getting to dummy in a notrump contract.

As example 6 indicates, it is important to pass without excess thought when your side has no chance for game. It is unethical to snap out the pass with machine-gun rapidity, but prolonged thought (while ethical) will warn the opponents and they will refrain from bidding. Study the above examples, giving partner a typical weak jump shift response (such as QJ9 x x x in his suit and no more than an outside queen) and see how good a hand opener must have for game to be possible after a weak jump shift response. This is one reason why the weak jump response is mandatory: it is likely to be the opponents' hand, and you must interfere with their bidding as much as safely possible in order to give them the best chance of getting to the wrong contract.

The weak jump responder has few problems after making his jump response. Most often, he will pass throughout the remainder of the auction. If partner invites game, accept his invitation with a maximum and pass with a minimum. Thus, if partner opens **one diamond** and raises your **two spade** response to **three spades,** proceed to **four spades** with

♠ QJ10987   ♡ 863   ◊ Q6   ♣ 32 (5 HCP and a good suit)

but **pass** with

♠ 1086432   ♡ 74   ◊ 643   ♣ Q2 (2 HCP and a poor suit).

If opener rebids **two notrump,** you must bid again. While the bid of a new suit is highly invitational but not forcing, support a bid of a new suit with three-card or longer support. Bid a new suit below the level of your first suit (or, with a good suit, three notrump) with a maximum hand. Rebid your own suit over two notrump and pass over a new suit bid with a minimum. Remember once again that partner is in charge of the auction once you have preempted, and you must accept his decision regarding passing, doubling the opponents, or bidding game. You are permitted to bid again only if partner invites game by raising your suit or forces you to bid by bidding two notrump.

Capsule Summary: The Weak Jump Response

JUMP RESPONSE BY	MEANING
Unpassed hand	Weak jump response.
Over competition by the opponents (passed or unpassed hand)	Weak jump response.
Passed hand, opponents silent	Maximum pass; urges partner to bid again but is not forcing.

REQUIREMENTS FOR WEAK JUMP RESPONSE

1. A maximum of 6 HCP.
2. A six-card or longer suit. (A good five-card suit is permissible for bidding at the two-level.)
3. Inability to support partner's major suit.

OPENER'S REBID OVER THE WEAK JUMP RESPONSE

BID	MEANING
Single raise of responder's suit	Invitational. Jump overcaller should bid game with a minimum and pass with a maximum.
2 NT	Forcing. Jump overcaller must bid again, and should raise with at least three-card support, bid a new suit (lower-ranking than his first suit) or three notrump with a maximum, and rebid his suit with a minimum.
	Jump overcaller must pass.
Any new-suit bid (jump or not)	Highly invitational, but not forcing.

REVIEW QUIZ FOR CHAPTER 18

For each problem, count your HCP and decide on your action. Remember that while your total point count is not vital for purposes of preemptive bidding, it is a good idea to keep in practice.

	PART.	OPP.	YOU	OPP.	VUL.	YOU HOLD
1.	1 ♦	Pass	?		Both	♠ Q109876 ♡ 863 ♦ 2 ♣ 543
2.	1 ♣	Pass	?		None	♠ J109843 ♡ 7 ♦ AQJ ♣ 432
3.	1 ♠	Pass	?		Both	♠ 8 ♡ J105432 ♦ 643 ♣ 762
4.	1 ♦	Pass	?		You	♠ 72 ♡ J86432 ♦ QJ8 ♣ 75
5.	1 ♦	1 ♡	?		None	♠ AQ1097 ♡ 643 ♦ 87 ♣ 942
6.	---	---	Pass	Pass	You	♠ 86 ♡ 72
	1 ♡	Pass	?			♦ KJ10987 ♣ 863
7.	1 ♠	Pass	?		You	♠ J85 ♡ 83 ♦ KQ10965 ♣ 72
8.	---	---	Pass	Pass	You	♠ K108643 ♡ 743
	1 ♦	1 ♡	?			♦ 92 ♣ 32
9.	1 ♡	Dbl	?		Opp.	♠ Q109865 ♡ 86 ♦ Q86 ♣ 32
10.	1 ♦	Pass	2 ♠	Pass	Both	♠ KQ9764 ♡ 863
	3 ♠	Pass	?			♦ 32 ♣ 32
11.	1 ♦	Pass	2 ♠	Pass	Opp.	♠ KQ9764 ♡ 863
	3 ♦	Pass	?			♦ --- ♣ 6432
12.	---	---	1 ♡	Pass	Both	♠ 8 ♡ AK876
	2 ♠	Pass	?			♦ AQ3 ♣ KJ85

(374)

	PART.	OPP.	YOU	OPP.	VUL.	YOU HOLD
13.	---	---	1 ◇	Pass	Opp.	♠8 ♡K1097
	2 ♡	Pass	?			◇AKJ65 ♣K63
14.	---	Pass	1 ◇	Pass	Both	♠K83 ♡AJ3
	2 ♠	Pass	?			◇AK876 ♣86
15.	---	---	1 ♡	Pass	Both	♠K6 ♡AK975
	2 ♠	Pass	?			◇AJ1064 ♣A

SOLUTIONS

1. 2 ♠   An ideal weak jump response. (3 Roth Points)

2. 1 ♠   With 8 HCP, you are too strong for a weak jump response. (11)

3. Pass   You are too weak for a jump to the three-level. (2)

4. 2 ♡   No problem when you are using weak jump responses. (7)

5. 2 ♠   A two-level weak jump response is acceptable on a good five-card suit. (6)

6. Pass   A jump by a raised hand is not a weak jump response. Your original pass was correct, as you must be within two tricks of your contract to make a weak two-bid when you are vulnerable and the opponents are not. (4)

7. 1 NT   Do not make a weak jump response when you meet the requirements for a raise of partner's major, either directly or via the forcing 1 NT response. Since you are raising partner's suit, do not count your side-suit Length Point. (8)

8. 2 ♠   When the opponents intervene, the 2 ♠ bid is a weak jump response. (4)

9. 2 ♠   The jump over a takeout double is a weak jump response. (5)

(375)

10.   4 ♠   Partner's bid is invitational and you have a maximum. (10)
11.   Pass   Perhaps spades would be better, but you have no choice; you are required to pass. (6)
12.   Pass   You are not going anywhere opposite a weak jump response. (17)
13.   4 ♡   It is somewhat puzzling how the opponents have managed to remain silent up to this point, but if you pass they will surely enter the bidding and they may even have game in spades. The favorable vulnerability suggests a preemptive raise to 4 ♡; you might even make it. (17)
14.   4 ♠   Partner's bid is invitational and you have an excellent hand. You should make 4 ♠ easily. (16)
15.   4 ♠   You have enough strength to make game a good bet. Slam is out of the question, so bid game directly in partner's suit. A diamond bid is pointless.

CHAPTER

19

Free Bids and the Negative Double

It is always a happy occasion when partner opens the bidding. Your side has struck the first blow in the battle for the final contract, and you may enter the auction armed with the knowledge that partner has at least 14 Roth Points. However, your opponents will not always succumb quietly. They may contest the issue by overcalling in a suit (possibly with a weak jump overcall or higher preempt). All too often, Standard American players have considerable trouble in these situations. There is general agreement that a bid after an overcall by the opponents should show greater values than that same bid had the opponents remained silent, but firm understandings about exactly how many points any given bid should show in this situation are conspicuous by their absence. Thus, the opener-responder relationship becomes a guessing game, and it is no surprise that inferior contracts are often reached after an overcall by the opponents.

The Roth approach to this problem differs from Standard American in two major ways: first, free bids (bids after the opponent to your right has overcalled) have clearly defined point ranges; second, the meaning of a double is changed to provide an answer to certain frequently-occurring problems that are impossible to solve using Standard American methods. We will consider each of these in turn.

Free Bids

When partner opens the bidding and the next player overcalls, you are relieved of the necessity of "keeping the bidding open" since partner is sure to get another chance. A bid made at this point is made freely, and is called a "free bid" (if in a new suit) or a "free raise" (if a raise of partner's suit). Since you are under no compulsion to bid, a free bid or free raise indicates a fairly good hand. With minimum values you would pass.

In discussing the requirements for free bids, it is important to take into account the level at which you are going to bid; the higher the level, the better hand you need. The requirements for free *major*-suit raises were given in Chapter 15. Here we will concern ourselves with other possible free bids.

LEVEL OF BIDDING	SAMPLE AUCTIONS			MEANING
	PART.	OPP.	YOU	
One-level	1 ♣	1 ♦	1 ♡	Minimum of 11 HCP.
	1 ♦	1 ♡	1 ♠	Guarantees another bid unless partner bids game.
Two-level, new suit	1 ♦	1 ♡	2 ♣	Minimum of 11 HCP.
	1 ♡	1 ♠	2 ♦	Guarantees another bid unless partner bids game.
Three- or four-level, new suit	1 ♦	2 ♠	3 ♣	A hand worth an opening bid (Minimum of 14 Roth Points and 10 HCP) and a good five-card or longer suit.
	1 ♡	3 ♠	4 ♦	
	1 ♡	2 ♦	3 ♣	

LEVEL OF BIDDING	SAMPLE AUCTIONS			MEANING
	PART.	OPP.	YOU	
Minor suit raise to the two-level	1 ◇ 1 ♣	1 ♠ 1 ♡	2 ◇ 2 ♣	7–10 Roth Points (not necessarily HCP) and four-card support*
Minor suit raise to the three- or four-level	1 ◇ 1 ♣	2 ♠ 3 ♡	3 ◇ 4 ♣	Minimum of 12 Roth Points and four-card or better support.

As you can see, free bids promise good values (usually* at least 11 points). Here are some illustrations:

	PART.	OPP.	YOU	YOU HOLD
1.	1 ♣	1 ♡	?	♠K842 ♡A843 ◇63 ♣Q85

Pass. You are not strong enough for a free bid.

| 2. | 1 ◇ | 1 ♡ | ? | ♠AJ876 ♡K103 ◇K842 ♣2 |

Bid 1 ♠. You are strong enough for a free bid at the one-level with 11 HCP. Prefer the more informative bid in a new (major) suit to raising partner's (minor) suit.

| 3. | 1 ◇ | 1 ♠ | ? | ♠85 ♡Q63 ◇432 ♣AK986 |

Do *not* bid 2 ♣. You need 11 HCP for a free bid at the two-level.

| 4. | 1 ♡ | 2 ♣ | ? | ♠K83 ♡32 ◇AKJ86 ♣432 |

Bid 2 ◇. You are just strong enough for the two-level free bid.

| 5. | 1 ♠ | 2 ♡ | ? | ♠83 ♡K83 ◇AKJ86 ♣432 |

Do *not bid 3 ◇.* For a free bid at the three-level, your hand must be worth an opening bid, and you have only 11 total Roth Points after DEMOTING your Distribution Points with a doubleton in partner's suit.

---

* When you have support for opener's *minor* suit, it is important to give an immediate free raise. If you do not raise at once, you may be forced to do so later, perhaps at an uncomfortably high level, and you may find opener with a three-card suit.

6.　1 ♡　　2 ◊　　?　　♠ AJ8　♡ 63　◊ 654　♣ AKQ84

Bid 3 ♣. Your hand is worth an opening bid, so you may make a free bid at the three-level.

7.　1 ◊　　3 ♠　　?　　♠ 86　♡ A75　◊ A10965　♣ Q108

Bid 4 ◊. Counting your PROMOTED doubleton, your hand is worth 12 total Roth Points—just enough for a free raise at the four-level.

The requirements for free bids and free raises are not changed if you are a passed hand.

Opener's rebid after any of the above free bids or free raises is straightforward, and is much the same as over any unlimited bid by responder. Since free bids are strong, opener will always bid again, and game is likely to be reached. If opener keeps the requirements for free bids and raises (and the priorities for bidding over an unlimited response) firmly in mind, he will have no trouble arriving at the proper decisions.

Capsule Summary: Free Bids and Free Raises

I. FREE BIDS (NEW SUIT)

LEVEL OF BIDDING	REQUIREMENTS
One-level	Minimum of 11 HCP. Guarantees another bid unless opener bids game.
Two-level	Minimum of 11 HCP. Guarantees another bid unless opener bids game.
Three- or four-level	Hand worth an opening bid (minimum of 14 total Roth Points and 10 HCP) Good five-card or longer suit.

II. FREE RAISES (MINOR SUITS)

LEVEL OF BIDDING	REQUIREMENTS
Two-level	7–10 Roth Points and four-card support. Opener must bid again.
Three- or four-level	Minimum of 12 Roth Points and four-card support.

The requirements for free-*major*-suit raises were given in Chapter 15.

_____

QUIZ

Count your Roth Points and your HCP and decide on your action on each of the following hands.

	PART.	OPP.	YOU	YOU HOLD			
1.	1 ◇	2 ♠	?	♠8	♡A1087	◇QJ76	♣Q964
		(weak)					
2.	1 ♣	1 ◇	?	♠8	♡A9865	◇Q432	♣J109
3.	1 ♠	2 ♡	?	♠97	♡865	◇AJ10965	♣A7
4.	1 ♣	1 ◇	?	♠KQ65	♡82	◇A108	♣A432
5.	1 ♡	3 ♠	?	♠8643	♡86	◇AKJ108	♣AK
6.	1 ♡	1 ♠	?	♠862	♡74	◇AK865	♣Q82
7.	1 ◇	1 ♠	?	♠1064	♡86	◇Q83	♣AKQ32
8.	1 ♠	2 ♣	?	♠976	♡108	◇AKQ87	♣Q75

SOLUTIONS

1. *Bid 3 ◇.* You have 12 Roth Points after PROMOTING your spade singleton and have just enough for the free raise.*

2. *Pass.* You are not strong enough for a free bid. (9 Roth Points)

3. *Do not bid 3 ◇.* You need a hand worth an opening bid to make a free bid at the three-level. This hand is worth only 9 Roth Points.

4. *Bid 1 ♠.* With 13 HCP, you have points to spare for the one-level free bid. Prefer the more informative bid of a new suit to a jump raise of partner's minor. (15 Roth Points)

5. Bid *4 ◇.* Your hand is well worth an opening bid and hence a free bid at the four-level. (15 Roth Points)

_____

* This bid is not ideal because although it shows the point count well, it risks missing a *major-suit fit* in hearts. The perfect solution will be presented in the next section.

6. *Do not bid 2 ◊*. You need 11 HCP for a free bid at the two-level. (9 Roth Points)

7. *Bid 2 ♣*. This time you do have the required 11 HCP. (12 Roth Points)

8. *Bid 2 ♠*. Just because free major raises were discussed back in Chapter Fifteen is no reason to fail to make one when your hand calls for it. With 12 Roth Points and three-card support for partner's major, you meet the requirements for the single major raise, which takes precedence over making a free bid of 2 ◊. Partner will be most interested to hear that you like his suit and is sure to bid again.

The Negative Double

Back in Chapter Fourteen, we presented you with the following problem:

You hold	PARTNER	OPP.	YOU
♠ 86	1 ♡	2 ♠ (weak)	?
♡ 72		or	
◊ AQ106	1 ♠	2 ♡	?
♣ KJ632			

No matter what system you are playing, you are supposed to pass, as this hand is not strong enough for a free bid. With support for both unbid suits, it would be pleasant if you could make a takeout double, but according to traditional Standard American bidding methods the double shows strength in the opponents' suit and indicates a desire to defend and exact a penalty.

Perhaps it seems so natural to you to play the double for penalties that you are reluctant to change the meaning of this bid. Yet consider: if your right-hand opponent opens the bidding with one heart and you double, are you expressing a desire to play one heart doubled? Of course not! You are making a takeout double and requesting partner to bid. If you have had some bridge experience before reading this book and have had the occasion to make such takeout doubles, it probably seems quite natural to you that this double is not an attempt to penalize the opponent. After all, how often do you get a hand where you wish to double one heart for penalties? Far more often, you have a hand such as

$$♠ AQ86 \quad ♡ 7 \quad ◇ KJ109 \quad ♣ K842$$

where you wish to compete but *would like partner to select the suit.* The double of your right-hand opponent's opening bid of one of a suit is not a penalty double because you almost never get such a hand, and a far more useful meaning can be assigned to the bid.

Although many players do not realize it, the same argument applies to the situation in which partner opens the bidding and the next player overcalls (possibly with a weak jump overcall or a preemptive bid). It is nice to be able to double for penalties with four or five trump tricks, but such situations just don't occur often enough to make the penalty interpretation of the double worthwhile (just as hands with which you would want to double an opening bid of one heart on your right for penalties don't occur often enough to use the double in this way). You are far more likely to get hands such as the one at the beginning of this section on which you would like to double as a takeout bid, requesting partner to bid one of the unbid suits.

Even if you have the hand with four or five trump tricks, your left-hand opponent is likely to run out to a better spot. In view of these considerations, you will discover that it is far more profitable to play the immediate double of a suit overcall as a takeout double.

Before we go any further, let us make clear that there will be hands on which the opponents step out of line and should be doubled and penalized. However, you will almost always be able to do so even when you are using the takeout interpretation that we recommend. We will see later exactly how this is accomplished. For now, let us see how this new kind of double works.

The basic principle involved is this: When responder makes an *immediate* double of a suit overcall, the double is for takeout and requests partner to choose between the unbid suits. This double is called a "negative double" to emphasize the fact that it is not an attempt to penalize the opponents. In fact, the negative doubler may be short in the opponents' suit, and will often have a poor holding in that suit.

Here are some illustrations of auctions in which a double is negative:

OPPONENT	PARTNER	OPPONENT	YOU
	1 ♠	2 ♣	Double
	1 ♣	1 ♠	Double
	1 ♡	2 ◇	Double
	1 ♡	3 ◇	Double
	1 ♡	4 ♠	Double
	1 NT	2 ♡	Double
	2 ♣	2 ♠	Double

Note that the double is negative even after a one-notrump or forcing two-club opening or after an overcall by partner. All of the above doubles convey the following message: "Partner, I do not have a very good holding in the opponents' suit and do not especially want you to pass for penalties. For the moment, please assume that I have good support for the unbid suits and would like you to bid one of them if you can."

The only time a double is *not* negative is when partner has opened the bidding with a weak two-bid or other preemptive bid. When partner opens with such a bid, he cannot possibly have holdings of great value in the unbid suits, so it would be pointless to use the double for takeout. Therefore, after a weak two-bid (or other pre-empt) and subsequent overcall by the opponents, a double is for penalties, and the opening bidder must pass:

PARTNER	OPPONENT	YOU
2 ♡ (weak)	3 ♣	Double (penalties)
4 ♠	5 ◇	Double (penalties)
3 ♡	3 ♠	Double (penalties)

If you remember the basic principle that the partner of a preemptive bidder is in charge of the auction and that the preemptive bidder must accept his decisions, you will have no trouble remembering this one exception to the negative double.

Now that we have discussed when a double is negative, let us turn to the question of when to use the negative double. One of the most important uses of the negative double is to indicate support for the two unbid suits but are too weak to make a free bid. Thus, with the hand given at the beginning of this section

(♠86   ♡72   ◇AQ106   ♣KJ632),

make a negative **double** after partner's **one spade** opening and a **two heart** overcall by your right-hand opponent, *or* after a **one heart** opening by partner and a **two spade** overcall by your right-hand opponent. This informs partner that you would like to hear him choose one of the two unbid suits if he is able to do so.

In addition to this highly valuable use of the negative double, there are two other situations where this bid solves vexing problems. If you have a good suit of your own but are two weak to make a free bid, the negative double may be just what the doctor ordered. For example:

PART.	OPP.	YOU	YOU HOLD			
1. 1 ◇	1 ♠	?	♠8	♡Q63	◇432	♣AK9865
2. 1 ♠	2 ♡	?	♠83	♡K83	◇AKJ86	♣432

If you remember these hands from the previous section, you will recall that the answer was somewhat ambiguous: "you should not make a free bid." However, you do not have to pass. In each case, you may make a negative double; if partner does not bid your long suit, bid it yourself at your next turn to bid. This will tell partner that you lack the values for a free bid but have a good suit that you would like to mention.

The other situation in which negative doubles are useful follows partner's opening of one of a major suit. Opponents overcall, and you have 9 points or less in support. You cannot make a single raise, as this would show a stronger hand; and your usual method for dealing with this kind of hand, a forcing one-notrump response followed by a return to partner's major suit, has been taken away by the opponents' interference. Consider the following hand from the review quiz from Chapter 15:

PART.	OPP.	YOU	YOU HOLD
1 ♠	2 ♣	?	♠ K86 ♡ 7 ◇ A10865 ♣ 8642

You may not raise to 2 ♠ for that would show 10 to 12 points. Instead, make a negative double and return to spades at your next turn to bid. This will convey the message that you have a weak spade raise (7 to 9 points and at least three-card support).

Thus, the negative double actually handles three kinds of hands: hands with support for both unbid suits; hands with one good suit of your own; hands with support for partner's major: all of which are too weak for a free bid or free raise. Before turning to more illustrations, let's summarize the requirements for a negative double.

LEVEL OF BIDDING AT WHICH OPPONENT OVERCALLS	REQUIREMENTS FOR NEGATIVE DOUBLE*
1. One-level	7–10 HCP with 1 to 2 defensive tricks Either: (1) Support for all unbid suits, or (2) A good suit of your own, or (3) Support for opener's major suit.
2. Two-level	7–12 HCP with 1 to 2 defensive tricks Either: (1) Support for all unbid suits, or (2) A good suit of your own, or (3) Support for opener's suit.

---

* Do not make a negative double if you meet the requirements for a free bid. Prefer a negative double to a minor-suit raise with four cards in the unbid major.

(386)

LEVEL OF BIDDING AT WHICH OPPONENT OVERCALLS	REQUIREMENTS FOR NEGATIVE DOUBLE
3. Three- or four-level	9 or more Roth Points (not necessarily HCP) with 1 or more defensive tricks Either: (1) Support for all unbid suits, or (2) Support for opener's *minor* suit (four cards or more).

Now for some illustrative examples:

PART.	OPP.	YOU	YOU HOLD
1. 1 ◇	1 ♡	?	♠KQ65 ♡72 ◇864 ♣A1043

Double. You need 11 HCP for a free bid at the one-level. Since you cannot bid one spade, and since you are most interested in hearing what partner has to say about the two unbid suits, the negative double is ideal.

2. 1 ♣	1 ♠	?	♠86 ♡A75 ◇9876 ♣KJ42

Bid 2 ♣. You meet the requirements for a free raise, so do not make a negative double. (Remember that the free *minor*-suit raise is weak.) (However, with one more heart instead of a spade or diamond, a double is preferable.)

3. 1 ♣	1 ♡	?	♠A63 ♡863 ◇K842 ♣654

Pass. The wrong kind of hand for a negative double, because you do not have good support for both unbid suits. Avoid making a negative double with 4-3-3-3 distribution.

4. 1 ♡	2 ♣	?	♠AK9876 ♡32 ◇432 ♣32

Double. You are too weak for a free bid of 2 ♠, but can show your suit by making a negative double and then bidding spades over any rebid by partner. Partner will not get carried away, because you have denied the values for a free bid and can have at most 10 HCP.

5. 1 ♡   1 ♠   ?   ♠ Q65   ♡ J742   ◊ A742   ♣ 75

Double. A direct raise to 2 ♡ would show 10 to 12 points. You will bid hearts the next time, showing 7 to 9 points and heart support.

6. 1 ◊   1 ♠   ?   ♠ A62   ♡ K742   ◊ A742   ♣ 92

Double. The counterpart of the situation in the previous example: You are too *strong* for a free *minor* raise. Double and support diamonds next time, unless partner bids hearts.

7. 1 ♣   1 ♠   ?   ♠ 863   ♡ Q742   ◊ A742   ♣ 64

Pass. You need a minimum of 7 HCP to make a negative double.

8. 1 ♣   1 ♠   ?   ♠ Q84   ♡ Q432   ◊ Q43   ♣ J53

Pass. You have 7 HCP, but do not have 1 defensive trick. Thus, the hand is not good enough for a negative double. Nor is it good enough for a free bid of one notrump.

9. 1 ◊   1 ♠   ?   ♠ KJ10943   ♡ K1086   ◊ 43   ♣ 2

Pass. A double would be negative. Wait for further developments.

10. 1 ♡   3 ◊   ?   ♠ 86   ♡ Q86   ◊ A1094   ♣ 5432

Pass. Two reasons: (1) you must have either support for both unbid suits or support for partner's minor suit opening to make a negative double at the three- or four-level; (2) you need 9 Roth Points and have only 7.

Check over these examples, try your hand at the following quiz, and you'll see that it's not as hard as it looks. It takes some practice at first, but you will soon get used to the negative double, which has been accepted by a majority of expert players because of its many advantages.

Capsule Summary: The Negative Double

I. WHEN A DOUBLE IS NEGATIVE

A double *is* negative: after an opening bid by partner of one of a suit, 1 NT, or 2 ♣ (forcing), and an overcall by your right-hand opponent.

A double is *not* negative: after an opening weak two-bid or preempt by partner.

II. REQUIREMENTS FOR THE NEGATIVE DOUBLE

GENERAL REQUIREMENTS: A hand not suitable for a free bid or raise *and*

(1) Support for all unbid suits, *or*

(2) A good suit of your own, *or*

(3) Support for partner's suit.

SPECIFIC REQUIREMENTS

LEVEL AT WHICH OPPONENT OVERCALLS	REQUIREMENTS
One-level	7–10 HCP
	1 to 2 defensive tricks
	Hand of type (1), (2), or (3).
Two-level	7–12 HCP
	1 to 2 defensive tricks
	Hand of type (1), (2), or (3).
Three- or four-level	9 or more Roth Points
	1 or more defensive tricks
	Hand of type (1)
	Hand of type (3), *minor* suit only.

- -

QUIZ

In each case, count your Roth Points and your HCP and decide on your action.

	PART.	OPP.	YOU	YOU HOLD
1.	1 ♠	2 ◇	?	♠85 ♡Q1064 ◇32 ♣AQ942
2.	1 ♡	1 ♠	?	♠643 ♡72 ◇A763 ♣J432
3.	1 ♣	1 ♡	?	♠AJ107 ♡642 ◇KQ84 ♣65
4.	1 ◇	1 ♠	?	♠863 ♡AQJ965 ◇32 ♣32
5.	1 ♡	1 ♠	?	♠1052 ♡K43 ◇K9865 ♣32
6.	1 ◇	1 ♡	?	♠J86 ♡432 ◇1097 ♣AK42
7.	1 ♠	3 ♡	?	♠84 ♡K63 ◇AQ6532 ♣82

(389)

8.	1 ♠	2 ♡	?	♠8 ♡KJ1097 ◇63 ♣A5432		
9.	1 ◇	3 ♠	?	♠7 ♡KQ108 ◇432 ♣A10864		
10.	1 ♣	1 ♡	?	♠J843 ♡J53 ◇QJ42 ♣Q8		
11.	1 ♠	2 ♡	?	♠86 ♡K87 ◇AKJ96 ♣K82		
12.	1 ♣	2 ♠	?	♠10764 ♡973 ◇K842 ♣AQ		
13.	1 ◇	2 ♠	?	♠865 ♡9842 ◇AQ87 ♣K4		
14.	1 ♠	2 ◇	?	♠Q84 ♡K862 ◇32 ♣A1042		

SOLUTIONS

1. *Double.* The negative double is perfect for hands like this. If partner rebids 2 ♠, pass. (8 Roth Points)

2. *Pass.* You need a minimum of 7 HCP to make a negative double. (5)

3. *Double.* An ideal hand for the negative double. You lack the 11 HCP needed for a free bid at the one-level. (10)

4. *Double.* You are too weak for a free bid of 2 ♡, but can mention your suit by making a negative double and bidding hearts next time. (10)

5. *Double.* A 2 ♡ bid would show 8 to 10 Roth Points. You will bid hearts, not diamonds, next time. (8)

6. *Pass.* You do not have good support for both unbid suits. Tend to avoid the negative double with 4–3–3–3 distribution. (8)

7. *Pass.* You do not have good support for both unbid suits, and you may not make a negative double at the three-level with a one-suited hand. Had your right-hand opponent overcalled 2 ♡, you would have doubled and bid diamonds the next time. (10)

8. *Pass.* The double is not for penalties. (8)

9. *Double.* A hopeless problem using old-fashioned Standard American. You will find a good heart or club contract if it exists. (11)

10. *Pass.* You do not have 1 defensive trick. (6)

11. *Bid 3 ◇.* With a hand worth an opening bid, you meet the requirements for a free bid at the three-level. (14)

12. *Pass.* You have enough points to double, but do not have good

support for both unbid suits, a good suit of your own, or support for partner's suit. (9)

13. *Double.* Try for a major-suit fit before raising to 3 ◊. You will not be unhappy if partner bids hearts and will correct a 3 ♣ rebid to 3 ◊, showing your support.

Had you held

♠ 8654   ♡ 98   ◊ AQ87   ♣ K43

discretion would suggest a bid of 3 ◊ as you would be forced all the way to the four-level if partner bid hearts over a double (11)

14. *Bid 2 ♠.* Do not make a negative double when you meet the requirements for a free raise. (10)

Rebids by Opener after a Negative Double

If you have opened the bidding, the next player has overcalled, and partner makes a negative double, you must keep firmly in mind the fact that *the double is for takeout.* Partner is asking you to bid; he is not trying to set the opponents and is likely to have nothing of value in their suit. Therefore, only rarely will you pass the double, and you will do so only when *you* wish to try for a penalty rather than proceed to a contract of your own. After a negative double, a pass is not a sign of weakness or indifference; it is a positive action stating that your best chance for a good result lies in trying to set the contract bid by the enemy. At low levels, the pass is justified only when you have a very strong holding in the suit bid by the opponents, a good defensive hand, and no particular desire to play in a contract of your own. At high levels

(e.g. 1 ♠ —4 ♡ —Double—Pass—?)

the pass is more frequent, as you have less bidding room to decide what to do if your action is not clear-cut. Most of the time, however, you will bid in response to partner's negative double, just as you usually respond when partner makes a takeout double of a bid of one of a suit.

After a negative double, opener's rebids are these:

1. With a minimum hand (14 to 16 points):

(1) Bid a new suit of at least four cards.

(2) If unable to bid a new suit, bid notrump with balanced suit distribution and at least one stopper in the suit bid by the opponents.

(3) If unable to bid a new suit or notrump, rebid your first suit.

(4) On *rare* occasions, with a very strong holding in the enemy's suit and a good defensive hand, pass.

None of the above bids are forcing. The negative doubler knows that you have 14 to 16 points, and if game is out of the question and you are in a playable contract, he can and should pass.

2. With a better than minimum hand (17 to 18 points):

(1) *Jump* in a new suit of at least four cards (but not past the game level).

(2) *Jump* in your own suit (but not past the game level).

(3) On rare occasions, with a very strong holding in the enemy's suit and a good defensive hand, pass.

These bids also are not forcing. The negative doubler knows you have 17 or 18 points and acts accordingly.

3. With a very good hand (19 points or more):

(1) Cue-bid the suit bid by the opponents. The negative doubler must bid again and describe his hand.

(2) Jump in notrump (but not past the game level) with balanced suit distribution and at least one (preferably more than one) stopper in the enemy's suit.

(3) If your own suit is reliable or self-sufficient, jump to game in your own suit.

(4) If you have a good new suit (good five-card suit or better) that you wish to bid, jump to game in that suit.

(5) On rare occasions, with a very strong holding in the enemy's suit and a good defensive hand, pass.

(6) Jump in notrump with 19 or more points. (With 20 points, jump to 3 NT from the one-level.)

If you are asked to bid at the three- or four-level, you are more privileged to use your judgment and may pass for penalties somewhat more frequently.

Here's how the rules work:

	YOU	OPP.	PART.	OPP.	YOU HOLD	
1.	1 ♣	1 ◇	Dbl	Pass	♠ 863	♡ A1042
	?				◇ K8	♣ AQ98

Bid 1 ♡. With a minimum hand, the best thing you can do is show a new suit if you have one.

	YOU	OPP.	PART.	OPP.	YOU HOLD	
2.	1 ♣	1 ◇	Dbl	Pass	♠ AJ85	♡ A83
	?				◇ 6	♣ AQ654

Bid 2 ♠. With 17 Roth Points, you are too good for a simple rebid of 1 ♠.* Your jump shows an interest in game, but partner is permitted to pass if he can support spades but sees no prospect of game opposite a 17 or 18 point hand.

	YOU	OPP.	PART.	OPP.	YOU HOLD	
3.	1 ♣	1 ♡	Dbl	Pass	♠ K83	♡ AJ8
	?				◇ 643	♣ AK42

Bid 1 NT. You have a minimum hand, no new suit to bid, and balanced suit distribution with stoppers in the enemy's suit.

	YOU	OPP.	PART.	OPP.	YOU HOLD	
4.	1 ♣	1 ◇	Dbl	Pass	♠ AQ8	♡ K10
	?				◇ KJ8	♣ AQ1064

Bid 2 NT. With 19 Roth Points, balanced suit distribution, and stoppers in the opponents' suit, jump to 2 NT. Remember not to count Distribution Points when bidding notrump.

	YOU	OPP.	PART.	OPP.	YOU HOLD	
5.	1 ◇	1 ♠	Dbl	Pass	♠ K83	♡ A86
	?				◇ AQ10965	♣ 3

Bid 2 ◇. Do not rebid notrump with unbalanced suit distribution. You have no new suit to bid, but can and should rebid your good diamond suit.

	YOU	OPP.	PART.	OPP.	YOU HOLD	
6.	1 ◇	1 ♡	Dbl	Pass	♠ K83	♡ AQ6
	?				◇ AQ10965	♣ 2

Bid 3 ◇. Jump to show 17 or 18 Roth Points.

---

* After a negative double, KEEP your Distribution Points if you have a new suit to bid, as an eight-card fit is probably present. (Also, as usual, KEEP your Distribution Points if your own suit is RELIABLE or better.)

7.   1 ◇   1 ♡   Dbl   Pass   ♠ 87   ♡ KJ95
     ?   ◇ AK43   ♣ K82

Bid 1 NT. It is extremely dangerous to pass for penalties at low levels. Prefer the notrump rebid.

8.   1 ♠   2 ♣   Dbl   Pass   ♠ AK987   ♡ AJ86
     ?   ◇ 86   ♣ 62

Bid 2 ♡. With a minimum, do not get excited. Just show your new suit.

9.   1 ♠   2 ♣   Dbl   Pass   ♠ AKQ87   ♡ AQ86
     ?   ◇ 86   ♣ 62

Bid 3 ♡. Compare with the preceding hand. With 17 or 18 points, you must jump to show a better than minimum hand, which still allows partner to pass.

10.   1 ♠   2 ◇   Dbl   Pass   ♠ KQ10987   ♡ AJ
     ?   ◇ 86   ♣ KQ9

Bid 3 ♠. Your most descriptive bid is to rebid your good spade suit. However, you must jump to show 17 or 18 points.

11.   1 ♠   2 ◇   Dbl   Pass   ♠ AKQJ65   ♡ 864
     ?   ◇ 3   ♣ AJ10

Bid 4 ♠. After doubling your Length Points with a self-sufficient suit, you have 19 Roth Points. Partner's double promises strength in hearts and clubs, which is just what you need. Game should be cold.

12.   1 ♠   2 ♣   Dbl   Pass   ♠ AQ864   ♡ 87
     ?   ◇ AK9   ♣ AQ10

Bid 3 NT. Better than rebidding the relatively weak spade suit. Partner should have strength in hearts for his negative double; if he was planning to support spades, he will go on to 4 ♠ anyway. Do not bid only 2 NT which would show 14 to 16 points.

13.   1 ♡   2 ◇   Dbl   Pass   ♠ 863   ♡ AK987
     ?   ◇ 4   ♣ AQ84

Bid 3 ♣. Respect partner's request to bid a new suit whenever you can do so.

14.	1 ♡	3 ♣	Dbl	Pass	♠ AQ87	♡ AKJ108
	?				◇ A86	♣ 7

Bid 4 ♣. With 20 Roth Points, you must make a forcing bid. Let partner clarify his hand. If he bids 4 ♡, pass. If he bids 4 ♠, you have a close decision, but a slam try would be justified.

15.	1 ♡	3 ◇	Dbl	Pass	♠ 85	♡ AKJ1064
	?				◇ A86	♣ K2

Bid 4 ♡. A 3 ♡ rebid would show a minimum hand.

As the above examples indicate, as opener you have two messages to convey to the negative doubler. First, you will tell him how strong your hand is by making a simple rebid with 14 to 16 points, jumping the bidding with 17 or 18 points, and making a forcing bid with 19 or more points. Second, you will describe what kind of hand you have by bidding a new suit in response to his request if you are able to do so, bidding notrump with a balanced hand and stoppers in the suit bid by the opponents, or rebidding a good suit of your own. It is almost never correct to pass for penalties at the one-level and rarely proper to do so at the two-level, and you should look for alternative bids if at all possible. At higher levels, however, it is permissible to "convert" partner's double from takeout to penalties if you have a good holding in the opponents' suit or if you are sure you have no clear action to take and are certain you can collect a sizable plus score by defeating the opponents in the contract they have bid.

Capsule Summary: Opener's Rebid after a Negative Double

YOU HOLD	YOUR CHOICES (IN ORDER OF PREFERENCE)
Minimum hand (14 to 16 points)	1. Bid a new suit.
	2. Bid notrump (balanced hand, enemy's suit stopped).
	3. Rebid your own suit.
	4. Pass (Almost never at the one-level Infrequently at the two-level Occasionally at high levels).

(395)

YOU HOLD	YOUR CHOICES (IN ORDER OF PREFERENCE)
Above minimum hand (17 or 18 points)	1. Jump* in new suit. 2. Jump* rebid your own suit. 3. Pass (same considerations as above).
Very good hand (19 or more points)	1. Cue-bid the opponents' suit with no clear-cut action to take. (Let partner clarify *his* hand). 2. Jump in notrump, or in a reliable or self-sufficient suit of your own, or in a new suit.

QUIZ

In each case, count your Roth Points and decide on your action.

	YOU	OPP.	PART.	OPP.	YOU HOLD
1.	1 ◊ ?	1 ♡	Dbl	Pass	♠ KJ85 ♡ 7 ◊ AQ106 ♣ K842
2.	1 ♡ ?	4 ♣	Dbl	Pass	♠ A1086 ♡ AKJ53 ◊ K93 ♣ 7
3.	1 ♠ ?	2 ♡	Dbl	Pass	♠ A7642 ♡ K83 ◊ A ♣ J532
4.	1 ♡ ?	2 ♣	Dbl	Pass	♠ 863 ♡ AQ1065 ◊ K3 ♣ KQ10
5.	1 ◊ ?	3 ♠	Dbl	Pass	♠ 85 ♡ K6 ◊ AQ10964 ♣ A84
6.	1 ♡ ?	2 ♠	Dbl	Pass	♠ 72 ♡ AKQ65 ◊ K1043 ♣ A7
7.	1 ◊ ?	1 ♡	Dbl	Pass	♠ AQJ6 ♡ 10 ◊ AKJ7 ♣ K984
8.	1 ♣ ?	1 ♡	Dbl	Pass	♠ Q4 ♡ AQ5 ◊ K83 ♣ AKJ102

* But do not jump above game.

	YOU	OPP.	PART.	OPP.	YOU HOLD
9.	1 ♠	2 ♣	Dbl	Pass	♠ KQ1086 ♡ AK97
	?				◊ A7 ♣ 32
10.	1 ♠	2 ◊	Dbl	Pass	♠ AK1085 ♡ AQ976
	?				◊ 2 ♣ K8
11.	1 ♡	2 ♣	Dbl	Pass	♠ 86 ♡ AK865
	?				◊ AQ3 ♣ AQ2
12.	1 ♡	3 ♣	Dbl	Pass	♠ 7 ♡ AK742
	?				◊ 863 ♣ KQ108
13.	1 ♠	3 ◊	Dbl	Pass	♠ KQ10642 ♡ AQ7
	?				◊ 83 ♣ 103
14.	1 ◊	3 ♠	Dbl	Pass	♠ A76 ♡ Q865
	?				◊ AQ987 ♣ 2
15.	1 ◊	3 ♡	Dbl	Pass	♠ 742 ♡ 8
	?				◊ AKJ10976 ♣ A5
16.	1 ♡	4 ◊	Dbl	Pass	♠ 83 ♡ AK432
	?				◊ K73 ♣ A105
17.	1 ♡	4 ♣	Dbl	Pass	♠ 87 ♡ KQ10976
	?				◊ AQ5 ♣ K8
18.	1 ♡	3 ♠	Dbl	Pass	♠ 85 ♡ KQ975
	?				◊ 42 ♣ AQJ9
19.	1 ♣	1 ♠	Dbl	2 ♠	♠ K83 ♡ KJ7
	?				◊ Q106 ♣ AJ42
20.	1 ◊	2 ♠	Dbl	Pass	♠ --- ♡ A7
	?				◊ AQJ1065 ♣ KQJ105

SOLUTIONS

	POINTS	BID	
1.	15*	1 ♠	Follow orders and show your new suit. With a choice, remember that game in a

---

* KEEP your Distribution Points. Since partner must be able to support spades or diamonds, an 8-card fit will be present. Remember that if partner makes a negative double and you have a new suit to bid, you can assume there is an 8-card fit present.

POINTS	BID	

major is easier than game in a minor (which requires 29 Roth Points).

2. 17   4 ♠   True, you have 17 points, but a jump to 5 ♠ is past the game level and therefore not to be considered. Perfect accuracy is impossible over high-level preempts; be glad that you have found your good spade fit. (Others won't).

3. 14   3 ♣   Show your new suit as requested by partner.

4. 14   2 NT   A notrump rebid without jumping shows 14 to 15 points and stoppers in the enemy's suit. With no new suit to bid, the notrump call is the best choice.

5. 16   4 ◇   You have no new suit to bid and cannot bid notrump with no stoppers in spades.

6. 18   4 ◇   Jump in your new suit to show 17 or 18 points.

7. 20   2 ♡   With 19 or more points, you must make a forcing bid. Find out whether partner's plan in making a negative double was to show support for the unbid suits, a good suit of his own, or to raise your minor suit, and you will then know where game should be played.

8. 19   2 NT   You have no new suit to bid, but meet the requirements for a notrump call. You must jump to show 19 points. With

♠ K10   ♡ AQ5   ◇ K83   ♣ AKJ102

you would bid 3 NT.

9. 18   3 ♡   Show you new suit, jumping to tell partner you have 17 or 18 points.

10. 19   4 ♡   This hand is too good for a jump to 3 ♡. Let partner choose between 4 ♡ and 4 ♠.

	POINTS	BID	
11.	19	3 NT	Partner can presumably stop spades.
12.	12	Pass	You have a fine holding in the opponents' suit and two potential defensive tricks in hearts. It is unlikely that your side is going anywhere, so try for a juicy penalty.
13.	12	3 ♠	No other choice is available. Do not count any Distribution Points; your suit is not RELIABLE and you have no new suit to bid.
14.	14	4 ♡	Don't be upset about bidding such a shaky suit on the four-level; you are merely complying with partner's request. Takeout doubles are meant for takeout! *Never* make a panicky pass.
15.	17	5 ◇	Game is no certainty, but you must jump with a well above-minimum hand. Partner has forced you to bid on the four-level and you could be much weaker.
16.	14	Pass	Partner may not make a negative double at the four-level with support for your major suit. Therefore, your side has no place to play the hand. Go for the sure plus score.
17.	17	4 ♡	No choice. A jump would put you past the game level.
18.	14	4 ♣	Comply with partner's request to bid a new suit whenever you can.
19.	14	Pass	You have an absolute minimum and your right-hand opponent's 2 ♠ bid has relieved you of the necessity to bid again. If partner also passes, nothing has been missed.
20.	22	6 ♣	Unusual hands require unusual action. Bidding slowly can only confuse the issue.

Opener's Rebid in the Balance Position

If you open the bidding, the next player overcalls, and partner and your right-hand opponent both pass, you are in what is called the "balance position." You and you alone have the fateful decision to make as to whether to allow the opponents to buy the contract or whether to continue the fight and try to reach a good contract of your own.

Using the Roth approach to bidding, *the opening bidder is expected to balance,* not pass and surrender to the opponents. Opener's action is quite simple. With a balanced or semi-balanced hand, and no great strength in the suit bid by the opponents, he should double. Responder may have a good holding in the enemy's suit and have been unable to double for penalties since a double would be negative. (If opener has strength and length in the opponents' suit, partner is probably passing because he has a bad hand. Opener may pass.) This represents the promised method for setting the opponents when they step out of line: responder passes, and opener balances with a double. Opener's double is for takeout, but responder "converts" it into a penalty double by passing.*
With an unbalanced hand, opener's action is usually clearly indicated: he has a good new suit to bid or a good suit of his own to rebid. With a very good hand (19 points or more), opener should jump the bidding. Some examples:

YOU	OPP.	PART.	OPP.	YOU HOLD	
1. 1 ♠	2 ◇	Pass	Pass	♠ AK1064	♡ J9
?				◇ 84	♣ AQ63

Double. In the balance position, double on all reasonably balanced hands. If partner had wished to make a penalty double of 2 ◇, he will simply pass; otherwise he will follow orders and treat your double as asking for an unbid suit. If he bids 3 ♣ or puts you back in 2 ♠, just pass; if he bids 2 ♡, a pass could be right but you

---

* Opener is expected to balance with a double, especially at low levels, with any hand on which he would have passed a standard penalty double, had one been made.

might as well return to 2 ♠ and play the hand yourself (unless partner is a superior dummy player, in which case you should surely pass).

2. 1 ♠   2 ♣   Pass   Pass   ♠ AQ976 ♡ K10864
    ?   ◇ K83 ♣ ---

Bid 2 ♡. Don't reopen with a double with a very unbalanced hand. (You would have taken partner out of a penalty double of 2 ♣ anyway.) You have a clear-cut action: bid your new five-card suit. Playing Standard American (a ghastly thought) you would not have stood for a double of 2 ♣, so don't double now and give partner a chance to pass.

3. 1 ♠   2 ◇   Pass   Pass   ♠ AQ10864 ♡ 64
    ?   ◇ A4 ♣ KJ4

Double. Note that when you have a reasonably balanced hand, you must go to considerable lengths to give partner a chance to penalize the opponents. If he had a hand worth a penalty double of 2 ◇, he will be very appreciative of your decision to double instead of rebidding spades. If partner takes out to 2 ♡, now is the time to go back to 2 ♠ (regardless of how good a dummy player partner is—spades must be a better contract).

4. 1 ♠   2 ♣   Pass   Pass   ♠ AK9765 ♡ AQJ102
    ?   ◇ 8 ♣ 8

Bid 3 ♡. With 19 Roth Points (counting the Length Point in spades), be sure to jump the bidding. Partner is permitted to pass, but your jump alerts him to the fact that you have a strong two-suiter and he will carry on to game when it is proper to do so. (Examples: he will pass with

♠ 84   ♡ 963   ◇ QJ75   ♣ QJ32

because you are obviously not interested in minor-suit queens and jacks, but will proceed to 4 ♠ with

♠ 842   ♡ 963   ◇ A764   ♣ 752

—spade support and a side ace—or to 4 ♡ with

♠ 8   ♡ K987   ◇ 7642   ♣ 9732

—you cannot possibly have more than three losers.)

    5. 1 ◇   2 ♠   Pass   Pass   ♠ AJ97   ♡ 63
        ?   ◇ AQ42   ♣ K83

Pass. Unless your left-hand opponent is just plain crazy, there aren't enough points in the deck for partner to be passing with spades. Therefore, his hand is limited and there is no chance for game. You are not required to reopen on *all* hands.

    6. 1 ♠   2 ◇   Pass   Pass   ♠ K9864 ♡ AQ83
        ?   ◇ 7 ♣ KJ7

Double. An ideal call. You don't mind if partner passes for penalties, and you have support for all unbid suits if he takes out the double. Note that the double does *not* promise extra values.

    7. 1 ◇   2 ♠   Pass   Pass   ♠ 85   ♡ AQ3
        ?   ◇ AQ1084 ♣ K97

Double. No choice. You have a reasonably balanced hand.

    8. 1 ◇   2 ♡   Pass   Pass   ♠ 106   ♡ 86
        ?   ◇ AKJ864 ♣ AJ2

Bid 3 ◇ . Too much of your strength is in diamonds to double.

    9. 1 ◇   2 ♠   Pass   Pass   ♠ AQ8   ♡ 76
        ?   ◇ AKJ84 ♣ KQJ

Bid 2 NT. If you double, partner (who cannot have spades) will take out to the three-level, and you will be on a guess as to what to do next. Bid 2 NT and let partner decide. This bid is natural and shows about 19–20 HCP with the opponents' suit well stopped. Partner is permitted to pass.

    10. 1 ◇   2 ♡   Pass   Pass   ♠ 8   ♡ 76
         ?   ◇ AKJ107 ♣ KQ1096

Bid 3 ♣. Do not reopen with a double with a two-suiter; your hand is too unbalanced.

    11. 1 ◇   2 ♠   Pass   Pass   ♠ 32   ♡ Q5
         ?   ◇ AK632 ♣ AJ75

Pass. Do not reopen minimum hands if there is danger that partner will bid a major suit you cannot support at a high level.

Capsule Summary: Opener's Rebid in the Balance Position

1. With a reasonably balanced hand and weakness in the enemy's suit, double.
2. With unbalanced hands, bid a new suit or rebid your own suit. Jump with 19 Roth Points or more.
3. Rebid notrump at the two-level with 19–20 HCP a balanced hand, and at least two stoppers in the enemy's suit.
4. With a minimum hand and strength and length in the suit bid by the opponents, pass. You are not required to reopen on all hands, and partner cannot have a penalty double.

QUIZ

In each case, count your Roth Points and decide on your action.

	YOU	OPP.	PART.	OPP.	YOU HOLD
1.	1 ♡ ?	1 ♠	Pass	Pass	♠ AQ8　♡ KJ1065 ♢ AQ7　♣ K8
2.	1 ♢ ?	2 ♣	Pass	Pass	♠ KJ64　♡ 32 ♢ AQ982　♣ K4
3.	1 ♡ ?	1 ♠	Pass	Pass	♠ 85　♡ AQ1086 ♢ 7　♣ KQJ32
4.	1 ♢ ?	3 ♠	Pass	Pass	♠ 8　♡ AQ9 ♢ AJ1065　♣ K1042
5.	1 ♡ ?	2 ♠	Pass	Pass	♠ 4　♡ KQ97432 ♢ AQ84　♣ 8
6.	1 ♡ ?	2 ♣	Pass	Pass	♠ 32　♡ AKJ85 ♢ AKJ72　♣ 8
7.	1 ♢ ?	2 ♠	Pass	Pass	♠ KQ84　♡ 73 ♢ AJ107　♣ A32
8.	1 ♡ ?	3 ♣	Pass	Pass	♠ A83　♡ KQ985 ♢ A2　♣ J73
9.	1 ♢ ?	2 ♠	Pass	Pass	♠ 87　♡ AQ8 ♢ AKJ85　♣ AJ3
10.	1 ♡ ?	2 ♣	Pass	Pass	♠ Q63　♡ AJ1084 ♢ AQ　♣ AQ10

	POINTS	BID	
1.	20	Double	You can always bid 2 NT next time. (A direct bid of 2 NT is acceptable.)
2.	15	Double	Your hand is reasonably balanced.
3.	15	2 ♣	Do not reopen with a double on a two-suiter.
4.	16	Double	A minimum hand, but no choice.
5.	17	3 ♡	Do not double with an unbalanced hand.
6.	19	3 ◊	You are too strong for a simple 2 ◊ re-bid.
7.	15	Pass	You are not going anywhere. Partner can't have spades and is passing because his hand is inferior.
8.	15	Pass	It is too risky to act at the three-level with a minimum hand *and* poor distribution.
9.	20	Double	Even with good hands, double when your hand is balanced and does not qualify for a notrump bid.
10.	19	2 NT	With strength in the enemy's suit, the notrump bid should be preferred to the double.

Some Helpful General Principles

When considering whether or not to make a negative double, you may find the following general principles helpful:

1. Make a free bid or free raise when you can do so. Use the negative double only when your hand does not qualify for a free bid or free raise.

2. Don't give partner a problem if you can avoid doing so. For example, suppose partner opens **one diamond,** next player bids **three spades,** and you hold

♠ AQ7   ♡ K83   ◊ 642   ♣ AJ87

You should bid **three notrump.** You have no chance for slam unless partner bids again, and notrump is likely to be the best spot.

3. Avoid making a negative double with 4–3–3–3 distribution.

4. At high levels, tend to make a negative double only with support (at least four cards) for the two unbid suits. At low levels, you may have either support for the unbid suits, a hand with support for partner's suit but too weak for a free raise, or a hand with a suit of your own but too weak for a free bid.

If partner has made a negative double, keep the following in mind:

1. At low levels, when in doubt, bid rather than pass for penalties.

2. At high levels, if you have no idea what to do, pass and take your plus score.

3. If you bid, make your most descriptive possible call. Remember that partner may pass any nonforcing bid.

Capsule Summary: Free Bids and the Negative Double

I. MAKE A FREE BID OR FREE RAISE WHEN YOU CAN

1. FREE BIDS (NEW SUIT)

LEVEL OF BIDDING	REQUIREMENTS
One-level	Minimum of 11 HCP.
Two-level	Minimum of 11 HCP.
Three- or four-level	Minimum of 14 Roth Points and 10 HCP; good five-card or longer suit.

IF YOU MAKE FREE BID, YOU MUST BID AGAIN UNLESS PARTNER BIDS GAME.

2. FREE RAISES, MINOR SUITS

LEVEL OF BIDDING	REQUIREMENTS
Two-level	7–10 Roth Points; at least four-card support.
Three- or four-level	Minimum of 12 Roth Points; at least four-card support.

3. FREE RAISES, MAJOR SUITS: See Chapter 15.

II. IF YOU CANNOT MAKE A FREE RAISE, CONSIDER THE NEGATIVE DOUBLE

1. A DOUBLE IS NEGATIVE: If partner opens with one of a suit, 1 NT, or a forcing 2 ♣, and next player overcalls.

A DOUBLE IS FOR PENALTIES: If partner opens with a weak two-bid or a preempt and next player overcalls.

2. REQUIREMENTS FOR A NEGATIVE DOUBLE

LEVEL OF BIDDING	REQUIREMENTS
One-level	7–10 HCP with 1 to 2 defensive tricks Any one of the following hands: (1) Support for unbid suits. (2) Good suit of your own. (3) Support for partner's suit.
Two-level	7–12 HCP with 1 to 2 defensive tricks Any one of the following hands: (1) Support for all unbid suits. (2) Good suit of your own. (3) Support for partner's suit.
Three- or four-level	9 or more Roth Points with 1 or more defensive tricks Preferably, support for all unbid suits; possibly, support for partner's *minor* suit.

3. OPENER'S REBID AFTER A NEGATIVE DOUBLE

OPENER'S POINTS	OPENER'S CHOICES (IN ORDER OF PREFERENCE):
14 to 16 points	1. Bid a new suit (at least four cards). 2. Bid notrump (balanced hand, opponents' suit stopped). 3. Rebid your own suit. 4. Pass (almost never at low levels).
17 to 18 points	1. Jump in new suit (but not past game). 2. Jump rebid your own suit (but not past game). 3. Pass (almost never at low levels).
19 or more points	With balanced hand, enemy's suit stopped: jump in notrump. With very powerful suit of your own: Bid game in your own suit.

OPENER'S POINTS	OPENER'S CHOICES (IN ORDER OF PREFERENCE):

With two-suited hand: Jump to game in new suit.

Otherwise: cue-bid the opponents' suit and let partner describe his hand.

4. PROTECTING PARTNER IN THE BALANCE POSITION: YOU OPEN, NEXT PLAYER OVERCALLS, PARTNER AND RIGHT-HAND OPPONENT PASS

YOUR ACTIONS (IN ORDER OF PREFERENCE):

1. With a reasonably balanced hand and no great length or strength in the opponents' suit, double for takeout. Partner will convert to penalties by passing if he wanted to double the opponents' overcall for penalties, and otherwise will bid his best suit.

2. With unbalanced hands, bid a new suit or rebid your own suit. Jump with 19 Roth Points or more.

3. Rebid notrump at the cheapest possible level with 17–20 HCP, balanced suit distribution, and at least two stoppers in the opponents' suit.

4. With a minimum hand and strength and length in the suit bid by the opponents (indicating that partner does not have a hand worth a penalty double), pass. You are not required to reopen on all hands.

REVIEW QUIZ FOR CHAPTER 19

For each problem, count your Roth Points (and your HCP where necessary) and decide on your action.

Part I

	PART.	OPP.	YOU	YOU HOLD			
1.	1 ♠	2 ♣	?	♠ 86	♡ AQ765	◇ KQ43	♣ 32
2.	1 ♠	3 ♡	?	♠ 104	♡ 865	◇ AK94	♣ Q1054
3.	1 ♣	1 ♡	?	♠ KQ7	♡ 432	◇ A432	♣ 1098

(407)

	PART.	OPP.	YOU	YOU HOLD
4.	1 ♡	2 ♠	?	♠K54 ♡72 ♢AKJ65 ♣K43
5.	1 ♢	1 ♡	?	♠A63 ♡32 ♢K843 ♣9842
6.	1 ♠	3 ♢	?	♠985 ♡AK42 ♢32 ♣KJ82
7.	1 ♠	2 ♢	?	♠8 ♡J65 ♢AQ1097 ♣J842
8.	2 ♠	3 ♡	?	♠7 ♡8642 ♢AQ86 ♣KJ75
	(weak)			
9.	1 ♣	1 ♡	?	♠KJ73 ♡85 ♢AK82 ♣743
10.	1 ♠	2 ♢	?	♠10843 ♡6 ♢A642 ♣7432
11.	1 ♢	2 ♡	?	♠AJ3 ♡94 ♢KQ65 ♣10942
12.	1 ♠	2 ♡	?	♠86 ♡1043 ♢A9865 ♣Q43
13.	1 ♠	2 ♣	?	♠84 ♡AJ10953 ♢Q83 ♣87
14.	1 ♣	3 ♡	?	♠Q106 ♡AQ7 ♢AQJ85 ♣104
15.	1 ♠	4 ♣	?	♠74 ♡AQ108 ♢KQ965 ♣92

Part II

	YOU	OPP.	PART.	OPP.	YOU HOLD
16.	1 ♢ ?	2 ♣	Pass	Pass	♠Q7 ♡A985 ♢AK876 ♣109
17.	1 ♢ ?	4 ♣	Dbl	Pass	♠10742 ♡AK3 ♢KQJ96 ♣6
18.	1 ♡ ?	2 ♠	Dbl	Pass	♠8 ♡AK10964 ♢AK3 ♣J108
19.	1 ♢ ?	2 ♣	Pass	Pass	♠QJ7 ♡K10 ♢AKJ65 ♣AQ7
20.	1 ♣ ?	1 ♡	Dbl	Pass	♠K1064 ♡72 ♢84 ♣AKQ98
21.	1 ♠ ?	2 ♣	Dbl	Pass	♠AQ642 ♡AK107 ♢AJ8 ♣9
22.	1 ♡ ?	2 ♣	Pass	Pass	♠KQ5 ♡AJ976 ♢742 ♣A8
23.	1 ♠ ?	2 ♡	Dbl	Pass	♠KQJ109 ♡86 ♢72 ♣AQ62
24.	1 ♠ ?	4 ♢	Dbl	Pass	♠AK975 ♡843 ♢K108 ♣A7

	YOU	OPP.	PART.	OPP.	YOU HOLD			
25.	1 ◇	2 ♣	Dbl	Pass	♠ AJ97	♡ 6	◇ AKJ95	♣ K108
	?							
26.	1 ♡	3 ◇	Dbl	Pass	♠ 853	♡ AJ1065	◇ AKQ2	♣ 4
	?							
27.	1 ♠	2 ♣	Dbl	Pass	♠ AQ654	♡ 108	◇ K106	♣ AQ9
	?							
28.	1 ♠	2 ♣	Pass	Pass	♠ K10965	♡ 7	◇ AQ1064	♣ A2
	?							
29.	1 ◇	2 ♣	Pass	Pass	♠ 86	♡ 743	◇ AKJ9	♣ KQ104
	?							
30.	1 ♡	2 ♠	Pass	Pass	♠ 973	♡ AQJ842	◇ AJ10	♣ 3
	?							

SOLUTIONS
Part I

	POINTS	BID	
1.	11	2 ♡	Make a free bid when you are strong enough to do so.
2.	9	Double	At high levels, the negative double is best with support for the unbid suits. You lack the requirements for a free bid but have a good negative double.
3.	9	Pass	It is best to pass on hands with 4–3–3–3 distribution that are unsuitable for a free bid, free raise, or notrump response.
4.	14	3 ◇	With a hand worth an opening bid, you may make a free bid at the three-level.
5.	9	2 ◇	The "weak" free raise in a minor.
6.	12	4 ♠	Do not make a negative double when you meet the requirements for a free raise. Be sure to jump; 3 ♠ would show a maximum of 10 points.
7.	8	Pass	If partner reopens with a double, you will pass for penalties.
8.	10	Pass	A double is not negative after an opening weak two-bid or preempt.

	POINTS	BID	
9.	12	1 ♠	Make a free bid when you are strong enough to do so. Bidding a new major suit takes precedence over bidding a new minor suit when the suits are of equal length.
10.	7	Double	When you next support spades, partner will know that you have 6 to 7 points and support for his suit.
11.	12	3 ◊	You are strong enough for a three-level free raise.
12.	6	Pass	You do not have support for the unbid suits, a good suit of your own, or support for partner's suit, and you have only 6 HCP, so a negative double is barred.
13.	8	Double	You plan to rebid hearts next, showing a good suit in a hand too weak for a free bid.
14.	15	3 NT	The most descriptive bid. Don't give partner a problem.
15.	11	Double	The negative double was invented for hands like this.

Part II

16.	14	Double	Reopen with a double when your hand is reasonably balanced. Partner could be "loaded" in clubs.
17.	15	4 ♠	Partner has asked you to bid a new suit. Do not pass in fright. Takeout doubles are for takeout!
18.	18	4 ♡	Game is not certain, but you should have good play for it. A 3 ♡ rebid would show a much weaker hand.
19.	20	2 NT	Partner is unlikely to be interested in doubling clubs for penalties. Make your most descriptive bid.

	POINTS	BID	
20.	14	1 ♠	Obey partner's request and show your new suit.
21.	20	3 ♣	You intend to commit the hand to game. Find out what kind of negative double partner has: support for the unbid suits, support for your suit, or a suit of his own.
22.	15	Double	You must protect partner by reopening.
23.	14	3 ♣	Partner has asked for a new suit, and you have one.
24.	14	Pass	At high levels, precise bidding is impossible. You have no good bid to make; "stay fixed" and take a sure plus score.
25.	18	3 ♠	You must jump to show 17 or 18 points.
26.	14	Pass	Your left-hand opponent has stepped out of line and should be punished. Since partner does not fit hearts, your offensive prospects look poor even in a notrump contract. Go for the penalty.
27.	15	2 NT	It is more important to describe the balanced hand and club stoppers than to rebid spades. Partner already knows you have a five-card spade suit.
28.	16	2 ◇	Do not reopen with a double on a two-suiter.
29.	14	Pass	Since partner was unable to make a free bid, your side isn't going anywhere on this hand. Besides, you have no good bid to make. Try for an undoubled penalty—it's probably "their hand" anyway.
30.	15	3 ♡	Your hand is unbalanced and you have too much of your strength in hearts to reopen with a double.

CHAPTER

20

The Light Takeout Double

Suppose that your right-hand opponent opens the bidding with **one club** and you hold

♠ K642   ♡ A763   ◇ QJ82   ♣ 6

According to traditional Standard American bidding methods, you must pass. Your hand is worth only 12 points, and you need a hand worth an opening bid (14 points) to make a takeout double. Nor is it permissible to overcall on a four-card suit. Therefore, the only possible choice is to pass.

As so often results from Standard American bidding methods, we have a pretty sad state of affairs. With excellent support for all three unbid suits, a pass is excessively timid. As a matter of fact, your hand will go up to 13 points if partner bids a new suit in response to your double, for no matter which suit he bids you have four-card support and will be able to PROMOTE your singleton club. Since you have a wide range of suits to choose from, it is very likely that you and your partner have a good suit fit somewhere—but you will never find it if you do not get into the auction.

(412)

It should be stressed once again that "cheating" on your point count is not the answer to this problem—nor to any problem. No matter what system you are playing, you should never lie about your point count. Partner, expecting you to live up to your promise, is quite likely to take an action that will place your side overboard, and the fault will be entirely yours for failing to produce the full number of points your bids have shown. You may get away with it for a hand or two, but lying about your point count is a sure road to eventual disaster.

As in previous chapters, the solution to this bidding problem lies in changing the meaning of yet another of Standard American's "wasted bids." In Standard American, the cue-bid of the opponents' suit shows a powerhouse hand and is forcing to game. As before, Standard American seems to have been developed by someone who spent a misguided evening playing bridge with a pinochle deck (in which no card is lower than a nine) or had an extremely fortuitous run of the cards. The strong (game–forcing) cue-bid comes up so rarely that it is poor strategy to assign this meaning to the bid.

Therefore, you will use the cue-bid of the opponents' suit as a strong takeout double. This will allow you to make a takeout double with weaker hands, hands with which Standard American players would be forced to pass. So long as partner is in tune with your methods, he will interpret your messages accurately, so there is no danger of getting overboard. The requirements for these two bids—the takeout double and the cue-bid of the opponents' suit—are as follows:

TAKEOUT DOUBLE*	CUE-BID
1. 13 to 19 total Roth Points.	1. 20 or more total Roth Points.
2. Support for all unbid suits.	2. Support for all unbid suits.
	3. Does *not* promise another bid.

When counting your points, assume that partner will bid your shortest suit aside from that bid by the opponent and count your

---

* With strong hands lacking support for all unbid suits, a takeout double must also be used. A subsequent bid of a new suit by the double shows 19–21 points (a jump shows more) and a hand lacking the perfect "shape" for a cue-bid.

Distribution Points accordingly. For example, if you hold a singleton in the suit bid by the opponents and four cards in each of the
other suits, assume that partner will bid one of your four-card suits
and PROMOTE your singleton by adding one extra point. However,
if you hold only three cards in any one of the unbid suits, you must
assume that partner will bid that suit, so do not PROMOTE any of
your Distribution Points.

Here's how these rules work:

OPP	YOU	YOU HOLD			
1. 1 ♣	?	♠ K642	♡ A763	◇ QJ82	♣ 6

Double. You have 13 Roth Points: 10 HCP and three points for
the PROMOTED singleton. You may PROMOTE your singleton
since you have four-card support for any suit that partner may bid.
Observe once again how the Roth Point Count and the Roth approach to bidding work in harmony: You PROMOTE your Distribution Points with strong holdings in the unbid suits, and thus have an
accurate idea as to the true value of your hand; and the light takeout
double allows you to make use of this information by entering the
auction when it is safe to do so. Standard American players would
make two errors on this hand: They would assume that they held
only 12 points, and they would pass because they "lacked the values"
for a takeout double.

2. 1 ♣	?	♠ KQ86	♡ AQ85	◇ KQ72	♣ 4

Double. With 19 Roth Points, you have a maximum takeout
double.

3. 1 ♣	?	♠ A642	♡ K963	◇ Q982	♣ 6

Pass. You have only 12 Roth Points and are too weak for a takeout
double. An accurate method of hand evaluation must also warn you
when you are too weak to enter the bidding, and the Roth Point
Count does so. Even though it is always more satisfying to take action than it is to pass, you must obey the rules of the system if you
expect it to work for you.

4. 1 ♡   ?   ♠ K642   ♡ A763   ◊ KQ85   ♣ 2

Pass. You do not have support for all unbid suits.

5. 1 ♠   ?   ♠ AQ8   ♡ KJ97   ◊ AJ6   ♣ Q108

Bid 1 NT. The direct one-notrump overcall shows a hand worth an opening notrump bid (16–18 HCP and balanced suit distribution) and stoppers in the suit bid by the opponents. Do not make a take-out double when you meet the requirements for the more descriptive 1 NT overcall.

6. 1 ◊   ?   ♠ AK85   ♡ KQJ6   ◊ 74   ♣ AQ4

Bid 2 ◊. Even assuming that partner bids clubs, you have 20 Roth Points: 19 HCP and one Distribution Point. The cue-bid does *not* promise another bid, so you can pass if partner shows no interest in game. Of course, 4–4–1–4 distribution would be preferable—but you can't have everything.

7. 1 ♠   ?   ♠ K1097   ♡ 8   ◊ AJ86   ♣ AQ76

Pass. You do not have support for all unbid suits and are too weak and too unbalanced for a 1 NT overcall, so you must pass and await developments.

8. 1 ♡   ?   ♠ KQ86   ♡ 7   ◊ A10965   ♣ Q109

Double. Assuming that partner bids clubs, your shortest unbid suit, your hand is worth 13 Roth Points—just enough for the double.

9. 1 ♡   ?   ♠ K4   ♡ 72   ◊ AKQJ86   ♣ A104

Double. You have 21 Roth Points: 17 HCP, two Length Points (double your Length Points with a SELF-SUFFICIENT suit), and two Distribution Points. The hand is much too strong for a mere 2 ◊ overcall; partner could pass with a hand which would produce a cold game. You plan to rebid in diamonds. See footnote on page 412.

10. 1 ♠   ?   ♠ 74   ♡ K7   ◊ AKQJ86   ♣ A104

Double. No matter what system you play, you should always plan your rebid. If you cue-bid 2 ♠ and partner bids 3 ♡, you will have to show your diamond suit at the four-level. This may get you too high and also precludes the possibility of playing in 3 NT, which may be the only makable game. We do not deny that it would be nice to be playing strong jump overcalls on *this* hand; any treatment is effective once in a while (else no one would *ever* play it). However, as we have seen, such hands arise much less frequently than hands calling for weak jump overcalls, and you do not want to be in the sorry position of Standard American players who must contest the auction with one hand tied behind their backs because of the numerous ineffective treatments with which they are saddled. In fact, strong jump overcalls are so infrequent that you will not run into any for the remainder of this chapter.

Since we have not had enough new material to justify a quiz, let us turn to the responses to the takeout double and the cue-bid.

Bidding after a Takeout Double

Since the takeout doubler has promised support for all unbid suits, you may bid a four-card suit with confidence. If you have a five-card suit, you should immediately PROMOTE by adding one point for a supported five-card or longer suit, since partner has promised this support by his takeout double. (Since you have been compelled to respond, it is possible that on some unfortunate occasions you may be called upon to bid a three-card suit. Partner has support, so you will not be in serious trouble; but it is best to avoid this whenever possible.)

You must keep in mind the fact that a non-jump response does not show *any* values. You have been required to bid by partner's takeout double, and may be forced to do so on a completely worthless hand. Therefore, when you do have good values, it is essential to take some special action to let partner know. Here is how the responses work:

1. A *non-jump bid in a new suit* shows 0–10 Roth Points and a probable four-card or longer suit.

2. *A bid of 1 NT* shows 8–11* HCP, balanced suit distribution, and at least one stopper in the adversely bid suit.

3. *A bid of 2 NT* shows 12–13 HCP, a balanced hand, and at least one stopper in the suit bid by the opponents.

4. *A jump in a new suit* shows 11–12 points and at least a four-card suit. Partner is permitted to pass and should do so if there is no chance for game.

5. *A cue-bid in the opponents' suit* shows a minimum of 12 Roth Points, and either support for all unbid suits or a good suit that will be bid later on. Partner must bid again, and game will probably be reached.

6. *A pass* promises five or more cards including three honors in the opponents' suit and a probable minimum of 6 Roth Points. Do not pass simply because you do not know what to bid! A pass is an aggressive action that promises great strength in the enemy's suit and states that your best chance for a good result is to defeat the contract bid by the enemy. Since this contract is at the one-level, you must have quite a good defensive hand. As a matter of fact, it is an unwritten law of bridge that if you pass, partner must lead a trump (if he has one) so that you can pull the enemy's trumps. If they can make tricks by "ruffability," you are most unlikely to set them. If you can't draw trumps, don't pass.

Some illustrations:

	OPP.	PART.	OPP.	YOU	YOU HOLD	
1.	1 ♡	Dbl	Pass	?	♠ 86	♡ A9654
					◇ 863	♣ Q95

Bid 2 ♣. Least of evils. Your heart suit is not nearly strong enough to draw trumps, so a pass is not to be considered, and you are too weak to respond 1 NT. Don't cheat on your point count!

	OPP.	PART.	OPP.	YOU	YOU HOLD	
2.	1 ♡	Dbl	Pass	?	♠ J975	♡ 86
					◇ AK8	♣ K642

---

* These requirements may be reduced slightly when the opening bid is a major suit. It is better to make a slightly light one-notrump bid than to force the bidding to the two-level.

(417)

Bid 2 ♠. With 11 Roth Points, you must jump. Bid your major suit in preference to your minor; game in a major requires only 26 Roth Points but game in a minor takes 29. Note that any four-card suit is biddable since partner has promised support.

3.	1 ♡	Dbl	Pass	?	♠ J976 ♡ A6
					◇ AK8 ♣ Q842

Bid 2 ♡. Now you are too strong even for a jump to 2 ♠.

4.	1 ◇	Dbl	Pass	?	♠ A83 ♡ 642
					◇ K1095 ♣ Q83

Bid 1 NT. The most descriptive response.

5.	1 ♠	Dbl	Pass	?	♠ 853 ♡ AK864
					◇ 9 ♣ J1042

Bid 3 ♡. You have 11 Roth Points: 8 HCP, two Distribution Points in diamonds, and one point for a supported five-card suit. (By doubling, partner has promised support for all unbid suits and has thereby supported your suit before you bid it!) Thus, you are too strong for a simple response and must jump to 3 ♡.

6.	1 ♡	Dbl	Pass	?	♠ 763 ♡ 85432
					◇ 74 ♣ 642

Bid 1 ♠. The point of this example is to emphasize that you must not pass simply because you do not know what to do. Partner will make allowances for the fact that you may have a worthless hand.

7.	1 ◇	Dbl	Pass	?	♠ 8 ♡ 643
					◇ KQJ986 ♣ 863

Pass. You would really like to have the ten of diamonds as well, but there is no better alternative. Your best chance for a good result lies in trying to penalize the opponents. However, don't be surprised if you don't set them as much as you would like. As you can see, you need quite a good holding in the enemy's suit to make a penalty pass.

After responder has made his bid, the auction proceeds in a

straightforward manner. As with any limited bid, the doubler adds his points to his partner's and evaluates game chances. If game is out of the question, just pass. If game is possible, invite it; if game is definite, bid it or make a bid partner cannot pass (such as a cue-bid of the enemy suit or a jump in a new suit).

Bidding after a Cue-Bid

If, instead of doubling, your partner cue-bids the suit bid by the opponents, he is showing at least 20 Roth Points. Thus, you need far fewer points to make an encouraging bid; as few as 6 points in your hand will give your side the total of 26 needed for game. Over the cue-bid, respond as follows:

1. A *bid in a new suit* shows 0–3 Roth Points and a probable four-card suit.

2. A *jump in a new suit* shows 4–5 Roth Points and at least a four-card suit.

3. A *bid of 2 NT* shows 3–5 HCP, stoppers in the opponents' suit, and balanced suit distribution. Note that 2 NT is not a jump since the cue-bid has driven the auction to the two-level.

4. A *bid of 3 NT* shows 6–9 HCP, balanced suit distribution, and stoppers in the opponents' suit.

5. A *cue-bid* shows 6 or more Roth Points and either good support for all unbid suits or a good suit of your own that you will bid later. Since partner has at least 20 Roth Points, your six points will produce game, and the cue-bid conveys this information.

You are compelled to bid over partner's cue-bid and may not pass under any circumstances.

Some examples:

	OPP.	PART.	OPP.	YOU	YOU HOLD
1.	1 ♠	2 ♠	Pass	?	♠ J1065 ♡ 843
					◇ 643 ♣ 643

Bid 3 ♣. You may not pass and are not strong enough to bid 2 NT.

2. 1 ♠   2 ♠   Pass   ?   ♠ 1072 ♡ 74
                                       ◇ Q843 ♣ 8642

Bid 3 ◇. With no major suit to bid, bid your better minor. You have only two Roth Points and are not strong enough for a jump response.

3. 1 ♡   2 ♡   Pass   ?   ♠ 9843 ♡ A63
                                       ◇ 10842 ♣ 32

Bid 3 ♠. This example illustrates several points: You should prefer to bid a major suit whenever possible; you should jump with 4–5 Roth Points; and you should not bid notrump with only one stopper in the suit bid by the opponents.

4. 1 ◇   2 ◇   Pass   ?   ♠ 742   ♡ 863
                                       ◇ KJ105 ♣ 642

Bid 2 NT. You have three Roth Points, balanced suit distribution, and two stoppers (possibly three) in the enemy's suit.

5. 1 ♣   2 ♣   Pass   ?   ♠ AQ86 ♡ K94
                                       ◇ 6432 ♣ 72

Bid 3 ♣. If you think about the fact that partner has 20 Roth Points, you will realize that this is quite a good hand. With six or more Roth Points, cue-bid to let partner know that game is definite. If partner does not bid spades, you will do so next time; you can bid spades below the level of game without fear of being passed since your cue-bid has already announced that game should be bid.

Just as was the case with a takeout double, the auction proceeds in a clear and simple fashion after the response to the cue-bid. The cue-bidder is permitted to pass if there is no chance for game and the contract is playable. If *responder* cue-bids, showing a powerful hand, the original cue-bidder simply makes the most descriptive bid; the bidding cannot die until game is reached. Usually, the original cue-bidder will have an excellent idea about game prospects after hearing his partner's first response, and can bid accordingly.

Capsule Summary: The Takeout Double and the Cue-Bid

TAKEOUT DOUBLE SHOWS:	CUE-BID SHOWS:

TAKEOUT DOUBLE SHOWS:
1. 13 to 19 Roth Points.
2. Support for all unbid suits,
   (or 3. 19+ Roth Points and
   improper distribution for a
   cue-bid)

CUE-BID SHOWS:
1. 20 or more total Roth Points.
2. Support for all unbid suits.

BIDDING AFTER A TAKEOUT DOUBLE

BID	MEANING
Bid in a new suit	0–10 Roth Points; probable four-card suit.
1 NT	8–11 HCP.
	Balanced suit distribution.
	At least one stopper in the enemy suit.
2 NT	12–13 HCP.
	Balanced suit distribution.
	At least one stopper in the enemy suit.
Jump in a new suit	11–12 Roth Points; at least a four-card suit.
Cue-bid	Minimum of 12 Roth Points.
	Either support for all unbid suits or a good suit of your own.
Pass	At least five cards headed by three honors in the enemy suit.
	Probable minimum of 6 Roth Points.

BIDDING AFTER A CUE-BID:

BID	MEANING
Bid in a new suit	0–3 Roth Points; probable four-card suit.
2 NT	3–5 HCP.
	One or two stoppers in the opponents' suit.
	Balanced suit distribution.
3 NT	6–9 HCP.
	Two stoppers in the opponents' suit.
	Balanced suit distribution.
Jump in a new suit	4–5 Roth Points; at least a four-card suit.
Cue-bid	6 or more Roth Points.

BID	MEANING
	Either good support for all unbid suits or a good suit of your own.
Pass	You have made an egregious error. You are not permitted to pass a cue-bid.

REVIEW QUIZ FOR CHAPTER 20

In each case, count your Roth Points and decide on your action. Remember to let the Roth Point Count and the Roth approach to bidding work in harmony by making whatever promotions and demotions are justified by the bidding.

Part I

	OPP.	YOU	PART.	OPP.	YOU HOLD
1.	1 ♦	?			♠ K843 ♡ 7
					♦ AQ42 ♣ A1064
2.	1 ♡	?			♠ AQ65 ♡ ---
					♦ AK1085 ♣ A942
3.	1 ♦	?			♠ K83 ♡ AJ64
					♦ AQ9 ♣ K108
4.	1 ♠	?			♠ 8 ♡ J1084
					♦ AK97 ♣ Q1042
5.	1 ♣	?			♠ KQ74 ♡ AQ86
					♦ QJ7 ♣ K2
6.	1 ♡	?			♠ J842 ♡ 7
					♦ K1043 ♣ A1084
7.	1 ♠	Dbl	Pass	2 ♡	♠ 86 ♡ AKQ2
	Pass	?			♦ K1043 ♣ 863
8.	1 ♦	Dbl	Pass	1 NT	♠ KJ106 ♡ AQ95
	Pass	?			♦ 2 ♣ AQ65
9.	1 ♣	Dbl	Pass	2 ♠	♠ QJ105 ♡ AK86
	Pass	?			♦ A103 ♣ 82
10.	1 ♦	2 ♦	Pass	2 ♡	♠ AK87 ♡ AK87
	Pass	?			♦ 2 ♣ A1042

(422)

Part II

	OPP.	PART.	OPP.	YOU	YOU HOLD
11.	1 ♣	Dbl	Pass	?	♠ AJ104 ♡ K83 ◇ K1042 ♣ 72
12.	1 ♡	Dbl	Pass	?	♠ A83 ♡ KJ94 ◇ 987 ♣ 1053
13.	1 ◇	2 ◇	Pass	?	♠ KQ65 ♡ 873 ◇ 643 ♣ 953
14.	1 ♠	Dbl	Pass	?	♠ Q10864 ♡ 73 ◇ J83 ♣ Q64
15.	1 ♡	2 ♡	Pass	?	♠ Q63 ♡ 7432 ◇ 983 ♣ 1062
16.	1 ◇	Dbl	Pass	?	♠ AQ1086 ♡ A83 ◇ 74 ♣ J105
17.	1 ♣	Dbl	Pass	?	♠ AQ3 ♡ 76 ◇ 10942 ♣ AQ105
18.	1 ◇	Dbl	Pass	1 ♠	♠ AKJ4 ♡ 63
	Pass	2 ♠	Pass	?	◇ 864 ♣ 10987
19.	1 ♣	2 ♣	Pass	2 ♡	♠ 76 ♡ J10432
	Pass	3 ♡	Pass	?	◇ 863 ♣ 1092
20.	1 ◇	Dbl	Pass	1 ♠	♠ Q1064 ♡ 7
	Pass	2 ♠	Pass	?	◇ A1064 ♣ 8432

SOLUTIONS

Part I

	POINTS	BID	
1.	13	Pass	You do not have support for all unbid suits and the spades are too weak for an overcall.
2.	21	2 ♡	You meet all the requirements for the cue-bid.
3.	17	1 NT	Prefer the 1 NT overcall to the takeout double when you meet the requirements.

POINTS	BID

4. 13 Double After PROMOTION, you are just strong enough for the light takeout double. Standard American players have to pass; you can compete for the contract.

5. 18 Double With such good support for the major suits and a shaky club stopper, the double is preferable to the 1 NT overcall.

6. 11 Pass You are not strong enough to double. Cheating on your point count is a sure route to losing bridge.

7. 14 Pass Partner has a maximum of ten points, so there is no chance for game. A raise can only get you overboard.

8. 16 2 NT There is a chance for game if partner has 10 or 11 points, so invite game by raising notrump. Partner has promised stoppers in diamonds.

9. 16 4 ♠ Partner has 11 to 12 Roth Points, so game is definite and slam is out of the question. Keep the auction simple.

10. 21 Pass Partner has a maximum of 3 Roth Points. Don't tell the same story twice.

Part II

11. 11 2 ♠ You must jump to show 11 Roth Points.

12. 8 1 NT You meet all the requirements for the 1 NT response.

13. 5 3 ♠ After a cue-bid, a jump in a new suit shows 4 to 5 Roth Points and at least a four-card suit.

14. 5 2 ♣ The spade suit is much too weak even to consider a pass and you are too weak for a 1 NT response. The club bid is the least of evils.

	POINTS	BID	
15.	2	2 ♠	You must respond. The worst thing you can do is to make a panicky pass and leave partner in the opponents' suit. Partnerships (and friendships) have broken up over less!
16.	13	2 ◇	After PROMOTING by adding one point for a supported five-card suit, you are too strong for the jump to 2 ♠, which partner can pass. Cue-bid to let partner know game is definite; you will bid spades next time.
17.	12	2 NT	The 2 NT bid shows 12 to 13 HCP, a balanced hand, and stoppers in the suit bid by the opponents.
18.	9	4 ♠	Partner is inviting game if you have a maximum, which you do. Do not confuse the issue with a pointless 3 ♠ bid that can only give partner a chance to make a mistake.
19.	3	4 ♡	It may strike you as unusual to accept a game invitation with "only" 3 Roth Points, but your 2 ♡ response showed 0 to 3 points yet partner is still interested in game. With a maximum, you must accept his invitation. (Do not forget to PROMOTE by adding one point for a supported five-card suit.)
20.	8	3 ♠	With a near-maximum, you are not strong enough to bid game yourself, but should make one further try. For all partner knows, you have a completely worthless hand. A 3 ◇ bid is also acceptable.

CHAPTER
21

The "Sound" Overcall

As previous chapters indicate, we are in favor of preemptive tactics that are designed to harass the opponents and disrupt their lines of communication. When properly used, weak two-bids, weak jump overcalls, and weak jump responses are effective bidding weapons that serve a dual purpose: they make it difficult for the opponents to reach the proper contract, and they make your own bidding easier by giving partner a full description of your hand in a single bid.

There is one bid, however, that should *not* be made without a "sound" hand, and that is the simple overcall. "Light" single overcalls accomplish none of the purposes achieved so well by the preemptive bids, and have numerous disadvantages. Simple overcalls do not use up a great deal of bidding room, so they are usually not overly bothersome to the opponents. Even worse, light overcalls can actually help the opponents by providing a road map that gives the enemy a good picture of the lie of the land. Often, the opponents can take advantage of the information obtained from your light overcall to stay out of a game that would have gone down, or to arrive at their best contract. A second problem with light overcalls is that they do not describe your hand very well. If an overcall can be either weak or strong, partner has a terrible problem. Thinking that you have a sturdy overcall, he may double the opponents when they are cold for their contract or get your side overboard. If, on the other hand, he tries to compensate for the possibility of a light overcall, game may be missed when you have a good hand.

Thus, the light single overcall has none of the advantages that make the preemptive bids so attractive. The overcall does not hinder the opponents; in fact, it often helps them. Also, it does not give partner a very good description of your hand, and makes it easy for him to make a mistake.

For these reasons, the overcall in the Roth approach shows a "sound" hand, one worth an opening bid. It is always made with game in mind. When the overcall is treated in this way, it becomes a useful weapon deserving of a place along with your array of preemptive bids. Partner has an excellent idea of your holding, and the constructive overcall represents an excellent first step on the road to game.

Requirements for the Overcall

The requirements for an overcall of an opponent's opening bid of one of a suit are quite straightforward:

1. A hand worth an opening bid (14 to 18 Roth Points with at least 10 HCP).*

2. A five-card or longer suit.

In order to follow expert practice, you should vary these requirements slightly depending on the vulnerability. If you are not vulnerable and the opponents are, you may overcall on one point less, since it is safer to enter the auction when vulnerability conditions are favorable. If, however, you are vulnerable and the opponents are not, you should have one *extra* point to overcall, since danger is lurking everywhere and the opponents will be most tempted to

---

* As noted in Part One, the *level* of the overcall is of importance. These requirements may be shaded by one point if your bid is at the one-level.

double because of the conditions of vulnerability. You must always have a five-card or longer suit, and preferably a good suit at that. With a close decision, be guided by the quality of your suit: if it is *strong*, take the plunge and overcall; but if your suit is sketchy and has a lot of holes, play safe and pass. Some illustrations:

	OPP.	YOU	YOU HOLD				VUL.
1.	1 ♠	?	♠ 832	♡ K84	◇ AQ965	♣ K7	Both

Pass. You are too weak to overcall, and cannot make a takeout double without support for all unbid suits. (13 Roth Points)

| 2. | 1 ♡ | ? | ♠ 87 | ♡ 65 | ◇ KQ4 | ♣ AKQ932 | You |

Bid 2 ♣. With 17 Roth Points, you have a near-maximum overcall. If partner bids 2 NT, raise to 3 NT.

| 3. | 1 ◇ | ? | ♠ AQJ64 | ♡ 863 | ◇ A8 | ♣ K42 | You |

Bid 1 ♠. A minimum overcall at "unfavorable" vulnerability. (15)

| 4. | 1 ◇ | ? | ♠ AKJ64 | ♡ 863 | ◇ A8 | ♣ 843 | Opp. |

Bid 1 ♠. A minimum overcall at "favorable" vulnerability. (13)

| 5. | 1 ♣ | ? | ♠ 109643 | ♡ 7 | ◇ AKQ7 | ♣ Q108 | Opp. |

Pass. Although you have 13 Roth Points, your spade suit is terrible. (13)

| 6. | 1 ♠ | ? | ♠ 7 | ♡ AKJ864 | ◇ A106 | ♣ A107 | You |

Double. You are too strong for an overcall. Rebid hearts over any response by partner, but do not be averse to the possibility of winding up in a minor suit if partner makes strong noises to that effect. (19)

| 7. | 1 ♣ | ? | ♠ K10 | ♡ AQ9 | ◇ K10765 | ♣ AQ9 | Both |

Bid 1 NT. You would have opened 1 NT, not 1 ◇, with this hand. Since you have stoppers in the suit bid by the opponents, you meet the requirements for the 1 NT overcall and should make this more descriptive bid. (18)

8.   1 ♣   ?   ♠ 87   ♡ AJ9   ◇ AK10765   ♣ K8   Both

Bid 1 ◇. Compare to the previous problem. It is surely more descriptive to show your fine diamond suit than to overcall 1 NT with a six-card suit and only a single club stopper. Since you are playing sound overcalls, you need not fear that you are underbidding or that partner will pass when game is cold. (18)

Responses to the Overcall

Since the overcaller has promised a good hand, responder need not be too timid about putting his two cents' worth into the auction. As responder, you have the following choices available to you:

1. Raise partner's suit. If your right-hand opponent has passed, a single raise shows 8 to 10 Roth Points; a double raise shows 11 to 12 points, and the triple raise is preemptive. If your right-hand opponent has bid, the single raise shows only 5 to 9 points; you are trying to fight for the contract and keep the opponents from stealing a cheap part-score by having a leisurely exchange of information. However, one requirement never changes: you must have at least three-card support to raise (to any level).

2. Bid notrump. A 1 NT response, (or a 2 NT response over a two-level overcall) shows 9–11 HCP. A *jump* in notrump promises 12 to 13 HCP. To bid notrump, you must have stoppers in all unbid suits. If you can raise partner's major, do so rather than bid notrump.

3. Cue-bid the suit bid by the opponents. This is forcing, of course, and promises at least 13 Roth Points. In addition, you should have either a good fit with partner, or an excellent suit of your own; you will clear up this minor mystery at your next turn to bid.

4. Invitational jump in a suit. The jump in a new suit is invitational (but not forcing) and shows 11 to 13 Roth Points, at least a six-card suit, and usually fewer than three cards in partner's suit.

5. Bid a new suit *without* jumping. This shows up to 11 Roth Points, at least a five-card suit, and usually poor support for partner's suit. This is *not* an invitational bid and partner can and often will pass (though he may bid again if he fits with your suit or has an extremely good hand). The reason for chiming in with your suit

is threefold: it will help your side if you wind up defending, as partner will know what suit you would like him to lead; it tells partner where your values are so that he can compete, bid game, or double the opponents; and it takes you off a possible later guess that could plague you if you pass with fairly good values and the auction grows hot and furious. Since partner has a sound overcall, you can mention your suit and gain these advantages in safety. However, remember that this bid will tend to slow partner down, so do not make it if you can support his suit or bid notrump. Don't fear a misfit at a low level. Get your bid in early—when it's safe!

Some examples:

	OPP.	PART.	OPP.	YOU	YOU HOLD	VULNER- ABILITY
1.	1 ◇	1 ♠	Pass	?	♠ K83 ♡ 72 ◇ 832 ♣ AQ965	None

Bid 2 ♠. Always raise partner's major suit when you can. With 10 Roth Points and three-card support, you meet the requirements for the single raise.

2.	1 ◇	1 ♠	Pass	?	♠ K843 ♡ 7 ◇ 843 ♣ AQ962	None

Bid 3 ♠. After PROMOTION, you have 12 Roth Points.

3.	1 ◇	1 ♠	Pass	?	♠ J843 ♡ 7 ◇ 8432 ♣ Q853	None

Pass. With only 6 Roth Points, you are too weak to raise.

4.	1 ◇	1 ♠	2 ◇	?	♠ J843 ♡ 7 ◇ 8432 ♣ A853	None

Bid 2 ♠. When your right-hand opponent has bid, the single raise is competitive and shows 5 to 9 Roth Points.

5.	1 ♠	2 ◇	Pass	?	♠ KQ10 ♡ A73 ◇ J842 ♣ Q109	You

Bid 3 NT. Since the enemy's suit is well stopped, notrump offers an easier route to game than the minor suit. The latter requires 29 Roth Points for game. (12)

6. 1 ♡   2 ♣   Pass   ?   ♠ J106 ♡3   Both
                              ◇ KJ10864 ♣987

Bid 2 ◇. You are too weak to raise to 3 ♣ and the opponents
have too many points to sell out to 2 ♣. Let partner know where
your strength lies; a diamond lead will be most welcome if you
wind up on defense. The bid of a new suit is not invitational and
partner will not get carried away. (7)

7. 1 ♣   1 ♠   Pass   ?   ♠ 85 ♡ J10865   None
                              ◇ J10653 ♣2

Pass. You have a terrible hand. Don't look for trouble. Unlike
problem 6, you do *not* have a suit that you especially wish partner
to lead. (2)

8. 1 ♣   1 ♠   Pass   ?   ♠ 3 ♡ KJ10642
                              ◇ 643 ♣ J62

Bid 2 ♡. Show your strong suit when you can do so conveniently. (6)

9. 1 ♣   1 ♠   Pass   ?   ♠ 3 ♡ AKQ942
                              ◇ J643 ♣54

Bid 3 ♡. Partner may pass or go to game. (11)

After the overcall and response, your bidding proceeds as in any
other situation. At each turn to bid, you and your partner evaluate
game prospects, based on your knowledge of the other's hand type
and point count. If game is impossible and your contract is at all
playable, pass; if game is possible but not definite, invite it; and if
game is definite, bid it or make a bid partner cannot pass (such as
a cue-bid of the opponents' suit).

Reopening the Bidding

Since the overcaller has a good hand, he may not want to give
up the fight even if partner has nothing to say the first time around.
Consider the following auctions:

OPP.	YOU	OPP.	PART.	OPP.	YOU	OPP.	PART.
1 ♠	2 ◇	Pass	Pass	1 ♠	2 ◇	2 ♠	Pass
2 ♠	Dbl			Pass	Dbl		

Since it is usually wrong to overcall with length in the opponents' suit, you cannot wish to make a *penalty* double of two spades. Thus, both of the above doubles are *for takeout*. You should have a hand like

♠8 ♡AQ3 ◇AQ10964 ♣K72

With a *strong* six-card suit, the overcall was preferable to a takeout double on the first round. Since you have a good hand, don't give up. Double to show support for the unbid suits. Since you did not double on the first round, partner should not expect more than three-card support in any of the unbid suits. He should bid a five-card heart or club suit if he has one, or return to three diamonds with diamond support and no new suit to bid. If partner is "loaded" in the opponents' suit, he may pass for penalties, but he must be careful since he is sitting in front of the spade bidder and may be finessed out of his trump tricks. To make this reopening double, you should have at least 17 Roth Points, and at least three-card support for all unbid suits.

The second example is similar to the first; your double is for takeout. Partner should bid a new five-card suit if he has one, or return to three diamonds with support and no new suit to bid. You should have at least 17 Roth Points for this reopening double, as well as support for the unbid suits.

The Responsive Double

There is one special response to an overcall you will find useful. It occurs when your right-hand opponent has bid over your partner's overcall.* Consider the following situation:

---

* Many players use the same treatment after a takeout double. This is sound, but unnecessary when playing the (potentially) light takeout double.

OPP.	PART.	OPP.	YOU	YOU HOLD
1 ♡	1 ♠	2 ♡	?	♠ A10 ♡ 763 ◊ KJ82 ♣ Q1032

You cannot bid notrump without any stoppers in the opponents' suit, and can hardly introduce a four-card suit at the three-level or raise with a doubleton. We suggest that you use a *double* in this situation for *takeout*. When your right-hand opponent has raised the suit bid by opener, you virtually never have good enough trumps to make a penalty double. It is far more useful to use the double to convey the following message: "Partner, I have a pretty good hand and don't dare pass for fear that you'll think I don't have anything. However, I have no good bid to make. Please help me out by making *your* most descriptive bid."

This double, which is called a responsive double, is for takeout and shows 8 to 11 points and support for the unbid suits. The overcaller simply bids his "best" suit, rebidding a *strong* suit or showing a new suit. He should almost never pass. Usually, the responsive doubler will pass the overcaller's rebid with a minimum (8 to 9 points) and raise with a maximum (10 to 11 points). Used in this way, the responsive double solves an awkward bidding problem by making use of still another of Standard American's "wasted bids," this time a penalty double which never arises.

Note that the responsive double applies only if partner has made an overcall. If partner has doubled or cue-bid, any double by you is for penalties.

- -

Capsule Summary: The Sound Overcall

I. REQUIREMENTS TO OVERCALL

1. 14 to 18 Roth Points and at least 10 HCP.°
2. At least a five-card suit.

   Not vulnerable against vulnerable, you may be a point weaker
   Vulnerable against not vulnerable, you should be a point stronger

---

° May be shaded if the overcall is made at the one-level.

II. RESPONSES TO OVERCALLS

BID	MEANING
1. RAISES	
Single raise (right-hand opponent passes)	8 to 10 Roth Points.
Single raise (right-hand opponent has bid)	5 to 9 Roth Points.
Double raise	11 to 12 Roth Points.
Triple raise	Preemptive.

All raises promise at least three-card support.
Prefer a major-suit raise to any other call.
Prefer a cue-bid or notrump bid to a minor-suit raise.

BID	MEANING
2. NOTRUMP BIDS	
Without jumping	9–11 HCP; stoppers in all unbid suits.
Jump in notrump	12–13 HCP; stoppers in all unbid suits.
3. CUE-BID	13 or more Roth Points; either a good fit with partner *or* an excellent suit of your own.
4. SIMPLE BID IN A NEW SUIT	Up to 11 Roth Points; *not* invitational (but partner may bid).
5. JUMP IN A NEW SUIT	Invitational (but not forcing). 11 to 13 Roth Points. At least a six-card suit.
6. DOUBLE	Responsive (for takeout).

REVIEW QUIZ FOR CHAPTER 21

In each case, count your Roth Points and decide on your action.

Part I

	OPP.	YOU	OPP.	PART.	VUL.	YOU HOLD
1.	1 ♠	?			You	♠ 1074 ♡ K9765 ◇ 2 ♣ AKJ9
2.	1 ♡	?			None	♠ KQJ102 ♡ A97 ◇ Q108 ♣ 92
3.	1 ♣	?			Opp.	♠ 87 ♡ AK1095 ◇ AJ83 ♣ A7
4.	1 ♡	?			Opp.	♠ AQ10965 ♡ 83 ◇ 983 ♣ 107
5.	1 ♠	?			You	♠ A86 ♡ 75432 ◇ 9 ♣ AK104
6.	1 ♡	?			Both	♠ K107 ♡ AQ6 ◇ AJ1065 ♣ K10
7.	1 ◇	?			You	♠ J9765 ♡ AK42 ◇ --- ♣ Q1042
8.	1 ♡	?			You	♠ A109 ♡ 763 ◇ AQJ962 ♣ 7
9.	1 ◇ Pass	1 ♠ ?	Pass	2 ♠	You	♠ KJ976 ♡ AQ3 ◇ KQ9 ♣ 42
10.	1 ♡ Pass	2 ♣ ?	Pass	2 ♠	Both	♠ 106 ♡ 853 ◇ AQ8 ♣ AKJ107

Part II

	OPP.	PART.	OPP.	YOU	VUL.	YOU HOLD
11.	1 ◇	1 ♡	Pass	?	Both	♠ AQ865 ♡ 987 ◇ 82 ♣ Q87
12.	1 ♠	2 ◇	Pass	?	Both	♠ 7 ♡ A986 ◇ KJ72 ♣ K1085
13.	1 ♣	1 ♡	Pass	?	You	♠ AQJ9876 ♡ 8 ◇ 963 ♣ 64

	OPP.	PART.	OPP.	YOU	VUL.	YOU HOLD
14.	1 ♣	1 ♠	Pass	?	None	♠ 86 ♡ QJ86 ◇ A103 ♣ KJ94
15.	1 ♠	2 ◇	Pass	?	None	♠ 865 ♡ AJ10976 ◇ 643 ♣ 32
16.	1 ♠	2 ♣	Pass	?	Opp.	♠ KJ98 ♡ AK32 ◇ J6 ♣ J95
17.	1 ♡	1 ♠	2 ♡	?	You	♠ A86 ♡ 7 ◇ 8632 ♣ 109865
18.	1 ◇	1 ♡	Pass	?	Both	♠ 853 ♡ J1042 ◇ AKJ4 ♣ 32
19.	1 ◇	1 ♠	Pass	?	Both	♠ 74 ♡ 109876 ◇ J8432 ♣ 5
20.	1 ◇	1 ♡	Pass	2 ♡	You	♠ 862 ♡ 983 ◇ 983 ♣ AQ42
	Pass	3 ♡	Pass	?		

SOLUTIONS

Part I

	POINTS	BID	
1.	13	Pass	You should have 15 Roth Points for an overcall at unfavorable vulnerability, and your heart suit is quite weak.
2.	13	1 ♠	A minimum but quite acceptable non-vulnerable overcall.
3.	18	1 ♡	A maximum.
4.	9	2 ♠	An ideal weak jump overcall.
5.	13	Pass	Your heart suit is much too weak to bid, and you may not make a takeout double without support for all unbid suits.
6.	17	1 NT	The most descriptive bid.
7.	14	Double	The spade suit is far too weak to bid, but you have an ideal takeout double.
8.	14	2 ◇	With a close decision, be guided by the quality of your suit.
9.	17	4 ♠	After PROMOTING for a supported-

POINTS	BID	

five-card suit, you must have game; partner has at least 9 Roth Points.

| 10. | 14 | Pass | You have no good bid to make. Partner's bid is not invitational. |

Part II

11.	9	2 ♡	You meet all the requirements for a raise of partner's suit. A 1 ♠ bid would indicate great doubt concerning game chances when you are actually quite optimistic.
12.	14	2 ♠	You are too strong for a raise.
13.	12	2 ♠	The jump is invitational.
14.	11	1 NT	You have 11 HCP and stoppers in all unbid suits.
15.	7	2 ♡	Show your suit while you can. Your bid is not invitational, so partner will not be misled.
16.	13	3 NT	With 12–13 HCP and stoppers in all suits, jump in notrump.
17.	6	2 ♠	When right-hand opponent has bid, a raise shows 5 to 9 Roth Points. Don't give up without a fight; it is likely to be the opponents' hand but the spade raise can't cost.
18.	11	3 ♡	After PROMOTING your doubleton, you are too strong for a single raise.
19.	1	Pass	There is no point whatsoever in bidding. You do not particularly care what partner leads; in fact, you would like to get on to the next hand as soon as possible.
20.	8	Pass	You had a rock-bottom minimum raise to 2 ♡ and must reject partner's game invitation. Two part–scores make game; they are too valuable to be thrown away.

CHAPTER

22

Responses to 1 NT Openings

When partner opens the bidding with 1 NT, you have an excellent picture of his holding: he must have 16–18 HCP and balanced suit distribution. As a result, you are often able to make an immediate decision regarding game or slam prospects at your very first turn to bid.

Unfortunately, old-fashioned Standard American bidding methods do not take full advantage of this situation. For example, suppose you hold

♠ AK10964   ♡ 653   ◇ 543   ♣ 2

partner opens **one notrump,** and with 12 Roth Points you know game is definite even if partner has a minimum of 16. Using Standard American methods, you respond four spades. This is undoubtedly the proper contract, *but the wrong hand will be dummy.* The defenders will be able to see exactly what the opening notrump bidder holds, and this valuable information will greatly help their defense. Also, partner is likely to hold one or more tenaces, such as AQ or KJ. If his hand is dummy, the opening lead will come through these tenaces, and your right-hand opponent will smile contentedly as he waits to capture dummy's high cards. However, if the opening one-notrump bidder plays the contract, the lead comes up to these tenaces, and the opponents will be forced to play their high cards before he has to commit himself—a much more favorable state of affairs. Thus, it would be nice if there were some way to make the opening notrump bidder the declarer in a four-spade contract.

A second problem with Standard American methods of bidding over notrump openings has to do with very strong hands. In Standard American, it is quite difficult to bid slams after a notrump opening bid. The reason for this is that there is no way responder can flash an immediate slam signal. In order to make a slam try, responder usually must pass the level of game. This can easily be dangerous; it is very unsettling to stop in *four* notrump and go down one. Therefore, responder often "plays safe" and refuses to pass the three-notrump level. As a result, slams are often missed either because the best suit fit was not discovered or because opener never learned that responder was interested in slam.

In this chapter, we will begin the discussion of the first complete bidding structure over 1 NT openings, a structure which will make it possible for you to get to the proper contract whether it be a part–score, game, or slam.

Texas Transfers and the Gerber* 4 ♣ Response

When you hold a long major suit and wish to bid game in your major over a 1 NT opening, it would be best if partner were the declarer. There is an easy way to accomplish this: use the four-diamond response as a command to partner to bid four hearts, and use the four-heart response as a command to partner to bid four spades. By doing this, you *transfer* the bid to your partner and make him the declarer. For example, with the hand given earlier

♠ AK10964   ♡ 653   ◊ 543   ♣ 2

---

* The Gerber Convention has many complex variations. What is presented here might well be called "the *basic* Gerber Convention."

bid **four hearts** over partner's **one-notrump** opening. Partner is under
orders to bid **four spades,** which you will pass. Had you held

♠ 653   ♡ AK10964   ◊ 543   ♣ 2

you would respond **four diamonds,** partner would bid **four hearts,**
and you would pass. These bids, which are called "Texas transfers,"
accomplish the valuable objective of making the opening one-
notrump bidder the declarer. Naturally, you must be sure that partner is playing the same system, or else a very embarrassing situation
will ensue.

The response of four clubs is reserved for the Gerber Convention,
which asks partner how many aces he holds. His responses are as
follows:

4 ◊ = 0 or 4 aces
4 ♡ = 1 ace
4 ♠ = 2 aces
4 NT = 3 aces

After partner's response, a 5 ♣ bid asks for kings and guarantees
that the partnership holds all four aces. The responses are:

5 ◊ = 0 or 4 kings
5 ♡ = 1 king
5 ♠ = 2 kings
5 NT = 3 kings

If the Gerber four-club bidder makes any rebid other than five
clubs, opener must pass.

As with the Blackwood Convention, the Gerber 4 ♣ Convention
is used to excess. The hallmark of the losing player is that he trots
out his ace-asking convention, smiling happily at the chance to use
his new toy, and then goes into a long huddle after partner's response
because he hasn't the slightest idea what to do. If you can't place
the contract after hearing how many aces partner holds, don't ask
for aces! For example, with

♠ KQJ108642   ♡ KQ8   ◊ 6   ♣ 6

you have an ideal **four-club** response to a **one-notrump** opening. If partner shows one or two aces (he cannot have none), you will sign off in **four spades**. If he shows three aces, you know there must be one loser and will simply bid **six spades**. If he shows all four aces you can count thirteen tricks and bid **seven notrump**. However, consider the following hand:

$$\spadesuit \text{KQ10986} \quad \heartsuit \text{AK3} \quad \diamondsuit \text{643} \quad \clubsuit \text{9}$$

When partner opens **one notrump**, slam is very likely, but you cannot place the contract after a Gerber four-club bid and response. Suppose partner shows three aces. This sounds fortuitous, but he could easily have

$$\spadesuit \text{A75} \quad \heartsuit \text{Q84} \quad \diamondsuit \text{AJ52} \quad \clubsuit \text{AJ6}$$

and slam will be nearly hopeless. On the other hand, you could be cold for *seven*

$$\spadesuit \text{A753} \quad \heartsuit \text{86} \quad \diamondsuit \text{AKQ} \quad \clubsuit \text{A1053}$$

If partner shows two aces, you could be cold for six

$$\spadesuit \text{A75} \quad \heartsuit \text{QJ2} \quad \diamondsuit \text{AK2} \quad \clubsuit \text{A876}$$

or have no play for slam

$$\spadesuit \text{A75} \quad \heartsuit \text{QJ2} \quad \diamondsuit \text{Q105} \quad \clubsuit \text{AK85}$$

Obviously, a Gerber four-club bid is a very poor choice on this hand—or on any hand with which you will still be in doubt after hearing partner's response. Also, never ask for aces with a void—you won't be able to tell whether or not partner has the right aces.

Perhaps ace-asking conventions are used so frequently because slam bidding is regarded as such a difficult task that players simply decide to be sure that they are not off two aces and then hope for the best. However, as we saw in Chapter 9, slam bidding after a suit opening bid is not difficult enough to justify this excuse. Over an opening one-notrump bid, however, the difficulties involved in slam bidding, using Standard American methods, are so staggering that we can sympathize with players who trot out the Gerber Convention simply because they have no idea what else to do. Therefore, let us see how slam bidding *should* take place after a one-notrump opening bid.

Slam-Try Stayman

The major problem with Standard American methods for bidding over one-notrump openings is that responder has no way to convey slam interest to opener *immediately*. As a result, he is often faced with an insoluble dilemma: to try for slam and risk going above the level of three-notrump (perhaps going down in four notrump when three notrump was cold), or to play safe, not get past the three-notrump level, and risk missing slam because there is not enough bidding room for an ample exchange of information.

All these problems are alleviated in one sweep by the use of an approach we call "slam-try Stayman." If responder is interested in slam after an opening bid of 1 NT, *he bids two diamonds.* Opener responds in a four-card major suit if he has one, and the bidding proceeds along normal lines *except that responder has already made a try for slam.* For example:

OPENER	RESPONDER	OPENER	RESPONDER
1 NT	2 ◇	1 NT	2 ◇
2 ♠	3 ♠ (slam try!)	2 ♡	2 NT (slam try!)

Look at the vast amount of space saved in these sequences. In the first, responder sets the trump suit and announces slam intentions below the game level. In the second auction, responder has shown a balanced hand with a slam try at the level of two notrump (when he would have had to bid *four* notrump in standard methods).

---

* Since the standard weakness response of two diamonds is rare and ineffective, "Slam-Try Stayman" can be superimposed on whatever method of responding to notrump you employ. Conversely, you can adopt this convention or not without disturbing the rest of the bidding structure we recommend. Slam-Try Stayman should be used only after specific agreement with your partner.

If responder does *not* wish to try for slam, yet has a hand calling for a Stayman bid, *he responds two clubs*. This shows an "ordinary" Stayman response with no interest in slam, and asks opener to show a four-card major suit if he has one.

After a 2 ◊ response, opener bids as follows:

1. 2 ♡ or 2 ♠ : shows four (or five) cards in the suit bid.

2. 3 ♡ or 3 ♠ : shows a five-card suit with a maximum for slam purposes.

3. 2 NT: shows no four-card major.

4. 3 ♣ : shows two four-card majors.

5. 3 ◊ : shows no four-card major with a maximum hand.

These responses to the immediate slam-try Stayman response are quite useful, although the convention may be used profitably even without them.

If responder starts with two clubs, a Stayman bid with no interest in slam, opener simply rebids two diamonds with no four-card major, two spades with four spades, and two hearts with four hearts.

Over a **two–notrump** opening, **three clubs** is slam-try Stayman* and **three diamonds** is Stayman with no interest in slam. This is particularly useful. There are many hands with which slam is possible, yet it is absolutely imperative for responder to state his intention at a level low enough so that he can stop in three notrump if there is no slam. For example, suppose partner opens two notrump and you hold

♠ KJ105   ♡ AJ86   ◊ 3   ♣ 5432

Under present methods of bidding, it is impossible to show slam interest with borderline holdings. If you make an ordinary Stayman response and find partner with four hearts or four spades, slam is quite possible. Yet there is no way to show an interest in slam and stop at four hearts or four spades if slam proves to be out of the question. Using slam-try Stayman, you merely bid three clubs over

---

* Slams and slam tries are very frequent after a *two*-notrump opening. So the lower bid, which leaves more room for investigation, is used for slam-Try Stayman.

two notrump and raise partner's three-heart or three-spade bid to four. If there is a slam, opener will now bid again, since your three-club bid has shown an interest in slam. If opener has a minimum, he will pass, and you will have stopped at four of a major after giving full investigation to slam prospects. Similarly, with

♠ KJ106   ♡ 3   ◇ A1042   ♣ J986

bid **three clubs** over partner's **two-notrump** opening. If he bids **three hearts,** sign off with **three–notrump.**

We cannot recommend slam-try Stayman too strongly. Players using the convention have found all sound slams are bid, no legitimate slams are missed, and many mild approaches may be made without getting higher than game.

Forcing Stayman

We mentioned in Part One that when ordinary (not slam-try) Stayman is being used, the two-club response may be treated as "nonforcing Stayman" or "forcing Stayman." The former is more popular, but forcing Stayman—under which a rebid of two spades or two hearts by the two-club bidder is forcing for one round—has a large number of adherents and is used in the Roth approach to bidding.

The only change this necessitates in your thinking about Stayman is that when responder *rebids* two of a major suit the opener must bid again. He can support his partner with three cards in the major suit, rebid notrump.

It follows that if responder holds a five-card major and the strength only to *invite* game he cannot start with two clubs but must simply bid two of his major suit. Therefore, opener is expected to bid again after a response of two spades or two hearts if he has a maximum hand (not only with the super maximum that was required when nonforcing Stayman was being used). However, as opener will have no reason to bid without a fit for responder's suit (if responder has a chance for game without a fit he would not make such a weak response), any bid he makes shows a fit for his partner. In particular, opener can:

Bid two notrump with a maximum hand in high cards (plus fit);

Raise to three of the major with good trump support;

Bid a new suit to show shortness (i.e., a doubleton).

This last bid is called a "'short-suit game try." It enables the responder to judge whether or not the hands mesh together properly. If responder has a difficult decision whether or not to bid game, he looks at his holding in the suit in which opener has shown a doubleton. If responder has a wasted honor (such as the queen) in this suit, he will pull in a notch and stop at three of the agreed major suit. But if responder has no wasted values in that suit (a small tripleton would be an ideal holding), he will continue to game. The short-suit game try is another modern device aimed at accurate bidding by using evaluation techniques which go beyond the mere counting of points.

Two Notrump for Minor Suits

Another response Roth players employ with favorite partners is an immediate response of **two–notrump** to ask for opener's longer minor suit. This bid may be made with a weak hand such as

♠ 3   ♡ 42   ◇ K10642   ♣ J10753

(on which responder wants to locate the partnership's better minor suit) or a fairly strong hand such as

♠ 3   ♡ A2   ◇ KJ1062   ♣ K10932

(on which responder wants to decide between game in notrump and in a minor suit).

With a hand of the first type (a weak hand), responder will simply pass opener's response; with a hand of the second type, responder *rebids in his major-suit singleton (or void)*. The latter call indicates a strong hand and pinpoints a potential weak spot in notrump. If opener is strong in responder's short suit, he rebids three notrump; if opener is weak in responder's short suit, a minor-suit game will be the indicated contract.

Of course, if you use this convention you can no longer raise to two notrump in the usual manner. But this is little loss for if responder holds a balanced hand with 8–9 Roth Points (with which he would give a "normal" raise to 2 NT), he simply responds **two clubs** (forcing opener to bid **two diamonds, two hearts,** or **two spades***** depending on his hand) and then *rebids* **two notrump.** This rebid is invitational to game and opener will pass with a minimum hand or continue to game with a maximum.

This simple (but effective!) convention can be added to your present arsenal or not as you choose. Also, as in the case of slam-try Stayman, the rest of the structure is not affected whether you include it or omit it. Of course, you will want to discuss it with your partner beforehand.

Weak Jump Responses (to 1 NT)

Over a one-notrump opening, responder, with slam interest, bids **two diamonds;** with game interest, he bids **two clubs.** Both ask opener to show a four-card major suit if he has one. With these bids available to you, there is no reason to use the jump response to a one-notrump opening as a strong bid, and the jump can therefore be used as a preempt designed to get you to the proper contract and interfere with the opponents at the same time. For example, if partner opens **one notrump,** bid **three clubs** on

♠8   ♡864   ◇732   ♣Q109764

Game is out of the question, and clubs should be your best spot. In standard American, you must first bid two clubs and then three clubs to "sign off" in a club contract, which allows the opponents to enter the auction cheaply at the two-level. Thus, the jump to

---

* With an established partnership, you may wish to add that with *both* majors, opener bids 2 NT with a minimum and 3 ♣ with a maximum. If responder had wanted to *invite* game in notrump, he passes 2 NT and converts 3 ♣ to 3 NT.

three of a *minor* is a very weak preempt, promising at least a six-card suit and indicating that game is out of the question; *the opening 1 NT bidder must pass.* The jump to three of a major is slightly stronger and is partially invitational to four of the major if opener has a maximum and a good fit. A minimum for this bid would be

♠8   ♡ KJ10964   ◇ J103   ♣742

(With a weaker hand, simply "sign off" in two of the major).

As you can see, the procedures involved in this chapter are quite simple and take place at responder's first turn to bid. A Texas transfer bid allows the opening one-notrump bidder to play a four-heart or four-spade contract; a slam-try Stayman bid of two diamonds immediately informs the opening bidder of responder's interest in slam; a Stayman bid of two clubs announces that slam is out of the question; a weak jump response announces a preemptive hand and at least a six-card suit. When a suitable hand occurs, the Gerber four-club bid asks for aces. We feel these simple and effective responses will improve your bidding after a one-notrump opening by partner.

Capsule Summary: Responses to 1 NT Openings

BID	MEANING
2 ♣	Stayman; no interest in slam. Opener rebids as follows:
	2 ◇ : no four-card major;
	2 ♡ : four hearts;
	2 ♠ : four spades.
2 ◇	Stayman; responder is interested in slam. Opener rebids as follows:
	2 ♡ : four-card heart suit (no four-card spade suit);
	2 ♠ : four-card spade suit (no four-card heart suit);
	2 NT: no four-card major suit, minimum hand;
	3 ♣ : two four-card major suits;
	3 ◇ : no four-card major suit, maximum hand;

BID	MEANING
	3 ♡ : five-card heart suit, maximum for slam purposes.
	3 ♠ : five-card spade suit, maximum for slam purposes.
2 ♡ , 2 ♠	Signoff. Opener must pass unless he has an absolute maximum.
3 ♣ , 3 ♢	Preemptive; at least a six-card suit; no chance for game. Opener must pass.
3 ♡ , 3 ♠	Preemptive, at least a six-card suit. Game unlikely; opener may bid game only with a good fit and a maximum hand.
4 ♣	Gerber; asks for aces. Opener rebids as follows:

> 4 ♢ : 0 or 4 aces;
> 4 ♡ : 1 ace;
> 4 ♠ : 2 aces;
> 4 NT: 3 aces.

A subsequent rebid of 5 ♣ asks for king; any other rebid must be passed. Responses are similar.

| 4 ♢ | Texas transfer. Opener must bid 4 ♡ . |
| 4 ♡ | Texas transfer. Opener must bid 4 ♠ . |

REVIEW QUIZ FOR CHAPTER 22

In each case, count your Roth Points and decide on your action.

	PARTNER	YOU	YOU HOLD
1.	1 NT	?	♠ 863 ♡ 7 ♢ 76 ♣ J1086432
2.	1 NT	?	♠ 6 ♡ AQJ965 ♢ 832 ♣ 1042
3.	1 NT	?	♠ KQ84 ♡ 72 ♢ AKJ4 ♣ K103
4.	1 NT	?	♠ Q10865 ♡ 743 ♢ 982 ♣ A5
5.	1 NT	?	♠ Q843 ♡ AQ62 ♢ 943 ♣ 32
6.	1 NT	?	♠ A109653 ♡ 83 ♢ 943 ♣ 72

	PARTNER	YOU	YOU HOLD
7.	---	1 NT	♠KQ8 ♡Q1043 ◇AQ82 ♣K8
	2 ◇	?	
8.	---	1 NT	♠87 ♡AKJ9 ◇KJ10 ♣AQ4
	4 ♡	?	
9.	---	1 NT	♠KJ8 ♡AQ6 ◇K1043 ♣A106
	2 ♣	?	
10.	---	1 NT	♠64 ♡AK108 ◇K93 ♣KQJ7
	4 ♣	4 ♡	
	4 ♠	?	

SOLUTIONS

	POINTS	BID	
1.	7	3 ♣	Preemptive. Warns partner to remain silent and obstructs the opponents' bidding.
2.	12	4 ◇	The Texas transfer. Partner is required to bid 4 ♡, which you will pass.
3.	16	2 ◇	If partner bids spades, your hand will be worth 18 points and slam is almost definite, and even if he does not bid spades slam on power is possible. The 2 ◇ bid—slam-try Stayman—announces your interest in slam in a single bid.
4.	7	2 ♠	Game is unlikely. Sign off in your five-card major suit. With only 7 points and a five-card major suit, even 3 ♠ might be too high, so do not make a jump response.
5.	8	2 ♣	You will raise a 2 ♡ or 2 ♠ bid to four, since PROMOTION will make your hand worth 10 Roth Points, but will bid 2 NT (invitational) after a 2 ♦ rebid.
6.	9	3 ♠	A good hand for a jump response. Prevents the enemy from getting together at a low

level, and you will be quite content if partner raises to 4 ♠ with a fit and a maximum.

7. 16   2 ♡   Show your four-card major, making a mental note that partner is interested in slam. If he likes hearts, you may be going places.

8. 18   4 ♠   No choice. Partner's 4 ♡ bid is a Texas transfer and commands you to bid 4 ♠. He could be void in hearts.

9. 17   2 ◊   Denies a four-card major. Note that partner is *not* interested in slam.

10. 16   Pass   No choice; partner's bid is a signoff. He has a long spade suit and has given up on slam chances (presumably because two aces are missing), so you must accept his decision.

CHAPTER
23

Defense against Preemptives

In this chapter we intend to note briefly a few techniques for dealing with opposition preemptive openings. In this area of bidding one's philosophy is important. It is vital to realize *and admit* that *there is no absolutely effective method available and you will at times concede a loss when faced with opponents' preemptive tactics.* We exhort you to do so gracefully. Let others take overbids and incur large sets over *your* preempts. Act cautiously, and you will show a substantial profit in the long run. In short, don't be goaded into dangerous action by an opponent's preemptive. Stay "fixed"!

Over high-level preempts (such as three hearts or four diamonds), a double in the Roth method shows a good hand and is basically for takeout (but may be passed). This is one instance in which responder can and should pass with no good idea of what to do: the doubler should have enough high cards to defeat the contract. Thus, if left-hand opponent opens **four spades**, partner **doubles**, and you hold

♠ 863   ♡ 743   ◇ 964   ♣ 5432

pass. To double a high-level preempt, you need quite a good hand (about 18 Roth Points). Thus, double a **four-heart** preempt on your right hand with

♠AK74　♡7　◇KQ86　♣KQ102　　　　　or
♠KJ3　♡72　◇AKJ86　♣AJ8

Since the double is primarily for takeout, you must *pass* over four hearts with a hand such as

♠83　♡AQ106　◇8643　♣A32

you are not strong enough to request partner to respond and a double is *not* a command to pass. Perhaps partner will double (for takeout) and you will be able to cash in your chips by passing.

Also, four notrump over a four-level major-suit preempt shows a good hand and is a minor-suit takeout. Partner *must bid* and should select his better minor suit.

Bidding Over Opponents' Weak Two-Bids

If the opponents are particularly enlightened, they also will be using weak two-bids, and you may find yourself under pressure from this device. Once again there is no simple effective answer to the problems posed by enemy weak two-bids. However, one must be as well prepared as possible and we suggest the following:

1. With a hand that would have opened one notrump (16–18 HCP and balanced suit distribution) and the opponent's suit well stopped (at least AJx), overcall 2 NT.

2. With an even stronger notrump-type hand (19 to 24 HCP and balanced suit distribution) and the opponent's suit well stopped, overcall 3 NT. (This is risky but nonetheless the "least of evils.")

3. Bid a strong suit (but not clubs) of your own (strong six-card suit or very strong five-card suit) provided you have 14 Roth Points with at least 10 HCP.

4. With 12–15 Roth Points and support for the unbid suits, double (for takeout).

(452)

5. With a strong hand and a strong suit, make a (strong) jump overcall.

6. With a very good hand that does not qualify for any of the above bids, bid **three clubs** (a takeout bid) or cue-bid the opponents suit. To bid three clubs you should have 17 to 19 Roth Points and some support for all unbid suits. Partner will be aware that you are bidding under pressure and may not have *ideal* support for all unbid suits. With 20 or more Roth Points and support for the unbid suits, cue-bid.

Some examples:

OPP.	YOU	YOU HOLD
1. 2 ♡	?	♠ AQ865 ♡7 ◇K864 ♣1032

Pass. The spades are not strong enough to bid and your hand is not good enough for a takeout double.

| 2. 2 ♡ | ? | ♠KQ87 ♡3 ◇A1065 ♣Q1032 |

Double. An ideal hand for the call.

| 3. 2 ♠ | ? | ♠8 ♡AKJ1065 ◇A83 ♣542 |

Bid 3 ♡ (vulnerable or not).

| 4. 2 ♡ | ? | ♠AKQ7 ♡6 ◇K1062 ♣A1032 |

Bid 3 ♣. This shows a strong takeout double. Do not overcall notrump without a heart stopper.

| 5. 2 ♡ | ? | ♠8 ♡A83 ◇AKJ965 ♣J108 |

Bid 3 ◇. It is too dangerous to double with poor support for an unbid *major* suit, but you have a good six-card suit of your own to bid.

| 6. 2 ◇ | ? | ♠KQ10 ♡AQ8 ◇AQ6 ♣9872 |

Bid 2 NT. This shows an opening 1 NT bid with the enemy suit well stopped.

Since the weak two-bid is an effective weapon, we can only suggest general guidelines for you to follow. One general principle may be helpful: Do not make risky or wild bids, such as overcalls on weak suits or takeout doubles without the necessary values. If, as must happen from time to time, you must lose out to the opponents' weak two-bid, do so by missing a contract rather than by taking a 1400-point set.

Capsule Summary: Defense against Preemptives

BIDDING OVER OPPONENTS' WEAK TWO-BIDS

BID	MEANING
2 NT	16–18 HCP; balanced suit distribution; stoppers in opponents' suit.
3 NT	19–24 HCP; balanced suit distribution; stoppers in opponents' suit.
Cue-bid of opponents' suit	Takeout double with 20 or more Roth Points and support for all unbid suits or a self-sufficient suit.
Three clubs	Similar to a cue-bid, but with 17–19 Roth Points.
Double	Takeout double with 16 points or less, or 17 or more points without perfect distribution.
Jump in a new suit	Strong (16–19) but not forcing.

BIDDING OVER HIGH-LEVEL PREEMPTIVES

Doubles of preemptives are for takeout but may be passed.
When in doubt, *stay "fixed"!*

REVIEW QUIZ FOR CHAPTER 23

In each of the problems below, you are vulnerable and your opponents are not. Your right-hand opponent opens with a weak 2 ♡ bid. What call do you make?

		POINTS	BID
1.	♠ 86 ♡ 64 ◊ AQ976 ♣ AQ82	_____	_____
2.	♠ AKJ976 ♡ 873 ◊ A8 ♣ 72	_____	_____

		POINTS	BID
3.	♠ KJ108 ♡ 7 ◇ AQ85 ♣ Q1087	_____	_____
4.	♠ AK875 ♡ 6 ◇ AQ103 ♣ KJ8	_____	_____
5.	♠ KJ8 ♡ AJ10 ◇ QJ96 ♣ KQ8	_____	_____

SOLUTIONS

1.	14	Pass	You have the wrong distribution for a take-out double, and an overcall in a weak suit could result in a serious penalty. You must be prepared to concede an occasional loss to the opponents' preemptive tactics.
2.	15	2 ♠	An overcall is quite safe with such a good suit.
3.	15	Double	The double shows a maximum of 15 points, so partner will not get your side overboard.
4.	19	Double	You have extra strength and plan to rebid in spades. Three clubs is inadequate as partner may pass (if clubs is his best suit) and a spade fit may be lost.
5.	17	2 NT	This bid shows a hand worth a strong 1 NT opening and stoppers in the opponents' suit.

CHAPTER

24

Bridge in the Space Age

Congratulations! Having reached this point in the book, you have learned to evaluate your hand accurately by using the Roth Point Count and to make use of this important information to arrive at better contracts, and also to disconcert your opponents by interfering with their normal bidding processes by applying the Roth approach to bidding. In accordance with your new status as a potential expert bidder, there will be no more quizzes or "Capsule Summaries" for the remainder of this book.

As we have seen, experts do not hesitate to change the meanings of bids when they believe it is to their advantage to do so. In today's jet-age bridge world, it is common to find people experimenting with new tools, modifying the requirements for bids, or attempting to find new ways to handle situations which have proved troublesome in the past. Naturally, care must be exercised in the course of this experimentation. It would obviously be absurd to use an opening bid of seven spades to convey the message "Partner, I have a terrible hand"; even if partner understood your message perfectly, you would still have to fulfill the requirement of taking thirteen tricks with spades as trumps. On the other hand, if partner opens **one spade** and you wish to indicate that game is definite and spades should be trumps, there is no reason why you must adhere to the old-fashioned Standard American procedure of a raise to three spades. A different response, such as **three clubs,** could easily be used to convey this message, since you are going to arrive at the *higher*-level contract of four spades (at least). The fact that a bid of three clubs theoretically offers to take nine tricks with clubs as trumps is totally irrelevant, since you are going to continue to bid at least until four spades has been reached. Thus, provided you and your partner are in full agreement as to the meanings of the bids that you are using, it is perfectly proper to experiment with new meanings such as this one.

Which new meanings are worth adopting? This is not a question that can be answered by armchair speculation alone. For example, the raise from one to three of a major could be used to show 13 to 15 points and support for partner's major; 10 to 12 points and support; or a very weak hand with which you wish to preempt the opponents' bidding room. Each of these possibilities has potential merit. The only way to decide among them is to subject each one to the acid test: Try them out at the bridge table and see which one produces the best results. In the end, the results obtained will dictate the new meanings which should be adopted.

Along with everyone else, Al Roth is continually inventing, testing, adopting and rejecting new bidding techniques. Some of his recent changes have led to exceptionally fine results. While these new "space-age" techniques represent some of the new frontiers of bridge, they are nevertheless well worthy of your attention; they have been tested out in the crucible of bridge play and have led to a considerable improvement in bidding accuracy. We believe that you will find them an exciting and profitable addition to your repertoire of expert bidding procedures. When you have completed this section, you may be quite sure that you are "up-to-date" on the very latest developments in the area of bidding; you will have completed the transition from the horse-and-buggy days of Standard American to present-day modern expert practices. Then watch your results at the bridge table!

CHAPTER

25

More on Major-Suit Raises

Suppose that partner opens the bidding with **one heart** and you
hold a hand worth 13 or more points with at least four-card heart
support. In line with our new space-age philosophy, you will not
blindly insist on a raise to three hearts as the best vehicle to convey
this information until all other avenues have been explored. Is
there an alternative which does the job better than the direct three-
heart raise?

If you are to change the meaning of an old bid to the new meaning of "partner, I have 13 or more points and heart support," you
cannot choose any of the low-level responses. These have such important meanings that you cannot do without them. This eliminates
using bids such as one spade, one notrump, any response at the
two-level. On the other hand, responses at the three-level are less
frequent, and you can spare one of them for this new meaning if
there is a good reason to do so. Change for the sake of change alone
is not a good idea and can only lead to confusion. There is, however,
a good reason for dispensing with the standard meaning of the
three-heart raise, namely that it takes up too much room and
makes slam investigation difficult. You certainly don't want to get

any higher than four hearts if there is no chance for slam; playing in five hearts and going down one means that you have lost a chance to score a game for no reason. On the other hand, if you play in four hearts and six hearts is cold, you have missed an opportunity to score a lucrative slam bonus. Yet, after a three-heart raise, the auction is in a terrible mess. Opener must rebid four hearts on any hand of 17 points or less, immediately cancelling slam chances. If opener wishes to try for slam, the partnership will find itself at the four-heart level with breath-taking speed, usually before either partner really knows whether it is worthwhile to venture on to the five-level. What to do?

To obtain additional bidding room, *we suggest using a response of three clubs as the strong major raise*. Thus, if partner opens one spade and you respond three clubs, you are showing 13 or more points and four-card or better spade support*; if partner opens one heart and you respond three clubs, you are showing 13 or more points and four-card or better heart support. This is a more valuable treatment than using three clubs as a weak jump response (or strong jump response!). Over the three-club response, opener *must* rebid 3 ◇ with a singleton in any suit. This bid says nothing about the quality of his diamond suit but merely announces the presence of a singleton, which is often very valuable for slam purposes. With a minimum hand and no singleton, opener should rebid so as to indicate his strength in the agreed trump suit (the suit he opened, about which precise information is crucial for accurate slam bidding):

> 3 ♡ with 2 of the top 3 honors;
> 3 ♠ with 1 of the top 3 honors;
> 3 NT with none of the top 3 honors.

All of these bids, however, deny the presence of a singleton (else opener would have rebid three diamonds).

The use of the three–club response allows you to obtain con-

---

* In general, it is a bad principle to respond three clubs without at least one ace.

siderable information below the level of four of opener's major suit and therefore facilitates accurate slam bidding. However, you do not want to have any wasted bids; can the raise to three of partner's major be used for a different purpose? Roth players have obtained good results playing the double raise as a distributional raise, showing 14 to 16 points with a void or singleton. For example, opposite an opening **one spade** bid, raise to **three spades** on

♠ J763   ♡ A   ◇ AJ96   ♣ 10864

Thus:

OPP.	YOU	OPP.	PARTNER	
Pass	1 ♠	Pass	3 ♠	14–16 points, spade support, a void or singleton, at most 9 HCP in aces and kings.
Pass	1 ♠	Pass	3 ♣	Strong spade raise: 13 or more points with at least four spades.

Triple Raises

Insofar as *triple* major raises are concerned, these can *always* be used as weak preempts. As we have seen, the direct raise of an *opening* bid from one to four of a major is preemptive in standard American methods (though responder must have enough strength to make the four-level contract reasonably safe). However, if opener bids one of a suit, responder bids a new major suit at the one-level, and opener raises to four, this also can be preemptive (showing a minimum opening bid which is highly distributional). To make the standard strong raise to four, *jump to three of the other major.** That is:

---

* Experienced partnerships may wish to add a further improvement. With a strong hand worth a triple raise of partner's major suit:
  (i) Jump to three of other major with balanced distribution.
  (ii) Jump to four of your original suit with a powerful six-carder and weak four-card support.
  (iii) Jump to four of a new suit with powerful holdings in *both* your suit and partner's suit.

OPENER	RESPONDER	
1 ♣	1 ♠ (♡)	Preemptive.
4 ♠ (♡)		
1 ♣	1 ♠	Hand worth a strong raise to
3 ♡		4 ♠.
1 ◇	1 ♡	Hand worth a strong raise to
3 ♠		4 ♡.

Even if you are a passed hand, *any triple major raise is preemptive*. Thus, if you have passed and partner opens **one spade,** a raise to **four spades** is weak; you should bid **three notrump** with a maximum pass and spade support (partner may not pass, since spades is the agreed trump suit) or **four clubs** with a near-maximum pass and spade support, or **four diamonds** with a hand just strong enough to drive to game. However, when you are a passed hand and partner opens with one of a major, the double raise is *not* weak and the three-club response is *not* the strong major raise, as we will see in the next chapter.

(461)

CHAPTER

26

Passed Hand Techniques

Like many other systems of bidding, the Roth approach recognizes that there is definitely a difference between opening the bidding in first or second position (when partner is not a passed hand) and opening the bidding in third or fourth position (when partner is a passed hand). For example, consider the following two auctions:

1.	YOU	PARTNER		2.	YOU	PARTNER
	1 ♡	2 ◇			---	Pass
	?				1 ♡	2 ◇
					?	

In the first example, you must bid again. Partner's hand is un-limited; he must have at least 11 Roth Points to bid at the two-level but could have as many as 18. Therefore, game is very likely, and you cannot pass partner's two-diamond response.

In the second example, however, partner's hand *is* limited by his original pass; he cannot have 14 or more Roth Points or else he would have opened the bidding. Therefore, partner's maximum is 13 points, and you have quite a good idea as to his general strength. If you have opened with only 12 Roth Points (which, as we will see in a moment, is permitted in third or fourth position), you may pass if two diamonds is a playable contract since you know game is out of the question; your 12 points plus partner's maximum of 13 adds up to 25, or one short of the total needed for game.

Thus, in the second example, partner's original pass conveys important information that you will find very helpful in determining the game prospects for your side. Because you possess this valuable information, you can open the bidding on certain holdings that you would have to pass were you in first or second position (when partner's hand is a complete mystery).

In third or fourth position, where partner is a passed hand, you *may:*

1. Open the bidding with 12 or more Roth Points (and at least 10 HCP).

2. Open the bidding in a strong four-card major suit.

For example, you would have to pass in first or second position holding

♠ Q83   ♡ AKQ10   ◇ 73   ♣ 8642

as you have only 12 Roth Points. However, in third or fourth position you should open the bidding with **one heart.** If partner makes a simple bid in a new suit, such as **one spade** or **two diamonds, pass.** Partner has not opened the bidding and can have at most 13 points, so game will not be missed. With

♠ J1073   ♡ A83   ◇ J84   ♣ AQ8

open **one club** in third or fourth position, as you have 12 Roth Points. However, **pass** in any position with

♠ Q8642   ♡ 7   ◇ 863   ♣ AK94

your 11 Roth Points are not enough for an opening bid.

Responses by a Passed Hand

If you have passed originally and partner opens the bidding in third or fourth position, it is very important to remember that (save

for a few exceptions) you cannot force opener to bid again. Therefore, you should make your first bid as descriptive as possible.
Many responses still retain their original meaning. For example:
one notrump over one of a major is still forcing, the triple major
raise is preemptive, the single major raise is strong (10–12 Roth
Points and support). As we have already seen (Chapter 25), three
notrump over one of a major shows a maximum pass and good
support, and four clubs, or four diamonds over one of a major shows
a *near*-maximum pass and good support. However, since you cannot
have a hand worth an opening bid, the meanings of some responses must be changed (else they would be totally useless).

For example, when you are a passed hand, it is pointless to play
a two-notrump response as showing 13 or more points; you cannot
have more than 13 points (for you would have opened the bidding).
Therefore, the two-notrump response by a passed hand shows specifically 12–13 HCP and a balanced hand with stoppers in all unbid suits. As usual, you should not have support for partner's major
suit when making the two-notrump response. Always prefer to
support a major if you meet the requirements. Also, if right-hand
opponent passes, remember that a jump in a new suit is *not* a
weak jump response. It shows a hand worth a "maximum pass"
with a good suit.* Partner need not bid with a complete minimum
—he need not fear you can support his suit for there are other bids
(such as 3 NT) available for this purpose. If you have support
for opener's suit with only 13 points, you should jump to three of
his suit (not forcing).

Here are some examples of responses by a passed hand:

	YOU	PARTNER	YOU HOLD
1.	Pass ?	1 ♣	♠ Q109 ♡ K86 ◇ J1097 ♣ AQ8

Bid 2 NT, showing 12–13 HCP, a balanced hand, and stoppers in
all unbid suits.

---

* Regular partnerships may find it valuable to use a jump to two hearts or
two spades to show 5–3–3–2 distribution and 12 HCP. See Example 3, below.

2. Pass   1 ♡   ♠ 87   ♡ K93   ◇ 864   ♣ AKJ65
    ?

Bid 2 ♡, just as you would have if you were not a passed hand.

3. Pass   1 ◇   ♠ AKJ96   ♡ Q72   ◇ 83   ♣ Q108
    ?

Bid 2 ♠, showing a maximum pass and a good spade suit. Partner is permitted to pass.

4. Pass   1 ♠   ♠ K843   ♡ 7   ◇ QJ85   ♣ A1063
    ?

Bid 3 ♠. This is invitational but not forcing.

5. Pass   1 ♡   ♠ 87   ♡ 105   ◇ 843   ♣ AKQJ87
    ?

Bid 3 ♣. You have a maximum pass and a long, strong suit.

Rebids by Opener

As with any limited bid, opener evaluates game chances after a response by a passed partner and bids accordingly. For example:

PARTNER	YOU	YOU HOLD
1. Pass	1 ◇	♠ A86 ♡ J107 ◇ K1085 ♣ AJ9
3 ◇	?	

Bid 3 NT. Partner's 3 ◇ bid shows a maximum pass (12 to 13 points) and diamond support. Game is not a sure thing, but you are so close that it must be right to try for it. Even if 3 NT can be defeated, the opponents may find the wrong opening lead.

2. Pass	1 ◇	♠ 863 ♡ A87 ◇ KQJ8 ♣ Q84
2 NT	?	

Pass. You have 12 points and partner has at most 13, so game is not a good bet. If the most that your side can have is short of the 26 points needed for game, discretion is the better part of valor.

3. Pass   1 ♡   ♠ 87   ♡ AKQ8   ◇ 1094   ♣ Q976
    3 ◇   ?

Pass. Partner's 3 ◇ bid is not forcing and you have a rock-bottom minimum.

4. Pass   1 ♡   ♠ Q83   ♡ AKQ10   ◇ 73   ♣ 8642
    2 ◇   ?

Pass. You are not going anywhere; don't look for trouble.

5. Pass   1 ♣   ♠ A73   ♡ J1085   ◇ 73   ♣ AK64
    1 ◇   ?

Bid 1 ♡. Show your new suit at the one-level. (Both players find passed-hand bidding easier when the specific sequence 1 ♣—1 ◇ is played as forcing.)

Some General Guidelines

1. *Third position is not forcing.* While you are permitted to "open light" in third or fourth position, it is well to remember that you are not forced to bid simply because your partner has passed. Do not "cheat" on the new point requirements for opening. For example, in third position pass with

♠ ---   ♡ J975   ◇ QJQ864   ♣ AJ84

as you lack the 10 HCP required to open the bidding.

2. *A passed hand must not temporize.* If you are a passed hand, always raise partner's major suit in preference to making a simple response in a new suit of your own. For example, if partner opens **one heart** and you hold

♠ 86   ♡ K83   ◇ AK987   ♣ 632

raise to **two hearts.** The hand belongs in hearts, and partner could pass a 2 ◇ response.

3. *If you do not want partner to pass, be sure to make a forcing bid.* We saw earlier that if partner opens **one heart** and you hold

♠ 7   ♡ QJ986   ◇ 84   ♣ AK1073

you should *not* jump to three clubs, which does not force partner to bid again. After the 1 ♡ opening, your hand is now worth 16 Roth Points, so game must be reached; do not make a bid which partner could pass. Instead, bid **three notrump** to show a superb heart raise.

CHAPTER
27
Special Slam Methods

This chapter is a catalog of special methods which can be employed in slam bidding.

Slam-try Stayman

We have seen that the use of slam-try Stayman is likely to lead to a great improvement in your slam bidding after a one-notrump opening bid. In addition, you will gain greater accuracy on your part-score and game hands, for both you and partner know after a two-club response that slam is out of the question.

Rather than present a long and detailed discussion of bidding after a slam-try Stayman response, we suggest you try it out at the table with your favorite partner. Some practice will be necessary before you gain maximum results from this convention; but you will soon find that there are numerous useful inferences that you can draw as the auction proceeds because of the strong foundation provided by the slam-try Stayman response. (Details in Chapter 22.)

Baby Blackwood

In the Roth approach to bidding, a response of two notrump to an opening bid of one of a suit by an unpassed hand shows 13 points or more (see Chapter 3); responder clarifies his point count at his second turn to bid. Therefore, the three-notrump response is now free to assume a new meaning, and we recommend using it as Blackwood, asking for aces. Opener rebids four clubs with 0 or 4 aces; four diamonds with one ace; four hearts with two aces; or four spades with three aces. The Blackwood bidder may now bid four notrump to ask for kings (provided that the partnership holds all four aces). Using "Baby" Blackwood makes it possible to stop at four of a major when your side is off two aces. Remember, however, that three notrump is "Baby" Blackwood *only when bid directly over partner's opening bid of one of a suit*. Also, you are still free to use the four-notrump ace-asking Blackwood bid in those situations in which it applies. The "Baby" Blackwood convention provides a useful meaning for the three-notrump response to an opening bid of one of a suit by an unpassed hand, which otherwise would be a wasted bid.

The 4 ♣ Opening Bid

Some hands contain many playing tricks but too little defense for an opening bid of one of a suit. As an example, consider

♠3　♡AKQJ7642　◇K7　♣65

This is a good hand but is far too weak for a two-club opening; you must therefore open one heart. This is unsatisfactory because you have very little in the way of defensive values, and it is quite possible that the opponents can make something in one of the other three suits. You would like to prevent this by making a preemptive bid, but—by classical standards—your hand is too strong for such an action.

To solve these problems, the Roth method uses an opening four-club bid as showing a hand with 8 to 9 tricks, mostly in one very good suit (not necessarily clubs). Thus, with the example hand given above, you would open **four clubs.** Partner is required to respond **four diamonds,** after which you name your suit (i.e., bid **four hearts** in the above example). Partner now has an excellent idea as to your hand and can pass or try for slam as he sees fit. Furthermore, by opening at the four-level, you make it very difficult for the opponents to enter the auction. You do give up the ordinary preemptive four-club opening, but such hands do not come up very often, and you will find it far more useful in practice to use the opening four-club bid in this new way. Of course, opening bids of four diamonds, four hearts, and four spades still retain the usual preemptive meanings.

Blackwood after Interference

Suppose you hold

♠ K8   ♡ AK98743   ◇ 7   ♣ KQ6

and open the bidding with **one heart.** Partner responds **three clubs,** which shows thirteen to fifteen points and heart support. This is clearly a case for Blackwood: If partner holds only one ace

(e.g. ♠ AQJ6   ♡ Q652   ◇ KJ8   ♣ J10)

you wish to stop in five hearts; if partner holds two aces, six hearts should be bid; and if partner holds three aces, you should bid the grand slam in hearts (partner must hold four or more hearts, so even if he does not hold the heart queen you cannot have any trump losers). Therefore, you correctly bid **four notrump,** asking for aces. To your horror, your left-hand opponent now bids **five diamonds.** What now? Partner can no longer bid five clubs to show no aces or five diamonds to show one ace. How can he convey the information you desperately need?

Very few bridge players have agreements to handle this situation, and even international stars have gone wrong. So that you will not miss any slams that should be bid or get to slams that go down because of confusion arising after the opponents' interference, we recommend the following treatment (as one of many possible methods):

Pass: shows no aces;

Double: shows one ace (and does *not* express a desire to try to set the opponents);

Bid of the next higher suit (5 ♡, in our example): shows two aces;

Bid of still higher suit (5 ♠, in our example): shows three aces.

Thus, in our example, suppose partner doubles, showing one ace. You return to **five hearts** since your side is missing two aces. Don't pass; partner's double is designed solely to tell you how many aces he has. If partner bids **five hearts,** showing two aces, go on to **six hearts;** and if partner bids **five spades,** showing three aces, bid **seven notrump.**

Similarly, if the auction proceeds

YOU	OPP.	PARTNER	OPP.
1 ♡	1 ♠	3 ♡	3 ♠
4 NT	5 ♠	?	

A pass shows no aces; a double shows one ace; five notrump shows two aces; six clubs shows three aces, and six diamonds shows four aces. Having a firm partnership agreement to cover situations like this will make your life easy and prevent unnecessary disasters.

Responding to a Preempt

It is also a good idea to have a firm understanding as to the meanings of various bids after partner has opened with a preempt (such as four hearts). In the Roth method, four notrump is Blackwood, and a raise to five of a major is invitational, asking partner to go on to six if his suit is solid missing only one of the top honors and to go all the way to seven with an absolutely solid seven-card or longer suit.

(471)

Finding a Suit After a 2 NT Opening

Suppose you hold

♠ A3 ♥ AK62 ♦ K73 ♣ AKQ8

With 23 HCP, you are just within the limits for a **two-notrump** opening. Suppose partner raises to **four notrump**. What now?

With a maximum, you would be justified in proceeding directly to six notrump, but a better bid is possible. You can be sure that partner does not hold a four-card or longer major suit (he would have used slam-try Stayman). Therefore, there is no point in considering hearts as a possible trump suit. However, it is quite possible that partner has four clubs, in which case six clubs may well be the best contract. Find out by bidding **five clubs!** If partner raises to six clubs, **pass;** if he returns to five notrump, go on to **six no-trump.** Roth actually held this hand in a rubber bridge game and bid five clubs. Partner,[*] holding

♠ Q102 ♥ 105 ♦ AJ94 ♣ J1093

raised to six clubs, and they thus arrived at the best possible slam contract. Since his partner was an expert, Roth knew that he would not pass five clubs regardless of his holding, so that Roth would be able to continue to six notrump if his partner did not like clubs. After all, with no interest in slam, Roth would have passed partner's four-notrump raise; when he bid five clubs, partner knew he was driving to slam and that the only question was *which* slam to bid.

---

[*] The late Harry Harkary, one of the all-time bridge greats.

CHAPTER

28

Special Defensive Methods

This chapter details techniques which are useful after the opponents open the bidding.

The Unusual Notrump Overcall

Let's try a bit of detective work. Take a look at the following auction. Can you figure out what the two-notrump bid means?

PARTNER	OPP.	YOU	OPP.
Pass	Pass	Pass	1 ♠
2 NT			

Can partner have a strong hand? No; for if he had a strong hand he would have opened the bidding. Obviously, something very unusual is happening, since partner cannot possibly have the strength for a legitimate two-notrump overcall. What can partner have in mind?

The solution is that partner wants you to bid a suit, and more specifically one of the *minor* suits. He doesn't know which suit to overcall and cannot make a takeout double for lack of heart support; he does not want you to make a penalty double of a contract you cannot set because you are expecting defensive values in his hand. On the other hand, he does not wish to pass because he has good offensive possibilities and wishes to contest the auction. A typical hand for the two-notrump overcall would therefore be

♠7   ♡2   ◇QJ1086   ♣KJ10965

Partner will be happy with as little as three-card support for diamonds or clubs, and wishes to show both his suits before the auction gets too high. Lacking the distribution for a takeout double or overcall, the "unusual" two-notrump overcall is the ideal solution.

The unusual notrump overcall is used by many players, and is one of the most abused bids in bridge. To make this convention work for you, be sure to follow these rules:

1. Have at least 5–5 distribution in the minor suits.

2. Have little in the way of defensive values. The unusual notrump often paves the way for a successful sacrifice, but it is most annoying to sacrifice against the opponents' game and pay a 300- or 500-point penalty only to find that the opponents could not have made the game that they bid because the unusual notrumper had quite a bit in the way of defensive values. Thus, do *not* make an unusual notrump bid in our example auction with a hand such as

♠7   ♡43   ◇AJ965   ♣AJ864

with two aces, you have much too much defensive potential. **Pass** and await developments. If your left-hand opponent bids **two hearts** and opener rebids **two spades,** pass again; their suits are higher-ranking and it appears to be their hand. If left-hand opponent instead bids **two spades** and opener passes, and you wish to compete, *now* bid two notrump. Partner will know that you have some points as the opponents have stopped short of game. If you use the unusual notrump overcall indiscriminately on hands which have good defensive values and on hands which do not, partner will never know whether to sacrifice against the opponents' game or try to defeat them, and your auction will become a guessing game.

3. Pay attention to the vulnerability. If you are vulnerable and the opponents are not, they are much more likely to double you for penalties, and you should have at least 6–5 distribution in the minors in such situations.

4. When responding to an unusual notrump overcall, trust your partner. Thus, in our example at the beginning of this chapter, what is your response to partner's two-notrump overcall holding

♠732   ♡AQJ86   ◇64   ♣853

Your correct bid is **three clubs.** True, you have a good heart suit, but partner has asked you to bid your better minor and you must respect his wishes. He *may* be void in hearts, but he *must* have at least five clubs!

When the opponents have bid two suits, a notrump overcall that is clearly unusual asks for a choice between the two unbid suits. Thus, suppose the auction proceeds as follows:

PARTNER	OPP.	YOU	OPP.
Pass	1 ♠	Pass	2 ◇
2 NT			

Here the two-notrump overcall asks you to choose between hearts and clubs. Partner cannot be interested in playing the hand in diamonds, as one of the opponents has already bid that suit and must have quite a bit of strength in it.

The unusual notrump bidder may bid notrump at a higher level if his hand calls for it. For example, suppose that you are not vulnerable and the opponents are. Your partner deals and passes, right-hand opponent opens **four hearts** and you hold

♠---   ♡87   ◇KQJ865   ♣KQJ92

Your hand is worth nine tricks in the minor suits, and the opponents may have a game in spades or your side may have game in a minor suit. Bid **four notrump.** This is not Blackwood but the "unusual" notrump. Partner must bid his better minor suit at the five-level.

One further caution: do not make the mistake of thinking that *every* notrump overcall is unusual. For example, if your right-hand opponent deals and opens with **one diamond,** a **one-notrump** overcall is strong, showing 16–18 HCP, a balanced hand, and stoppers in the opponents' suit. *A notrump overcall is unusual only when it cannot reasonably have any other meaning.*

When the Opponents Open 1 NT

If the opponents open the bidding with one notrump, you will rarely want to make an ordinary overcall. The opening bidder has announced so much strength that it is far too likely that you will be doubled for penalties. Furthermore, since the opening bidder is so strong, it is unlikely that your side has game, and there is therefore no strong inducement to bid.

The picture changes, however, when you have a two-suited hand (at least 5–5 distribution). Now your distribution can offset the opener's high-card strength, as you will be able to ruff in your short suits. Therefore, there is more chance that your side has game, and it is safer to enter the auction (provided that you have sufficient high-card strength). For these reasons, in the Roth method most bids after a one-notrump opening bid by the enemy are used to show two-suited hands, since it is better to pass with a one-suited hand that is not exceptionally strong. One such system of bidding that has already been developed is called "Astro," after the originators (Paul Allinger, Roger Stern, and Lawrence Rosler). The procedures of the Roth method are similar in some respects but quite different in others, so they are called "Roth-Astro." After a 1 NT opening by the opponents, we use the following procedures:

1. A *double* shows a two-suited hand with hearts and spades as your long suits. It asks partner to bid his better major, and is not an attempt to try to set the opponents.

2. A two-club overcall shows a two-suited hand with clubs and spades as your long suits.

3. A two-diamond overcall shows a hand with diamonds and spades as your long suits.

4. A three-club overcall shows clubs and hearts.

5. A three-diamond overcall shows diamonds and hearts.

6. A two-heart or two-spade overcall shows a one-suited hand, with considerable strength and length in the suit bid.

7. A two-notrump overcall shows four hearts and six or more cards in one of the minor suits.

All of these bids show a hand worth at least an opening bid.* If your right-hand opponent opens **one notrump,** and you (vulnerable) hold

♠8 ♡QJ642 ◇73 ♣KJ1065

pass whatever system you are playing. You are not strong enough to enter the bidding; even though you have a two-suited hand, you do not have sufficient high-card strength to ensure that you will not be severely penalized. However, with

♠8 ♡AK1065 ◇73 ♣KQJ102

overcall **three clubs,** showing clubs and hearts. You should be safe in one of your two suits and may well have game in spite of the one-notrump opening because of your excellent distribution. With

♠KQJ65 ♡AK965 ◇43 ♣2

double, showing at least 5–5 in the major suits. With

♠87 ♡643 ◇7 ♣AKJ8532

just pass; a club overcall would accomplish nothing. Aside from the fact that it would show a two-suited hand, you have no reason to overcall. Game for your side is unlikely, and all you can accomplish is to warn the opponents that they had better not bid three notrump unless they have a club stopper.

These methods will take a bit of memorization, but it will be worthwhile for you. You will reach games that you would otherwise miss and still stay out of auctions when it is too dangerous to bid. The method is therefore well worth learning.

---

* However, *playing strength* (in accordance with the vulnerability) is paramount. You are attempting to overcome a strong high-card hand with distributional values—make sure these values are sound!

The Negative Slam Double

In competitive auctions, it often becomes clear that the opponents are likely to have a play for slam. The question then arises, should you allow them to play in slam and try to set the contract, or should you sacrifice? If the opponents are cold for a vulnerable small slam (worth approximately 1400 points) and your non-vulnerable sacrifice will cost only 700, you should obviously take it; but you do not want to pay out 700 points if the opponents are not going to make their slam.

Bidding will never be completely accurate and you cannot guess right in all situations, but you can improve your percentage of correct decisions by using the negative slam double. Here's how it works: When you are not vulnerable, *or* when you are vulnerable and the opponents are also vulnerable, *the double of an opponents' slam contract after a competitive auction shows no defense at all and suggests a sacrifice.* For example:

OPP.	YOU	OPP.	PARTNER	(Opponents vulnerable)
1 ♡	2 ♠	3 ♡	5 ♠	
6 ♡	Pass	Pass	*Double*	

Partner's double shows *no* defensive tricks at all and asks you to sacrifice in six spades unless you can defeat the six-heart contract in your own hand, in which case you should pass. A typical hand for partner might be

♠ K1086   ♡ 7   ◇ QJ10965   ♣ 82.

It is important to remember that the double is *not* negative if you are vulnerable and the opponents are not, because it is usually too expensive to sacrifice in such situations. Also, the double is negative only in competitive auctions. Consider the following situation:

OPP.	YOU	OPP.	PARTNER
1 ♠	2 ◇	3 ♣	Pass
3 ♠	Pass	4 ♠	Pass
5 ◇	Pass	5 ♡	Pass
6 ♠	Pass	Pass	*Double*

Here the double is *not* negative. There has been no semblance of a competitive auction; no possibility of your side taking a sacrifice. Partner is doubling simply because he thinks he can defeat six spades, and you should pass regardless of your holding.

Assuming that the final contract is six spades doubled, what do you lead? This is a most important question! If partner is following standard expert practice, he is not doubling to increase the size of the penalty; slams rarely go down more than one trick, so such doubles are not profitable. Even if partner holds two aces, he has no right to double as the opponents are likely to be void in one of those suits. (Even if they are not, the increased penalty from a one-trick set is simply not enough to justify a double.) Partner is doubling *to request an unusual lead,* because only in this way can the slam be beaten. If the opponents are using standard methods and you hold a hand such as

♠8   ♡86   ◇AKJ965   ♣K842

the club lead stands out. The complete deal might well be:

NORTH
♠1094
♡AJ
◇Q72
♣AJ763

WEST (you)		EAST
♠8		♠A53
♡86		♡1097432
◇AKJ965		◇10843
♣K842		♣---

SOUTH
♠KQJ762
♡KQ5
◇---
♣Q1095

With any lead but a club, South makes his contract. The slam double to demand an unusual lead, called the Lightner double after its inventor, Theodore Lightner, is used by most experts, and is a valuable device to have at your disposal. Your choice of leads may not always be this clear-cut, but after you have eliminated the "usual" leads (such as a suit you or your partner have bid, or an unbid suit) you will usually have a good idea as to what partner wants. A long suit in your own hand should suggest the possibility that partner is void in that suit and wishes to ruff the opening lead. If you are completely confused and have absolutely no idea what to lead, lead the first suit (other than the trump suit) that has been bid by the dummy.

Principles of Balancing

Consider the following auctions:

OPP.	PARTNER	OPP.	YOU	OPP.	YOU	OPP.	PARTNER
1 ♡	Pass	Pass	?	1 ♠	Pass	2 ♠	Pass
				Pass	?		

In each case, you are in what is called the "balancing" position. You must decide whether to let the opponents play the contract or whether to try for a contract of your own.

In the first example, it is usually right to bid. The exceptions occur when you have a very weak hand

(**pass** with ♠863 ♡74 ◇A843 ♣7532, as you cannot have a game)

or when you have length in the opponents' suit and no good bid to make

(**pass** with ♠832 ♡Q10976 ◇A83 ♣Q2)

In this situation, a major-suit overcall shows approximately 7 or more Roth Points and a reasonably good five-card suit. A suit jump is similar to a weak two-bid.

In the second sequence, you must be more careful, as you are bidding at the three-level. It is usually right to pass with length in the opponents' suit. Since both opponents have spades and you do also, partner must be short in the suit, yet he did not overcall or make a takeout double. Therefore, you are unlikely to be going anywhere. However, with a hand such as

♠ K7   ♡ J1064   ◇ AQ108   ♣ 1073

a non-vulnerable balancing double is in order. Partner must have some strength since the opponents stopped in a meek two spades. So why give up cheaply? You have reasonable support for any suit partner can bid, and may be able to set the opponents if they persist to three spades (though you will *not* double). You are unlikely to get hurt, and while making two spades gives the opponents "only" 60 points below the line, this might well cost you a subsequent game. Similarly, if you hold

♠ AK864   ♡ 732   ◇ K108   ♣ 63

and right-hand opponent opens **one heart,** you must pass since you are not strong enough to overcall.

Suppose left-hand opponent raises to **two hearts** and this is passed back to you. You should definitely balance with **two spades.** Since hearts have been bid and supported, partner is likely to be short and should have some support in spades. You may even have a game and should raise to **four spades** if partner bids three spades. By passing, you have obtained valuable information (the opponents have a heart fit, and spades are not bunched behind you since your left-hand opponent did not respond one spade) and conveyed the general strength of your hand to partner. However, suppose that left-hand opponent had instead responded **one notrump** (not forcing) and right-hand opponent rebid **two hearts.** Now you should pass. Since the opponents have not found a fit, your side may not have one either, and it is too dangerous to enter the auction.

In a balancing auction, be careful not to tell the same story twice. If you make a balancing double, partner makes a simple response, and the opponents outbid you, pass. You have pushed them up one and have a better chance of setting them. Don't keep on bidding and wind up paying out a substantial doubled penalty when the opponents do not have a game. Good balancing technique requires an understanding of when to stop. A simple rule is this: if you balance once and partner shows no signs of life (he simply replies to your double by bidding a suit without jumping, or passes your balancing bid in a suit), pass and live to fight another day.

Special Methods against Weak Two-Bids

Though strong jump overcalls are usually ineffective, we have found them useful when the opponents have opened with a weak two-bid, and we recommend this treatment to you. The Roth method also uses (over a weak two-bid) a three-club overcall that is primarily for takeout but may be passed; thus, it shows respectable club *support* but also a tolerance for a major-suit bid by partner. (See also pages 336 to 343.)

CHAPTER

29

Special Competitive Methods

We now investigate techniques for situations in which both sides are bidding.

Doubles of Artificial Bids

We have seen that if you open the bidding with one notrump and the next player overcalls, a double by partner is negative. There is, however, one exception to this. Many players use an overcall of a one-notrump opening as a conventional bid. Some play "Ripstra" (an overcall of two of a minor shows the suit bid plus both major suits); some play "Landy" (an overcall of two clubs is for takeout with emphasis on the major suits); and some use "Astro" (a two-diamond overcall shows spades plus a second suit, and a two-club overcall shows hearts plus a minor suit). After such a conventional bid, a double is *not* negative, but shows a reasonably good hand (8 HCP or more). With this information, the opening one-notrump bidder can double for penalties if the opponents bid a suit in which he is particularly strong, and pass to give his partner a chance to double if he is not strong in the suit they bid. You certainly want to penalize the opponents for their presumption in entering the auction after a one-notrump opening if you can do so; if not, you wish to look for your own game. The "general strength" double after a conventional overcall gives you a chance to do both.

The Cue-Bid after an Overcall

Suppose that partner opens **one club** and the next player overcalls **one heart.** A **two-heart** cue-bid by you is an "idle" bid that has no apparently useful meaning. Can we find one for it?

It is often important to play a three-notrump contract from the correct *side* of the table. If, in our example, you hold ♡A32 and partner holds ♡Q7, you have two stoppers *if partner is the declarer* and your right-hand opponent is forced to lead away from his ♡KJ10xx(x) into your partner's queen. However, if *you* become declarer, the lead comes through your partner's queen and you have only one stopper. Therefore, we suggest using the two-heart response as showing a hand worth a 2 NT bid (13 to 15 HCP and balanced suit distribution) with which you wish partner to be declarer in a notrump contract. In our example, a sample hand would be

$$♠ KJ3 \quad ♡ A32 \quad ◇ KQ106 \quad ♣ J32$$

Partner is not compelled to bid notrump (and should not if he is weak in the opponents suit and/or has an unbalanced hand), but if he has a holding such as ♡Q7 and does so, you will play three notrump from the right side. (Partner rebids two notrump with any opening bid when he wishes to play in notrump and there is no chance for slam, and you will raise to three.) However, be sure to bid two notrump yourself on your first turn to bid if you have the opponents' suit well stopped; respond **two notrump,** not two hearts, with

$$♠ Q108 \quad ♡ KQ10 \quad ◇ AQ106 \quad ♣ J32$$

When the Opponents Overcall 1 NT

If your partner opens the bidding with one of a suit and the next player overcalls one notrump (showing a hand worth a strong opening 1 NT with partner's suit stopped), a two-club bid in the Roth method is a weak takeout asking partner to bid his best new suit. With 8 or more HCP, you should double the overcall. This is as much for takeout as for penalties, but partner will leave your double in if he expects to obtain a lucrative penalty.

The Care and Handling of Freak Hands

Once in a while, you will pick up a true freak hand, such as

♠ A108642   ♡ A   ◇ J106432   ♣ ---

Suppose partner astounds you by opening **one spade** and the next player overcalls **two hearts.** What is your general strategy? (Your side is vulnerable.)

First of all, you should realize that there is going to be a lot of bidding by the opponents. They also must hold considerable distributional features, and will not sell out to a low-level contract. In the second place, your objective should be to play the hand in spades at any level. Bidding four spades and making six, worth 680 points, is better than setting seven hearts doubled two tricks (300 points) or even three tricks (500 points). While your hand is an offensive powerhouse, you have very little in the way of defense and cannot expect to take many tricks if hearts are trumps. If you show your true colors by jumping to six spades, the opponents are likely to save in seven hearts, which is exactly what you do *not* want. To avoid this, bid only **two spades!** There will be more bidding, and by bidding spades slowly you may persuade the opponents that you are sacrificing. You do not know if slam is certain (you could be off two diamond tricks) but it must be right to play in spades at *any* level.

If you want the opponents to sacrifice, you bid in exactly the opposite fashion. Suppose that you hold

♠ AJ98   ♡ K10432   ◇ AJ9   ♣3

and the auction proceeds:

YOU	OPP.	PART.	OPP.	(Neither side vulnerable)
1 ♡	1 ♠	2 ♡	2 ♠	
?				

You should bid **four hearts.** You think you can make game, but not slam, and will be quite happy to double a four-spade sacrifice. In actual play, the opponents did bid four spades and went down 700 points against the non-vulnerable game (worth 420).

CHAPTER
30

Expert Responses

As we have seen, there are two guidelines you should follow in your study of expert bidding methods: *don't* have "wasted" bids in your bidding repertoire, but *do* have a firm agreement as to what various bids mean. This chapter is devoted to a further discussion of these principles, insofar as they pertain to responder's first bid.

Bidding over Takeout Doubles

We have already observed that if partner opens and the next player makes a takeout double, a jump response is weak and a redouble promises 10 or more Roth Points (with at least 8 HCP). It is also important to have a firm understanding as to what other bids over a takeout double mean, so that you and your partner will proceed with the auction with confidence and without the guess-work that pervades much of Standard American bidding methods.

Over a takeout double, a suit bid *at the one-level* promises 6 to 11 HCP, a good four-card or any five-card or longer suit, and is forcing for one round. Thus, if partner opens **one diamond** and the next player doubles, bid **one spade** on

♠ A10986   ♡ 743   ◇ 64   ♣ K52

or

♠ AKJ7   ♡ 643   ◇ 32   ♣ 8743

Opener is not permitted to pass (unless your left-hand opponent bids).

A suit bid *at the two-level* promises 6 to 10 HCP, and a five-card or longer suit. This is *not* forcing and opener is permitted to pass, for with a really good hand you would have redoubled. Thus, if partner opens **one heart** and the next player doubles, bid **two clubs** with

♠ 86   ♡ 73   ◇ J832   ♣ AKJ97

However, do not bid a new suit if you can raise partner's major, or have sufficient strength to redouble.

If you cannot support partner's suit or bid a new suit, you may bid one notrump with 7–10 HCP and balanced suit distribution. For example, if partner opens **one heart** and the next player doubles, bid **one notrump** with

♠ KJ8   ♡ 62   ◇ Q1084   ♣ QJ97

(You should not bid a four-card suit at the two-level.) Over a take-out double, the one-notrump bid is not forcing and partner may pass. With

♠ 62   ♡ KJ8   ◇ 10842   ♣ QJ97

raise to **two hearts.** Since you did not redouble, you cannot have ten or more Roth Points, so the single raise over a takeout double shows 6 to 9 Roth Points.

Responses of Two of a Suit

If partner opens the bidding and you respond with two of a new suit, you must have at least 11 Roth Points to bid at the two-level. We have already discussed this point in Part One of this book. It is well, however, to have a firm agreement regarding the following aspects of a two-over-one response:

1. A two-over-one response in a minor suit guarantees at least four cards in the suit bid and promises a rebid. No matter what opener rebids, responder must bid again at his next turn.

2. A two-over-one response *in hearts* guarantees at least a five-card suit and promises a rebid. Do not bid two hearts over a 1 ♠ opening with only four hearts; you must have at least five. Again, no matter what opener rebids, responder must bid again at his next turn.

The 1 NT Response over a 1 ♣ Opening

Roth players have found it useful to use the one-notrump response over a one-club opening to show 9–11 HCP (and balanced suit distribution) with no four-card major suit to bid. Remember that a one-notrump response to one of a *minor* is *not* forcing. Over a one-diamond opening, the one-notrump response shows the usual 6 to 10 HCP.

The Unlimited 2 NT Response

According to traditional Standard American, the three-notrump response to the opening bid of one of a suit promises 16–18 HCP and balanced suit distribution. This is an extremely poor method. In the first place, the jump to three notrump preempts the opening bidder. With many minimum hands, the opening bidder is reluctant to bid over three notrump, for fear that the bidding may get out of control. Also, even if the HCP do not add up to slam, slam may be there if a suit fit is found and PROMOTION can take place. For example, suppose you hold

♠ AK1064   ♡ 7   ◇ AJ32   ♣ J84

You open **one spade,** and partner makes a Standard American **three notrump** response. What now? If partner fits diamonds, slam in diamonds is very likely; but if partner has fewer than four cards in diamonds, slam is unlikely and a four-diamond bid at this point could easily get your side too high.

This problem can be solved by using the two-notrump response to show 13 points *and up*. Opener now has room to show his distribution on the three-level, after which responder can clarify the range of his original response. If for example the bidding proceeds

OPENER	RESPONDER
1 ♠	2 NT
3 NT	?

responder will now pass if he has the usual 13 to 15 point hand, and will bid again with a stronger hand. The Roth method uses a rebid of four notrump to show 16–17 points; four diamonds, 18 points; four clubs, 19 points or more. (The theory is that the cheapest bid should be the strongest as it leaves the most room for slam investigation.)

The main advantage of this treatment is that responder need not bid three notrump at once with a hand like

♠ K6   ♡ A842   ◇ A103   ♣ KQ75.

Look at the horrible things that can happen to you if you respond three notrump on this hand: opener will pass with a weak hand with five spades and four clubs, and three notrump may even go down when *six* clubs is cold. Or, partner may guess wrong and make a four-diamond slam try when notrump is the best contract and slam cannot be made, and your side may get too high. However, when *two* notrump is used as the strong response, opener will rebid his second suit at the three-level and you can drive to a club slam if he bids three clubs or play in notrump if his second suit is diamonds.

Observe that in this situation, it is not at all bothersome that your slam try gets you past the game level. For you to bid over partner's three-notrump rebid, you must have at least 16 points. Since partner has at least 14 for his opening bid, you will be quite safe should you stop short of slam in four notrump.

CHAPTER
31

When Not to Count Roth Points

After the great emphasis we have placed on the importance of counting your Roth Points, it is only fitting that we conclude this book with a discussion of when *not* to count your Roth Points. There are certain times when you can decide the proper action simply on the basis of logical inference, and counting your points will only confuse the issue.

The Theory of Suit Distributions

On some hands, it is best to evaluate your hand by considering the bidding and determining the number of winners and losers that you are likely to hold. When doing so, keep the following rules in mind:

1. If your side has found a trump fit and you have a side suit of five or more cards, partner is likely to have no more than two of that suit.

2. If your side has found a trump fit and you have a singleton or doubleton, partner is likely to have three or more cards in that suit.

3. If you have three or more cards in a suit which has been bid and raised by the opponents, partner is likely to have no more than a doubleton, usually only a singleton.

Here's how these rules work:

PARTNER	YOU	YOU HOLD
1. 3 ♠	?	♠ AQ8 ♡ 7 ◇ AKJ863 ♣ A42

Bid 6 ♠. You have no losers in spades (partner surely has the king for his preempt); one loser in hearts (partner should *not* have the ace); no losers in diamonds or clubs (partner must have at least seven spades for his preempt and should have at least three hearts since you have a fit and a singleton; therefore he cannot have more than three cards in the minors, which will be taken care of by your ◇ AK and ♣ A). Partner actually held

♠ KJ109763   ♡ 842   ◇ 5   ♣ 93

and slam was cold.

YOU	PART	YOU HOLD
2. 1 ♠	3 ♣ *	♠ AK1093 ♡ AK864 ◇ K3 ♣ 2
?	* strong raise	

Bid 4 NT. Following the theory of suit distributions, partner is unlikely to hold more than a doubleton in hearts since your side has a spade fit. You plan to bid *seven* spades if partner shows both aces, and 6 ♠ if he shows one ace. Partner's actual hand:

♠ QJ85   ♡ 72   ◇ AJ8   ♣ AJ106

YOU	PART	YOU HOLD
3. 1 ♠	3 ♣	♠ KQJ763 ♡ 7 ◇ AK543 ♣ 2
?		

Bid 4 NT. If partner shows three aces, bid a grand slam in spades; if he shows two aces, bid 6 ♠. Partner will probably have no more than two diamonds.

YOU	OPP.	PART.	OPP.	YOU HOLD
4. 1 ♠	2 ◇	2 ♠	3 ◇	♠ AKJ103 ♡ A73 ◇ 9842 ♣ 7
?				

Bid 4 ♠. Since the opponents have bid and supported diamonds, partner should have at most a singleton, and game is likely. Counting points will only confuse the issue.

Thus, following these distribution rules, you can visualize partner's holding in certain key suits and bid accordingly. Such hands will not come up every rubber, so remember to count your Roth Points on the vast majority of hands; but when hands such as those discussed in this chapter do occur, remember the theory of suit distributions and you will get to cold games and slams other players miss.

Hands Requiring One-Sided Action

Once in a long while, you will have a hand where you should take complete charge of the bidding. For example, suppose you hold

♠ AKQJ63   ♡ 7   ◇ AJ98   ♣ A6

You properly open **one spade,** planning to jump shift to **three diamonds** next time to show a powerful hand and drive to game. Unfortunately, partner foils you in your plan by passing your opening bid, and your right-hand opponent balances with a double. Can you make four spades even though partner has passed? We don't know, but we do know that you will never find out by bidding scientifically. We suggest you jump directly to **four spades.** You cannot be severely penalized, and it is worth the risk that you will be one down because there are so many holdings that will make game cold in spite of partner's original pass.

Similarly, suppose you hold

♠ Q108　♡ AJ32　◇ K106432　♣ ---

As dealer, you have 13 Roth Points and must **pass.** Partner opens **one diamond,** and your right-hand opponent preempts **three hearts.** No amount of scientific gadgetry can help on this hand, and we suggest that you jump straight to **six diamonds.** It may be cold; the opponents may make the wrong opening lead; or they may sacrifice. In any case, bidding slowly *cannot* help you but *can* give the opponents room to decide what to do.

Situations such as these are occurring every day in every rubber bridge game and tournament competition. Here is a decision which arose in a game at Al Roth's Mayfair House of Bridge while this book was being written. With both sides vulnerable, South held:

♠ AQJ642　♡ AJ1032　◇ 3　♣ 7

The bidding went this way:

South	West	North	East
1 ♠	Pass	Pass	2 ◇
2 ♡	3 ◇	3 ♡	4 ◇
?			

North's failure to respond initially marks him with a very weak hand; even his competitive raise to three hearts shows little strength (with a *really* improved hand he could have bid four). There is no point-count evaluation method which will give South enough "points" to bid **four hearts,** but we think he should. (In practice South passed; four diamonds was defeated one trick but four hearts was "cold" for North-South.) North probably has four hearts to an honor and not much else. Even so, game will probably be made if he has a singleton spade, or may depend on as little as a spade finesse if his heart honor is the king. Furthermore, even if four hearts is defeated a trick perhaps four diamonds would be made. (One hundred points is a cheap price to pay to prevent an opposing vulnerable part-score.)

Sometimes you must stop to visualize the possible holdings for partner. Point count, even the dynamic Roth Point Count, is not sacred.

APPENDIX

Special Sequences

I. Partnership Auctions

1. *Major Suit Auctions*

OPENER	RE- SPONDER	MEANING, STANDARD AMERICAN	MEANING, ROTH SYSTEM
1 ♡ or 1 ♠		At least a four-card suit.	At least a five-card suit.
1 ♡ (♠)	1 NT	6–10 points. Opener may pass.	6–11 points. Opener must bid again.
1 ♡ (♠)	2 ♡ (♠)	7–10 points. Opener may pass.	10–12 points. Opener must bid again.
1 ♡ (♠) any bid	1 NT 2 ♡ (♠)	6–10 points.	6–9 points.
1 ♡ (♠)	3 ♡ (♠)	13–15 points; at least four-card support.	14–16 points; at least four-card support; void or singleton.
1 ♡ (♠)	3 ♣	18 points or more; good club suit.	13 HCP or more; at least four-card support for partner's major.

OPENER	RE-SPONDER	MEANING, STANDARD AMERICAN	MEANING, ROTH SYSTEM
1 ♡ (♠)	4 ♡ (♠)	Preemptive; 11–15 points.	Preemptive; 11–15 Roth Points.
1 ♣ (◇) 4 ♡ (♠)	1 ♡ (♠)	20 or more points; at least four-card support.	Preemptive.
1 ♣ (◇) 3 (♠)	1 ♡	Undefined.	20 or more points; at least four-card support for hearts.
1 ♣ (◇) 3 ♡	1 ♠	20 or more points; at least four hearts and five clubs.	20 or more points; at least four-card spade support.
1 ♠ 3 ♣	2 ♠	Forcing.	Forcing (invites game).
1 ◇ 1 ♠	1 ♡ 3 ♠	Forcing.	Nonforcing (10–12). The only nonforcing secondary jump in the Roth method.
Pass 4 ♡	1 ♡	Strong.	Weak.
1 ♡ 2 ♣	1 NT 2 ♠	Undefined.	Strong club raise.

2. Auctions after Notrump Openings and Rebids

OPENER	RE-SPONDER	MEANING, STANDARD AMERICAN	MEANING, ROTH SYSTEM
1 NT	2 ♣	Stayman; minimum of 8 points, strength undefined.	Stayman; minimum of 8 points, no interest in slam.

OPENER	RE-SPONDER	MEANING, STANDARD AMERICAN	MEANING, ROTH SYSTEM
1 NT	2 ◊	Signoff.	Stayman, interest in slam.
1 NT	2 ♡ (♠)	Signoff.	Signoff.
1 NT	3 ♣ (◊)	No standard treatment.	Signoff.
1 NT	4 ♣	Undefined, but often used as Gerber.	Gerber, asking for aces.
1 NT	4 ◊	Undefined.	Transfer; opener must bid 4 ♡.
1 NT	4 ♡	Signoff.	Transfer; opener must bid 4 ♣.
1 NT 2 ♡	2 ♣ 4 NT	Ambiguous.	*Not* Blackwood (notrump raise).
1 ♡ 1 NT	1 ♠ 2 ♣	Nonforcing.	Forcing, to avoid jumps with questionable hands.
1 ♣ 1 NT	1 ♠ 3 ◊	Forcing, strength unspecified.	Interest in slam (as 2 ◊ in forcing).
2 ♣ 2 NT	any 3 ♣	Undefined, widely used as Stayman.	Stayman.
2 NT 4 ♣	3 ♣ (or 3 ◊)	Undefined.	Two four-card majors.

3. *Higher-Level Responses and Rebids*

OPENER	RE-SPONDER	MEANING, STANDARD AMERICAN	MEANING, ROTH SYSTEM
1 ◊ 1 ♣	2 ♡ 2 ◊	18 or more points; at least four cards in	Maximum of 6 Roth Points; at least five

OPENER	RE-SPONDER	MEANING, STANDARD AMERICAN	MEANING, ROTH SYSTEM
1 ♡ 1 ♠	2 ♠ 3 ◇ etc.	suit bid.	and probably six cards in suit bid.
1 of a suit	3 NT	16–18 HCP and balanced suit distribution.	"Baby" Blackwood, asking for aces.
1 of a suit	2 NT	13–15 HCP and balanced suit distribution.	13 or more points (unlimited); balanced distribution.
1 of a suit 3 NT	2 NT 4 NT	Undefined, sometimes used as showing 19–20 HCP.	16–17 HCP.
1 of a suit 3 NT	2 NT 4 ◇	Undefined, sometimes used to show 19 HCP, balanced distribution and five diamonds.	18 HCP.
1 of a suit 3 NT	2 NT 4 ♣	Undefined, or used as four diamonds.	19 HCP.
1 ♠ 5 NT	2 ♡	Undefined, widely used as grand-slam force.	Grand-slam force in hearts.*
1 ♣ 4 ♣	1 ♡	Undefined.	Distributional raise to four hearts with strong clubs and weak hearts.

* The grand-slam force requests partner to bid seven of the agreed suit with two of the top three trump honors.

OPENER	RE-SPONDER	MEANING, STANDARD AMERICAN	MEANING, ROTH SYSTEM
1 ◇ 2 ♡	1 ♠	Theoretically non-forcing, but used as forcing by a majority of experts.	Forcing for one round (reverse).

4. Higher-Level Openings

OPENER	RE-SPONDER	MEANING, STANDARD AMERICAN	MEANING, ROTH SYSTEM
2 ◇ (♡, ♣)		Strong; forcing to game.	Weak; 7–10 HCP nonvulnerable, 9–11 HCP vulnerable; six-card suit.
2 ◇ (♡, ♠)	2 NT	Negative response.	Forcing; asks opener to bid side strength with maximum and rebid suit with minimum.
2 ◇ (♡, ♠)	3 ◇ (♡, ♠)	Forcing.	Signoff.
	4 ◇ (♡, ♠)	No ace, king, void or singleton.	Signoff.
2 ♡ 2 ◇ 2 ♠	3 ♠ 3 ♡ 4 ◇	Solid Suit.	Preemptive.
3 NT		25–27 HCP; balanced suit distribution.	Solid seven-card minor suit with one outside ace or king.
2 NT		22–24 HCP; balanced suit distribution.	21–23 HCP; balanced suit distribution.

OPENER	RE-SPONDER	MEANING, STANDARD AMERICAN	MEANING, ROTH SYSTEM
2 ♣		Strong; forcing to game; good club suit.	Strong; forcing to game; may be strong two-bid in any suit or strong notrump hand.
2 ♣	2 ♦	Positive response;* shows diamonds.	7 or more "quality" points; diamonds may be weak.
2 ♣	2 ♡	Positive response; shows hearts.	Less than 6 points; no good suit.
2 ♣	2 ♠, 3 ♣, 3 ♦, 3 ♡	Positive response; shows suit bid.	Maximum of 6 points; shows suit bid.
2 ♣	2 NT	Negative response.	7–8 points queens and jack.
2 ♣ 2 NT	2 of suit	Club suit; unbid suits stopped.	24–26 HCP; balanced suit distribution.
2 ♣ 3 NT	2 of suit	Club suit; unbid suits stopped; extra values.	27–29 HCP; balanced suit distribution.
2 ♣	*jump in new suit*	Solid suit.	Long, strongish suit but less than positive response.
4 ♣		Preempt in clubs.	Strong preempt (8–9 tricks) in any suit.
4 ♡	5 ♡	Undefined.	Invitation to six or seven, asking about solidity of the trump suit.

* Used as negative if 2 ♣ is artificial.

OPENER	RE- SPONDER	MEANING, STANDARD AMERICAN	MEANING, ROTH SYSTEM
4 ♡	4 NT	Blackwood.	Blackwood.
4 ♡	5 ♣	Ambiguous.	Signoff.
	or		
4 ♡	4 ♠		
3 ◇	3 ♡	Forcing.	Nonforcing.

II. Competitive Auctions

OPENER	OPP.	PARTNER	OPP.	MEANING IN STANDARD AMERICAN	MEANING IN ROTH SYSTEM
1 ♡	2 ♣	*Double*		For penal- ties.	Takeout for the unbid suits.
1 ◇	1 ♠	*Double*			
1 NT	2 ♡	*Double*			
2 ♣	2 ♠	*Double*			
1 ◇	2 ♠	*Double* etc.			
1 ♡	1 ♠	3 ♡	3 ♠	Not ace- showing.	Shows no aces. Double would show one ace, next higher bid two aces, and so on.
4 NT	5 ♠	*Pass*			
1 ♣	1 ◇	2 ♠		19 or more points.	Weak jump response.
1 ♡	Double	2 ♠		Used in var- ious ways.	Weak jump response.

OPENER	OPP.	PARTNER	OPP.	MEANING IN STANDARD AMERICAN	MEANING IN ROTH SYSTEM
---	1 ♢	Double	1 ♡	Nonforcing; May be rescue.	Forcing; shows some values (6–10)
1 ♠	2 ♣	2 ♠		8–10 points.	10–12 points.
1 ♠	3 ♢	3 ♠		9–11 points.	9–10 points.
---	1 ♡	1 ♠	2 ♠	Slam try.	Temporarily treated as a two-notrump bid asking partner to take the notrump.
2 ♠	3 ♣	*Double*		Penalties.	Penalties.
4 ♡	4 ♠	*Double*			
1 ♢	1 NT	2 ♣		Weak hand; club suit.	Takeout.

III. Defensive Auctions

OPP.	PTNR.	OPP.	YOU	MEANING IN STANDARD AMERICAN	MEANING IN ROTH METHOD
4 ♡	*4 NT*			Undefined.	Takeout for the minors.
1 NT	*Double*			16 or more points.	Two-suiter in hearts and spades.

(502)

OPP.	PTNR.	OPP.	YOU	MEANING IN STANDARD AMERICAN	MEANING IN ROTH METHOD
1 NT	2 ♣			Club suit.	Two-suiter in clubs and spades.
1 NT	2 ◇			Diamond suit.	Two-suiter in diamonds and spades.
1 NT	3 ♣			Used various ways.	Two-suiter in clubs and hearts.
1 NT	3 ◇			Used various ways.	Two-suiter in diamonds and hearts.
1 NT	2 ♡ (♠)			Shows suit bid.	Shows suit bid.
1 NT	2 NT			Forcing.	Four hearts and a six-card minor.
1 ♡	2 ♠			Strong hand, good suit.	Weak hand, good suit.
1 ◇	2 ♡				
1 ♡	3 ♣ etc.				Preemptive.
1 of suit	Double			Takeout; 14 or more points.	Takeout; 13–19 points.
1 ♡	2 ♡			Takeout; forcing to game.	Takeout; 20 or more points. Cue-bidder may pass at his next turn.
1 ♠	2 ♠ etc.				

OPP.	PTNR.	OPP.	YOU	MEANING IN STANDARD AMERICAN	MEANING IN ROTH METHOD
weak 2-bid	2 NT			Undefined.	16–18 points.
weak 2-bid	3 NT			Undefined.	19–24 points.
weak 2-bid	cue-bid			Forcing to game.	Takeout; 20 or more points.
weak 2-bid	3 ♣			Club suit.	Takeout; 17–19 points.
weak 2-bid	Double			Takeout; range un-specified.	Takeout; maximum of 16 points.
1 ♡ 6 ♡	1 ♠ Double	3 ♡	4 ♠	Penalties.	Negative (in competition only).
1 ♣	1 NT			16–18 points.	Maximum: 18–19.
1 ♣ Pass	Double 1 NT	Pass	1 ♡	Ambiguous.	Minimum: 16–17.
4 ♠	Double			For penalties.	For takeout.
4 ♠	4 NT			Ambiguous.	Takeout for the minor suits.
1 ♣	Pass	1 ♡	2 ♣	Ambiguous.	Club suit.
1 C	Pass	1 ♡	2 ♡	Cue-bid	Heart suit.
1 ♠ 2 ♠	2 ♣ Double	Pass	Pass	For penalties.	For takeout.

OPP.	PTNR.	OPP.	YOU	MEANING IN STANDARD AMERICAN	MEANING IN ROTH METHOD
1 ♠	2 ♣	2 ♠	Pass	For penalties.	For takeout.
Pass	Double				
1 ♠	Double	Pass	4 NT	Blackwood.	Minor-suit takeout.
1 ♣	Pass	Pass	2 ♠	Ambiguous.	Similar to weak two-bid.
1 ♡	Pass	Pass	D'ble	May be shaded.	At least 10 HCP.

APPENDIX
II

The Roth Method in Action

In this section we present a few recent examples of the use in actual play of the Roth method. Some of these hands were played by experts in major championships; others by average players in ordinary rubber-bridge games. In each case, observe not only that the correct final contract was reached, but that the East-West players (using the Roth method) had available the tools they needed to solve the particular problems they faced.

— —

Double Reverse by Opener to Show Old-Fashioned Strong Raise in Major

West	East	West	East
♠ A1087	♠ KQ632	1 ♣	1 ♠
♡ A2	♡ 953	3 ♡ (1)	3 ♠ (2)
◇ A3	◇ 54	6 ♠	Pass
♣ AQ1098	♣ K32		

(1) Double reverse to show the equivalent of the old-fashioned jump to 4 ♠.

(2) Mild slam try showing a good spade suit, but no ace.

By using this method, room is left open to explore for a possible slam below the level of game.

The eventual direct jump to 6 ♠ is considered a good gamble, once partner can make a slam try without an ace.

Preemptive Jump to Game (or Its Equivalent) by Opener

West	East	West	East
♠ A987	♠ KQJ64	1 ♣	1 ♠
♡ 52	♡ A87	4 ♣ (1)	4 NT
♢ 3	♢ A642	5 ♡	7 ♠
♣ AKQ987	♣ J	Pass	

(1) Jump bid shows strong clubs and poor spades.

You, too, might get to this slam, but not this easy and fast.

Slam—Try Stayman—2 NT Opening

West	East	West	East
♠ Q1064	♠ AJ	---	2 NT
♡ 5	♡ AKQ2	3 ♣ (1)	3 ♡
♢ 963	♢ A87	3 NT	4 ♣ (2)
♣ AQ874	♣ KJ103	6 ♣	Pass

(1) Slam—try Stayman.
(2) Looking for the 2nd suit with a quality 2 NT opening. Remember, you can always stop at 4 NT if necessary.

Slam—Try Stayman—1 NT Opening

West	East	West	East
♠ A1064	♠ K3	1 NT	2 ♢ (1)
♡ K2	♡ AQ86	2 ♠	2 NT(2)

(507)

West	East	West	East
◊ AQ87	◊ KJ92	3 ◊ (3)	4 ◊ (4)
♣ KJ9	♣ Q32	6 ◊	Pass

(1) Slam—try Stayman.
(2) Warning—high cards may be short.
(3) Seeking 2nd suit fit with more than a minimum.
(4) Confirming 2nd suit.

REMEMBER: Both hands pick up a ROTH POINT WHEN THE SUIT FIT IS FOUND. THUS, IN ORDER TO PRODUCE A SLAM WITHOUT 33 HCP YOU MUST HAVE A SUIT FIT.

Passed Hand Jump in the Majors

West	East	West	East
♠ Q10642	♠ AK873	Pass	1 ♠
♡ -----	♡ K872	3 NT(1)	4 ◊ (2)
◊ K10873	◊ A42	4 ♡ (3)	6 ♠
♣ A109	♣ 8	Pass	

(1) Raise in spades with maximum interest in slam.
(2) Cue-bid.
(3) Cue-bid.

Baby Blackwood

West	East	North	South
♠ AK10876	♠ 5	1 ♠	3 NT(1)
♡ A4	♡ KQJ10	4 ♡ (2)	5 ♣
◊ KQ62	◊ 3	Pass	
♣ 3	♣ KQJ1098765		

(1) Baby Blackwood.
(2) Shows 2 aces.

(508)

Slam—Try Stayman—2 NT Opening

West	East	West	East
♠ AK3	♠ 52	2 NT	3 ♣ (1)
♡ AQ87	♡ KJ942	3 ♡	4 ♡ (2)
◇ KQJ6	◇ 43	4 NT(3)	5 ◇
♣ K2	♣ A1098	6 ♡	Pass

(1) Slam—try Stayman (a minimum).
(2) Merely game—warning partner.
(3) Blackwood.

NOTE: THE ROTH POINTS ARE THERE.

Artificial 3 ♣ Raise to Show Strong Major Raise

West	East	West	East
♠ J9873	♠ Q1042	1 ♠	3 ♣ (1)
♡ AK8	♡ 5	3 ◇ (2)	3 NT(3)
◇ 5	◇ AKQ6	4 ♠ (4)	Pass
♣ KQJ2	♣ A876		

(1) Showing strong major raise.
(2) Forced; shows some singleton.
(3) Denies the A or K of trumps.
(4) The end.

Immediate Cue-Bid as Strong Takeout Double

West	East	Opp.	West	Opp.	East
♠ KQ109	♠ J32				
♡ 5	♡ 108762	1 ♡	2 ♡ (1)	Pass	2 ♠ (2)
◇ AK87	◇ J63	Pass	Pass(3)	Pass	
♣ AQ43	♣ J2				

(509)

(1) Cue—bid showing strong takeout double.

(2) Responding with most convenient suit at the lowest possible level.

(3) Going no further—too dangerous.

The contract of 2 ♠ was in jeopardy, but was made. Note how important it is not to get higher.

---

2 ♣ Takeout Over Opponent's 1 NT Overcall

West	East	Opp.	West	Opp.	East
♠ KQ3	♠ J10976	---	1 ♣	1 NT	2 ♣ (1)
♡ AK64	♡ Q10983	2 NT	3 ♡ (2)	Pass	4 ♡
◇ J8642	◇ 5	Pass	Pass	Double	Pass
♣ 2	♣ Q2	Pass	Pass		

(1) For takeout—leans to the majors.
(2) Seeking 2nd suit fit.

4 ♡ doubled was made.

---

1 NT—2 NT Response for the Minors (by Partners)

West	East	West	East
♠ A98	♠ 53		
♡ A10642	♡ 9	1 NT	2 NT(1)
◇ A2	◇ J9863	3 ♣ (2)	Pass
♣ KJ9	♣ Q10872		

(1) Asking for best minor.
(2) Complying with request.

(510)

Unusual NT (Strong) over Opponent's Weak Two-Bid

East-West vulnerable

West	East	Opp.	West	Opp.	East
♠5	♠A42				
♡9	♡108763				
◇AKJ876	◇Q109	2 ♡	4 NT(1)	P	6 ◇ (2)
♣KQJ102	♣A3				

(1) Strong minor-suit holding.
(2) Enough to bid a slam in a minor with only a three-card suit.

Opening Game Preempt in Major; Slam Try for Suit Quality

Non-vul. vs vul.

West	East	West	East
♠QJ109876	♠2		
♡---	♡AK87	4 ♠	5 ♠(1)
◇QJ10	◇AK62	P(2)	
♣KJ10	♣AQ32		

(1) Asking partner to bid six or seven depending on how solid and long the suit is.
(2) Must pass missing the AK of trumps.

Artificial "Impossible Bid" to Show Strong Raise of 2nd Suit

West	East	West	East
1 ♡	1 NT	♠K2	♠A93
2 ♣	2 ♠ (1)	♡A10876	♡3
4 NT (2)	5 ♡	◇A	◇10987
5 ♠ (3)	7 ♣ (4)	♣KQ982	♣AJ1076
Pass			

(511)

(1) Artificial impossible bid to show strong club raise. (Remember, partner may have a 3 card suit.)

(2) Blackwood.

(3) Grand slam try, asking for an additional value.

(4) The singleton heart must be the key.

Roth-Astro over the Opponent's 1 NT Opening

North-South Vulnerable

West	East	Opp.	West	Opp.	East
♠ K10876	♠ QJ932				
♡ 5	♡ J9876				
◇ 52	◇ 9	1 NT	2 ♣ (1)	3 NT	4 ♠ (2)
♣ AQ876	♣ J4	Double	Pass	Pass	Pass

(1) Showing clubs and spades.

(2) Taking a save with the possibility of making.

The contract was fulfilled with the club finesse working.

Negative 3 ♣ Response after a 2 ♣ Opening

West	East	West	East
♠ AKQ642	♠ 3		
♡ AK	♡ 542	2 ♣	3 ♣ (1)
◇ K2	◇ 987	4 NT	5 ♣
♣ AKQ	♣ J109873	6 ♣	Pass

(1) Showing a long club "bust".

West was able to bid the slam without even bothering to show the spades. Slam is virtually unbeatable from the West side. How would you bid this slam?

THE ROTH POINT COUNT

	HIGH-CARD POINTS		DISTRIBUTION POINTS		LENGTH POINTS
BASIC COUNT	Ace[1] King Queen Jack	4 3 2 · 1	Void Singleton Doubleton	3 2 1	6-card major 1 GOOD 6-card minor 1 7-card major 2 GOOD 7-card minor 2
FOR SUIT BIDDING	SUBTRACT 1 for each unguarded honor holding[2]		If partner shows a suit: Fit Adjustment 0–2 DEMOTE to zero[3] 3 KEEP 4(5+) ADD 1 for *one* doubleton ADD 1(2) for *each* void or singleton If partner does not show a suit: KEEP with known 8-card or better trump fit; otherwise DEMOTE to zero[3]		When raising partner's suit do not count Length Points in your own suit. If partner shows support,* ADD 1 for each card over 4 in the longest supported suit. DOUBLE all Length Points with a SELF-SUFFICIENT suit.
FOR NOTRUMP BIDDING	KEEP		DEMOTE to zero		KEEP only if based on a GOOD suit (otherwise DEMOTE to zero)

A GOOD suit is one containing two of the top three honors.
A RELIABLE suit is KQ109xx, KQxxxxx, or better.
A SELF-SUFFICIENT suit is KQJ10xx, KQJxxxx, or better.

1 ADD 1 point for all four aces; *for opening only* SUBTRACT 1 for no aces.
2 K, Q, J, KQ, KJ, QJ, Qx, Jx
3 But KEEP if you have a RELIABLE suit

* For example, by raising, showing a balanced hand, or making a takeout double